In the Path of Conquest

T0369706

In the Path of Conquest

Conquest

Resistance to Alexander the Great

WALDEMAR HECKEL

OXFORD
UNIVERSITY PRESS

OXFORD
UNIVERSITY PRESS

Oxford University Press is a department of the University of Oxford. It furthers
the University's objective of excellence in research, scholarship, and education
by publishing worldwide. Oxford is a registered trade mark of Oxford University
Press in the UK and certain other countries.

Published in the United States of America by Oxford University Press
198 Madison Avenue, New York, NY 10016, United States of America.

Library of Congress Cataloging-in-Publication Data
Names: Heckel, Waldemar, 1949– author.
Title: In the path of Conquest : resistance to Alexander the Great / Waldemar Heckel.
Identifiers: LCCN 2019033836 (print) | LCCN 2019033837 (ebook) |
ISBN 9780190076689 (hardback) | ISBN 9780190076702 (epub) |
ISBN 9780190076696 (updf) | ISBN 9780197501146 (online) |
ISBN 9780197671559 (paperback)
Subjects: LCSH: Alexander, the Great, 356 B.C.–323 B.C. |
Greece—History—Macedonian Expansion, 359–323 B.C. |
Generals—Greece—Biography. | Greece—Kings and rulers—Biography. |
Greece—History—Macedonian Expansion, 359–323 B.C.—Sources.
Classification: LCC DF234.2 .H375 2020 (print) |
LCC DF234.2 (ebook) | DDC 938/.07092 [B]—dc23
LC record available at https://lccn.loc.gov/2019033836
LC ebook record available at https://lccn.loc.gov/2019033837

1 3 5 7 9 8 6 4 2

Paperback printed by Marquis, Canada

This book is dedicated to my grandson,
Alexander James DeWolfe

Contents

Preface

IN ORDER TO reach a wider audience and make this book more lively, I have included numerous passages from the ancient sources, believing their words more effective than any paraphrase. The majority of the passages quoted have been translated by my friend John Yardley; there are a few exceptions, which are acknowledged in the footnotes. Therefore, my first and greatest debt is to him. I am also grateful to the usual group of Alexander scholars to whom I have regularly turned for guidance and instruction. Stefan Vranka of Oxford University Press has given support and encouragement throughout the process. I am particularly indebted to Fred Naiden, who read and criticized a preliminary version, and to my sister, Anneli Purchase, who corrected numerous mistakes in my writing and forced me to simplify the most convoluted arguments. Special thanks go out also to Sheila Ager, Ed Anson, Liz Baynham, Pierre Briant, Beth Carney, Monica D'Agostini, Konrad Kinzl, Franca Landucci Gattinoni, and Yossi Roisman and to my former students Erin Garvin, Carolyn Willekes, and Graham Wrightson. Most of all, I acknowledge the continuing friendship and support of Tim Howe and Sabine Müller (both of whom generously sent me published material that I found difficult to obtain), as well as Larry Tritle, John Vanderspoel, and Pat Wheatley. Of course, I thank my family, and it is to the youngest (for now) of them that I dedicate this book.

Calgary, October 15, 2018

List of Maps

Abbreviations

Atkinson I–II	J. E. Atkinson, *A Commentary on Q. Curtius Rufus' Historiae Alexandri* (Amsterdam, 1980, 1994).
Barr. Atlas	Richard A. Talbert, ed., *Barrington Atlas of the Greek and Roman World* (Princeton, 2000).
Beloch I²–IV²	K. J. Beloch, *Griechische Geschichte*, 2nd ed., 4 vols. (Strasbourg, 1912–1927).
Berve I–II	H. Berve, *Das Alexanderreich auf prosopographischer Grundlage*, 2 vols. (Munich, 1926).
BHLT	A. K. Grayson, *Babylonian Historical-Literary Texts* (Toronto, 1975).
BNJ	*Brill's New Jacoby*. Online.
Bosworth I–II	A. B. Bosworth, *A Historical Commentary on Arrian's History of Alexander* (Oxford, 1980, 1995).
Briant, *HPE*	P. Briant, *A History of the Persian Empire from Cyrus to Alexander*, translated by Peter Daniels (Winona Lake, 2002).
Brunt I-II	P. A. Brunt, *Arrian*. 2 vols. Loeb Classical Library (Cambridge, MA, 1976, 1983).
CAH²	*Cambridge Ancient History*, 2nd ed.
Carney, *King and Court*	E. D. Carney. *King and Court in Ancient Macedonia: Rivalry, Treason and Conspiracy* (Swansea, 2015).
Davies, *APF*	J. K. Davies, *Athenian Propertied Families, 600–300 B.C.* (Oxford, 1971).
Develin, *AO*	R. Develin, *Athenian Officials, 681–321 BC* (Cambridge, 1989).
FGrH	*Die Fragmente der griechischen Historiker.*
Geiger, *Feldzüge*	W. Geiger, *Alexanders Feldzüge in Sogdiana* (Neustadt, 1884).
Hamilton, *PA*	J. R. Hamilton, *Plutarch*, Alexander: *A Commentary* (Oxford, 1969).

Hammond, *MS*	N. G. L. Hammond, *The Macedonian State. The Origins, Institutions and History* (Oxford 1989).
Head, *HN*²	B.V. Head, *Historia Numorum.* 2nd ed. (London 1911).
Heckel	W. Heckel, *Who's Who in the Age of Alexander the Great: Prosopography of Alexander's Empire* (Oxford and Malden, 2006).
Heckel, *Marshals*²	W. Heckel, *Alexander's Marshals: A Study of the Makedonian Aristocracy and the Politics of Military Leadership*, 2nd ed. (London and New York, 2016).
HMac I	N. G. L. Hammond, *A History of Macedonia*, Vol. 1 (Oxford, 1972).
HMac II	N. G. L. Hammond and G. T. Griffith, *A History of Macedonia*, Vol. 2 (Oxford, 1979).
HMac III	N. G. L. Hammond and F. W. Walbank, *A History of Macedonia*, Vol. 3 (Oxford, 1988).
Hofstetter	J. Hofstetter, *Die Griechen in Persien: Prosopographie der Griechen im persischen Reich vor Alexander* Archäologische Mitteilungen aus Iran, Ergänzungsband 5 (Berlin, 1978).
Hoffmann	O. Hoffmann, *Die Makedonen: ihre Sprache und ihr Volkstum* (Göttingen, 1906).
How and Wells	W. W. How and J. Wells, *A Commentary on Herodotus.* 2 vols. (Oxford, 1912).
IG	*Inscriptiones Graecae.*
Justi	F. Justi, *Iranisches Namenbuch* (Marburg, 1895).
Kaerst, *Hellenismus*	Julius Kaerst, *Geschichte des Hellenismus*, 2 vols. (Berlin and Leipzig, 1926).
Kirchner, *PA*	J. Kirchner, *Prosopographia Attica*, 2 vols. (Berlin, 1901–1903).
Kuhrt, *Corpus*	A. Kuhrt, *The Persian Empire: A Corpus of Sources from the Achaemenid Period* (London and New York, 2007).
LPGN	*A Lexicon of Greek Personal Names* (Oxford).
Niese	B. Niese, *Geschichte der griechischen und makedonischen Staaten seit der Schlacht bei Chaeronea* (1893–1903; reprint Darmstadt, 1963).
*OCD*⁴	*Oxford Classical Dictionary*, 4th ed. (Oxford, 2003).
Poralla	P. Poralla, *Prosopographie der Lakedaimonier bis auf die Zeit Alexanders des Großen* (Breslau, 1913).
Rhodes and Osborne	P. J. Rhodes and Robin Osborne, *Greek Historical Inscriptions 404–323 BC* (Oxford, 2003).

Rolfe I-II	J. C. Rolfe, *Quintus Curtius.* Loeb Classical Library, 2 vols. (Cambridge, MA, 1971, 1976).
Schwarz, *Feldzüge*	F. v. Schwarz, *Alexanders des Grossen Feldzüge in Turkestan* (Munich, 1893).
Tarn I–II	W. W. Tarn, *Alexander the Great*, 2 vols. (Cambridge, 1948).
Tod I–II	M. N. Tod, *Greek Historical Inscriptions*, 2 vols. (Oxford, 1946, 1948).
Welles, *Diodorus*	C. Bradford Welles, *Diodorus of Sicily*, Vol. 8, Loeb Classical Library (Cambridge, MA, 1963).
Westlake, *Thessaly*	H.D. Westlake, *Thessaly in the Fourth Century B.C.* (London, 1935).
Yardley and Heckel	J. C. Yardley and W. Heckel, *Justin: Epitome of the* Philippic History *of Pompeius Trogus*, Vol. 1, Books 11–12, *Alexander the Great* (Oxford, 1997).
Yardley, Wheatley, and Heckel	J. C. Yardley, Pat Wheatley, and W. Heckel, *Justin: Epitome of the* Philippic History *of Pompeius Trogus*, Vol. 2, Books 13–15, *The Successors to Alexander the Great* (Oxford, 2011).

Introduction

THE FIFTH-CENTURY GREEK historian Herodotus wrote his *Histories* in order that "the great and marvelous deeds [*erga megala te kai thōmasta*] performed by the Greeks and the barbarians would not be without fame [*aklea*]." He viewed the wars fought by the Greeks against Darius I and Xerxes as the continuation of an age-old struggle between East and West that began well before the legendary Trojan War. And, indeed, that conflict continued into the fourth century, providing a justification for politicians, kings, and historians alike to write the final chapter in the struggle between the "free" Greeks and the "oppressive" Achaemenid Empire. Whatever the true size of Xerxes' army,[1] danger of annexation by the Persian juggernaut was, at the time, very real, even if the Greeks were mistaken in their belief that following their paradoxical repulse of the barbarian, the Great King was obsessed with gaining revenge.[2] In fact, the events of the 490s and the following decades were, for the Persians, misadventures on the fringes of an empire with more pressing concerns.[3] Nevertheless, Greek paranoia was fertile ground for motivational speeches by politicians and propagandists.

---

1. Herodotus estimated the Persian army at well over 5 million, including camp followers and naval forces. The attempt by Cuyler Young 1980 to debunk Herodotus' figures on the basis of logistical concerns is flawed by faulty mathematics. More convincing is the work of Maurice 1930. If we reduce the Persian army by 90%, we are still looking at a substantial invasion force. There was a similar exaggeration of Persian numbers in the accounts of the battle at Cunaxa and in the Alexander historians (on which see Hyland 2017, 76–78).

2. See Herodotus' well-known but apocryphal story (5.105.2): "[Darius I] instructed one of his servants to tell him three times when dinner was set for him, 'Master, remember the Athenians.'"

3. See Momigliano 1979; Cartledge 1987, 185; and, recently, now the salutary comments of Ruzicka 2012, xx: "Because Persia was continuously so central to Greek affairs, Greeks believed that Greece was similarly of paramount importance in Persian affairs." Economically, the Eastern satrapies were of far greater importance.

In the Path of Conquest. Waldemar Heckel, Oxford University Press (2020). © Oxford University Press.

DOI: 10.1093/oso/9780190076689.001.0001

In the fifth century, the Athenian Empire (the Delian League) could be justified, maintained, and enlarged by propaganda that depicted the Persian Empire as an inveterate enemy and ever-present danger.[4] Whatever the true aims of the Macedonian conquest of the East were, fear of Persia proved an effective, if specious, way of uniting the Greek states, who were bound to Philip II and his successor in the League of Corinth and whose forces served under compulsion. The rhetorician Isocrates, following in the footsteps of his teacher Gorgias of Leontini, who promoted Panhellenism at Olympia in 408, had long anchored his pleas for Greek unity in the image of the Great King as the "Common Enemy of the Greeks," although it remained for Philip to give the idea military underpinning.[5] Indeed, participation in a Panhellenic crusade against the age-old enemy gave luster to the servitude imposed upon the Greeks by their new masters. Through the Greco-Macedonian lens, and with the benefit of hindsight, it is hard to imagine that the expedition against Persia would not have been a success.[6] This book examines the campaign of Alexander from the viewpoint of the conquered peoples, both in mainland Greece and in the East, to the extent that this is possible without resorting to fantasy. Nevertheless, many of the interpretations are speculative, but they are based on the evidence available and attempt to add another dimension to the traditional story of Alexander's conquests.[7]

It is, of course, difficult to write an account from the vantage point of the defeated when the losers of the struggle recorded very little about the conquest, much less about their own view of the enemy, their predicament, intentions,

---

4. Cf. Eddy 1973; Hall 1989. Philip and Alexander were not the first to use such propaganda to their advantage. Agesilaus, when he set out on his Asiatic campaign, sacrificed at Aulis and cast himself in the role of Agamemnon (Xen. *Hell.* 3.4.3-4; Instinsky 1949, 24–27; Rehork 1969, 257–58; Cawkwell 1976, 66–67; 2005, 163).

5. Panhellenism in Lysias: Kleinow 1987. For Panhellenic/anti-Persian sentiment in the 370s, on the part of Jason of Pherae, see Westlake 1935, 119; Buckler 2003, 517. Philip II had already used the vengeance theme in the Sacred War against the Phocians, posing as what Latin writers termed *ultor sacrilegii*, and Xerxes' destruction of the Athenian temples formed part of the Persian crimes against Greece. For the use of vengeance propaganda by Philip and Alexander, see Squillace 2010.

6. Cf. Wiesehöfer 2009, 92: "Only in retrospect, from the perspective of later Greek authors, did his victory against the doomed Persians appear easy."

7. Thus, Schachermeyr 1976, 47, prefaced his study in the following manner: "Ich könnte aber auch die Frage aufwerfen, wie sich die verschiedenen Nationen ihrerseits zu Alexander verhielten und ich glaube, dass das eine neue und interessante Fragestellung wäre. Leider mangelt es mir zu ihrer Beantwortung aber an hinreichendem Material." One notable attempt to broaden our understanding of Alexander's expedition (from both the Macedonian and Persian standpoints) is the excellent cartographic account of Seibert 1985, which I have used extensively in this study. See his comments on pp. 191–94, and especially 198–204.

motivations, and actions. To most living in the Persian Empire, written history was an alien concept, and much of the information concerning the Achaemenid Empire, if it found its way into Greek histories, was filtered through the lens of the victor, who constructed a world for the barbarian that reinforced Western prejudices.[8] The barbarian was defeated not only on the battlefield, or through tenacious sieges, but also in the court of public opinion. No war-crimes tribunals afforded the losers—for it is only losers who are subjected to such inquisitions—a chance to argue their cases.[9] Those whom Alexander regarded as the worst offenders were summarily executed, even if (as in the case of Bessus) the aim was to mollify the native population. How the barbarians viewed Bessus and Barsaentes—whether as regicides or martyrs—we cannot say.[10] Nor, given the opportunity, would they have been permitted to speak freely in condemnation of the new master,[11] for even the Macedonians voiced objections at their own peril. What the defeated thought of men such as Mazaeus or Artabazus is also unknown, but one may imagine that they were regarded by many as shameful collaborators.[12] There are official documents—not many—from the losing side; these are simple records of fact, some taking the form of "prophecies" of events that had already occurred, others preserving practical measures taken to meet the crisis, but all devoid of meaningful comment or judgment.[13]

----

8. Some details about the Persian court and customs came, presumably, from Deinon (*FGrH* 690) via the history of his son Cleitarchus (cf. Brunt 1962, 146). For the changing scholarly approach to Greek sources for Persian history, see Wiesehöfer 2015, 96: "The Greek sources are now examined increasingly less on their value as testimonies for phenomena of the history of events and political structures—even if this remains important. Rather, scholarship focuses on their relevance to the history of ancient mental and intellectual debates on 'foreigners,' i.e. as—equally real—statements of 'foreign' contemporaries (or non-contemporaries) on a 'barbaric' act or institution."

9. In 1948, B. H. Liddell Hart published *The Other Side of the Hill*, which was based on discussions he had with German generals in the period before the Nuremberg trials. Some of the claims have been disputed, but the book at least presents the view from the losers' perspective.

10. For the Iranian nobility, the reader may consult Shayegan 2007, 97–126, which came to my attention only after I had completed this study.

11. That is, in an account published in Alexander's lifetime. Brunt 1962, 141 n. 4, however, points out that pro-Persian (viz. anti-Macedonian) sentiment would have found favor in many Greek cities that were hostile to Alexander.

12. Cf. Curt. 5.8.12. The existence of Persian factions and political tensions is clear from numerous passages in the Alexander historians (esp. Curt. 5.9-12). On Artabazus' dealings with Alexander, see Heckel 2019.

13. The dearth of evidence from the Persian side can be seen in Kuhrt's sourcebook (*Corpus* 418–65). For Gaugamela and the surrender of Babylon, see A27 (cf. Wiseman 1985, 116–21); for

But although the surviving accounts were written in Greek and Latin (all of them long after the Conqueror's death),[14] there is more information about the defeated than many imagine. Greek mercenaries who fought in the Great King's armies supplied the contemporary historians of Alexander with details concerning numbers, deployment, even tactics. If they themselves were not present at war councils, they could learn the essential arguments presented there from those empowered to relay instructions to their men; there were probably also "leaks" of more sensitive discussions.[15] The activities of Memnon of Rhodes, whose importance is clearly exaggerated, must certainly have been reported by Greek eyewitness informants.[16] But far more important were the accounts of affairs given by Persians who either were captured or came voluntarily into Alexander's service. Captives could be, and were, routinely interrogated. Laomedon of Mitylene, a naturalized Macedonian with estates in Amphipolis and described as bilingual (*diglossos*), was placed in charge of the barbarian prisoners of war.[17] Furthermore, some prominent Persians had lived for an extended period at the court of Philip II. Hence, they were both well placed to assess the situations before, during, and after the war and able to communicate, to some extent at least, with their conquerors in Greek. Plutarch (*Alex.* 5.1-2) tells a story of Alexander as a boy questioning "Persian ambassadors" about the state of affairs in the Persian Empire, perhaps a reference to his dealings with the exiles at Philip's court. The most important of these, Artabazus, had married a Rhodian woman, whose brothers spent many years in Persian service. He and at least some of his children

---

the ahistorical "Dynastic Prophecy," see Kuhrt, *Corpus* 462, A41 (= *BHLT* 34–35), and Hyland 2017, 84–85; provisions for Bessus (Mairs 2014, 33, 43).

14. The earliest extant account was written three hundred years after the events it describes. For what follows, see especially Brunt 1962.

15. Cf. Clearchus' participation in the council of the younger Cyrus and the information he gave to his friends (ἐπεὶ δ' ἐξῆλθεν, ἀπήγγειλε τοῖς φίλοις τὴν κρίσιν τοῦ Ὀρόντα ὡς ἐγένετο· οὐ γὰρ ἀπόρρητον ἦν), which shows that information of other sorts could also become known to mercenary troops.

16. I do not subscribe to Hammond's simplistic view that accounts of Greek (and some earlier Persian) affairs came ultimately from Diyllus of Athens (1983, 32–35), of whose work only three fragments survive (*FGrH* 73).

17. Arr. 3.6.6: Λαομέδοντα . . ., ὅτι δίγλωσσος ἦν [ἐς τὰ βαρβαρικὰ γράμματα], ἐπὶ τοῖς αἰχμαλώταις βαρβάροις [sc. κατέστησε]. Laomedon's career: Heckel 146; *Marshals*[2] 317–18; Berve II 231–32 no. 464. Mithrenes, the former *phrourarchos* of Sardis, was apparently bilingual; *peritum linguae Persicae* comes as no surprise when speaking of a man who was himself a Persian; Curt. 3.12.6 must be taken to mean that he also spoke Greek. Less plausibly, Curt. 5.11.4 says that Darius himself had some knowledge of Greek. On the matter of language and interpreters, see Kuhrt, *Corpus* 840–48, B1-21; also Rochette 1997.

(particularly his daughter Barsine,[18] who became Alexander's mistress) must have been functionally bilingual. What they reported no doubt found its way into the account of Alexander's official historian Callisthenes.

In many cases, however, we must draw inferences. We know from the histories that lauded the achievements of the Conqueror that resistance took different forms and in some cases did not materialize at all. This is surely significant, and it is fruitful to examine why certain groups—some Greeks of Asia Minor, some Phoenicians, the Egyptians—chose surrender and accommodation with the enemy over armed opposition.[19] The history of their deeds (or sufferings) in the years, or even the century, before the Macedonian invasion explains their actions and by extension their anxieties and attitudes toward not only the Conqueror but also their current overlord. Some hesitated to submit because their countrymen were virtual hostages in the armed forces (both on land and at sea) of the Persian Empire. Others were kept loyal to the Great King by tyrants or oligarchies who owed position and prosperity to Achaemenid power.[20] Yet others were more concerned with neighboring arch-rivals and saw in the Conqueror a protector or an opportunity to settle old scores. And of course, there were those who gladly changed allegiance for recognition and retention of local power. Just as we can infer the aims of the Conqueror from the nature of his treatment of the defeated and the administrative settlements that concluded hostilities, so we may assume that many of the empire's officials (at a variety of levels) were caught in a tug of war between loyalty to the Achaemenids and self-interest and preservation.

There remains the question of what exactly constituted resistance. In light of the fact that Alexander's campaign was primarily one of military conquest, resistance means first and foremost the act of opposing the invader on the battlefield with the aim of driving him, if not out the empire entirely, then at least from one's own territory. Then there was the failure to surrender a city or to co-operate with the invader. Those who resisted in this way held out the vain hope of exhausting the patience of the besiegers or of deterring them by inflicting heavy casualties and destroying their siege engines. Others defended their territory by employing guerrilla warfare and disrupting the invader's lines of supply and communication, while some submitted but subsequently failed to honor the terms of their surrender.[21] Some clung to the naive belief that the Conqueror could be

---

18. Her linguistic skills are mentioned by Plut. *Alex.* 21.9: πεπαιδευμένη δὲ παιδείαν Ἑλληνικήν.

19. Nevertheless, the autobiography of Somtutefnakht (Kuhrt, *Corpus* 458 no. 38) shows that some Egyptians did fight on the Persian side.

20. Thus, Schachermeyr 1976, 53.

21. Cf. Seibert 1985, 199.

bought off by the extradition of their leaders or of rebels who had taken refuge in their territory. There were even a few who promised neutrality in return for their independence. Such offers were invariably rejected. In the end, it was often a choice between contrition and annihilation. The attitudes and actions of the resisters varied according to their circumstances, their past interactions with foreign overlords, and their forms of government. Nor should we overlook commercial/economic interests. But the determination to resist came, for the most part, from the top, from the ruling elites concerned about local autonomy. The lower strata of society had seen overlords come and go, and they sought assurance that their patterns of life would suffer only minimal disruption. This was especially true of the non-Greek portion of the Persian Empire. In the Greek cities, the masses saw in the overthrow of oligarchies and the establishment of democracies opportunities for greater power.[22] Enslavement was a high price to pay for protecting the interests of the ruling classes.

This book deals with resistance in a number of forms: the attempt by certain peoples to prevent their subjugation by the Conqueror (military resistance), perhaps more aptly described as confronting aggression; the efforts of those who sought to overthrow the new governments that followed defeat on the battlefield or negotiated surrender (rebellion or insurgency);[23] malfeasance on the part of officials who were either newly appointed or retained in their former positions; and, finally, the unwillingness of the Macedonian troops to condone the policies or the behavior of their own king (conspiracy, insubordination, and mutiny).[24]

22. Cf. Schachermeyr 1976, 54. For an excellent discussion of the plight and actions of Achaemenid soldiers in defeat, see Hyland 2017.

23. For this problem and the application of modern terminology to ancient history, see the animated discussion in Howe 2015a; cf. also Brice 2015.

24. Seibert 1985, 198, notes: "Denn die in den Quellen bezeugten Arten der Unterwerfung—freiwillige Übergabe, Übergabe nach vertraglicher Regelung, Einnahme beim ersten Angriff oder Einhame nach längerer Belagerung—waren für die Behandlung der Unterworfenen von ausschlaggebender Bedeutung." On military insubordination, see Roisman 2012, 61–86.

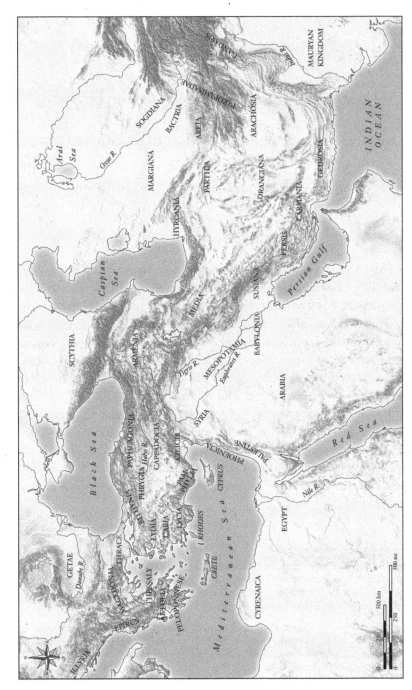

MAP 1.1 Map of Alexander's empire.

I

In the Face of Panhellenic War

GREECE AND THE EASTERN MEDITERRANEAN, 340–334

ALEXANDER'S CROSSING OF the Hellespont in May 334 surprised no one in Asia Minor.[1] A war against Persia, whether for control of the littoral or for a larger purpose, had been expected by Achaemenid officials since 340 at the latest.[2] Philip II's long and unsuccessful siege of Perinthus, followed by an attack on Byzantium via Selymbria, had been countered not only by military support from various Greek states (most notably Athens) but also by aid authorized by Artaxerxes III Ochus, the Persian king who had done so much to revive the empire's fortunes after the ineffectual reign of his father, Artaxerxes II.[3] Although Philip's domination of European Greece was not yet guaranteed, signs of an impending war with Persia were clearly visible to those who cared to turn their attention to East-West relations. Such an undertaking was already being promoted in certain circles south of Thermopylae. Indeed, Isocrates had written in his *Letter to Philip* of 342, when the Macedonian king was engaged in his Thracian war:

---

1. Date of Alexander's crossing of the Hellespont: Arr. 1.11.3 says that Alexander began his expedition "at the beginning of spring"; the battle at the Granicus was in the Macedonian month Daisios (Plut. *Alex.* 16.2), the Attic month Thargelion (May/June). See Hamilton, *PA* 39; Beloch IV² 2.26–28 for the Macedonian calendar.

2. Siege of Perinthus (Arr. 2.14.5, adding Persian intervention in Thrace) and Byzantium and its implications concerning the "state of war" between Athens and Philip II: Worthington 2008, 131–35; Buckler 2003, 475–88. See also Ruzicka 2010, 4–5 (cf. 1992, 127) for the pro-Persian forces campaigning in defense of Perinthus, though perhaps overestimating Pixodarus' role; also Ruzicka 1985.

3. Diod. 16.75.1-2 (Kuhrt, *Corpus* 417 no. 80).

In the Path of Conquest. Waldemar Heckel, Oxford University Press (2020). © Oxford University Press.

DOI: 10.1093/oso/9780190076689.001.0001

As for the barbarians with whom you are now at war, however, it will be enough for you to subdue them only to the point of establishing security for your own land; but you must try to crush the king now called "great" so as to boost your own reputation and also make clear to the Greeks who the enemy is that they must fight.[4]

The Peace of Philocrates of 346, which ended the Sacred War,[5] had gone a long way toward improving Philip's relationship with the Greeks to the south (especially Athens and Thebes), but he was far from prepared, politically or militarily, for a full-scale attack on the "traditional" or "common enemy of the Greeks."[6] The combined lack of overarching authority and common purpose led only to the deterioration of affairs as the reluctant signatories sought to regain lost power.[7] Indeed, the attack on Perinthus was either a sign of or the stimulus for the breakdown of Macedonian relations with Athens.

The new contest—or, rather, the resumption of hostilities between Philip and the Athenians, who were incited by the bellicose speeches of Demosthenes and his ilk—would settle the matter once and for all. On the plain of Chaeronea at the beginning of August 338,[8] Philip with an army of 30,000 infantry and 2,000 cavalry defeated a slightly larger coalition force of Athenians and Boeotians,[9]

---

4. Isoc. *Ep.* 2.11. The reference is, of course, to the Persian king, also known as the Great King. Cf. *Ep.* 3.5: "You can rest assured that you will have incomparable glory, worthy of everything that you have done in the past, when you make all barbarians except those who have championed your cause become serfs to the Greeks, and when you make the now so-called 'Great King' do whatever you command." For the concept see also Isoc. *Paneg.* 133–37, 162–66, 186; cf. Atkinson (in Atkinson and Yardley 2009, 134–35), who believes that the conquest of Asia was limited to Asia Minor. On panhellenism, see Flower 2000. For Isocrates' views, see the illuminating discussion in Pownall 2007, who sees the goal of such propaganda as economic and in the interests of the Greek elites.

5. For Philip and the Sacred War, see Buckler 1989.

6. Dem. 14.3 (ἐγὼ νομίζω κοινὸν ἐχθρὸν ἁπάντων τῶν Ἑλλήνων εἶναι βασιλέα), cf. 10.51. For Philip's unpreparedness at the time, see Judeich, *Kl. Stud.* 299.

7. Perlman 1973, 104 (in a reprint of Perlman 1957) comments: "The peace was . . . more of the nature of a respite, or truce, with both sides suspiciously watching each other and preparing for the next trial of strength."

8. Date of Chaeronea: Metageitnion 7, 338 (Plut. *Cam.* 19.5, 8) [= August 2]. Accounts of the battle: Polyaenus *Strat.* 4.2.2, 7; Diod. 16.86; Plut. *Pelop.* 18.7; Justin 9.3.4-11; Plut. *Alex.* 9. Modern discussions: Griffith, *HMac* II 596–603; Hammond 1994c, 147–54, *MS* 149–51. See also Beloch III² 2.299-304.

9. Size of Philip's forces: Diod. 16.85.5; cf. Beloch III² 2.299. The Greeks are said by Diod. 16.85.6 to have been inferior in numbers; but Justin 9.3.9 says the "Athenians" (*sic*) far outnumbered the Macedonian forces. See the discussion in Beloch III² 2.299-301; also Hammond 1994c, 148–49, who estimates the Greek strength at 35,000, of whom 30,000 were hoplites. The

crushing them in an engagement that saw the first display of Alexander's military leadership and the destruction of the vaunted Theban "Sacred Band."[10] The
victor was able to translate military success into political advantage, forming the
League of Corinth, which recognized Philip as hegemon, in short, its director
of foreign (viz. military) affairs, and giving an immediate purpose to the union
by declaring a war of vengeance against Persia.[11] The agreement stipulated the
contributions of the allies and penalties for opposing the League's initiatives, the
last point pertaining directly (though not exclusively) to Greeks who took up
mercenary service in opposition to Philip and his allies.[12]

Although a war against Persia to avenge past atrocities had little attraction
for the Macedonian soldiers who were to form the core of the army of invasion,
neither Philip nor Alexander was oblivious to the value of Panhellenic propaganda. Indeed, Alexander commissioned Callisthenes of Olynthus, a nephew of
Aristotle, to promulgate the Panhellenic aspects of the campaign.[13] Among the
allied Greeks, most will have recognized these as empty slogans, though (as is always the case with the masses) there were doubtless others who were taken in or
simply chose to believe in a higher purpose.[14] But this was yet to come. Philip's
war on Persia was inaugurated in the spring of 336, when an advance force of some
10,000 under the command of Attalus, Parmenion, and Amyntas crossed into
Asia Minor. It appears that the bulk of the invading army was to join them in the
following spring, for Philip was still selling his mission to the Greek ambassadors
in October of 336, when he celebrated the marriage of his daughter Cleopatra
to Alexander I of Epirus. As it turned out, this was also the occasion of his own

Greek alliance included Leucas, Corcyra, and Acarnania from the west and Euboea, Achaea,
Megara, and Corinth.

10. Alexander's role at Chaeronea is, admittedly, exaggerated to his benefit by Plutarch (*Alex.*
2-4). Diod. 16.86.1 mentions that Philip stationed Alexander alongside his most notable generals; cf. Hamilton, *PA* 23. For the destruction of the Sacred Band: Plut. *Alex.* 9.2; Diod. 16.86,
following a pro-Greek source, says only that "many Boeotians were killed," without specifying
the Sacred Band. Their monument appears to be the Lion of Chaeronea (Paus. 9.40.10; cf.
Strabo 9.2.37 C414). See also Tuplin, *OCD*⁴ 1305; Ma 2008.

11. Diod. 16.89.2-3; Polyb. 3.6.12-13.

12. The heavily restored lines 5-7 of *IG* II² 236 show that the parties to the Common Peace
swore not to take up arms against Philip or any of those who abided by the peace. See also
Parke 1933, 181; Trundle 2004, 71. Oddly, Diod. 16.1.5 says that Philip left behind such resources
(δυνάμεις) that his son Alexander had no need to call upon allies to overthrow Persia (ὥστε τὸν
υἱὸν Ἀλέξανδρον μὴ προσδεηθῆναι συμμάχων εἰς τὴν κατάλυσιν τῆς Περσῶν ἡγεμονίας). On the
background, see Buckler 1994.

13. On the alleged role of Aristotle in recommending Callisthenes to Alexander, see the cau-
tionary remarks of Bosworth 1970.

14. For discussion of the *Rachekrieg* and the origins of the war against Persia, see Seibert 1998
and the response by Bloedow 2003.

death. The heir to both the throne and the direction of the Panhellenic War would be his son, Alexander III, who by virtue of his conquests has come to be known by the epithet "the Great."[15]

I

The consolidation of Macedonian power came at an opportune time. In early 338, Artaxerxes III Ochus was murdered by his vizier Bagoas, who became the power behind the throne, upon which he placed one of the king's sons, Arses.[16] This young man took the regnal name Artaxerxes (IV), but his reign was so brief and ineffectual that few modern historians have taken note of his official title.[17] Greek sources and the Roman writers who used them were fond of court intrigue, especially when it appeared to involve the harem and much-despised eunuchs. Bagoas was, in all likelihood, physically a eunuch, but his power and competence were far greater than what the ancients ascribed to the guardians of the harem.[18] He was both general and chiliarch: in short, he was powerful in the military and at the court, commanding the Great King's armies on occasions and controlling access to his person.[19] Through the agency of a court physician he administered poison to Ochus but found Arses less compliant than he had hoped and eliminated him as well, along with his children. The unsuccessful experiment had lasted two years. From the depleted royal family Bagoas now promoted Darius son of Arsanes, the latter a nephew of Artaxerxes II, to the kingship. But when the vizier sought to remove the new king by poison, his plot was discovered and the perpetrator

---

15. Cartledge 2004, 190, aptly calls it "Alexander's inescapable legacy." He inherited the mission but not the ideology associated with conquest and consolidation, as Kaerst, *Hellenismus* I[3] 313 notes: "Sein Sohn Alexander, der so im jugendlichsten Alter seinem Vater auf dem Throne folgte, trat allerdings in das Erbe der Pläne und der Macht Philipps ein, aber er tat dies mit der Selbständigkeit einer ungewöhnlich früh entwickelten, eigenartigen Herrscherindividualität, die, auch indem sie an das Werk des Vater anknüpfte, doch von Anfang an ihre eigenen Wege ging, ihre besonderen Ziele verfolgte."

16. Olmstead 1948, 489.

17. In fact, Bessus (when he made his claim to the kingship) is often referred to by modern scholars as Artaxerxes IV, although he was the fifth to assume the name. See Badian 1977b. For Arses as Artaxerxes IV, see the Babylonian Tablet in Kuhrt, *Corpus* 424 no. 2.

18. For the role of eunuchs in Assyria, see Grayson 1993; similarly, Hdt. 3.4.2 attributes greater authority to an Egyptian eunuch of the pharaoh Amasis; Myśliwiec 2000, 177, accepts Aelian's claim (*VH* 6.8) that Bagoas was Egyptian. Whatever the historical value of the *Persika* of Ctesias of Cnidus (on whom see now Llewellyn-Jones and Robson 2010), it is clear that that author—and certainly his informants—considered eunuchs politically influential. See also Lenfant 2012; Briant, *HPE* 919; Llewellyn-Jones 2010, 260.

19. Persian chiliarchs: Charles 2015; earlier literature in Collins 2001, 259 n. 1.

forced to drink his own deadly concoction. Such, at least, is the version given by Diodorus of Sicily (late first century B.C.).[20]

Olmstead, in his *History of the Persian Empire* (1948), remarks: "Bloodthirsty as Ochus had shown himself to be, he was an able ruler, and it is not too far wrong to say that, by his murder, Bagoas destroyed the Persian Empire." That the change of rulers marked a turning point appears true only in retrospect, but the opportunity presented to Philip and Alexander by the destabilization at the Achaemenid court is undeniable, at least in the short term. This view should not be taken to revive the now (rightly) discredited view of Persian decadence and decline in the fourth century.[21] Indeed, Pompeius Trogus (in the abbreviated work of Justin) puts a far more positive spin on the accession and career of Darius III. Before ascending the throne, he was known as Codommanus, and he gained fame for himself and his countrymen when he defeated in single combat a champion of the rebel Cadusians. The reputation for cowardice that has adhered to the man for more than two millennia was clearly unfounded and based on a willful misinterpretation of his later actions. Pompeius Trogus' source was far more generous—and, indeed, truthful—when he wrote that "Darius fought a protracted war against Alexander the Great *with varying success and great courage* but eventually he was defeated by Alexander and murdered by his own kinsmen."[22]

Justin's summary of regime change places Darius and Ochus in sharp contrast. There is no mention of Arses or the kingmaker, Bagoas, and it is unclear whether this can be attributed to Justin's careless abbreviation or to the possibility that Pompeius Trogus used a different source for Book 10 from what he used for the following two books, which dealt with Alexander. Achaemenid court politics were, of course, far more complex than Greek historians were able to comprehend.[23] Nevertheless, it is true that there was a destabilization that allowed the Macedonians, despite a succession crisis of their own, to initiate the campaign in the face of lesser opposition. That is not to say that the Persian satraps, or Darius himself, would have mounted a more serious challenge to the invader at this point, for it is highly likely that they regarded the forces at their disposal—that is, the satrapal armies supported by a large contingent of Greek

---

20. Diod. 17.5.3-6.

21. Cf. Briant, *HPE* 1008.

22. Justin 10.3.6.

23. The intrigue at the court is mentioned in a Babylonian document: see *BHLT* 34–35, where the "eunuch" in question is clearly Bagoas; cf. Kuhrt, *Corpus* 425 no. 4(i).

mercenaries—as sufficient.[24] The advance force under Parmenion and his staff had enjoyed only limited success in the years 336 and 335, proving scarcely more dangerous than the Spartan contingents who harassed northwestern Asia Minor in the 390s. Experience, it seems, had taught different lessons to the antagonists. Persia measured Greek invading armies by the ineffectual campaigns of Agesilaus and his predecessors. The notion that Agesilaus could have brought Persia to its knees is fantasy, and it is pure exaggeration to say he "overran a large part of Asia, mastering the open country, and finally would probably have succeeded, had not the Spartans recalled him because of political affairs, in reducing the whole Persian Empire to the direst straits."[25] Nevertheless, the Greco-Macedonians believed that the expedition of Cyrus the Younger had exposed the vulnerability of the Persian Empire. Xenophon himself remarks in his *Anabasis*:

> It was clear to anyone who paid close attention to the size of the King's empire that it was strong in terms of lands and men, but weak on account of the great distances of road and the dispersal of its forces, if someone made a quick military strike against it.[26]

Indeed, the Athenian general Chabrias was said to have remarked that Pharnabazus was quick with words but slow in action, to which the satrap replied that his words were his own but that the Great King was master of his actions.[27] The picture of inefficiency endured: Plutarch observed that the escape of the Ten

---

24. Briant, *HPE* 818: "the central authority had probably been alerted by Arsites and taken appropriate action." Kaerst, *Hellenismus* I³ 335 questions the Achaemenid response, which failed to give sufficient support to Memnon ("seine Unternehmungen fanden keine wirksame Fortsetzung und tatkräftige Unterstützung von der persischen Reichsleitung") and relied on the "blinde Vertrauen des Großkönigs auf seine Massen, auf die Überlegenheit der äußeren Mittel." It is, furthermore, a commonplace that Darius underestimated his young opponent, though much of this reflects the bias of the sources.

25. Diod. 15. 31.3. See Hamilton 1991, 86–103; Cartledge 1987, 180–202; cf. Plut. *Ages.* 15.1-2; Paus. 4.17.5. Cawkwell 2005, 172 n. 29, rightly notes: "he [Agesilaus] was probably lucky to be recalled to the war in Greece. This enabled him to continue his big talk."

26. Xen. *Anab.* 1.5.9. See also Judeich, *Kl. Stud.* 190.

27. For the sluggishness of the Persians, see also Diod. 15.41.5 (ὡς ἐπίπαν γὰρ οἱ τῶν Περσῶν στρατηγοί, τῶν ὅλων οὐκ ὄντες αὐτοκράτορες, περὶ πάντων ἀναφέρουσι τῷ βασιλεῖ, καὶ προσαναμένουσι τὰς περὶ ἑκάστων ἀποκρίσεις). Cf. Diod. 15.41.2. Rawlinson 2005, 206, sees the achievements of both the Ten Thousand and Agesilaus as indicative of Persian weakness: "The expedition of the younger Cyrus, and the return of the Ten Thousand under Xenophon, had made patent to all the internal weakness of the empire. The campaigns of Agesilaus had shown how open Asia Minor was to attack by an enterprising enemy." See also Kaerst, *Hellenismus* I³ 332–33. Cf. Briant, *HPE* 817: "the relative permeability of the Persian defenses."

Thousand from the heart of the empire made clear that the Great King's empire, though rich in gold, luxury, and women, was nothing but "smoke and mirrors" and thus encouraged the Greeks to despise the barbarians.[28]

II

The arrival of the advance (or expeditionary) force in the spring of 336 gave hope to those in coastal Asia Minor who thought to use the power of Macedon to bring about revolution at home, with the concomitant independence from Persian control. It should be noted, however, that liberation and regime change went hand in hand. "Freedom" was little more than a political slogan. Local politics and factional strife dictated that since the ruling party was propped up by Persian power, its overthrow demanded a champion of equal or greater power. Whatever words were used to justify revolution, the truth remained that the Greeks of Asia Minor were on the verge of exchanging one overlord for another.[29]

In Ephesus and the town of Eresus on Lesbos, however, the "liberators" anticipated the full-scale invasion (which at this time they expected Philip to lead) by erecting altars to Philip and instituting regime change.[30] The Ephesians made their intentions clear: democratic revolution, with the expulsion of the pro-Persian oligarchs, occurred very soon after the arrival in Asia of the expeditionary force under Parmenion and Attalus. The promise of Macedonian protection was surely what gave the democrats the courage to act, and they sought the king's patronage by placing a statue of him in the temple of Artemis. Whether this was in keeping with Philip's evolving view of his position or the stimulus for further connections with the "divine" world is unclear; certainly there was an earlier cult of Amyntas III in Pydna and one of Philip in Amphipolis.[31] We are told that

---

28. Plut. *Artox.* 20.2-3: ἀποφήναντες τὰ Περσῶν καὶ βασιλέως πράγματα χρυσὸν ὄντα πολὺν καὶ τρυφὴν καὶ γυναῖκας, τὰ δ᾽ ἄλλα τῦφον καὶ ἀλαζονείαν, πᾶσα μὲν ἡ Ἑλλὰς ἐξεθάρρησε καὶ κατεφρό νησε τῶν βαρβάρων.

29. Cf. Wiemer 2011, 125, for the case of the Rhodians, who "were unable to form a foreign policy of their own and had no option but to follow wherever they were led. The arrival of Alexander the Great did little to change this pattern: when the Rhodians submitted to the king who had won the battle of Issus, they only changed masters again."

30. For the situation in Ephesus, see Bosworth 1988a, 251–52. Eresus is a more difficult case, and it is uncertain whether the pro-Philip tyranny, which established a cult of Zeus Philippios, came to power long before Parmenion and Attalus crossed into Asia or as a result of their presence; see Heisserer 1980, 27–78, and Lott 1996 for earlier dates; Rhodes and Osborne 414–15 favor 336.

31. Dreyer 2009, 229. In his final year, Philip was honored as *synnaos* and *synthronos*, but neither implied "divinity." Badian 1996, 13: "This does not amount to deification. But it clearly raised

on the day of his daughter's wedding, he arranged a procession in the theater in Aegae (Vergina), in which the statues of the twelve enthroned Olympian gods were displayed, along with a thirteenth—Philip himself—seated among them.[32]

But this display was followed by the assassination of Philip in front of a crowd that included foreign dignitaries, an act that put the invasion of Asia on hold and left the Ephesian democrats in a precarious state with regard to both their political enemies and their Persian overlords. How long they held on to power is unclear, but it is certain that by the time of Alexander's crossing in 334, the oligarchs had staged a successful counter-revolution under the leadership of Syrphax and his family and with military support from Memnon of Rhodes.[33]

The primary purpose—and thus the actual progress of the expeditionary force under Parmenion and Attalus—is unclear, and we know only of the occupation of Magnesia, attempts on Gryneum and Pitane, and the activities of a subordinate officer, Calas, in the region of the Propontis.[34] Vital to our understanding of the campaign of 336–335 is the question of whether the expeditionary force occupied Magnesia on Sipylus or Magnesia on the Maeander. The latter is close to Ephesus, but the former is much farther north and in the vicinity of Gryneum and Pitane. It has been argued that Philip's concern was to gain a foothold in Asia by winning over the Greek cities. To this end, Ephesus may have been intended as the starting point for the Macedonian conquest of Asia. Magnesia on the Maeander was then a natural place to establish a Macedonian garrison.[35] Such

---

Philip to a status above that of other mortal men." See Habicht 1970, 11–16; also Hamilton 1984, 9–10; Carney 2007a, 36. See also Carstens 2009, 125–26, and especially Schultz 2007 on the Philippeum.

32. Diod. 16.92.5.

33. Syrphax and his relatives are known only from the fact of their overthrow and murder (Arr. 1.17.12). Memnon's interference in Ephesus is dated by Judeich, *Kl. Stud.* 305, to a point very soon after the Macedonian withdrawal from Magnesia, but this assumes that the city is Magnesia on the Maeander.

34. On the Macedonian campaign in 336 and 335, see detailed discussion by Kholod 2018, which appeared after this study had been completed.

35. Thus, Judeich, *Kl. Stud.* 303 n. 1: "Es ist . . . anzunehmen, dass die Makedonen, wie sechzig Jahre früher die Spartaner, Ephesos zum Ausgangspunkt ihrer Operationen machten und von hier aus das wichtige Magnesia am Maeander besetzten." But unlike the Spartans, the Macedonians did not control the sea and were forced to begin their campaign in the Hellespontine region. Badian 1966, 63 n. 20, rightly observes: "Anyone who tries to follow the campaign will agree that this is probably Magnesia on Sipylus, not the better-known city on the Maeander." Since the minor victory of Memnon at Magnesia (described by Polyaenus, *Strat.* 5.4.44) did not dislodge the Macedonians from the city, this makes it harder to explain the counter-revolution in Ephesus (but see Bosworth I, 131). Beloch III² 1.620 regards Magnesia as a staging point for a Macedonian march on Sardis. This would have followed the course of the Hermus River. Kholod 2018, 420 n. 39 is noncommittal.

action, so close to the borders of Caria, was sure to affect Pixodarus' thinking about his future in the new world order.

This interpretation has its weaknesses. First of all, since the expeditionary force crossed the Hellespont and landed (in all probability) at Abydus, it is strange that it should move so far south immediately, leaving Gryneum and Pitane to be dealt with later. Second, the limited information we have about the upheavals in Ephesus says nothing about the presence of the Macedonian army.[36] Finally, our sources, when they do tell us something about the activities of the expeditionary force and the measures taken to limit its success, speak only of Memnon, as if he were the sole military commander in that region. This man, who would play such a major role in the West in 334/3, was in the spring of 336 nothing more than a regional military commander.[37] What is more, his territories—which had been given to him and his brother, Mentor, by Artabazus—were in the Troad, very close to the region in which Parmenion and Attalus were active upon their arrival in Asia.[38] The expeditionary force was thus probably tied up on the mainland opposite Lesbos, encouraging the anti-Persian party there to throw its support behind Philip but failing to gain much support on the mainland. Their base of operations was thus probably Magnesia on Sipylus.[39]

Many of the Asiatic Greeks were content to wait for events to unfold, whether motivated by caution or indifference. Certainly, not all were crying out for change, either within their individual poleis or in relation to their Persian overlords. The actions of the Delian League and (in its later form) the Athenian Empire, as well as the broken promises of the Spartans, sufficed to remind them that freedom was illusory and came at a cost.[40] In the short term, their inaction proved beneficial.

---

36. Green 1991, 186: "Ephesus had been taken by Parmenio, and on that occasion its citizens went so far as to institute a quasi-cult of Philip in the temple of Artemis." This (reiterating comments on p. 98) is pure speculation. Heisserer 1980, 59, holds a similar view.

37. Briant, *HPE* 820: "Diodorus exalts the figure of Memnon and confers on him an authority and influence he certainly did not have in the spring of 334." Not long after the Granicus battle, he would become ὕπαρχος τῆς κατὰ τὴν Ἀσίαν παραλίας. It was the position held by Mentor before his death. On Memnon and Mentor, see Hofstetter 125–27 no. 215 and 129–31 no. 220. Their sister was the wife of Artabazus, and it appears that they were the successive husbands of Artabazus' daughter Barsine (see Brunt 1975).

38. Scepsis, Cebren, and Ilium. Arr. 1.17.8 speaks of this area as "Memnon's Land"; cf. Polyaenus, *Strat.* 4.3.15.

39. See also Buckler 2003, 520 n. 31.

40. Briant, *HPE* 856: "Generally, the enthusiasm of the Asia Minor Greeks for the 'war of liberation' must be considered from the perspective of hindsight." Heisserer 1980, 58 n. 9: "for the city of Gryneum (and almost for Pitane) . . . 'liberation' meant the sale of its citizens into slavery." Ruzicka 1997, 124, writes: "Given the absence of reports of fighting, it is most likely that Parmenion received spontaneous submissions, like that reported at Ephesus." But it is

Important details are lacking, but inscriptional evidence from Eresus, Mitylene, and Chios appears to show that these states defected to the Macedonian side in 336, if not earlier. An added incentive may have been the relative weakness of the Persian naval forces in 336 and the prospect of naval support from the member states of the League of Corinth. The latter did not materialize, since the death of Philip preempted a full-scale invasion. Nevertheless, it was not until 334/3 that Memnon and the Persian fleet could effect counter-revolution on the islands.

It was not only the Greeks of Asia Minor who saw either opportunity or danger in the planned Macedonian expedition. Pixodarus, the dynast of Caria and youngest brother of Mausolus (whose magnificent tomb in Halicarnassus was considered one of the Seven Wonders of the World),[41] hoped to gain a measure of independence by anticipating the invasion and hitching his wagon to the Macedonian cause. His position was precarious: upon the death of his brother, Idrieus, in 341/0, Pixodarus usurped power from his sister (Idrieus' wife), the elder Ada.[42] The coup was apparently not treated with disfavor by Ochus, who was preoccupied with affairs elsewhere, nor by his ephemeral successor Arses. But the ousted queen (*basilissa*) withdrew with her entourage to the safety of Alinda and remained a useful pawn in any future power struggle. Other non-compliant dynasts succumbed to the power of the Great King in due course, and a Macedonian invasion encouraged defectors to hope for protection. Pixodarus thus offered his daughter, also named Ada, in marriage to one of Philip II's sons. Philip was not blind to the advantages of a Carian ally, nor was he unaware of the prestige of the thoroughly Hellenized Hecatomnid dynasty.[43] Whether Pixodarus proposed Arrhidaeus as his prospective son-in-law or was merely content to cement an alliance at any cost hardly matters in terms of the military and political considerations of the two rulers. Some scholars have suggested that Pixodarus himself had wanted Arrhidaeus as a son-in-law, knowing that he was the most likely heir to the Macedonian throne.[44] Plutarch does, in fact, depict Pixodarus as the one who initiated the process:

---

exactly the absence of reports of any kind that makes it difficult to reconstruct events. On Greek freedom, see Nawotka 2003; 2010, 125–37.

41. See Waywell 1988; on the Mausoleum in particular, see Carstens 2009, 65–74.

42. Carney 2005, 68–70.

43. On the Hecatomnids, see especially Hornblower 1982, 34–51; also Ruzicka 1992 and 2010; cf. Bean 1971; Carstens 2009; LaBuff 2017. For Pixodarus, see Berve no. 640; Heckel 223.

44. Thus, Badian 2012, 502 [= Badian 2007]: "Philip's intention of invading Asia had been known there ever since Memnon and Artabazus, obviously well informed about it, returned from honoured exile in Macedonia, to inform Memnon's brother Mentor, who had secured his recall. By the time of Alexander's and Olympias' flight from Macedon, the plans were common

> When the satrap of Caria, Pixodarus, was trying to inveigle his way into an alliance with Philip by means of a family bond, he wanted to marry the eldest of his daughters to Philip's son Arrhidaeus. He sent Aristocritus to Macedonia about the matter, and once again talk and slanderous comments would come to Alexander from his friends and mother to the effect that Philip was trying to settle the kingdom on Arrhidaeus through a glorious marriage and an important connection.
>
> Very worried by this, Alexander sent the tragic actor Thessalus to Caria to talk with Pixodarus and tell him that he should forget about his illegitimate brother, who was not sound of mind, and switch the marriage connection to Alexander. (Plut. *Alex.* 10.1-2)

Since primogeniture was hardly the deciding factor—though in many cases (and especially in the family of Amyntas III) the kingship passed to sons in order of age—Pixodarus must not have had high hopes for the marriage of Ada to Arrhidaeus, for only a fool would have interpreted the temporary displeasure of Philip with his son, Alexander, as an indicator that the half-witted Arrhidaeus was destined for the throne. That Pixodarus understood the implications of the turmoil at the Philip's court but remained totally unaware of Arrhidaeus' mental condition is doubtful. In itself it was hardly a "deal breaker."[45] Alexander got wind of the arrangement and, through the agency of Thessalus, offered himself as a suitor for Ada's hand. The very fact that Pixodarus preferred this offer makes it clear that the Carian dynast had not pinned his hopes on the prospect of Arrhidaeus' kingship and that legitimacy and succession were secondary matters. What he wanted, in fact, was an alliance with Philip and security in the postinvasion era.

---

knowledge. But as we shall see, Pixodarus in fact *waited until Macedonian forces actually stood in Asia before sending his messenger.* After their first successes it was clear that Caria would be invaded before long—and Ada, whose claim to legitimate sovereignty clearly surpassed his, was still secure in her mountain fastness. With support of a powerful and victorious army, she was likely to be acclaimed by large sections of the population as their legitimate ruler" (emphasis added).

45. Lane Fox 1973, 36, rightly comments on Philip's thinking: "a half-witted son was a light price for such an alliance." Ruzicka 2010, 4, draws attention to Plutarch's description of the marriage as "brilliant" (γάμοις λαμπροῖς) but fails to note that Plutarch is referring to the distorted account (διαβολαί) given by Alexander's *hetairoi*. Also, he believes, despite Plutarch's explicit statement to the contrary, that it was Philip who approached Pixodarus (Ruzicka 2010, 7). Philip himself, speaking to Alexander, is said to have called Pixodarus Καρὸς ἀνθρώπου καὶ βαρβάρῳ βασιλεῖ δουλεύοντος ("a mere Carian and the slave of a barbarian king"). The Pixodarus affair serves to enhance our picture of the tensions at the Macedonian court, but it is easy to lose track of the true intentions of Philip and the Carian dynast. For the chronology of the affair, see Heckel 1981a, 57; French and Dixon 1986.

The negotiations fell through, largely on account of Alexander's meddling and much to Philip's chagrin, for an alliance would have been mutually beneficial, and Pixodarus offered substantial military resources.[46] The limited success of the advance force, which had become bogged down in northwestern Asia Minor, and the news of Philip's death forced the dynast to reconsider his options. Perhaps his treasonous negotiations with the Macedonian king had been exposed. Darius, newly established on the Persian throne, may have become wary of him. Strabo says that Pixodarus, "having espoused the Persian cause, asked for a satrap to share his rule."[47] The younger Ada was promptly married to Orontopates,[48] who was sensitive to the dynastic tradition in Caria. This self-preservation was short-lived, for Pixodarus soon died, apparently of natural causes. The sudden administrative change does, however, suggest that Orontopates was the instrument of the Great King's displeasure.[49]

In short, there were some in Asia Minor who anticipated the Macedonian invasion, only to be alarmed by the news of Philip's assassination and forced to endure the consequences of what they believed was the end of the undertaking. Alexander, of course, set affairs in Greece in order, had himself recognized as hegemon of the League of Corinth, and crushed resistance and talk of Medizing, with the destruction of Thebes. But most inhabitants of Asia Minor found it expedient to bide their time and await the arrival of the Macedonian force. Those who had acted prematurely discovered that the winds of change were themselves changeable and unpredictable. The impact of Alexander's presence on Asian soil will be examined in a later chapter.

---

46. Thus, Ruzicka 2010, 4, but Ruzicka 1992, 130, paints a different picture: "Idrieus' dispatch of thousands of mercenaries to Cyprus in the mid 340s had, it appears, substantially and permanently reduced Hecatomnid military resources."

47. Strabo 14.2.17 C657: περσίσας δὲ μεταπέμπεται σατράπην ἐπὶ κοινωνίᾳ τῆς ἀρχῆς.

48. Orontopates: Heckel 186; Berve II, 295–96 no. 594 s.v. Ὀροντοβάτης. His name appears on Carian coinage as *ROONTOPATES* (*BMC Caria* LXXXIV; Head, *HN²* 630), but the literary texts call him Orontobates.

49. Cf. Heckel 2008, 39. Diod. 16.74.1-2 says Pizodarus (*sic*) ruled for five years (ἐδυνάστευσεν ἔτη πέντε ἕως ἐπὶ τὴν Ἀλεξάνδρου διάβασιν εἰς τὴν Ἀσίαν). His death can probably be dated to the spring of 335. Olmstead 1948, 491, remarks: "So sure was Pixodarus that Persia would be the victor that he married Ada—once offered to Arrhidaeus—to the satrap Orontobates in sign of return to Persian allegiance." Orontopates could hardly have been recognized as "satrap" before the marriage, which in turn made Pixodarus expendable. Ruzicka 1992, 134, speaks of "Darius' new arrangements and a period of shared rule with Orontobates."

2

The Long Road to Asia Minor

RESISTANCE IN MACEDONIA AND GREECE

THE YEAR THAT followed Philip's ill-fated union with Cleopatra-Eurydice was marked by turmoil at the court, destabilization of the northern and western frontiers, and political opportunism in the south. Whatever long-term plans the king had for his new bride and her prospective offspring, these had to take a back seat to military and political expediency. But just as Alexander was precocious and ambitious, so, too, did he distrust any act that threatened his right to succeed his father.[1]

I

The seeds of Alexander's conquest and subsequent greatness were sown in his boyhood, but the events that catapulted him into the limelight of national and international affairs were played out at a wedding banquet in Pella, Macedon's capital since the reign of Archelaus I (413–399).[2] Philip, the victor of Chaeronea, new hegemon of a Greek League (albeit united by force), had returned to his northern homeland, there to plan his great expedition against Persia and—if the

---

1. The impact of these events at court cannot be underestimated. The point is illustrated by Plut. *Alex.* 9.12-13, describing an exchange between Philip and Demaratus of Corinth: "Meanwhile the Corinthian Demaratus came to visit Philip—he was a guest friend of his house and a straight-talking man—and after the initial greetings and courteous exchanges, Philip asked him how the Greeks were getting along with each other. 'After filling your own house with such bitter dissension and troubles [στάσεως τοσαύτης καὶ κακῶν ἐμπέπληκας],' replied Demaratus, 'it is really appropriate for you to be concerned for Greece.'" The sarcastic remark had its desired effect.

2. But see the comments of Borza 1990, 296; also Petsas 1978. For the city, see Akamatis 2011, who accepts a foundation date in the reign of Archelaus I; cf. Greenwalt 1999.

In the Path of Conquest. Waldemar Heckel, Oxford University Press (2020). © Oxford University Press.

DOI: 10.1093/oso/9780190076689.001.0001

fates allowed—to unwind from the stress of his annual military campaigns. He had collected wives as he acquired territory, though truth be told, the two were generally part of inseparable packages. At the age of forty-six, he had already brought six wives into the palace, many of them from fringe areas that branded them as barbarians, if only some dared to say so. The biographer Satyrus, in his now-lost *Life of Philip*, lists the names of the wives taken by Philip in the course of his campaigns in the "twenty-two years" of his reign. These included one Illyrian (Audata), two Thessalians (Philine and Nicesipolis), an Upper Macedonian from Elimeia (Phila), princesses from Epirus (Olympias) and Thrace (Meda), and then, finally, a Macedonian noblewoman named Cleopatra, subsequently known also as Eurydice. And Satyrus concludes that "by bringing her home as another wife alongside Olympias he made a total shambles of his life."[3]

The new bride was hardly to blame for the events that unfolded. A girl of tender years and the darling of a besotted middle-aged man, Cleopatra-Eurydice was the pawn of her uncle and guardian Attalus, whose ambition and fondness for drink robbed him of his wits. Falsely secure in the power of his relationship with his new "son-in-law," he unwisely proposed a toast at the wedding banquet, praying that the union would produce "legitimate heirs." Whether he added the words "and not bastards" or if this was merely a natural inference on the part of Alexander (and later writers) matters little.[4] The words—undoubtedly reflecting Attalus' true feelings—were fueled by alcohol but no more forgivable on that account.[5] What was done or said without reflection—both the words of Attalus and Philip's drunken outburst at the wedding feast—was greeted by the prince with impulsive rage and indignation. Withdrawing from the court, and in the company of his mother, Alexander fled first to Epirus and thence to Illyria. The impression of Macedonian weakness, or at least temporary instability, was not lost on the Illyrians, whether they received a tainted version from the exile himself or merely read between the lines. Nor was the news slow in reaching the Greeks to the south. Though they had cowered after the Macedonian victory at Chaeronea,

---

3. Athen. 13.557b-d.

4. Γνήσιον ἐκ Φιλίππου καὶ Κλεοπάτρας γενέσθαι διάδοχον τῆς βασιλείας (Plut. *Alex.* 9.7), but Athen. 13.557d says γνήσιοι . . . καὶ οὐ νόθοι βασιλεῖς. The importance of Cleopatra-Eurydice and her offspring has been debated. Palagia (2010 and 2017, 152–53) believes the Eurydice of the Philippeum was Philip's last wife. Her inclusion in the statue group indicated her importance as "potential mother of future heirs" (2017, 153). See, however, Carney, *King and Court* 89–90 (an "Afterword" to Carney 2007a); Bowden 2017a, 176, like Carney, identifies her as "Philip's mother."

5. Kaerst, *Hellenismus* I³ 316, rightly calls the views of Attalus and his relatives "ehrgeizigen Hoffnungen."

they were quick to believe reports of any weakness that might be exploited. The conflagration that followed Philip's murder had been sparked by events before his death.[6]

The outburst at the wedding banquet was just the tip of the political iceberg. There were others who accepted Philip's kingship grudgingly but certainly did not welcome Alexander as his successor. Philip had come to the throne in 360/ 59, when his brother, the reigning king, Perdiccas III, was killed in battle against the Illyrians. At that time, the heir to the throne, Perdiccas' son Amyntas, was a small child, and it appears that the Macedonians in a time of national crisis accepted Philip as king in his place—though some have argued for a brief period of regency.[7] Amyntas grew up at the court and was eventually married to one of Philip's daughters, appropriately the granddaughter of the very king against whom Perdiccas III died fighting.[8] Neither Amyntas nor his new wife could have been expected to look with favor upon Philip's heir, whether this proved to be Alexander or, as some have speculated, a son borne by Cleopatra-Eurydice. And there were rival claims as well. Aëropus of Lyncestis, who belonged to a branch of the royal family, had three living sons: Arrhabaeus, Heromenes, and Alexander. He himself was apparently exiled by Philip in 338 and may have died soon afterward. But his sons were prepared to challenge the succession when the time came.[9] Such were the dynastic politics that formed the backdrop against which the affairs of Greece and the north were played out between October 336 and May 334.

The celebration of the wedding of Alexander I of Epirus to Philip's daughter Cleopatra was accompanied by a lavish ceremony in the theater of Aegae designed

---

6. For the most recent discussion, see Heckel, Howe, and Müller 2017, with references to previous literature. See also Howe 2015a and Müller 2016, 269–76. For Attalus' role, see Heckel, *Marshals*[2] 7–12. It must be stressed, however, that until the crisis resulting from the wedding banquet, the relationship between father and son had been a good one, indeed exemplary. Cf. Kaerst, *Hellenismus* I[3] 316; see also Köhler 1892.

7. Amyntas Perdikka: Justin 7.5.10; Athen. 13.557b; Diod. 16.1.3; Aes. 3.51. Modern discussions: Aymard 1950; Ellis 1971; Errington 1974; Prandi 1998; Worthington 2003; Hammond, *HMac* II 651; Müller 2016, 236–37; Heckel, *Marshals*[2] 287–90. Similarly, Alfred the Great became king in Wessex in place of Æthelwold, son of Æthelred I, in a time of crisis. Æthelwold sought the crown for himself after Alfred's death (Stenton 1971, 250, 321).

8. Death of Perdiccas III: Diod. 16.2.4 (in battle with the Illyrians); Justin 7.5.6 (at the hands of his own mother, Eurydice; on whom, see Carney 2019). Since one of Philip's first battles was against Bardylis, he is probably the king who defeated Perdiccas. He is also thought to have been the father of Audata, whose daughter Cynnane married Amyntas Perdikka. The marriage probably dates to the late 340s, but see the unconvincing arguments of Lane Fox 2011, 31–32.

9. For the Lyncestians and their claims, see Heckel, *Marshals*[2] 19–32; Bosworth 1971b. Exile of Aëropus: Polyaenus, *Strat.* 4.2.3; cf. Heckel 5.

to impress the gathered representatives of the Greek states. But it ended with the spectacular assassination of the most powerful man in the Greek world. The procession that moved into the theater at dawn was a display of Philip's power and status. In fact, it proclaimed the not-too-subtle message that Philip was no ordinary man, for the parade included a likeness of the Macedonian king seated among the enthroned Olympian gods. But as the man of the hour walked into the theater, flanked by two Alexanders, his son and his new son-in-law, he was ambushed by an assassin. Pausanias of Orestis, a young man of the king's guard, rushed upon Philip and thrust a Celtic dagger between his ribs. Killed as he attempted to flee, Pausanius had nevertheless accomplished his goal, although the motive for the murder remains a matter for debate.[10] Olympias, the jilted wife, greeted the news with sardonic satisfaction, but in political circles, both in Macedon and beyond its borders, any rejoicing or sense of liberation was soon to be met with disappointment and, indeed, punishment.

Scapegoats were easy to find. Two sons of Aëropus of Lyncestis, Arrhabaeus and Heromenes, were arrested and executed—if there was a trial, there is no evidence of it[11]—more likely because they posed a threat to Alexander than for their role in the assassination. Nor was Amyntas Perdikka destined to survive:[12] his supporters, Amyntas son of Antiochus and Aristomedes of Pherae, were not slow to flee, eventually finding their way to the Persian king. The son of Perdiccas III and husband of Cynnane (half-Illyrian daughter of Philip II) was executed on a charge of conspiracy. Only months later, Alexander was already offering to marry the widow to Langarus, king of the Agrianes.[13]

---

10. Plut. *Alex.* 9–10; Diod. 16.91-95; Justin 9.6.1–7.14. For the much-discussed problem of the background to Philip's murder, see particularly Willrich 1899; Badian 1963; Hamilton 1965; Kraft 1971, 11–42; Ellis 1971; Bosworth 1971b; Fears 1975; Heckel 1981a; Develin 1981; Carney 1983; 1992; 2006; Will 1987; Whitehorne 1994, 43–56; Antela-Bernárdez 2012; Heckel, Howe, and Müller 2017. Against the view that the Macedonians were politically divided along geographical lines (Upper and Lower Macedonians), see Heckel 2017b. Pausanias was a member not of the seven-man guard but of a younger group of guardsmen known as *somatophylakes basilikoi* or *hypaspistai basilikoi* (see Heckel 1992, 250–53).

11. Despite the imaginative interpretation by Hammond 1978 and 1991b, 401, of P.Oxy. 15.1798, there is no evidence of a trial in this second century A.D. document. Hammond also believes that τοὺς τ]ε περὶ θρόν[ον are the "Friends" of the king (i.e., Philip), but Palagia 2018 argues persuasively that there is no evidence for a royal throne in Macedonia in this period. The "throne" in the papyrus fragment must be that of a god or a priest.

12. His death: Arr. *Succ.* 1.22; cf. Arr. 1.5.4. See Heckel 23 s.v. "Amyntas [1]"; Berve II, 30-1 no. 61.

13. Langarus and Cynnane: Arr. 1.5.4; Heckel 100–101.

MAP 2.1 Map of Greece and Macedonia.

II

In the south, reaction was swift but ineffectual. Plutarch remarked that Philip lacked sufficient time "to tame Greece and put it under the yoke."[14] Nevertheless, the suddenness of his death left the Greeks ill prepared to take concerted countermeasures. Many states were, in fact, shackled by Macedonian garrisons.[15] The Thessalians were among the first to show signs of disaffection. Their proximity to Macedonia and their potential military strength made them an immediate concern. At the height of their power in the fourth century—from the time that Lycophron was tyrant of Pherae and laid the foundations for the unification of Thessaly until the murder of his son and successor, Jason—Thessaly was a force to be reckoned with in a Greek world riven by the competing ambitions of Sparta, Thebes, and Athens.[16] In the years that followed the death of Amyntas III, when his first three successors had but a tenuous grip on power, the affairs of Thessaly led to Theban intervention in Macedonian politics.[17] Despite the vicissitudes of the Thessalians' fortunes after the death of Jason of Pherae, it remained clear that they had great military potential, especially with respect to cavalry, in which resource they rivaled their northern neighbors. They would eventually contribute a sizable and effective contingent to the armies of both Philip and Alexander. The father had exploited divisions between Larisa and Pherae, in the first instance, and his role in the Sacred War against the Phocians, soon afterward, in order to bring Thessaly securely into the Macedonian orbit. His successes won for him the position of archon of the Thessalian League, and he sealed his alliances with marriages to Philine of Larisa and Nicesipolis of Pherae.[18]

---

14. Plut. *Alex.* 11.2.

15. See Roebuck 1948.

16. Thessaly was a prominent state in the sixth century but declined after the Persian invasion. Between Lycophron and Jason, Thessaly was controlled by Polyalces, possibly Lycophron's eldest son. For the period of dominance by the tyrants of Pherae, who held also the *tageia* of the Thessalian League, see Westlake, *Thessaly* 47–159. Jason's reputation appears to have exceeded his real power, something that is reflected in modern scholarship (cf. Borza 1990, 189: "Jason . . ., had he lived, might have anticipated Philip II's organization of the Balkans"). He had given his support to Thebes as it rose to its brief period of greatness, but he was assassinated in 370. The years 370-358, in which Alexander of Pherae dominated Thessalian affairs, were a time of instability and decline (cf. Roy 1994) as Thessaly found itself pressured by Thebes and gravitating towards Athens. Westlake 159 calls Alexander's role "sensational rather than important." His death in 358 opened the door to Macedonian intervention. See also Graninger 2010, 312–13.

17. The pro-Macedonians in Larisa summoned the aid of Alexander II of Macedon, but his ambitions merely drew the Thebans into Thessaly and beyond (Buckler 1980, 112–14; Roy 1994, 194–95; Müller 2016, 219–22; Borza 1990, 189–91).

18. The Sacred War: Buckler 1989; Griffith, *HMac* II 259–95; Müller 2016, 52–54. Philip's marriages: Athen. 13.557c; cf. Ogden 1999, 18–19, and Carney 2000b, 60–61, though I doubt Carney's suggestion that both marriages were contracted before 357. See also Ehrhardt 1967.

The Thessalian rising against Alexander was premature and easily crushed by the young king, who entered their territory unopposed by cutting steps into the side of Mount Ossa and creating what was to be known as "Alexander's Ladder."[19] The contrite Thessalian League promptly elected him archon, and the Amphictyonic Council of Delphi recognized his authority.[20] Similarly, the first moves by the Thebans, Athenians, and Spartans to regain lost ground were stopped in their tracks by the king's sudden arrival. No longer were they amused by Demosthenes, who had ridiculed Alexander, calling him a child, and compared him with Homer's fool, Margites.[21] The League of Corinth was renewed and Alexander elected as Philip's successor,[22] thus affirming his leadership of the Panhellenic War against Persia. The Spartans, though stymied by the quick actions of the young king, remained aloof from the League and its grand designs, arguing that it was their prerogative to lead rather than follow.[23] Official recognition of Alexander did little to alleviate Greek discontent, and an extended absence by the king in the north allowed his enemies to organize a more serious rebellion, the suppression of which would leave them in no doubt about Macedonian supremacy.

The barbarians to the north and west of Macedon had long been attuned to their powerful neighbor's internal troubles. The Illyrians especially kept an uneasy peace with Philip, and, because they comprised strong tribal units with individual rulers, they were unpredictable by the very fact of their disunity.[24] The various

---

19. Polyaenus 4.3.23: Ἀλεξάνδρου κλίμακα. The Thessalians had blocked his entrance at the Vale of Tempe. Westlake, *Thessaly* 218, is cautious in view of the difficulties of defending Tempe, as the Greeks discovered at the time of Xerxes' invasion. In addition to military surprise, Alexander could use claims of kinship with the Thessalians, tracing his descent back to a common ancestor, Heracles, and to the family of Achilles (Diod. 17.4.1; Justin 11.3; cf. Graninger 2010, 317).

20. As Westlake, *Thessaly* 219, points out, the Thessalian oath to Philip was valid only in his lifetime (but Diod. 17.4.1 speaks of Alexander's πατροπαράδοτον ἡγεμονίαν). Cf. Justin 11.3.1. For the Amphictyony, see *OCD*⁴ 73. The Delphic Amphictyony held its meeting at Thermopylae (Diod. 17.4.2). Thessalian League: Sordi 1958. For the office of archon and *tagos*, see Griffith, *HMac* II 288–89; Hornblower 2002, 96; also *OCD*⁴ 1467.

21. Dem. 23.2; cf. Aes. 3.160. In the coming year, Alexander would fulfill his prophesy that Demosthenes, who called him a child when he was among the Illyrians and Triballians and a stripling among the Thessalians, would discover that he was a man before the walls of Athens (Plut. *Alex.* 11.6; *Dem.* 23.2). See also *OCD*⁴ 898 s.v. "Margites." See also Moloney 2015.

22. Diod. 17.4.9: ἔπεισε τοὺς Ἕλληνας ψηφίσασθαι στρατηγὸν αὐτοκράτορα τῆς Ἑλλάδος εἶναι τὸν Ἀλέξανδρον καὶ συστρατεύειν ἐπὶ τοὺς Πέρσας.

23. Arr. 1.1.2: Λακεδαιμονίους δὲ ἀποκρίνασθαι μὴ εἶναί σφισι πάτριον ἀκολουθεῖν ἄλλοις, ἀλλ' αὐτοὺς ἄλλων ἐξηγεῖσθαι.

24. Hammond 1966 and 1994c, 423, against the views of Papazoglou 1965. The most prominent tribes were the Ardiaei, Autariatae, Dardani, and Taulantii. The struggles of the Illyrian

Illyrian campaigns of the fourth century that merited the attention of our historical sources are merely highlights of a perennial struggle. Illyrians drove Amyntas III, temporarily, from the throne (393/2–391/0), and they may have defeated him again in 383.[25] Another major battle with the Illyrians brought an abrupt end · to the reign and life of Perdiccas III. Here some 4,000 Macedonians fell—a catastrophe of epic proportions, given the military resources of the day.[26] As late as 344/3 and 337/6, they were still inflicting serious casualties on Macedonian armies.[27] Political marriages, on both a dynastic and an aristocratic level, provided a measure of stability, but they were often indicators of past struggles rather than guarantees of long-term peace. The frontiers were rugged and porous,[28] and what garrisons existed were rarely sufficient to preempt hostilities. Bardylis was defeated, with heavy casualties, by Philip at Heraclea Lyncestis and made the transition from most dangerous enemy to ally in 358. The victor married his daughter or granddaughter, Audata (renamed Eurydice, perhaps in honor of her mother-in-law).[29] But even this did not end hostilities in the west; for Philip's general, Parmenion, defeated the forces of Grabus (perhaps ruler of the Grabaei)

---

tribes against one another and with Macedon made it difficult to establish a peaceful relationship with the region as a whole. It is easy to view the Illyrians as a thorn in the side of the burgeoning Macedonian kingdom and thereby ignore that they had their own geopolitical concerns. See Greenwalt 1988; Howe 2017.

25. Diod. 14.92.3. See the highly speculative view of Mortensen 1991, 55, who thinks that Sirrhas was the Illyrian king who expelled Amyntas. A second expulsion at the hands of the Illyrians in 383/2 is mentioned by Diod. 15.19.2 (accepted by Hammond, *HMac* II 174). See Müller 2016, 202–3; Wilkes 1992, 118; also Greenwalt 1988.

26. Death of Perdiccas III: Diod. 16.2.4-5; Polyaenus 4.10.1; Müller 2016, 233; Borza 1990, 197: "This was more than a border raid, as evidenced by the size of the Macedonian force sent out."

27. Diod. 16.69.7 attributes Philip's campaign of 344/3 to "ancestral hatred" (πατρικὴν ἔχθραν); for 337/6, see Diod. 16.93.6 and Curt. 8.1.25. For the background, see also Dell 1970 and 1980. These two campaigns, against Pleuratus and Pleurias, should not be conflated on the false assumption (Beloch III² 1.606 n. 2; cf. Badian 2012, 449) that the kings in question are the same individual (see Hammond 1966, 245).

28. Cf. Strabo 7.7.9 C327. Garrisons on the Illyrian border: Hammond 1994a, 438.

29. It was Bardylis who defeated Perdiccas III. Philip's victory: Diod. 16.4. The marriage must have occurred soon after Philip's victory. Reuss 1881: "König Philipp hatte damals bereits die Paionen und Illyrier besiegt und ihren König Bardylis getötet." I see no evidence for his death: [Lucian] *Macrob.* 10 says that he was eighty-nine when he fought on horseback against Philip. The dead man was Agis, king of the Paeonians (Diod. 16.4.2); [Lucian] *Macr.* 10 also mentions Atheas the Scythian as falling in battle against Philip when he was more than ninety years old. His career: Mortensen 1991. Victory over Bardylis: Diod. 16.4.4-7; Frontinus *Strat.* 2.3.2; Polyaenus 4.2.17. Marriage to Audata: Athen. 13.557c; Arr. *Succ.* 1.22 calls her Eurydice; see Carney 2000b, 57–58; Heckel 64. It is unlikely that Grabus was Bardylis' successor (Tod II 170, following Schaefer 1887, II, 20).

in 356.[30] The Illyrians and Epirotes, who as neighbors had their disputes,[31] also had dynastic connections, perhaps reflecting the common interests of the barbarous west.[32] But Epirus had become a virtual puppet of Macedon after Philip's marriage to the princess Olympias and was not a pressing concern; in due course, Alexander the Great would call his namesake, the Epirote king, both uncle and brother-in-law.[33]

It was standard practice for subjects and neighboring states—some of them reluctant allies—to reassess their relationships with the dominant power when there was a change of rulers, particularly when this was accompanied by internal, dynastic disputes and effected by violent means.[34] A campaign of consolidation by the new king of Macedon may have been intended, at least in the northern regions, as preemptive,[35] but it soon provoked active military opposition.[36]

---

30. Plut. *Alex.* 3.8 and Justin 12.16.6, who do not name Grabus, but he was an ally of the Athenians in 356 (along with Cetriporis the Thracian and Lyppeius the Paeonian): *IG* II² 127 = *SIG*³ 196 = Tod II no. 157 = Rhodes & Osborne no. 53; also Diod. 16.22.3; cf. Beloch III² 1.231 n. 1; Hammond 1966, 244. On the background to the alliance, see Archibald 2010, 334; cf. Loukopoulou 2011 for Macedon and Thrace.

31. Diod. 15.3.1-3 (385/4); Frontinus *Strat.* 2.5.19 (c. 360).

32. The Hellenization of Epirus came later than that of Macedon, but the royal house's adoption of Greek names (asserting descent from the Aeacids, the mythical ancestors of the Molossians; cf. Strabo 7.7.8 C326; also Funke 2000) is prominent in the fourth century (see Cross 1932, 7–9, 24–25; Heckel 1981b, 80–82). Politically, it was perhaps more progressive than Macedon (Hornblower 2002, 199). For the history of the region, see Hammond 1967 and 1994c; for relations with Macedon, see Greenwalt 2010. Philip's marriage to Olympias in 357 must have had as one of its aims to drive a wedge between Epirus and the Illyrians. Connections between the two barbarian regions can be seen in the time of Pyrrhus, though it probably points to long-standing relationships. Beroa, the wife of Glaucias, was an Aeacid (Justin 17.3.18-19), and Bircenna was one of Pyrrhus' two Illyrian wives, of whom he was exceptionally fond (Plut. *Pyrr.* 9.2-3 and 10.7: Λάνασσα μεμψαμένη τὸν Πύρρον ὡς μᾶλλον προσέχοντα ταῖς βαρβάροις γυναιξίν).

33. For Epirus, see Cross 1932 and Hammond 1967. Alexander I of Epirus: Heckel 10 s.v. "Alexander [1]"; Berve II, 19–21 no. 38. Since both Macedonia and Epirus were threatened by Bardylis in 360, it is likely that some alliance was made by the two states against a common enemy (Hammond 1967, 533). After 350, hostilities between Arybbas and Philip were followed by the annexation of some Epirote territory and eventually (342) the establishment of Alexander I on the Epirote throne (Justin 8.6.5; but see Errington 1975; Heskel 1988).

34. As evinced by the early years of Philip II, who, although his predecessor died at enemy hands and his accession—despite the presence of Perdiccas' young son—was relatively smooth, was beset by foreign enemies. His position is aptly summed up by Müller 2016, 236: "Er sah sich mit einem komplizierten Geflecht aus außenpolitischen, militärpolitischen und innerdynastischen Konflikten konfrontiert."

35. Schachermeyr 1976, 48, notes that the basis for relations between Macedon and the northern states had been established already in the time of Philip II.

36. Arr. 1.1.4 says Alexander learned that the Triballians and Illyrians were on the point of "rebellion" (νεωτερίζειν ἐπύθετο Ἰλλυριούς τε καὶ Τριβαλλούς), a peculiar word to apply to people

Whatever impulse the young king had to seek glory in the East, he did not neglect the security of his European realm.[37] The first of Macedon's northern neighbors to take a stand against Alexander were the so-called autonomous Thracians, who inhabited the lands beyond Mount Haemus to the northeast of Amphipolis.[38] Their aim was not to challenge Macedonian authority but rather to contest his right to pass through their lands under arms. They attempted to block his advance through the Shipka Pass (or perhaps the Trojan Pass)[39] by unorthodox means:[40]

[The Thracians] were preparing to prevent him from advancing and had occupied the crest of Haemus on the path that their enemy was taking. They had assembled carts and positioned them in front of themselves like a palisade; they intended using the carts as a barrier from which to defend themselves in the case of emergency, but they also had the idea of letting them loose on the phalanx of the Macedonians at the point where they came up the most precipitous part of the mountain. Their thinking

who were not in fact subject to Macedonian authority. In the case of the Triballians, some had perhaps submitted to Philip II, but, as Bosworth I 53 notes, they "cannot have been completely subjugated, for by their demands of passage-money in 339 they showed themselves both independent and hostile."

37. Schachermeyr 1973, 111.

38. Alexander set out from Amphipolis at the beginning of spring 335. It was a ten-day march to Mount Haemus (Arr. 1.1.4-5). Hammond 1974, 80, estimates that he did not reach the Getae on the north shore of the Danube until "June or so."

39. The Shipka Pass: thus, Burn 1973, 57; Schachermeyr 1973, 111 n. 96; Lane Fox 1973, 82; Hammond 1981, 46; but Bosworth I 54 prefers the Trojan Pass farther to the west (more cautiously, Bosworth 1988a, 29). This is indeed the easier and faster route, but it depends also on the location of the Triballians themselves. Since Alexander had planned to meet ships sent from Byzantium to the mouth of the Danube, we may assume that the Triballians were located somewhat farther downstream—though, of course, not at the river mouth itself. Cf. Kaerst, *Hellenismus* I³ 321 n. 3.

40. The Macedonian countermeasures: Heckel 2005. Wagons and shields: Bloedow 1996. English 2011, 24, speculates: "If the wagons were released down the slope, and there is no real reason to doubt this, then they must have been manned. If they had not been then they would have veered off course and straight into the walls of the pass long before they reached the advancing Macedonians, even if the drive mechanism had been fixed in place. None of our sources mentions any drivers, but it must have been the case that some brave souls were steering the wagons as they careered down the slope, a role that they would have known before they started would have meant their certain death." But the reason the Macedonians were successful in breaking ranks to avoid the wagons must surely have been that they were driverless. For this reason, too, English's analogy with the scythed chariots at Gaugamela is not convincing. The troops who parted ranks were not *sarissa*-bearing *pezhetairoi* in either case, and at Gaugamela, where the chariots did exploit a gap, they did extensive damage precisely because they could be maneuvered by their drivers. On this, see Heckel, Willekes, and Wrightson 2010.

was that the more densely packed the phalanx as the carts came tumbling down on it, the more their violent descent would scatter it.

Alexander contemplated the safest way of traversing the mountain; and since it seemed that the risk had to be taken—there was no other way around—he issued the following orders to his hoplites. When the carts came down the slope, those for whom flat terrain provided an opportunity for breaking ranks were to separate and allow the carts to fall between them; those who were hemmed in were to crouch down together, some actually falling to ground, and tightly link their shields together so that the carts bearing down on them would probably, by their impetus, jump over them and continue forward innocuously.

In the event Alexander's recommendation proved correct. A part of the phalanx divided, and the carts rolled over the shields of the others, inflicting little damage and with no one dying under them. (Arr. 1.1.6-10)

When this tactic failed, some of the Thracians moved forward to meet the Macedonians who were surging up the hill, only to be driven back by the enemy's archers; for they lacked sufficient defensive armor. The Macedonians drove them from the high ground, killing about 1,500 in the process. The remainder fled, leaving their women, children, and possessions as booty for the victors.[41]

The victory cleared Alexander's path to the Danube, where he encountered first the Triballians, who were clearly the object of his campaign, and then the Getae, who lived beyond the river. The Triballians were a Thracian tribe that occupied the southern lands of the lower Danube.[42] Although they had suffered defeats at the hands of the Macedonians, they were hardly subdued. As late as 339, they had inflicted a serious thigh wound on Philip as he was returning from his campaign against the Scythian Atheas.[43] The Triballian king, Syrmus, learning of Alexander's intention to march against them, took the women and children to the Danube, where they found shelter on the island of Peuce. The Triballian fighters meanwhile encamped at the Lyginus River,[44] about three days'

---

41. Arr. 1.1.5-13; Polyaenus 4.3.11; Fuller 1958, 220–21; Lonsdale 2007, 112; English 2011, 22–25.

42. Mócsy 1966, 103–4.

43. Marsyas of Pella (*FGrH* 135/6 F17) = Didymus, *Demosth.* col. 13, 3–7. A *sarissa* was driven through Philip's thigh, laming him (τ[ρ]ίτον τραῦμα λ[α]μβάνει κατὰ τὴν εἰς Τριβαλλοὺς ἐμβολὴν τὴν σάρισάν τινος τῶν διωκόντων εἰς δεξιὸν αὐτοῦ μηρὸν ὠσαμένου καὶ χολώσαντος αὐτόν). The weapon passed right through Philip's thigh and killed his horse (Justin 9.3.1-2). Philip's wounds: Riginos 1994. Atheas (or Ateas): Justin 9.2.

44. The location is uncertain, but Hammond 1981, 46, identifies it with the Rositsa River; cf. Velkov 1987, 263.

march from the Danube, placing themselves behind Alexander's army. But the Macedonians turned back to deal with them:

> Caught like that, the Triballians formed up at the glen by the river. Alexander, however, also marshaled his phalanx in deep formation, led it forward, and ordered the archers and slingers to rush ahead and let fly their arrows and stones at the barbarians, in the hope of drawing them into the open out of the glen.
>
> When the barbarians were within range and under fire, they proceeded to charge out against the archers in order to engage them hand-to-hand, archers being otherwise unarmed. But having drawn them out of the glen, Alexander now instructed Philotas to take the Upper Macedonian cavalry and charge their right wing at the point where they had advanced furthest in their sortie. Heracleides and Sopolis he ordered to lead against their left wing the cavalry from Bottiaea and Amphipolis. The infantry phalanx and the rest of the cavalry, deployed before the phalanx, he led against the center.
>
> While it was still a matter of skirmishing on both sides, the Triballians did not come off worse; but when the dense phalanx launched a vigorous charge at them, and the cavalry, no longer hurling javelins but thrusting at them with their mounts, were falling on them at various points, they turned to flee through the glen to the river. (Arr. 1.2.4–6)

Three thousand Triballians were killed in the engagement, but only a few were captured. Dense woods and darkness cloaked their flight.[45] The noncombatants on the island of Peuce were, however, spared indignities at the hands of the Macedonians, since the banks of the island were steep and it proved difficult for the enemy's ships to land there.[46] The prize, in short, was not worth the risk. Furthermore, the Getae, who lived beyond the river, had made a demonstration on the banks with 4,000 horse and 10,000 foot. But the intended warning only invited a military response, particularly from a king who refused to back down from a challenge, no matter how great the odds.

---

45. Arr. 1.2.7. The Macedonians were said to have lost eleven cavalrymen and about forty infantry. For this campaign, see Fuller 1958, 221–22; English 2011, 26–28.

46. Arr. 1.2.2-3, 3.3-4; Strabo 7.3.8 C301, 7.3.15 C305. For the location of the island, see Bosworth I 57, rejecting the view that it was at the mouth of Danube (noted also by Velkov 1987, 263–64), since this would place the Triballians too far to the east and because the reference to the steep banks of the island and the rapid flow of the river does not suit the flat and marshy Danubian delta, where the river is sluggish.

Crossing the river at night on hides stuffed with straw and on boats used by the local fishermen, the Macedonians landed behind the shelter of a cornfield. At dawn they marched through the field, holding their *sarissai* at the level and scything the crop—thus causing devastation while also guarding against any natives who might have concealed themselves in the field. The cavalry, which followed the infantry formation, shifted to the right wing as soon as the Macedonians emerged from the cornfield; their sudden assault engendered panic and headlong flight in the Getae, who took as many of their women and children as they could to safety on horseback. Their city and all their possessions fell into Macedonian hands.[47]

Following this setback, the barbarians of the north were prepared to acknowledge the king's authority, giving him the stability he needed on his northern frontier. The recently defeated Triballians were among the first, and they contributed cavalry forces to Alexander's Asiatic campaign.[48] They were joined also by representatives of the Celts who lived farther to the west. The latter were motivated more by curiosity than by fear.[49] Their dealings with Alexander give some insight into the arrogance of the young king. Believing that the news of his exploits— at this time relatively limited, if truth be told—had intimidated the Celts, he asked their envoys what it was the Celts feared most. The pages of history are filled with examples of barbarians who fail to show proper deference to would-be conquerors,[50] and the Celts responded with equal bravado, saying that "their greatest dread was that the sky would fall upon them."[51]

III

Now that he had established the Danube as his northern frontier, Alexander moved south and west to launch a strike on his most bitter enemies, the Illyrians. To this end he moved into the lands of the Agrianes and the Paeonians, both of

---

47. Arr. 1.3.5-4.5. The campaign served as a trial run for that against the Scythians beyond the Iaxartes in 329 (noted by Kaerst, *Hellenismus* I³ 321), although the opposition on that occasion was more determined. Bosworth 1988a, 30, calls it "a gratuitous act of terrorism on a helpless people, but it demonstrated yet again the efficiency and ruthlessness of the invaders and proved that the Danube was no defence against them." But Velkov 1987, 265, points out the strategic importance of the area.

48. Diod. 17.17.4.

49. Arr. 1.4.8: Ἀλέξανδρόν τε ἀγασθέντες οὔτε δέει οὔτε κατ᾽ ὠφέλειαν πρεσβεῦσαι παρ᾽ αὐτόν.

50. E.g., the response of the Ethiopians to the Fish-eaters, who arrived as agents of Cambyses in the sixth century (Hdt. 3.21).

51. Arr. 1.4.8; Strabo 7.3.8 C308, based on Ptolemy, *FGrH* 138 F2.

whom were securely in his camp.[52] The menacing gestures of the Autariatae were derided by Langarus, king of the Agrianes, a stout ally who called them "the least warlike tribe in those parts"[53] and kept them in check while Alexander moved to the region south of Lake Ochrid to confront a rising by two Illyrian chieftains, Glaucias and Cleitus.[54] The latter, king of the Dardanians, took up a position in Dassaretis, on the borderlands with Macedonia. He gathered his forces at Pellium, probably located at Goricë, at the bend of the Eordaicus (Devoll) River.[55] Hostilities were preceded by an otherwise unattested human sacrifice—three boys and three girls—along with that of an equal number of black rams. These offerings, still visible when the Macedonian troops arrived before the city, may have had less to do with religious practice than with a desire to intimidate the enemy.[56]

Forced to retreat within the city, Cleitus found himself besieged until Glaucias, the Taulantian king, arrived with his forces and threatened to pin the Macedonians down between two armies. Nor could the Macedonians allow the two kings to unite their forces. An attempt by Glaucias to catch Philotas and his foraging party while they were cut off from their main force was thwarted by the quick action of Alexander. But the Illyrians retained a tactical advantage, occupying the high ground with a substantial cavalry force that was supplemented

---

52. Arr. 1.5.1. They occupied "the upper Strymon valley and the country between that valley and the upper Vardar (Axios) valley" (Hammond 1974, 78; cf. *HMac* I 78, 202). See also Strabo 7.5.12 C318. A part of Paeonia had already been in Macedonian hands in Thucydides' time (Thuc. 2.99.4; cf. Borza 1990, 87–88); see Diod. 16.4.2 and Dem. 1.13 for their defeat at the hands of Philip, early in his reign; but their continued resistance is seen in the treaty with Athens made by Lyppeios (Rhodes and Osborne no. 53). The Paeonians found themselves caught between the Illyrians and the Thracians and probably regarded Macedon as their best option and supplied troops to its king (Ellis, *CAH* VI² 747). Paeonian cavalry served with Alexander from 334 onward (Diod. 17.17.4). See also Merker 1965. Alexander's route: Hammond 1974, 78, writes, "Alexander took the quickest route to western Macedonian via Sofia, Kjustendil (ancient Pataulia), Kratovo (Tranupara) and Štip (Astibus), and the from the upper Vardar valley via Gradsko and Prilep into Pelagonia and Lyncus. . . . From Lyncus the most direct route to Pelion was via Florina, Pisodherion, Kariai and the Gryke e Ujkut." But then he proposes an alternate route "via Vatokhorion and Bilsht." For the most part, we are reduced to guesswork.

53. Arr. 1.5.3: ἀπολεμωτάτους τῶν ταύτῃ. This is perhaps boastfulness on the part of Langarus. They were once a powerful tribe (Strabo 7.5.11 C317-318). For their location and that of the Dardanians, see Strabo 7.5.1 C313, 7.5.7 C316 (cf. Mócsy 1966, 104).

54. Bosworth 1988a, 31, links the danger from the west with possible disaffection in Lyncestis after the execution of Heromenes and Arrhabaeus. For the Illyrian campaign, see Arr 1.5-6; cf. Hammond, *HMac* III 56–66; Hammond 1974; Bosworth 1982; also Fuller 1958, 85. For a good and concise discussion of Alexander's campaigns in the north, see King 2018, 138–41.

55. Arr. 1.5.5; cf. Livy 31.40 (a city of the Dassaretii). For the location, see Hammond 1974.

56. Arr. 1.5.7. Bosworth I, ad loc., has no comment.

by both light-armed units and hoplites. If Alexander moved against them, there was the threat of an attack from the city, and the route that the Macedonians must take was through a wooded area between river and cliff that restricted the width of the advancing column to no more than four abreast.[57]

The invader countered with a dazzling display of military discipline which at first mesmerized and then terrified the Illyrians into abandoning their positions. The Taulantians retreated to the safety of the city and their compatriots. But there were sufficient numbers who held the high ground, and these were now attacked by Alexander's forces:

> The enemy left the hill when they saw Alexander's onslaught and turned off to the mountains on both sides. Together his with companions Alexander then took the hill and sent for his Agrianians and archers, about two thousand in number. He gave the order for the hypaspists to cross the river and for the Macedonian squadrons to follow them. When they had successfully completed the crossing they were to fan out to the left so the phalanx would appear solid as soon as they crossed. Alexander was in a forward outpost himself and from the hill had a full view of any enemy assault. When they saw the Macedonian force make the crossing, the enemy charged down the mountains in order to attack the rear of Alexander's troops as they went off, but when they were already approaching the king himself ran out with his retinue, and the phalanx raised a shout as it advanced through the river. The enemy, with everything coming at them, turned and fled, and Alexander meanwhile brought the Agrianes and the archers up at the double toward the river. He was himself the first across, but when he saw the enemy putting pressure on those at the rear he set up his ballistas on the riverbank and gave the order for every kind of projectile that can be launched from ballistas to be launched at them at the furthest range, and for his archers, who had already entered the water, to shoot at them from the middle of the river. (Arr. 1.6.68)

The Macedonians had extricated themselves from a dangerous position, but the Illyrians, given the chance to unite their forces, squandered any hope of success. Two days later they kept careless watch as they encamped for the night and were attacked while many were still in their beds. Panic ensued. The Taulantians under Glaucias fled with heavy losses. Cleitus torched the city of Pellium and hastened

---

57. Arr. 1.5.12.

to join his fleeing ally.[58] The Illyrians were still a force to be reckoned with, but these were no longer the days of Amyntas III.[59] Not only had the Macedonian state been consolidated and secured, but the military efficiency had now attained a level—in training and equipment and most of all in leadership—that made it virtually irresistible. Illyria proved to be a valuable training ground for campaigns in the hill country of Asia.[60]

IV

Alexander's lengthy campaigns on the northern marches gave the Greeks to the south of Thermopylae a chance to reconsider their situation. Many now repented what must have seemed a premature capitulation in 336. By summer 335, there were rumors that the impetuous young king had been killed in Illyria. Surely some wished it to be true, but the story was a deliberate fabrication by the enemies of Macedon, especially in Athens. Demosthenes allegedly confirmed the report by bringing into the *ekklesia* a witness, who claimed that he himself had been wounded in the engagement in which the king died. [61] Demosthenes and his supporters did what they could to move the Thebans to rebellion, and their attempt to oust the Macedonian garrison from the Cadmea was clearly influenced by the report. There was also the bitter legacy of Chaeronea. Philip's treatment of Thebes—scene of his early years of political captivity—had been relatively harsh: the opponents of the king were executed and the government entrusted to an oligarchy of three hundred, maintained by a Macedonian garrison.[62] The Boeotian League continued to exist, but the reconstitution of Thespiae, Plataea, and Orchomenus subverted Thebes' earlier dominance. Confident of Athenian, and apparently Persian, support, the anti-Macedonian party, led by Phoenix and

---

58. Arr. 1.6.9-11. Full discussion of the campaign: Hammond 1974, 77–87; Fuller 1958, 223–26. Illyrian casualties appear to have been significant, but Arrian provides no numbers, not even about the strength of the army.

59. Wilkes 1992, 124: "The escape and victory of Alexander and his army brought home to the Illyrians, or at least some of them, how much had changed since they had brought Macedonia to its knees barely 50 years before."

60. Cf. Howe 2017, 107.

61. Justin 11.2.8: "[Demosthenes] qui Macedonum deletas omnes cum rege copias a Triballis adfirmaverit producto in contionem auctore, qui in eo proelio, in quo rex ceciderit, se quoque vulneratum diceret."

62. Worthington 2014, 97–98.

Prothytes and armed in exile by Demosthenes,[63] besieged the garrison on the
Cadmea, proclaiming their intention to liberate Greece from Macedonian control with the help of Persia.[64]

Alexander hurried south from western Macedonia to Boeotia, reaching
Thebes in less than two weeks and outpacing the news of his march.[65] The suddenness of his arrival stunned even those who had treated the rumors of his death
with skepticism. Still there were those who suggested that the army had been sent
by Antipater and was being led by his son-in-law Alexander the Lyncestian.[66]
Demosthenic Athens, which had voted to support Thebes, prevaricated, content
to watch events unfold; reinforcements from the Peloponnese likewise delayed,
perhaps restrained by the diplomacy of Antipater.[67] Their inaction proved fatal
for Thebes.[68]

At the time of the king's arrival, the Thebans were besieging the Macedonian
garrison on the Cadmea.[69] Alexander offered to forgive them if they surrendered
the fomenters of the rebellion, but the Thebans responded with outrageous
counter-demands and stated their determination to liberate Greece from
Macedonian oppression.[70] To the king's surprise, the size of the Macedonian
army—some 30,000 infantry and 3,000 cavalry, all battle-ready veterans—did

63. Prothytes and Phoenix: Plut. *Alex.* 11.7; Heckel 222 s.v. "Phoenix [1]", 233; cf. Berve II, 328
no. 661; II, 399 no. 809. Demosthenes: Plut. *Dem.* 23.1.

64. Persian aid: Diod. 17.9.6.5; Justin 11.3.9. It is tempting to dismiss the claim of Persian support
as another sign of Theban Medism, but Kholod 2011, 150, rightly notes that both Macedon and
Persia conducted a propaganda war to win the hearts of the Greeks, since "the outcome of the
campaign as a whole, especially at the beginning of the military operations, largely depended
on the Greeks' position." Persian attempts to bribe the Athenians: Aes. 3.239.

65. Alexander marched south to Pelinna and then continued to the Sperchius River valley; the
Thebans learned that he was nearby when he reached Onchestus (Arr. 1.7.6). For his route, see
Arr. 1.7.5; Hammond 1980b and *HMac* III 57–59. Bosworth 1988a, 32, believes that Alexander
bypassed Thermopylae. But see Plut. *Alex.* 11.6: εὐθὺς ἦγε διὰ Πυλῶν τὴν δύναμιν.

66. Arr. 1.7.6.

67. Diod. 17.8.5-6; cf. Frontinus, *Strat.* 2.11. 4; Din. 1.18.

68. The Theban campaign: Arr. 1.7-9; Diod. 17.8.2–14.4; Plut. *Alex.* 11.6-13; Justin 3.6–4.8 (cf.
Oros. 3.16.2); Fuller 1958, 85–88.

69. The Cadmea was the Theban acropolis, not nearly as imposing as its Athenian counterpart. The city lay at its foot and to the north. Buckler 1980, 7: "Though by no means lofty, the
Cadmea easily commands the adjacent hills."

70. Plut. *Alex.* 11.7-8; cf. Diod. 17.8.3-4. Hamilton, *PA* 30, wrongly assumes that Philotas and
Antipater were officers of the Macedonian garrison. Berve II 46 rightly calls the demand
"hönisch."

nothing to deter the rebels,[71] who gained false confidence from thoughts and talk of past glories.[72] For the first of many times, Alexander meant to use the terror of destruction and annihilation to make an example of those who dared to defy him, thinking that "the Greeks would be shocked by a disaster of such proportions and thus frightened into inaction."[73]

Arrian's account of the Theban campaign is pro-Macedonian and based, at least in part, on Ptolemy's *History*; the latter may have used the opportunity to malign his later rival Perdiccas.[74] But the actions of this general contributed to the taking of the city, though they nearly cost him his life. Ptolemy says Perdiccas acted without the king's orders,[75] but his attack on the palisades set up outside the city by the Thebans drew into the fray the battalion of Amyntas son of Andromenes and, eventually, the whole army. Perdiccas' men overran the first palisade and moved against the second. Here their general was seriously wounded and needed to be carried from the battlefield.[76] Nevertheless, the Thebans, under pressure, retreated within the walls and in the process allowed the Macedonians entry. A counterattack by the Greeks, now cornered in the vicinity of the Heracleum, inflicted casualties on the lightly armed troops who had been sent in advance of the phalanx battalions,[77] but when the Macedonians pushed through to the Cadmea, they were joined by the garrison troops who threw the defenders into turmoil.

---

71. In contrast to the fear (φόβος) experienced by the Thebans at the appearance of Alexander's army in the previous year (Diod. 17.4.4).

72. Macedonian numbers: Diod. 17.9.3. Theban determination: Diod. 17.10.6; cf. Plut. *Alex.* 11.9: "the Theban defense was conducted with courage and spirit above and beyond their actual strength."

73. Plut. *Alex.* 11.11: προσδοκήσαντος αὐτοῦ τοὺς Ἕλληνας ἐκπλαγέντας πάθει τηλικούτῳ καὶ πτήξαντας ἀτρεμήσειν.

74. This, at least, is the opinion of Errington 1969, 236–37, and it has been accepted by the majority of scholars. I am not sure that it follows from Ptolemy's account that Perdiccas was responsible for the ultimate fate of Thebes, as Errington suggests. Roisman 1984, 375, concludes that "Perdiccas' blame . . . for the fate of the city was practically negligible." It was clear that Alexander had made his offer, and when the Thebans rejected it, he was prepared to attack. It was not a case of if but of when. King 2018, 142, goes so far as to suggest that "Ptolemy sanitizes and heroizes Alexander's role *and* points a finger at Perdiccas, his later mortal enemy" (emphasis in the original).

75. Arr. 1.8.1: Περδίκκας . . . οὐ προσμείνας παρ' Ἀλεξάνδρου τὸ ἐς τὴν μάχην ξύνθημα. Diod. 17.12.3 says that Alexander ordered Perdiccas to initiate the attack.

76. Arr. 1.8.3. Perdiccas' career: Heckel 197–202 s.v. "Perdiccas [1]" and *Marshals*² 153–84. Amyntas son of Andromenes: Heckel 24–25 s.v. "Amyntas [4]" and *Marshals*² 189–91.

77. Arr. 1.8.4. Eurybotas, commander of the Cretan archers, was killed at this point of the battle.

Diodorus, on the other hand, follows a strongly pro-Greek source and emphasizes the courage and manliness of the Theban soldiers, who fought against incredible odds.[78] Enemy numbers, and the ability to bring up reserves, wore down the defenders (who had even resorted to pressing slaves into military service),[79] though their desperation only drove them to sell their lives dearly. But in truth, it was a lost cause right from the start and aggravated by the pusillanimous response of their fellow Greeks. Some, like the Spartans, could not get beyond the animosity that had built up over the course of the fourth century, for after a lengthy struggle that went back to the time of the Corinthian War, the Thebans put an end to Spartan military supremacy in 371 on the battlefield of Leuctra.[80] The Athenians and the Peloponnesians outside the orbit of Sparta failed to match their words with deeds, and the perennially hostile neighbors—including former members of the Boeotian League—threw their lot in with the Macedonians; they served as convenient scapegoats for the atrocities that accompanied the fall of the city.[81]

Alexander needed to make an example of an important Greek polis and found a convenient target: in addition to a long history of Medism, the city had won few allies despite its comparatively benign hegemony of the 360s. Alexander could destroy Thebes, claiming to fulfill the infamous "Oath of Plataea," and set

---

78. The information about the prisoners fetching 440 talents in silver came from Cleitarchus (*FGrH* 137 F1 = Athen. 4.148d-e). Hammond's belief that the description of Greek affairs in Diodorus comes primarily from Diyllus, while the sensational passages can be ascribed to Cleitarchus (*THA* 12–51), is simplistic at best.

79. Diod. 17.11.2: τοὺς δ' ἐλευθερωθέντας οἰκέτας. It is not clear whether they were previously manumitted slaves or ones who were freed for this very purpose. Welwei 1977, 45, uses the words "Freigelassene" and "emanzipierten Oiketai" in the same sentence and appears to make a distinction between two groups, since on the following page he includes among those who were sold into slavery by Alexander "gefangengenommenen Sklaven und Freigelassenen."

80. The Thebans were dissatisfied with the settlement that ended the Peloponnesian War, in which they had been stout allies of the Spartans, and they resented their high-handed conduct following the fall of Athens. They joined Athens, Corinth, and Argos in a quadruple alliance and waged the so-called Corinthian War (394–387), which was concluded by the Peace of Antalcidas (better known as the King's Peace, because it left Artaxerxes II as arbiter of Greek affairs, on which see Urban 1991 and Hyland 2018, 14–68; on the concept of Common Peace, see Ryder 1965 and Jehne 1994). Sparta used the support of Persia to insist upon the disbanding of the Euboean League (on which see Buck 1994; also *Hell. Oxy.* XI 3–4, with Bruce 1967, 104–9), thus attempting to destroy the underpinnings of Theban power. Spartan defeat at Leuctra: Buckler 1980, 46–69; Beloch III² 1.168 n. 1 with references to the primary sources. For the subsequent relationship between Thebes and Persia, see Cawkwell 2005, 185–90.

81. Not only were they charged with making the decision to destroy the city and enslave its inhabitants (Arr. 1.9.9-10; Diod. 17.14.1-4; Justin 11.3.8-9; Plut. *Alex.* 11.11-12), but they also participated in the slaughter (Arr. 1.8.8; Diod. 17.13.5).

an example for the rest of Greece without striking out "one of its two eyes."[82] It was an act of terror that carried with it the message of the Panhellenic crusade: this was the beginning of the war on Persia. On a less elevated plain, responsibility for razing the city and enslaving its population could be laid at the feet of the Phocians and disaffected Boeotians, whose more immediate grievances demanded the destruction of an ancient enemy. Even among compatriots, bonds of kinship and ethnicity meant little as the pro-Macedonian party drove up the price of captives in their zeal to enslave political enemies.[83] Athens could bemoan the Thebans' fate, but the hypocrisy is brought home by the story that the orator Hyperides purchased a Theban captive named Phila for twenty minae and kept her as his mistress in Eleusis.[84]

Predictably, Athenian opposition melted away, as the specter of Chaeronea, their worst disaster since the Peloponnesian War, loomed before them. News of Philip's death had been greeted by the city with joy and thanksgiving. Honors were even proposed for the king's assassin, and moves were made to rally anti-Macedonian support throughout Greece,[85] for Demosthenes was not alone in despising Philip's successor. If his sudden appearance in the south in 336 did not send an unequivocal message, the destruction of Thebes certainly did. Bellicose oratory and resolutions passed on emotion gave way to prudence and fear with the Macedonian army encamped nearby. They had prepared to resist Philip after Chaeronea, but he had treated their allies with at least a measure of restraint. Now they could only hope that the lion's appetite for slaughter had been sated.[86] Persuaded by Demades, the Athenians sent an embassy to Alexander, offering him belated and utterly disingenuous congratulations on his "safe return from Illyria" and punishment of Thebes.[87] Thus they sought forgiveness for their own part in

---

82. Justin 5.8.4 (referring to the Spartans' rejection of the demand to wipe Athens off the map): "they would not dash out one of the two eyes of Greece." See also Graßl 1987. On the Oath of Plataea, see Hdt. 9.86-88. Tod II, 204 = Rhodes and Osborne no. 88; Lycurg. *Leocr.* 81; Diod. 11.29.2; Theopompus, *FGrH* 115 F153 (with Shrimpton 1991, 80–81); Burn 1984, 512–15; Barron, *CAH²* IV 604; Siewert 1972, esp. 63–75.

83. Justin 11.4.8.

84. Idomeneus, *FGrH* 338 F14 (= Athen. 13.590d). Not much attention is given to the fate of the civilian population, although the story of Timocleia (Plut. *Mor.* 259e–260a; *Alex.* 12; Polyaenus 8.40) does not demonstrate that Alexander was concerned about the fate of women in general. See Heckel and McLeod 2015, 253–58.

85. Plut. *Dem.* 22; cf. Diod. 17.3.2. Demosthenes was also in contact with Alexander's bitter enemy, Attalus.

86. Plut. *Dem.* 23.6: ὥσπερ λέοντα φόνου κεκορεσμένον.

87. Arr. 1.10.3: ὅτι τε σῶος ἐξ Ἰλλυριῶν καὶ Τριβαλλῶν ἐπανῆλθε. For the checkered career of Demades, see Heckel 107; Berve II, 131–32 no. 252; and Davies, *APF* 99–101. Plut. *Dem.* 23.6 says

the uprising. The king at first demanded the surrender of ten prominent orators and generals[88] but in the end insisted on only one intractable enemy: Charidemus of Oropus, who promptly fled to the court of Darius III.[89] Military action against Athens would have been costly and counterproductive. Not only did Alexander have to consider, as Philip II did in 338, the ancient reputation of Athens, but he needed the city's naval strength for the impending war in the East. In the event, the role of Athenian sea power was negligible, but Alexander's clemency had served its purpose. For the duration of his reign, the Athenians remained idle, refusing to join in Agis' war and rebuffing Harpalus in 324. When they did finally join the Hellenic uprising against Antipater in the following year, taking a lead in the so-called Lamian War, the results were tragic. But for the moment, Athens had gained by not putting its military strength to the test.

For the Greek world in general, the winter of 335/4 was one of bitter disappointment. But the leading states had only themselves to blame; this was the legacy of a pernicious struggle for hegemony that had divided and debilitated Athens, Sparta, and Thebes, along with their adherents.[90] The Sacred War, which had opened the door to central Greece for Philip II, had divided Thebes from Athens and Sparta. When Thebes and Athens combined to resist Philip in 338, Sparta held aloof. And so it was to continue, through the war of Agis[91] and later the Lamian and Chremonidean wars. In 335/4 there was nothing to do but cooperate openly, while pursuing a hostile policy through diplomatic channels.

---

that Demades had received five talents from the men whose extradition Alexander demanded. The man who once chastised Philip II for playing Thersites when history had cast him in the role of Agamemnon (Diod. 16.87.1-2) took a more cautious approach with Alexander.

88. See Plut. *Dem.* 23.4; *Phoc.* 17.2; Arr. 1.10.4; *Suda* A2704. The names vary according to authors; only Demosthenes, Charidemus, and Lycurgus are in all four lists. See Heckel 347 for all the names.

89. Arr. 1.10.6; Justin 11.4.11-12; Curt. 3.2.10; Diod. 17.30.2; cf. Kelly 1990.

90. The Athenian, Spartan, and Theban hegemonies: Cargill 1981 and 1982; Marshall 1905; Hamilton 1979, 1982, and 1991; Buckler 1980 and 1982. See also Buckler 1989.

91. On this and the role of Athens and Demosthenes, see Plut. *Dem.* 24.1. For Spartan resistance to Macedon, see Cartledge in Cartledge and Spawforth 2002, 16–27.

3

First Clash in Asia Minor

SEVENTY YEARS SEPARATED Alexander's invasion from the end of the Peloponnesian War and the fall of Athens in 404.[1] The consequent supremacy of the Spartans and the participation of Greek mercenaries in the rebellion of Cyrus the Younger brought the affairs of Asia Minor into clear focus.[2] The victor of the fraternal war was the rightful king, Artaxerxes II, even though Cyrus had the support of his mother and a powerful faction at court. Artaxerxes comes across as lethargic at best, quite possibly the weakest man to ascend the Persian throne; his reputation defies attempts at rehabilitation, but the limitations of the Greco-Roman historians and an insufficient amount of information from the center of the empire are clearly to blame.[3] The impact of the events that followed his accession is undeniable. Entanglements in the politics of the city-states beyond the Aegean had a destabilizing effect on the Achaemenid far west. Despite his role as arbiter of Greek affairs as a result of the Peace of Antalcidas (aptly called the King's Peace), Artaxerxes' court was faction-ridden (at least in the early and the final years), and there were signs of rot in the fabric of the western satrapal administration. Some problems could be explained in terms of ambition and rivalries,

---

1. With it came the collapse of the Athenian Empire. The main accounts of the war can be found in Thucydides and the first two books of Xenophon's *Hellenica*, along with certain relevant *Lives* of Plutarch and Diodorus, Books 12–13. Modern accounts are too numerous to itemize, but the reader is directed to Kagan's four-volume study (published between 1969 and 1987), now brought together in a revised single volume in Kagan 2003. See also Hanson 2005; Tritle 2010. On the Athenian Empire, the best account is still Meiggs 1972; McGregor 1987 is intended for the general reader. Most important for the affairs in Asia Minor is Lewis 1977.

2. See Xenophon, *Anabasis*, Book 1. Spartan supremacy: Hamilton 1991; Clauss 1983, 59–69.

3. See Plutarch, *Artoxerxes*, the only biography of an Achaemenid ruler. Briant, *HPE* 612–81 provides a balanced account of his reign, stressing the deficiencies of the Greco-Roman sources. For a positive view of Persian policy in the time leading up to the Peace of Antalcidas, see Hyland 2018.

In the Path of Conquest. Waldemar Heckel, Oxford University Press (2020). © Oxford University Press.
DOI: 10.1093/oso/9780190076689.001.0001

some in the difficulties posed by the central government's vacillating support for Sparta, Athens, and later Thebes. The Greek cities of the coast found Spartan leadership oppressive, for it had been the policy of Lysander to control them by means of dekarchies and garrisons, each under a Spartan harmost. The end of Spartan hegemony meant the welcome return of Persian overlords,[4] who were content with minimal interference in local politics.

In fact, many Greeks worked with—rather than under or against—the Great King's satraps, as did local dynasts. The Persian Empire had a long history of localized rebellions, but nevertheless the centralized government of the Achaemenids managed to prevent its dissolution. Quarrels between satraps were sometimes regarded as useful checks on provincial rulers.[5] Certainly there were sufficient mechanisms to control the ambitions of the noble families—some of whom, such as the Pharnacids of Dascyleum, treated satrapal rule as a hereditary right[6]—both internally and through neighboring officials.[7] But there was also a tendency on the part of such officials to inform against their rivals, bringing slanders or at least misrepresentations of the truth to the attention of the king. To his credit, Artaxerxes II was cautious in his interpretation of such reports and often willing to bring about reconciliation with the alleged offenders.

I

In the 370s and 360s, the Achaemenid Empire, already weakened by the Egyptians, who defied repeated attempts to end their independence, and by stubborn resistance in Cyprus, was confronted with uprisings in Asia Minor. The so-called Great Satraps' Revolt is depicted as a full-scale challenge to the central authority and, indeed, an existential crisis for the empire:

> During Molon's archonship in Athens, Lucius Genucius and Quintus Servilius were elected consuls in Rome. While they were in office the people living on the coastline of Asia defected from the Persians and some

4. We must avoid the simplistic interpretation that Greek domination and democracy were always regarded as preferable to Persian rule and oligarchy. If the Greeks of Asia had learned anything from the Athenian and Spartan supremacies, it was that "liberation" did not necessarily mean freedom.

5. Xen. *Anab.* 1.1.8.

6. See Abe 2012, 2.

7. The view of Kaerst, *Hellenismus* I³ 343 ("Im persischen Reiche war die große Selbstständigkeit der Satrapen zu einer Gefahr für den Bestand der Achaemenidenherrschaft selbst geworden") is, to my mind, excessive, even if he had the Great Satraps' Revolt in mind.

of the satraps and army officers opened hostilities against Artaxerxes. At the same time as this Tachos, the king of the Egyptians, decided on war with the Persians, prepared a fleet of ships, and assembled infantry forces. He enlisted many mercenaries from the Greek cities and persuaded the Spartans to join his war—the Spartans were at loggerheads with Artaxerxes because the Messenians had been put on the same footing as the other Greeks by the king in the communal peace treaty.

When the uprising against the Persians reached this level, the king also prepared for war. For he was obliged to fight simultaneously the Egyptian king, the Greek cities in Asia, the Lacedaemonians, and the allies of these peoples, namely satraps and military leaders who governed the coastal areas and had agreed to join them. The most famous of these were Ariobarzanes, satrap of Phrygia, who had even taken over Mithridates' kingdom when he died, and Mausolus, suzerain of Caria and master of many fortresses and notable cities, of which Halicarnassus, possessing a famous acropolis and the palaces of Caria, was the hearth and metropolis. There were also, besides these, Orontes, satrap of Mysia, and Autophradates, satrap of Lydia. Apart from the Ionians there were also Lycians, Pisidians, Pamphylians, and Cilicians, as well as Syrians, Phoenicians, and virtually all the peoples on the coast. Such being the extent of the rebellion, half the king's revenues had been cut off and the remainder was not enough to cover his war expenses. (Diod. 15.90)

Thus Diodorus sums up the outbreak of the satraps' revolt, which he presents as both a concerted effort and a set of virtually simultaneous uprisings, dating it to 361 and thus conflating the events of several years into a short period of time. Was this a direct challenge to the Great King's authority, a coordinated rebellion, or a case of opportunism on the part of the satraps, fueled by personal rivalries? Unfortunately, we must rely primarily on the evidence of Greek authors, some of them writing long after the events they describe, and accounts that offer little in the way of historical context.[8] The defections occurred at different times, though within a limited time frame, and several of the key players vacillated in their loyalties to the Great King or to their erstwhile allies. Some scholars have tended to downplay the notion of a concerted effort, and the general lack of success

8. The evidence of the Athenian orators is contemporary but lacks a clear chronological framework; Nepos' *Life of Datames* appears to have made use of Deinon, a fourth-century author of *Persika*; and Diodorus' account may be based on Ephorus. The extant accounts are greatly compressed and suffer from selective abbreviation. Trogus, *Prol.* 10, shows that it was discussed at some length in the *Philippic History*, but Justin omitted the satraps' revolt entirely.

enjoyed by the satraps may point in this direction.[9] Others see it as an organized undertaking and a dangerous threat to the central government.[10]

The first of the rebels was Datames son of Camisares, a man who distinguished himself in the service of Artaxerxes II and was, since perhaps 385 or 384, satrap of Cappadocia.[11] Despite his popularity with his troops and a reputation for military daring, he was betrayed first by his own son Sisines and then by his father-in-law Mithrobarzanes; finally, he succumbed to the treachery of Mithridates.[12] That man had the dubious distinction of having betrayed his own father, Ariobarzanes, satrap of Hellespontine Phrygia, who refused to relinquish authority to Artabazus. Ariobarzanes enlisted the aid of Greek troops against the Great King's general Autophradates but was likewise the victim of intrigue. Orontes of Mysia (who figures prominently in Diodorus' account) also revolted—perhaps he was the ringleader of the rebels.[13] He, at least, managed to make peace and retain his command. In light of the combination of Egyptian support for the rebels, Spartan aid, and the ineffective military campaigns of the aging Artaxerxes II, the poor performance of the satraps suggests a lack of joint purpose and strategy, to say nothing of mutual suspicion and military incompetence. The Achaemenid Empire had demonstrated that it could bend without breaking and that the forces that gave rise to disunity—for the empire had been content to allow a great deal of local autonomy and was flexible in its methods of control—were the same ones that, in the long run, denied common purpose to potential traitors. In the end, they were more at ease with their role as subjects of the Achaemenids than with their fellow rebels.[14]

9. See particularly Weiskopf 1989, although I believe he underestimates the importance of political alliances (i.e., factions) among the Persian nobility. Dusinberre 2013, 45: "Epigraphic evidence from Anatolia and Egypt demonstrates that this so-called revolt probably consisted of a series of local uprisings rather than a concerted and unified effort."

10. Hornblower, *CAH*[2] VI 84–90, sees a far more serious threat, developing in four stages and over a period "nearly twenty years" (84). For much of this period, Judeich, *Kl. Studien* 190–225, published in 1892, is still a useful guide. For the satrapal rebellion in the context of Persia's dealings with Egypt, see especially Ruzicka 2012, 122–44. See also Osborne 1973; Sekunda 1988; Moysey 1991 and 1992; Briant, *HPE* 674–75; Hornblower 1982, 170–82; cf. Bing 1998.

11. Thus Sekunda 1988, 44.

12. Mithrobarzanes: Nepos, *Datames* 6.3-8 (= 14.6.3-8). Sisines (Sysinas): Nepos 14.7.1. 14.10.1-5 claims that he was murdered by Mithridates, the son of Ariobarzanes. Sekunda 1988 serves as an indispensable commentary on Nepos' *Life*. Cook 1983, 221, dates his uprising to 368; Hornblower, *CAH*[2] VI 84, puts it in the 370s; cf. Brosius 2006, 26 (c. 372).

13. Hornblower, *CAH*[2] VI 86.

14. We should not, however, ignore the impact of the new ruler, Artaxerxes III, who, despite his reputation for savagery, restored Egypt to the empire and suppressed rebellion in the West.

The turmoil of the 360s and 350s did little to weaken the bond between the Great King and his satraps, although it doubtless made the satrapal families more circumspect in their dealings with one another as well as with their own relatives. But more important, during this period of instability, there were several Persians who sought refuge in Pella with Philip II. Among these was Artabazus, who took his entire family into exile and proved later to be a convenient instrument of Alexander's orientalizing policies. As a young man, Alexander questioned these exiles about the nature of the Achaemenid Empire, and their answers doubtless confirmed what could be gleaned from a careful reading of Xenophon's *Anabasis*.[15] On the other hand, the Persian exiles appear to have learned relatively little about Philip's true intentions with regard to Achaemenid Asia.[16] Three decades of instability had certainly shaken the empire, but the central authority knew well how to exploit the political divisions of both the satraps and the Asiatic Greeks.

II

The advance force of 10,000 sent by Philip II to Asia Minor in the spring of 336 met with only limited success.[17] Darius, who had just recently come to the throne,[18] assigned the task of defending the coastal areas to a group of commanders, among

Nor was the support of the Greek city-states anything more than tepid. In fact, the Athenians, with their own concerns about the integrity of the Second Athenian League, had gravitated toward Ochus—or, at any rate, they were eager not to offend him.

15. Plut. *Alex.* 5.1-3 speaks of "ambassadors of the Persian king who had come in Philip's absence" (τοὺς δὲ παρὰ τοῦ Περσῶν βασιλέως πρέσβεις ἥκοντας ἀποδημοῦντος Φιλίππου), but it is more likely that these were the exiles at Philip's court. Given the presence of Artabazus and his followers, there was no need for the prince to interrogate ambassadors. For Artabazus' revolt, see the thorough discussion in Rop 2019, 119–47.

16. Cf. Ellis 1976, 172–73. It is necessary to add here a note about Hermias of Atarneus, the eunuch tyrant who had carved out a small fiefdom for himself between Mount Ida and the coastline opposite Lesbos. If he was eager to gain an alliance with Philip II, perhaps with Aristotle (who had married Hermias' niece; Diog. Laert. 5.3) acting as an intermediary (see Guthrie 1981, 35–36, summarizing Jaeger 1934), it never came to fruition. Some of his alleged dealings with Philip appear to reflect Demosthenes' paranoia more than actual events (Dem. 10.33, though the speech may not be genuine). He was arrested by Mentor, who had learned a thing or two about treachery in years of Persian service, and taken to Artaxerxes III, who had him tortured and executed. See the intriguing discussion in Green 2003.

17. The advance force and chronology: Justin 9.5.8 (*initio veris*); Diod. 16.91.2 (cf. 16.93.9). The number 10,000 comes from Polyaenus, *Strat.* 5.44.4. The third commander was Amyntas, whose identity is not certain. Possibly he was the son of Arrhabaeus.

18. Diod. 17.7.1-2 says that Darius ascended the throne before Philip's death (indeed, he was later charged with instigating the Macedonian king's murder) but mentions the appointment of Memnon only in the context of the threat from Alexander.

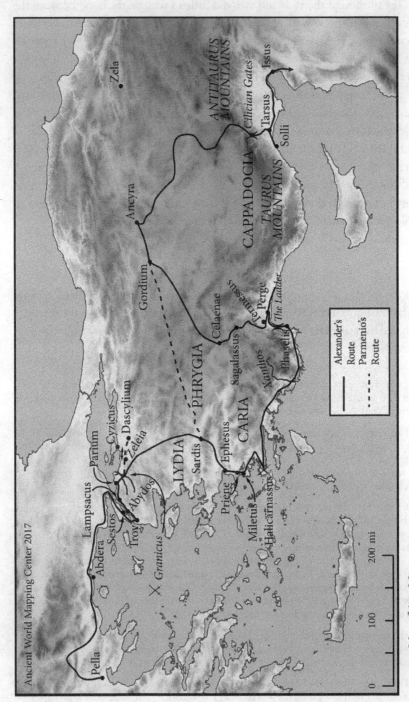

MAP 3.1 Map of Asia Minor.

whom was Memnon the Rhodian, brother of the famous condottiere Mentor.[19] As a Greek, he was, of course, singled out by the historians, to the exclusion of the Persian leaders who acted in concert with him. They were probably the satraps of the coast, the same men who later shared the command at the Battle of the Granicus—Spithridates of Lydia and Arsites of Hellespontine Phrygia, in whose territory the invading force found itself.

The invaders enjoyed initial success, gaining control of Magnesia on Sipylus. But the Macedonians did not remain there for long, and the reason for their retreat is unclear.[20] It has been suggested that it was part of a move against the new king, Alexander. One of the leaders of the expedition was Attalus, the very man who insulted the prince at the wedding feast in 337 and who now feared reprisals. If he withdrew to the Hellespontine coast with the intention of bringing his forces back into Europe—something he may have done in collusion with Memnon[21]— then this must have been done either without the knowledge or with the agreement of his colleague, and father-in-law, Parmenion.[22]

The role of Parmenion, who clearly acquiesced in the removal of Attalus and whose power was, in all likelihood, enhanced by the new king, suggests that this was not the case. Even though Attalus received a letter from Demosthenes urging him to rebel and promising support in central Greece, he appears not to have acted on it, and there is no good reason to believe that such a policy had widespread support in the expeditionary army. Alexander sent a trusted agent, Hecataeus, to arrest and execute Attalus, something he accomplished without a great deal of resistance.[23] We next learn of Parmenion's successful siege of Gryneum and the

---

19. For Mentor, see Hofstetter 129–31 no. 220.

20. The only reference to the occupation of Magnesia is Polyaenus, *Strat.* 5.44.4, which tells of a victory by Memnon over some of the Macedonians, who subsequently retreated to Magnesia. Later there must have been a strategic withdrawal by the entire army—it was not in Macedonian hands in 334—since Memnon with limited manpower could not have expelled the Macedonian force.

21. This is the view of Judeich, *Kl. Stud.* 305: "Wir werden uns deshalb die Entwicklung der Ereignisse etwa so zu denken haben, dass sich Attalos auf die Nachricht von Philipps Ermordung, *wahrscheinlich ohne Vorwissen seines Schwiegervaters Parmenion,* mit Memnon heimlich verständigte und den Abzug des makedonischen Heeres nordwärts veranlasste" (emphasis added). This strikes me as highly implausible, unless we assume that Parmenion held a subordinate position and did not question Attalus' decision.

22. For the relationship, which came back to haunt Parmenion's son, Philotas, see Curt. 6.9.17.

23. Hecataeus is unlikely to have been the Cardian mentioned by Diod. 18.14.4 and Plut. *Eum.* 3.6-8. (This is contrary to the views I expressed in Heckel 131.) Diod. 17.2.5 calls him one of Alexander's *philoi.* He was apparently a Macedonian. Attalus is said to have sent Demosthenes' letter to Alexander in a vain attempt to prove his innocence (Diod. 17.5.1).

military actions of Calas. Memnon, although he was unable to capture Cyzicus, did prevent Parmenion from taking Pitane.[24] The Macedonians may have withdrawn their forces from Magnesia on Sipylus[25] and entrenched themselves in the Hellespontine region; by the time of Alexander's crossing, they kept only a toehold in Asia, having fallen back on Rhoetium.[26] Certainly, the death of Philip and the apparent collapse of the fortunes of the expeditionary force led to the overthrow of the pro-Macedonian party in Ephesus and on Lesbos. Hence, by the time of Alexander's crossing, the expeditionary force was bottled up in the Hellespontine region. It had started well, but the combination of changes in leadership and the quick actions of Memnon and his Persian colleagues turned the tables on the invader. Everything would depend on the army from Macedonia and its young leader.

III

The Macedonian army that crossed the Hellespont in May 334 numbered just under 50,000. The high estimates, in all likelihood, include the units from the expeditionary force.[27] A visit to Ilium (Troy) gave symbolic significance to the undertaking,[28] but it was in the interests of both the Persians and the Macedonians to bring about a quick military decision. The former could not afford defections

---

24. Diod. 17.7.3, 8-9. Cf. Polyaenus 5.44.5. Diod. 17.7.2 says that Darius gave Memnon 5,000 mercenaries. It must have been as a mercenary commander that Memnon, at this point, held any military authority. His appointment as commander-in-chief in the west came after the Battle of the Granicus.

25. Magnesia, which surrendered to Alexander along with Tralles, is the city on the Maeander (Arr. 1.18.1).

26. Anson 1989 takes a different view. The Macedonians had secured enough of the Hellespontine coast—with the notable exception of Lampsacus—to deprive the Persian fleet of a base from which to operate and thus prevented them from opposing Alexander's crossing in 334.

27. Anaximenes of Lampsacus (*FGrH* 72 F29): 43,000 infantry, 5,500 cavalry. Ptolemy (*FGrH* 138 F4): 30,000 infantry, 5,000 cavalry. Aristobulus (*FGrH* 139 F4): 30,000 infantry, 4,000 horse. Diod. 17.17.3-4: 32,000 infantry, 1,800 Macedonian horse and an equal number of Thessalians, 600 allies, and 900 Thracians and Paeonians. Plut. *Alex.* 15.1: 43,000 infantry, 5,000 cavalry. Frontinus, *Strat.* 4.2.4: 40,000 men in Alexander's army.

28. Arr. 1.12.1-5. The sacrifices at Ilium were preceded by other gestures that called to mind the Trojan War and sought to place the expedition on a higher plane. Alexander sacrificed at the tomb of Protesilaus, to Poseidon and Nereids and even to the ghost of Priam (Arr. 1.11.5-8). See also Plut. *Alex.* 15.7-9; Diod. 17.17.2-3; cf. Cic. *Pro Archia* 24; cf. Instinsky 1949. These acts were intended more for the Greek audience at home than for those of Asia, who required more than slogans.

that the presence of the enemy force might encourage, especially since there had been those who had—prematurely, as it turned out—jumped ship at the news of a Macedonian invasion. To that end, they secured cities with garrisons. The concerns of the Macedonian king were more mundane but no less pressing for all that: he was short of money, and by the time he crossed to Asian soil, the army was living from hand to mouth.[29]

The Persian forces marshaled in the satrapy of Hellespontine Phrygia, interposing themselves between the invading army and Cyzicus, which had held out against Memnon. This man now advised the Persians to withdraw before the enemy, leaving destruction in their path.[30] But the war council at Zeleia was dominated by local satraps and hyparchs whose parochial concerns showed little regard for larger imperial interests. There were at least signs that the Greek cities were not rushing to join the invader[31]—the perils of showing one's cards prematurely were clear to them—and the poor performance of the expeditionary force gave the satraps reasons for optimism. Alexander, by contrast, had only omens associated with sweating statues of bards or fallen representations of satraps past.[32] The Persian brain trust overruled Memnon and chose to meet the enemy at the Granicus River.

The march of the invading army took it from Ilium past Arisba, Percote, and Lampsacus to the Pactius River (Bergas Çay), which flowed, at least according to Arrian, from Mount Ida into the Propontis (Sea of Marmara); in fact, it drained into the Hellespont.[33] By the time the Macedonians camped here, they had all but

---

29. For Alexander's financial crisis, see Plut. *Alex.* 15.2; *Mor.* 327e, 342d: his war chest amounted to seventy talents (sixty according to Curt. 10.2.24). See also Engels 1978a, 27–30; Austin 1993, 206. Memnon's alleged advocacy of a scorched-earth policy would make more sense if he understood the Macedonian predicament. See also Green 1991, 489–90; for a different view, Holt 2016, 23–43, esp. 32–33; also Franz 2009.

30. Memnon's strategy: Arr. 1.12.9; Diod. 17.18.2. Curtius clearly mentioned it in one of his lost books; it is alluded to at 3.4.3. Persian distrust of Greeks in their service was also a factor (McCoy 1989; cf. Green 1991, 490). Briant argues that it is doubtful that the council at Zeleia debated overall strategy and that it dealt only with tactics. It is likely that the Persian leaders were convinced of their superiority in cavalry warfare, having not yet experienced the tactics and fighting styles of their Macedonian and Thessalian opponents (see Gaebel 2002, 159–83).

31. Lampsacus is a case in point. Arr. 1.12.6 passes over the question of Lampsacene Medism. See Paus. 6.18.2-4; Val. Max. 7.3 ext. 4. Bosworth I, 107–8. The city was probably garrisoned by the Persians.

32. The sweating statue of Orpheus at Leibethra: Plut. *Alex.* 14.8-9. The fallen statue of Ariobarzanes: Diod. 17.17.6.

33. Arr. 1.12.6; but see Strabo 13.1.21 C590 (cf. 13.1.4 C583); Seibert 1985, 31; Bosworth I, 108. Lane Fox 1973, 515, attempts to resolve the problem by emendation (rightly rejected by Engels 1978a, 30 n. 21).

used up the provisions that had been supplied by the fleet.[34] From here the army moved to Hermotus, Colonae, and Priapus, which surrendered to Alexander's scouting force under Amyntas son of Arrhabaeus.[35] The Persians by now had left Zeleia and taken up a position on the Granicus River (Biga) near the village of Didymoteichos (Dimetoka). It appears that the Persians occupied the eastern bank of the Granicus very close to where it is joined by a tributary (Koçabas Çay).[36] Nikos Nikolitsis studied the area in 1971 and observes:

> The river Granicus is noticeably uneven, with deep reaches up to 20 m long, up to 4 m across and 0.30 m deep. The bottoms of these reaches are muddy. The river has both high and gently sloping banks. The banks are made of clay and are up to 4 m high. The east bank is steeper than the west.[37]

Kenneth Harl, who visited the site in 1996, remarks: "The only fordable points for a large force lay along the four to five kilometers between the marshy lower reaches of the Granicus and the confluence of the Granicus and the Koça Çay." An unopposed crossing would have to be attempted downstream, but here the marshes made such a maneuver all but impossible: "A Macedonian crossing south of the confluence was precluded by the steep, narrow banks of the swiftly flowing upper Granicus, rough terrain thick with undergrowth and sinkholes, and the second river barrier posed by the Koça Çay."[38]

What we know of the command structure of the Persian forces is limited by the fact that, particularly in these early stages of the campaign, the Greek historians—drawing their information primarily from Callisthenes of Olynthus—placed Alexander firmly in the center of their discussions. Even the

---

34. Engels 1978a, 29–30.

35. If he was, indeed, one of the commanders of the expeditionary force (Justin 9.5.8), he would have been familiar with the area.

36. Hammond 1980b, 79 (fig. 2).

37. Nikolitsis 1974, 10. Somewhat different conditions are described by Hammond 1980a (summarized by Devine 1986a, 267), but on Hammond's own interpretation the riverbed has shifted since antiquity. This is surely a problem for any attempt to link sources to topography. Thompson 2007, 53, identifies the Granicus with the Biga and argues that there is no evidence for the river having shifted its course. The ancient lake, Ece Göl, now drained, does not figure in any of the extant sources for the battle and needs no further comment.

38. Both quotations are from Harl 1997, 307.

other Macedonians and the allies were given little attention.[39] The Persians were thus little more than a collection of exotic names that gave color to the spectacle. Nevertheless, we can say that in the absence of Darius, the defense of Asia Minor devolved upon a coalition of satraps, each mustering his territorial levies. Leadership may have been entrusted to Arsites of Lesser Phrygia, in whose satrapy the battle took place, and to Spithridates of Lydia, whose family also had connections with the Hellespontine satrapy. They were supported by the Cilician satrap Arsames, Atizyes of Phrygia, and Mithrobuzanes of Cappadocia.[40] Other leaders—Niphates and Petenes—may have been local hyparchs.[41] On the other hand, the presence of royal relatives, Mithridates, Arbupales, and Pharnaces, suggests some sort of imperial oversight.[42] There were, in addition to the satrapal armies, units from Hyrcania, Media, and Bactria, some under the command of Rheomithres; the barbarian mercenaries under Omares may also have been recruited elsewhere.[43] These troops from beyond Asia Minor may have been detached from a royal army that had earlier dealt with the uprising in Egypt. Finally, there was also Memnon of Rhodes, who, as noted above, tended to be given pride of place by the contemporary historians despite his true position in the barbarians' chain of command.

The sizes of the armies were roughly equal, by some accounts, although this was the only major battle in which the Persians might have been slightly

---

39. Those who are mentioned also served the Panhellenic propaganda: the Thessalians (Diod. 17.21.4) and Demaratus of Corinth (Arr. 1.15.6). Diodorus notes the valor of the Thessalians but gives us very little detail about their movements. They were, of course, on the Macedonian left with Parmenion, whose role is regularly downplayed or undermined.

40. Diod. 17.19.4; Arr. 1.12.8. Diodorus has Arsam[en]es, which is surely an error for Arsames, who is known to have been the Cilician satrap (Curt. 3.4.3; Arr. 2.4.5).

41. Bosworth I, 111: "They may have been generals specifically sent down for the campaign, or possibly large landowners in Asia Minor."

42. Seibert 1985, 33: "Der Perserkönig hat den Krieg keineswegs auf die leichte Schulter genommen, wofür auch die Entsendung naher Verwandter spricht." Berve II 263 assumes that Mithridates was from Pontus-Cappadocia. His wife must have been Darius' daughter by a wife other than Stateira. Arbupales was a son of that Darius whose father was Artaxerxes II (Arr. 1.16.3; cf. Plut. *Artox.* 26–27; Briant, *HPE* 680–81). Pharnaces was either also from Pontus-Cappadocia (thus Berve II 380) or from the ruling house of Hellespontine Phrygia.

43. Rheomithres may be the father of Phrasaortes, who was later appointed satrap of Persis (Arr. 3.18.11). Bosworth I, 111 identifies him with the duplicitous leader in the so-called Great Satraps' Revolt in 362 (Diod. 15.92.1; cf. Stylianou 1998, 542–43; Heckel 241; Berve II 346 no. 685). Omares is otherwise unknown. I was wrong to doubt the presence of these troops in Heckel 2008, 177 n. 11.

inferior in numbers.[44] They did, however, have a distinct advantage in cavalry, who outnumbered their Macedonian counterparts by a ratio of 2:1 on the low estimate and by as much as 4:10n a high one.[45] But it was not a shortage of numbers that proved decisive; nor, as the most scholars have maintained, was it the unorthodox deployment of the troops that tipped the balance in favor of the invader. The Persians stationed their horsemen on top of the eastern banks of the Granicus River, keeping their infantry—at least, their Greek mercenaries—in reserve. This has been dismissed as motivated by fear of treachery. If this is true, the Persians failed to understand that Alexander's Panhellenic propaganda (and his interpretation of the charter of the League of Corinth) made taking up arms against fellow countrymen a criminal offense, punishable by death or hard labor. Hence, the Persian satraps are thought to have robbed themselves of a vital tool, for the cavalry alone could not stand up to the surge of the *sarissa*-bearing phalanx. It is virtually certain that they supported their cavalry with light infantry, particularly archers,[46] but these, like the cavalrymen, found it impossible to stand up to the Macedonian onslaught.

Such an interpretation does not take into account the nature of the Iranian and Anatolian cavalry, which comprised not heavily armed shock troops but fighters armed with javelins and trained (along with their mounts) to maneuver quickly among and around their opponents. From the high ground, they hoped to rain down javelins on the attacking force, thereby disrupting their advance and demoralizing—and, ideally, even defeating—them. It was when the enemy cavalry came to grips with the defenders and engaged in hand-to-hand fighting that the superiority of Macedonian weaponry and technique put the Persians at a serious disadvantage. That the Persian "knighthood" wanted to settle the issue with its Macedonian counterpart[47] may have been part of the mindset of ancient warriors, but it does not adequately explain the Persian tactical dispositions.[48]

---

44. Cf. Fuller 1958, 147. Schachermeyr 1973, 168, is probably correct in assuming that the Persian numbers for both cavalry and Greek mercenaries are far too high.

45. Diod. 17.19.4 says the Persians had 100,000 infantry and 10,000 cavalry; Arr.1.14.4 gives the Persian force 20,000 cavalry and 20,000 mercenary infantry. Justin 11.6.11: *sescenta milia* is rhetorical hyperbole. Plut. *Alex.* 16.15 claims that the dead alone numbered 2,500 cavalry and 20,000 infantry.

46. Plut. *Alex.* 16.4.

47. Schachermeyr's notion about "Junker gegen Junker" (1973, 169–70). Cf. Fuller 1958, 149: "Throughout history the cavalry soldier has despised the infantryman, and to have placed the Greek mercenaries in the forefront of the battle would have been to surrender to them the place of honour. Military etiquette forbade it."

48. Rightly noted by Harl 1997, 307–10.

The version of the battle given by Arrian and supported by Plutarch can be summarized as follows. On their left wing, the Persian cavalry under Arsames and Memnon was attacked by the squadrons of Socrates son of Sathon, who was supported by Amyntas son of Arrhabaeus. As they moved against the attackers, they were drawn away from the center, and this created an opening into which Alexander and the main force of Companions moved, crossing behind the initial attacking force and coming to grips with Arsites' horsemen. The Persians had observed that the king and his Companion cavalry had taken up a position on their far left, and they massed their horsemen accordingly. But Alexander's shift back to the right (i.e., toward the center) allowed him to cross the river in the direction of its flow.[49] The hand-to-hand fighting did not favor the Persians, who relied more on the javelin than the thrusting spear (*xyston*) used by the Macedonians.[50] As they came to grips, the Persians, fighting now with their swords, were no match for the pikes of the enemy which gave them a distinct advantage in reach.

One such contest is described in detail by the pro-Alexander sources, highlighting the personal prowess (*arete*) of the Macedonian king, who plunged into the river with the cavalry squadrons. Plutarch describes his leadership style as "madcap and senseless rather than prudent" and notes that the battle quickly degenerated into hand-to-hand fighting by the individual cavalrymen, with the king himself drawing a crowd of adversaries, for he was conspicuous "because of his shield and the crest on his helmet, on each side of which there was a plume striking for its whiteness and its size."[51]

This forms an integral part of the "official" account of the first major engagement fought by Alexander, a magnificent piece of propaganda in which the young king displayed courage and fighting skills worthy of a Homeric hero. In fact, after a general overview of the troop deployment and the beginning of the clash, the historian—in this case, Callisthenes, who was himself well acquainted with the Homeric epics—draws the reader's attention to the actions of Alexander

---

49. Arr. 1.14.7. Ancient accounts of the battle: Arr. 1.13-16; Diod. 17.19-21; Plut. *Alex.* 16; *Itiner. Alex.* 18; Justin 11.6.10-13; cf. Oros. 3.16.4. Modern discussions are numerous: Fuller 1958, 147–54; Nikolitsis 1974; Badian 1977a; Foss 1977; Hammond 1980a; Devine 1986b and 1988; McCoy 1989. For earlier literature, see Seibert 1972a, 83–85. See also Green 1991, 489–512; Keegan 1987, 78–81; Harl 1997; Thompson 2007; English 2011, 33–60; and the counterfactual discussion of Ober 1999. Consider also the interesting comments of Delbrück 1990, 1.190: "I have not undertaken a real study of the battle on the Granicus, since it appeared to me, in view of the status of the sources, to offer too little prospect of a fruitful result."

50. Noted by Arr. 1.15.1; see also Gaebel 2002, 161–63.

51. Plut. *Alex.* 16.4-7.

himself. He attacks without regard for his safety, rushing madly up the banks of the river and overpowering his enemies before narrowly avoiding the barbarian's potentially lethal blow. The brothers Spithridates and Rhoesaces—the former was satrap of Lydia—bore down on Alexander. The Persians are praised for their bravery and spirit, and Spithridates himself is described as "a Persian by birth and son-in-law of King Darius, a man of superior courage."[52] It is against him that Alexander directs his attack:

> The Persian thought that the opportunity for single combat was a gift from heaven—if it should transpire that by his own personal courage Asia could be freed of its greatest fears, the much-vaunted courage of Alexander checked by his hands, and the reputation of the Persians not sullied. He made the first move, hurling his javelin at Alexander and hitting his target with such formidable impetus as to pierce Alexander's shield and his right shoulder and to penetrate his breastplate.
>
> The king threw aside the weapon that he now had hanging from his arm; then, putting the spurs to his horse and capitalizing on the momentum of his charge, he drove his spear right into the satrap's chest. With that, the nearby squadrons of both armies cried out in reaction to the superhuman demonstration of manly prowess; but the spear tip shattered on impact with the breastplate, and the damaged weapon sprang back. The Persian then drew his sword and bore down on Alexander, but the king, grasping his spear shaft, anticipated him by plunging it into his face and then thrusting it home. At that point, as the satrap was falling, his brother Rhosaces rode up and brought down on Alexander's head such a blow with his sword as to split his helmet and graze his scalp; but as he was aiming a second blow at the same split, Cleitus, nicknamed "The Black," rode up and lopped off the barbarian's arm. (Diod. 17.20.3-7)

The quick and heroic action of Cleitus finds its way into all accounts of the battle because it left Alexander forever in his debt, one he later repaid in the most disgraceful manner. For it was at a dinner party in Maracanda in 328 that he killed Cleitus in a drunken rage.

---

52. Diod. 17.20.2. The relationship to Darius may be an error. Alexander had killed in this battle a son-in-law of the king named Mithridates (Arr. 1.16.3).

Despite a noble effort by the leading Persians, including the so-called Relatives (*syngeneis*),[53] they were worsted in hand-to-hand combat and pressed by the surging formations of the *pezhetairoi* (Foot Companions). Many illustrious leaders died in the engagement, notably Pharnaces, the brother of Darius' queen, and Mithrobuzanes, who commanded the Cappadocians.[54] But ultimately, they broke ranks and fled. The light infantrymen were helpless against the better-equipped enemy, but at least they had the advantage of mobility—though even that did little good against the Macedonian and Thessalian horsemen. The Greek mercenaries formed a square and fought for their lives. To no avail. The Macedonians killed all but 2,000,[55] and these they sent to Macedonia as slaves on account of their "betrayal" of the Greeks. It would be three years or more before any of them were released.

If the Battle of the Granicus occurred on the same day as the Macedonian army arrived at the river, and in the late afternoon, it was certainly mismanaged by the Persian leaders. But the actual course of events cannot be reconstructed with certainty. Both Plutarch and Diodorus offer information that when combined suggests that Alexander took a more cautious approach to the river crossing.[56] Plutarch and Arrian tell us that the Macedonian leadership, upon surveying the topography, especially the natural obstacles, advised Alexander not to give

---

53. The *syggeneis* were the so-called King's Relatives, a group found in both the Persian court and military hierarchy. Here they are a corps of elite horsemen. See Briant, *HPE* 309–10.

54. Pharnaces: Diod. 17.21.3; Arr. 1.16.3. He was perhaps a member of the Pontic-Cappadocian aristocracy. His sister was almost certainly not Stateira, the woman captured at Issus. See Heckel 206–7, 274 F5; Berve II, 380 no. 767. Mithrobuzanes: Heckel 168–69; Berve II, 263 no. 527; Justi 209. Diodorus mistakenly says that Atizyes died in this battle, but he lived to fight again (and die) at Issus.

55. It is generally assumed that the Greek mercenaries numbered 20,000 (Arr. 1.14.4, 16.2, calls them ξένοι πεζοὶ μισθοφόροι, and so not necessarily all Greeks). But Memnon was given 5,000 Greek mercenaries by Darius with whom to attack Cyzicus (Diod. 17.7.3), and it is doubtful that the Greek contingent at the Granicus was larger. Certainly, it is highly improbable that the Macedonians killed 18,000 Greeks in the aftermath of the battle, a kill rate of 90%. Schachermeyr is surely right when he observes: "Letztere können somit unmöglich 20 000 Mann gezählt haben, da das einem Verlust von 18 000 gefallenen Griechen gegenüber nur 30 gefallenen Makedonen ergeben würde" (1973, 168 n. 69).

56. Diod. 17.20.3 and Plut. *Alex.* 16.7 agree also that Alexander carried a shield (*aspis* or *pelte*), which is not supported by the other sources or by artistic representations (the Alexander Sarcophagus and the Alexander Mosaic, admittedly depicting later battles). The shield may be an invention, based on Homer. Cf. Homer, *Iliad* 3.355-60, describing the duel between Paris and Menelaus: "He spoke, balanced his long-shadowed spear and hurled it. It hit Paris' round shield. The heavy weapon pierced the glittering shield, forced its way through the ornate body-armor and ripped right into the side of Paris' tunic. But Paris had swerved and so avoided dark death" (R. Lattimore translation).

battle at once. Parmenion, it is said, added that it was too late in the day to com-
mence hostilities. But the impetuous young king replied that "the Hellespont
would blush for shame, if, after having crossed that strait, he [Alexander] should
be afraid of the Granicus."[57] Diodorus omits the exchange between Alexander
and his old general but speaks of the Macedonian army crossing the river unopposed at dawn the following day. In this respect, Diodorus' account, for all its
Homeric qualities, is at odds with those of the other extant historians. If his version is correct, the Persians at least were right to mass their cavalry on the banks
of the river, for it forced the Macedonians to avoid a frontal attack.[58] Instead, the
Macedonian army declined to fight on the day they arrived, moving downstream
at dawn to ford the river before attacking their foes on the same side of the river.[59]
Nevertheless, if the battle really did unfold in this way, we are still left to wonder
why the Greek mercenaries did not play a greater role. It appears that Diodorus,
in the process of abbreviating his source, assumed that Parmenion's advice was
accepted.[60] Alexander's role in this version of the battle was equally distinguished
and equally suspect.

    Whichever version of the battle one accepts, it is clear that the Persian lead-
ership did not shrink from the engagement but fought with exceptional courage.
Of the commanders listed above, only a handful—Arsites, Arsames, Atizyes,
Rheomithres, Memnon—escaped the slaughter. Arsites later committed suicide,
accepting the responsibility for the ineffectual battle plans.[61] The fact that the

---

57. Plut. *Alex.* 16.3. Cf. Arr. 1.13.6-7: "Alexander replied, 'I am well aware of that, Parmenion.
But I would be ashamed if, after crossing the Hellespont with ease, this little stream (this was
his term to disparage the Granicus) is to prevent us getting across just as we are. I would take
this as false to Macedonian prestige and false to my own short way with dangers: and I imagine
that it would encourage the Persians to begin thinking themselves a match for Macedonians, if
they have met with no immediate justification for their fears.'"

58. Green 1991, 495: "Diodorus offers us not only a quite different picture but an eminently
sane one."

59. I am inclined to accept the interpretation of Green 1991, 496 and 566 n. 43, with regard to
Polyaenus, *Strat.* 4.3.16.

60. Green 1991, 489–512, makes an intriguing case for the basic reliability of Diodorus' version,
suggesting that there were, in fact, two confrontations at the Granicus. In the first, Alexander
(after ignoring Parmenion's advice) suffered a setback in the river. The casualties suffered "in
the first onslaught" (Arr. 1.15.2: ἐν τῇ πρώτῃ προσβολῇ) are thought to belong to the first battle.
The Greek mercenaries were, to a great extent, responsible for the defeat, for which reason
Alexander later took vengeance on them. On the second day, the Macedonians crossed the
river uncontested and won the victory. The "official" account of the battle was thus intended to
cover up for the poor generalship (cf. Plut. *Alex.* 16.4) of the inexperienced young king.

61. Suicide of Arsites: Arr. 1.16.3. His satrapy was given by Alexander to Calas son of
Harpalus: Arr. 1.17.1. For the question of how much authority a satrap could exercise in relation
to the directives of the Great King, see Briant, *HPE* 822–23. Diod. 17.21.3 mentions the death

Persian forces were marshaled in his satrapy probably gave him the supreme command. The outcome was devastating not only in that it meant the collapse of military resistance in northwestern Asia Minor but also because it destroyed the flower of the Anatolian aristocracy in a single stroke. Memnon fled south to join forces with Orontopates, the satrap of Caria,[62] and his appointment as supreme commander of the forces on the littoral, although it may be an indicator of his merits as a general, shows that the Granicus battle created a vacuum in the military leadership of the West.[63]

_____

of Atizyes (omitted by Arrian) but then at 17.34.5 names a certain Atixyes (*sic*) among the dead at Issus (confirmed as Atizyes by Arr. 2.11.8). The false report of his death is, at least, an indicator of his presence at the Granicus, which is what we should expect at any rate. Atizyes and Arsames bought time to join Darius when Alexander turned back to the Aegean coast.

62. Memnon and other survivors of the Granicus fled first to Miletus (Diod. 17.22.1).

63. Memnon's appointment after the fall of Miletus: Diod. 17.23.5-6. Memnon sent his wife and children to Darius as hostages; they were later captured by Parmenion at Damascus (Curt. 3.13.14; Justin 11.10.2; for wives and children as hostages, see Xen. *Anab.* 1.4.8). In addition to Memnon, the Persian king relied upon Pharnabazus son of Artabazus and on Autophradates, who was in command of the Persian fleet. Pharnabazus sent his nephew Thymondas to Darius before the battle of Issus.

4

From the Aegean to Cappadocia

DESPITE THE NUMBERS of dead tallied by the Alexander historians,[1] the greatest impact of the slaughter was, as we have noted, on the Persian leadership. But the effect of the Macedonian victory on the Greek cities of Asia Minor was far more consequential. Of course, the Persian fleet was still active in the Aegean, threatening those of the islanders or the coastal cities who contemplated defection. The imposition of the first Macedonian satrap, Calas son of Harpalus, in Hellespontine Phrygia sent a clear message that Alexander was no Agesilaus; victories were consolidated and a permanent presence established.[2] Not surprisingly, it was the northwest that saw the first significant changes. Still, it would take a full campaigning season, followed by a determined winter campaign, before Anatolia was securely in Macedonian hands.[3] Whether resistance in this area reflected loyalty to the Achaemenid rulers or an unwillingness to trade one overlord for another remained to be seen.

1. Persian casualties: about 1,000 Persian cavalry (Arr. 1.16.1) and all the Greek mercenaries except 2,000 (Arr. 1.16.2; since the number is normally given as 20,000, the dead must have numbered 18,000, but probably only about 3,000; see above); the prisoners were sent to hard labor camps in Macedonia (1.16.6). Diodorus 17.21.6 says 10,000+ infantry killed and 2,000 cavalry, with 20,000 captives (cf. Plut. *Alex.* 16.7: 2,500 horse and 20,000 foot); but Diodorus omits the fate of the Greek mercenaries. Arrian sets the Macedonian dead at 60 cavalry, 25 members of the Companion cavalry, 60 other cavalrymen, and 30 infantry (1.16.4), figures that belie the tenacity of the Persian resistance.

2. For the importance of the Dascyleum satrapy (Hellespontine Phrygia), see Briant, *HPE* 697–700. Description of the satrapy: Seibert 1985, 206; see also Bakir 1995 and 2006; Abe 2012.

3. Even after Issus, there were remnants of Persian resistance that had to be suppressed by Alexander's newly appointed satraps.

In the Path of Conquest. Waldemar Heckel, Oxford University Press (2020). © Oxford University Press.

DOI: 10.1093/oso/9780190076689.001.0001

I

Of the survivors of the Granicus, Atizyes and Arsames retained some hope of reorganizing the resistance in their satrapies, Greater Phrygia and Cilicia, respectively. Memnon and the others probably fled to the coast of the Propontis and, from there, south to Miletus. Alexander was quick to follow, leaving Alexander the Lyncestian and Calas son of Harpalus to consolidate the victory at the Granicus. At Sardis, the Persian garrison commander, Mithrenes, a subordinate of the now-deceased satrap, Spithridates, surrendered the citadel to the Conqueror and was received into his entourage. A position of responsibility would have to wait for some time, and in the end it was the thankless task of ruling Armenia.[4] Sardis received a Macedonian garrison that supported the new satrap, Asander son of Philotas, but the provision that the Lydians could retain their old customs and enjoy local autonomy was offset, at least symbolically, by the construction of a temple of Olympian Zeus on their acropolis.[5]

The large Greek populations of coastal Asia Minor were now placed in an awkward position, caught between the victor of the Granicus, who controlled the land, and the Persians, who were still powerful at sea. It was not at all certain that the Macedonians were destined to win the contest, and the perils remained very real for the denizens of the coast. When news from the Granicus arrived, the Macedonian defector, Amyntas son of Antiochus, took flight from Ephesus, along with the mercenary troops who had garrisoned the city.[6] Alexander, on his arrival, restored the democracy but ordered the Ephesians to assign what they had formerly paid in tribute to the temple of Artemis. Ephesus had been one of the Greek cities that rebelled against its pro-Persian oligarchy in anticipation of Philip's invasions, presumably at the time of Parmenion and his expeditionary

---

4. Mithrenes: Arr. 1.17.3 (garrison commander: ὁ φρούραρχος τῆς ἀκροπόλεως τῆς ἐν Σάρδεσι); Diod. 17.21.7 calls him satrap. Like Mazaces after the death of Sauaces, he must have assumed the dead satrap's position, although in that case Darius had time to make the appointment. Armenia: Arr. 3.16.5; Diod. 17.64.6; Curt. 5.1.44. Description of Lydia and Ionia: Seibert 1985, 206–7.

5. Arr. 1.17.3-7. Asander was not, as many have argued (Berve II 87; Badian 1960, 329), a brother of Parmenion (Heckel 1977b and 1992, 385; Bosworth I 130). He was supported by a citadel commander, Pausanias, and a tribute collector, Nicias. Asia Minor kept its satrapal organization but was now governed by Greeks and Macedonians. Kaerst, *Hellenismus* I[3] 341 believes that Lydian rights had been suppressed by the Persians (see the doubts of Brunt I 71 no. 4).

6. Arr. 1.17.9-10. For the city itself, which had a substantial barbarian population, see Bean 1979[2] 128–50. Its famous temple of Artemis was destroyed by fire, allegedly, at the time of Alexander's birth in 356 (Plut. *Alex.* 3.5-7; on the city and its temple, see also Strabo 14.1.21-23 C640-641).

force.[7] They had set up a statue of Philip in the temple of Artemis. But the waning
fortunes of the expeditionary force resulted in counter-revolution, supported by
Memnon, and the pulling down of Philip's statue; it was at this time that the mercenary garrison was imposed. Restoration of the democracy saw the brutal execution of Syrphax and his family, who had sought refuge in the temple but were
dragged away and publicly stoned.[8] Alexander intervened before the predictable
atrocities could advance too far. Not long afterward, he held a symbolic victory
procession in Ephesus.[9] But the real work along the coast was yet to be done.

The cities of Aeolia received Alexander's envoy, Alcimachus son of Agathocles,
and according to his instructions deposed their local oligarchies and replaced
them with democracies. The process was lubricated with a show of force—
Alcimachus had close to 3,000 troops at his disposal—and promises of the remission of tribute.[10] What exactly were the laws that Alexander swore to uphold
is a matter of debate. Magnesia on the Maeander and Tralles made formal surrender, as did Priene, but the focus of the Persian resistance was now Miletus and
Mycale.[11]

II

Miletus played a prominent role in the Panhellenic propaganda that gave
meaning to the campaign. An old Greek city, it had been at the center of the
so-called Ionian Revolt of the early fifth century, and it had suffered grievously
for its actions. The Athenian playwright Phrynichus brought the plight of the
Milesians before an Athenian audience in 493/2 in his now-lost play *The Capture*

7. See Ruzicka 1997, 124.

8. Arr. 1.17.11-12. Syrphax: Heckel 259; Berve II, 366 no. 731; *Tyrannis* I 335–36, II 690;
Hofstetter 169–70.

9. Arr. 1.18.2. It was perhaps a signal to other cities, an encouragement to defect, but it was also
intended to inspire the troops to redouble their efforts, since the strength of Memnon and his
army was increasing steadily at Miletus.

10. Alcimachus may have been a brother of the later king of Thrace, Lysimachus. For his mission
and the number of his troops, see Arr. 1.18.12. Remission of tribute to Persia did not exempt the
cities from contributions to Alexander's war effort, as Brunt I li notes. The status of these cities
in relation to the League of Corinth is unknown, but this has not prevented speculation. See
especially Badian 1966 and Bosworth 1988a, 250–58; cf. Kholod 2017.

11. Magnesia and Tralles: Arr. 1.18.1; Priene: Badian 1966, 47–48.

of Miletus.[12] Their cruel treatment at the hands of Darius I could not have failed to influence Alexander's decision on how to deal with the city once it was captured.

The *phrourarchos* of Miletus sent Alexander an offer of surrender, but news that a Persian force was nearby lifted his spirits.[13] He now hoped to hold the city for Darius. Nevertheless, the Macedonian admiral, Nicanor, managed to secure the island of Lade before the Persian fleet could arrive and, landing some 4,000 Thracians, thus hampered the Persians' ability to support the city, even though they had a distinct numerical advantage: their flotilla comprised 400 ships in comparison with the mere 160 vessels of the Greco-Macedonian fleet.[14] At this point, Alexander began to view his allied fleet as a potential liability, and he must have raised his concerns in a meeting of his council. Arrian presents it as an issue on which the king and Parmenion disagreed:

> Parmenion nevertheless advised Alexander to fight a sea battle. He expected the Greeks to win at sea and gave various reasons for it, and in particular he was persuaded of it by an omen—-an eagle was seen settling on the beach at the stern of Alexander's vessels. Winning, he said, would bring great benefits for the whole conduct of the campaign, while losing would entail no great loss for them, involving only continued Persian supremacy at sea. In fact, he said, he himself was willing to board the ships and face the danger. (Arr. 1.18.6)

---

12. The events were clearly known to Callisthenes, who remarked that the Athenians had fined Phrynichus 1,000 drachmas for bringing the horrors to life (*FGrH* 124 F30 = Strabo 14.1.7 C635; cf. Hdt. 6.21). For the date, see Lesky 1966, 230. See also Hall 1989, 63–64. Ionian Revolt: Hdt. 5.97–6.32. Fall of Miletus: Hdt. 6.18-20 says the male population was killed, the women and children sold into slavery, and the shrine at Didyma plundered and destroyed. Some Milesians were relocated to the town of Ampe at the mouth of the Tigris.

13. Arr. 1.18.4. The *phrourarchos* was Hegesistratus (Heckel 132; Berve II, 166–67 no. 346; Hofstetter 76 no. 135). The allied force appears to have been that of Memnon. Diod. 17.22.1 says that Memnon had taken refuge in the city. But Arrian shows that Alexander captured the outer works of the city, which would have made it virtually impossible for Memnon's force to gain access. Nor does either source mention Memnon's escape from the city when it was captured.

14. Arr. 1.18.4-5: the island of Lade, which Stark 1958a, 103, describes as "now a hummock in the Maeander reaches, but . . . then one of the estuary islands." Justin 11.6.2 says Alexander's fleet numbered 182 (Oros. 3.16.2: 180 ships); the additional ships may be the cargo ships mentioned by Arr. 1.11.6. Diod. 17.17.2 mentions 60 ships under Alexander's direct command at the time of the crossing into Asia (unless this is the Macedonian fleet of Proteas). Diod. 17.29.2, 31.3 says the Persians had 300 ships in the following year. But 300 is a common figure for Persian fleets. For Alexander's fleets and their commanders, see Hauben 1972; cf. Hauben 1976. On the naval war, see Brunt I, 453–56. I do not accept the view of Kaerst (*Hellenismus* I³ 330) that the admiral Nicanor was the son of Parmenion. See Heckel 176 s.v. "Nicanor [2]."

This is, of course, one of the many passages in the Alexander historians in which the strategy or tactics of the king are pitted against the conservative advice of Parmenion.[15] Invariably, the young king proves to be right, the old general discredited. But it is an effective way of presenting the alternatives that confronted the Macedonians. In this case, Alexander responds that it would be too risky to engage a superior force, since a loss at sea would be a serious blow to the campaign in general as well as to Macedonian—by which he clearly meant his own—prestige. Rightly, he points out the proficiency of the Cypriote and Phoenician sailors, in comparison with whom the Macedonians were unskilled and inexperienced.[16]

Nevertheless, the order to disband the fleet did not go into immediate effect, for Alexander could not abandon the advantage he held. The island of Lade was occupied, and the Macedonians blockaded the harbor of Miletus, positioning their ships with their prows pointing outward. The Persians, for their part, could neither break the blockade nor lure the Macedonian fleet into open water for a full-scale engagement. Furthermore, they could not remain for long under Mount Mycale for lack of supplies and water.[17] These necessities drew them away to Samos and left the Milesians to be invested by land and sea. The city sent Glaucippus to offer terms of surrender that allowed it to give equal access to Macedonians and the Persians. In effect, they were asking for neutrality. More than a year later the Tyrians would propose something similar, although in their case they would refuse to admit either party to their city. Any concession to the Persians that left a coastal city without a Macedonian garrison was clearly unacceptable, and Glaucippus was sent back to Miletus with orders to prepare his people for an attack:[18]

---

15. Arr. 1.18.6-9. For the exchanges between Parmenion and Alexander, see Bearzot 1987; Carney 2000a.

16. Arr. 1.18.7-8. This, at least, was the official explanation. Alexander in early years of the campaign showed a distrust of his Greek allies, who were underrepresented in the land army and overrepresented in the navy.

17. One minor skirmish saw ten Macedonian ships confront five from the Persian fleet, and it turned out badly for the latter. One slower vessel manned by Iasians was captured; the other four escaped, and the fleet abandoned Miletus (Arr. 1.19.10-11). The Persians were prevented from disembarking at Mycale by a force of cavalry and three battalions of infantry under the command of Philotas son of Parmenion (Arr. 1.19.8: the reference to τῶν πεζῶν τάξεις τρεῖς suggests that they were light infantry; cf. Heckel 1992, 329).

18. Difficulties of the Persian fleet: Arr. 1.19.3, 7-11. Glaucippus: Arr.1.19.1-2; cf. Heckel 126; Berve II, 112 no. 229; also Bosworth I, 138.

The besieged initially found defending themselves from their walls easy; many soldiers were gathered in the city, and they had a plentiful supply of projectiles and other implements useful for countering the siege. However, when the king, with greater determination, proceeded to batter the walls with his siege engines, and to prosecute the siege with utmost force by land and sea at the same time, and when the Macedonians also began forcing their way through the collapsing walls, they at that point gave way and took flight. The people of Miletus at once prostrated themselves before the king with olive branches and surrendered to him their own persons and their city. Some of the barbarians were killed by the Macedonians, others fled after being driven from the city, and all the rest were taken prisoner. (Diod. 17.22.2-4)

In the course of the siege, some 300 mercenaries, who no doubt had heard of Alexander's actions at the Granicus, fled the city and paddled on inverted shields to an island near the harbor. Although they were prepared to fight to the death, Alexander reversed his usual policy and took them into his service.[19]

With Miletus in his power, the Conqueror disbanded the fleet. It was one of his most risky moves and at least partially overturned in the following spring:[20]

Alexander decided to disband the fleet; he was lacking funds at that time and could also see that his own fleet was no match for the Persian. He was therefore unwilling to take a risk with any part of his forces. Furthermore, he reckoned that since he now had Asia in his possession with his army, he had no need of a fleet, and by capturing the coastal cities he would also put an end to the Persian navy; they would have no source from which to make up their crews and nowhere in Asia to put in. This was how he

---

19. Arr. 1.19.4 (cf. Diod. 17.22.4). Others who tried to escape in boats were captured by the fleet. Lane Fox 1973, 133, suggests that the 300 who escaped to the island "were the richer citizens who had domineered the city with Persian support." Arr. 1.19.6 makes it clear that they were mercenaries. Nevertheless, Arr. 1.19.4 speaks of οἱ Μιλήσιοί τε καὶ οἱ μισθοφόροι, and the former may have been those who took to the boats and were captured.

20. Bosworth, *CAH²* VI 801, calls it "one of his few military blunders." On the other hand, Buckler 2003, 506, concludes: "Philip imposed no indemnity on Athens, no[r] did he garrison it. Although some have attributed this lenience to his desire to command the Athenian fleet, neither he nor later Alexander ever used it. Its actual importance has received much more attention than it deserves. Its operational quality had markedly declined since the Social War, and its days of glory lay shrouded in the mists of the past. For Macedonian purposes it served a more valuable function as a captive, aging in the harbor."

interpreted the eagle: it was a message to him that he would overcome the ships from the land.[21]

These arguments are not convincing. Many ports remained for the Persian fleet, and in fact its real strength came from Cyprus and Phoenicia. Claims of financial restraints—even though it required more than one hundred talents per month to maintain the fleet—seem disingenuous, as every conquest added to the king's war chest or, at least, increased his tax base for future endeavors.[22] His primary concern must have been anxiety about a naval defeat, particularly one caused by the defection of his allies.[23] The success of the fleet at Miletus did little to change the Conqueror's thinking. No doubt he believed himself fortunate to have escaped disaster. But the disbanding of the fleet had what can only be regarded as predictable consequences: the siege of Halicarnassus was made far more difficult, Miletus was soon recaptured, and the Persians were presented with an opportunity to launch a counterstrike in the Aegean.[24] But that was yet to come.

III

The Persian forces withdrew and solidified their base in Caria. Here, on the Myndus peninsula, the city of Halicarnassus (modern Bodrum) faced south with an excellent harbor on the Gulf of Cos, which served as the primary base for the Persian fleet. Endowed with natural defenses, supplemented by walls that reached to a height of forty-five feet in places, the city proved to be a greater obstacle than Miletus. Memnon, now entrusted with the defense of coastal Asia Minor,[25] worked in tandem with the local satrap Orontopates. But many of the

---

21. Arr. 1.20.1. On this episode and divination in general, see Bowden 2017b.

22. Brunt I, 454, notes that since the majority of the ships were supplied by the Greek allies, the League members should have assumed the cost (cf. the case of Chios, Tod no. 192; for the decree and its date, see also Heisserer 1980, 79–95).

23. For a careful analysis, see Bosworth I, 141–43.

24. Alexander retained twenty Athenian ships in order to transport the siege equipment (Diod. 17.22.5). They did this when the Conqueror moved south to Halicarnassus (Diod. 17.24.1), and it is hard to imagine that they could have done so in safety with the Persian fleet nearby. Recapture of Miletus: Curt. 4.1.37, 5.13. I omit from this part of my narrative the vexed question of Didyma and the Branchidae, on which see now Nudell 2018, with earlier literature. The punishment of the Branchidae in Sogdiana is discussed in chapter 11.

25. Diod. 17.23.4-5 says that Memnon sent his wife and children to Darius to serve as hostages in the expectation that Darius would promote him to the supreme command, and he adds that "this was what happened" (ὅπερ καὶ συνέβη γενέσθαι). Darius then wrote letters to all those who dwelt on the coast instructing them to obey Memnon. Now, all of this would have taken

Carian cities submitted without a fight, some out of fear as the towns between Miletus and Halicarnassus fell to the Macedonians;[26] others, loyal to the exiled ruler, the elder Ada (who had taken refuge in Alinda), welcomed Alexander, who now reinstated the woman as legitimate ruler of the satrapy.[27] Her brother Mausolus had recognized the natural advantages of Halicarnassus; when he came to power in 377, he enlarged and fortified the city and transferred his satrapal capital there from Mylasa.[28] Memnon, who occupied the city with a large force of Persians and mercenaries, had been diligent in reinforcing any weak points in the city walls, with mortar and manpower. In their stubborn opposition, the defenders exhibited the heroism of desperation; mercenaries with long records of service under Memnon were both loyal to their commander and fearful of the punishment meted out to Greek "traitors";[29] they were inspired (and occasionally led) by the Conqueror's most bitter enemies, exiles who likewise could expect no mercy in the event of defeat.

Approaching the city from the northeast, Alexander encamped five stades from the city on the Mylasa road, and from there he made his first assault, driving

up a considerable amount of time, and we must assume that the sending of hostages, the appointment of Memnon, and the sending of letters by Darius all occurred before the siege of Halicarnassus (thus Arr. 1.20.3; cf. 2.1.1). Most likely the hostages were required to guarantee the appointment and not sent as an inducement for such a promotion. For the Halicarnassian campaign, see Arr. 1.20.4–23.8; Diod. 17.24.1–27.6; Plut. *Alex.* 17.2; Fuller 1958, 200–206; English 2009, 47–55; Ashley 1998, 206–10.

26. Arr. 1.20.2.

27. Diod. 17.24.2-3; cf. Arr. 1.23.7-8. Ada at Alinda: Strabo 14.2.17 C657; Heckel 3 s.v. "Ada [1]"; Berve II 11–12 no. 20. Arrian mentions her reinstatement after the defenders of Halicarnassus had been effectively hemmed in, but it is likely that he used his support for Ada as a device to win over the population (cf. Diod. 17.24.3), thus giving his attention to what Fuller 1958, 267, calls the "inner, or psychological, front" (cf. Lonsdale 2007, 50). Stark 1958a, 106, suggests that the meeting with Ada is an indicator of Alexander's route; that he actually came to Alinda may find support in Plut. *Mor.* 180a (Diod. 17.24.2 is ambiguous). For the site, see Bean 1971, 161–68. The case for identifying Ada with the Carian princess unearthed at Halicarnassus (Özet 1994; Prag and Neave 1994) strikes me as very weak. The woman was probably in her early forties.

28. The natural strengths of the city: Bean 1971, 81; Arr. 1.20.3; cf. Vitruv. 2.8.11. Mausolus: Hornblower 1982, 76 ff.; Ruzicka 1992, 33–45.

29. One wonders whether the generous treatment of the mercenaries captured at Miletus (Arr. 1.19.6), which came so soon after the Conqueror had made an example of their compatriots at the Granicus, was perhaps intended to dangle the prospect of clemency before the eyes of Memnon's troops. As the later treatment of the mercenaries in Hyrcania shows, Alexander was capable of devising sophistries in order to disguise inconsistencies of policy (Arr. 3.24.5; Bosworth I 140 believes that Alexander used the same argument in the case of the 300 mercenaries at Miletus, namely, that they had taken up service before the general peace and the formation of the League of Corinth).

back those who sallied forth and putting the city under siege. Upon receiving word that some within Myndus, which lay on the promontory to the west of Halicarnassus, were prepared to betray the city, Alexander moved under the cover of night to a position beneath its walls. But the betrayal did not materialize— either because the traitors had a change of heart or because their plan was exposed—and the king, without siege equipment, could not breach the walls. An attempt to sap the walls was only marginally successful, and the invader moved back to his main target.[30]

Alexander appears to have shifted his forces away from the Mylasa Gate to the Tripylon, which faced to the north, and here he ordered his men to fill in a moat, which the defenders had dug to a width of thirty cubits and a depth of twenty, so that he might bring up his siege engines:[31]

> Alexander established camp close to the city and mounted a vigorous and
> fearful blockade, first launching a series of attacks on the walls in rapid
> succession and then spending all day piling on the pressure. He brought
> up all kinds of war engines, filled the ditches before the city with siege
> sheds of every sort, and with battering rams shook the towers and the
> walls connecting them. Whenever he brought down a section of the wall,
> he followed up by attempting to force his way into the city over the fallen
> masonry by hand-to-hand fighting.
>
> At first Memnon easily repelled the Macedonians attacking the walls
> since there were many of his soldiers in the city; and to counter the barrage
> from the siege engines he would make night sorties from the city with large
> numbers of men and set the engines on fire. In the furious encounters that
> took place before the city the Macedonians were far superior in fighting

---

30. Arr. 1.20.5-7. In the process, Alexander considered, but rejected, the possibility of directing his attack on the Myndus Gate of Halicarnassus.

31. There is no indication that he shifted his camp, but this appears to be the case (cf. Fuller 1958, 20). Arr. 1.20.8; cf. Diod. 17.24.4. A cubit is the length of the forearm, roughly eighteen inches. Hence the moat was forty-five feet wide and just over twenty-two feet deep. How and where the siege equipment was landed remain a mystery. For the retention of the transport ships, see Diod. 17.22.5. Brunt I 453 rightly asks: "how could he [Alexander] venture to send artillery by sea, when the ships might be sunk or captured by the superior Persian forces?" English 2009, 49, simply assumes that the transports managed to evade the Persian navy and land their cargo, a remarkable covert operation. Given the nature of the peninsula, with Myndus at its tip and Halicarnassus facing south, it may have been possible for the Macedonians to land the siege engines on the northern coast. The unsuccessful venture at Myndus may perhaps have been a diversion to draw Persian naval forces there (Arr. 1.20.7: καὶ ἐκ τῆς Ἁλικαρνασσοῦ κατὰ θάλασσαν πολλοὶ ἤδη παραβεβοηθηκότες)—or hold the ships that were on patrol off the headland at Myndus—while the transports landed in the north.

ability, but the Persians had the advantage in numbers and military equipment; they were helped by men who supported their fight from the walls with missile-hurling equipment, killing some of their foes and wounding others. (Diod. 17.24.3-6)

During the night sortie, the garrison troops of Halicarnassus were beaten back by the Macedonians, with heavy casualties on both sides. Some 170 of the defenders fell, among them Neoptolemus son of Arrhabaeus, a member of Lyncestian royal house. The Macedonians registered 16 dead but 300 wounded.[32]

For a second time, the troops of Perdiccas' battalion led what was said to be an unauthorized attack on an enemy city. At Thebes there was a malicious rumor that their commander attacked without orders; on this occasion the troops who led the others through a breach in walls were allegedly drunk. The affair ended badly for the Macedonians: Perdiccas' men, launching an undisciplined assault, were killed or driven back, and although Alexander brought up reinforcements, the defenders kept control of the walls.[33] Among those who served with Memnon were Ephialtes and Thrasybulus, two Athenians whose extradition Alexander had sought after the destruction of Thebes. When the king asked for a truce to bury his dead, these two were said to have urged Memnon to refuse his request. Memnon acted in accordance with the norms of warfare, but the advice of the two Athenians demonstrates the bitter hatred that existed within the Greco-Macedonian world.[34]

Where the towers had collapsed, the Persians hastily erected a crescent wall, against which Alexander now directed his siege engines. The defenders had little choice but to attempt to destroy these before they could be brought up:

32. Casualty figures: Arr. 1.20.10, who attributes the wounds to the night fighting and the lack of protection (ὅτι ἐν νυκτὶ γενομένης τῆς ἐκδρομῆς ἀφυλακτότεροι ἐς τὸ τιτρώσκεσθαι ἦσαν). This must mean, as Bosworth I 145 notes, that they were aroused from their sleep and did not have time put on their defensive armor. Arrian says Neoptolemus died fighting for the Persians and was "one of those who had defected to Darius" (τῶν παρὰ Δαρεῖον αὐτομολησάντων). Diod. 17.25.5 says he was fighting on the Macedonian side (accepted by Welles, *Diodorus* 188 n. 1, and Bosworth I 145), which is probably incorrect. He was a grandson of Aëropus of Lyncestis, and his father had been executed for alleged complicity in the murder of Philip II. At least two of his relatives—his brother Amyntas and his uncle Alexander—were at the time serving in Alexander's army (Heckel 174 s.v. "Neoptolemus [1]" and *Marshals*[2] 19–32 for the family).

33. Diod. 17.25.5-6; Arr. 1.21.1-4 mentions only two soldiers who were drunk.

34. Diod. 17.25.6. Arrian omits the episode, probably because it brings no credit to the Macedonian king. Cf. Fuller 1958, 203: "That the garrison had the best of this encounter is supported by an incident which Ptolemy does not mention, presumably because it would be derogatory to Alexander." The story that some of Perdiccas' men were drunk may also be apologia—it served at once to discredit their general and to exculpate Alexander himself.

A meeting of the commanders followed, at which Ephialtes recommended that they not wait until the city was captured and they became prisoners. Rather, he said, the leaders of the mercenaries should themselves be the first to face the dangers and launch an attack on the enemy. Memnon could see that Ephialtes was eager to demonstrate his valor, and, since he had great expectations of him because of his courage and physical strength, he gave him free rein. Ephialtes then took 2,000 hand-picked mercenaries and, distributing burning torches among half of them and forming the rest up facing the enemy, suddenly flung all the gates open. Charging out at dawn with these men, he used some for setting the siege engines on fire— and there was immediately a great conflagration—while he himself led the others, closely packed in a deep phalanx, and attacked those Macedonians coming up to help put out the fires. (Diod. 17.26.1-4)

The attack caught the Macedonians by surprise, and Ephialtes' force killed many of them, whereupon Memnon threw additional men into the fray. But as the Macedonians were wavering, the veterans, who had thus far been held out of the battle, came up to turn the tide of battle:[35]

The greatest carnage occurred right at the gates. Shutting them prema- turely in panic (because they feared the Macedonians might rush in along with the fugitives they were pursuing) led to their also keeping out many who were on their side, and the Macedonians dispatched these right at the walls. In fact, the city actually came close to capture and would have been had Alexander not recalled his troops; he still wished to pre- serve Halicarnassus if there were any indication of surrender from the Halicarnassians. Of those in the city some one thousand died and of Alexander's men about forty, including the bodyguard Ptolemy, Clearchus commander of the archers, the chiliarch Addaeus, and other not undistin- guished Macedonians. (Arr. 1.22.6-7)

Once again Diodorus and Arrian present the encounter in different ways. Diodorus' focus is on the Greek mercenaries and the leader, Ephialtes, who dies a noble death but only after inflicting heavy casualties on the attackers. Arrian omits all mention of Ephialtes and minimizes the Macedonian casualties. In Diodorus' account, the engagement concludes with Alexander drawing back his

---

35. Diod. 17.27.1. Arr. 1.21.5, in a different context, mentions Philotas and Hellanicus, and Curt. 8.1.36 names Atarrhias, all members of the hypaspists who were later promoted for their valor (Curt. 5.2.5).

men on account of darkness, but Arrian attributes his withdrawal to a concern for the population of Halicarnassus.

Despite a valiant defense, Memnon and Orontopates realized that the walls could no longer be defended. They set fire to a wooden tower, built in order to rain down missiles on the attackers, as well as other makeshift structures. Buildings near the walls were torched, either deliberately or by accident. Thereupon the Persian forces withdrew to the island fortress of Zephyrium and the Salmacis citadel, where they left a force "of their best soldiers" before moving the rest of the army and its supplies to the island of Cos.[36] For the citizens there was little that could be done. Those supporters of Memnon who were engaged in torching the city were put to death by the Macedonians, but the remainder were spared on the king's orders. Nevertheless, once those who had surrendered were removed, the Conqueror ordered the city razed and a force of 3,000 mercenary infantry and 200 cavalry left behind to guard the area and the rest of Caria. The elder Ada, who had met him upon his entry into Caria and surrendered Alinda to him, was confirmed as ruler of Caria.[37]

IV

Although the defenders of Asia Minor were quickly running out of options, the disbanding of the Macedonian fleet did allow them to make counterattacks on the islands. This program of reconquest was part of a larger plan to create problems for the invader as he moved east, as well as an attempt to join forces with the Spartans who were fomenting discord in the Peloponnese.

Alexander meanwhile sent home to Macedonia those men who had taken wives shortly before the beginning of the campaign (*neogamoi*), for the purpose of "recreation and procreation";[38] Cleander son of Polemocrates was dispatched to the Peloponnese to recruit mercenaries; and Parmenion placed the bulk of

---

36. Diod. 17.27.5. The garrison: τοὺς ἀρίστους τῶν στρατιωτῶν. Arrian says nothing more about Memnon until he recounts his campaign on Lesbos and his death (Arr. 2.1.1-3).

37. Arr. 1.23.8. She adopted Alexander as her "son," a gesture that the king accepted, for, indeed, it signified that he was the legitimate heir to the territory. I do not accept the view of Abramenko 1992a that she is the "mother of the King" exposed the treachery of Alexander Lyncestes (Diod. 17.32.1). Her claims had been recognized earlier (Diod. 17.24.2). The occupation forces were placed under a certain Ptolemy, most likely the brother of Antigonus the One-Eyed (thus Billows 1990, 426): Arr. 1.23.6; Heckel 234 s.v. "Ptolemy [2]"; Berve II 336 no. 671. For the satrapy, see Seibert 1985, 207.

38. Bosworth, *CAH*[2] VI 802. Arr. 1.24.1: their leaders were Coenus, Meleager, and Ptolemy son of Seleucus, all commanders of phalanx battalions. Their return: Arr. 1.29.4. Cummings 2004, 144, rightly notes that this "seems designed to serve the double purpose of popularizing his victories in Macedonia and Greece, and attracting thence the desired type of young and adventurous recruits to his ranks." Cf. also Bosworth I 154.

the allied troops in winter quarters in Phrygia.[39] The king himself, with the remainder of the army, moved toward Lycia and Pamphylia. Arrian insists that the purpose of the march was to secure the coastline there and render the Persian fleet useless.[40] This argument was accepted by Freya Stark, who comments: "Nothing but the need to destroy, or rather to take over, the Persian naval power at its source—the half-Greek half-barbarian cities of the coast with their population of sailors and hillsides of timber—can explain the choice of this wild and dangerous route for the march through Asia Minor."[41] But such a methodical approach to eliminating naval bases—which in Lycia were not particularly good ones—is at odds with the fact that the invader left all of southern Caria (including Myndus, Theangela, Cnidus, and Caunus) in Persian hands.[42] The force left with Ptolemy at Halicarnassus was scarcely sufficient to conquer these regions, and even the renewed presence of Ada could not have won them over as long as the full Persian fleet operated off their shores. Alexander's plans for securing southwestern Asia Minor are thus a matter of conjecture.

Despite the fact that the Lycians long exhibited a blend of Hellenic and Near Eastern culture, here it was no longer possible to rely on Panhellenic propaganda or exploit the kinds of political divisions that existed within the cities on the Aegean coast.[43] Lycia had been under Hecatomnid rule since the time of Mausolus,[44] but it could easily reassert its independence in the absence of Carian overlordship.[45] Whereas the unconquered cities of southern Caria could be dealt with by Ada and the Macedonian force under Ptolemy, Lycia could not safely be

39. Cleander's mission: Arr. 1.24.2; Curt. 3.1.1. He rejoined the king at Sidon with 4,000 mercenaries: Arr. 2.20.5; cf. Curt. 4.3.11. Parmenion in Phrygia: Arr. 1.24.3, 25.4-10; cf. Diod. 17.27.6.

40. Thus Arr. 1.24.3: ὡς τῆς παραλίου κρατήσας ἀχρεῖον καταστῆσαι τοῖς πολεμίοις τὸ ναυτικόν. Bosworth, *CAH*[2] VI 802 notes that Alexander did not go to the coastal region and, furthermore, the cities of the Lycian coast were not important as naval bases (cf. Bosworth I 156). For discussions of Alexander's route, see Stark 1958a; Seibert 1985, 50-54; and Keen 1996. On his way to Lycia, Alexander bypassed Caunus, which was held by the Persians (Arr. 2.5.7).

41. Stark 1956, 294.

42. Seibert 1985, 50.

43. There were nevertheless intercity rivalries that were exploited, as in the case of the Pisidian Selgians and Termessians. For the Lycian people, see Keen 1998, 13-33. For Lycia in the Achaemenid period, see also Treuber 1887, 95-116. The actions of the Lycians in the fifth century show that they were torn between support for Persia and for Athens. They are attested on the Athenian Tribute Lists for 446 (Treuber 1887, 98-99). Description of Lycia, Pamphylia, and Pisidia: Seibert 1985, 208.

44. Keen 1998, 172-74; Hornblower 1982, 119-23; Briant, *HPE* 706-9.

45. See Keen 1998, 148-70, for the reign of King Pericle of Limyra.

bypassed. Areas left untouched, as the Conqueror was to find on later occasions, would serve as a refuge and even a recruiting ground for the remnants of the Persian resistance.[46]

In all likelihood, the Macedonian army followed the road east to Telmessus (modern Fethiye) and the Xanthus River and then moved south to Xanthus itself. Telmessus surrendered voluntarily, possibly influenced by the presence in the Conqueror's army of their countryman, the famed seer Aristander. Xanthus and many surrounding settlements also submitted.[47] From there the invaders followed the coast to Limyra before striking inland and then moving to the coast again at Phaselis.[48] There is certainly an indication of resistance, but details are lacking except for the fact of Macedonian success.[49] It appears that the attack on Milyan territory was a diversion into the interior, perhaps starting out from Limyra up the valley of the Arycandus River, which led to the southern limits of Milyas.[50]

En route, ambassadors came from Phaselis, surrendering their town and offering a golden crown. Their territories were annexed and Macedonian agents

---

46. For example, Cappodocia, to which those of Darius' generals who escaped from Issus fled (Curt. 4.1.34; cf. Diod. 17.48.6). Cf. Stark 1958a, 109.

47. Surrender of Telmessus (also Telmissus, not be be confused with Termessus: see *Barr. Atlas* 65 B4, D4); Arr. 1.24.4. For the location, see Strabo 14.3.4 C665. Polyaenus 5.35, referring to Nearchus' capture of Telmessus, must date to the age of the Successors. Nearchus' friendship with Antipatrides (who is called παλαιὸς φίλος) was probably the result of his time as satrap of Lycia. It is difficult to explain what Nearchus was doing entering the harbor of Telmessus by ship in 334/3. Surrender of other towns: many cities in Lycia had Hecatomnid garrisons (Keen 1996, 111), and these may have surrendered on orders from Ada (Arr. 1.24.4 speaks of the surrender of Pinara, Patara, Xanthus, and thirty *polismata*)—if they were inclined to heed her commands. Of these, Patara, once the port of Xanthus, had developed into one of the most important bases on the Lycian coast (Treuber 1887, 116). App. *BC* 4.80 says Alexander destroyed Xanthus. This is otherwise unsubstantiated. For Aristander, see Greenwalt 1982; Nice 2005; also Heckel 45–46; Berve II 62–63 no. 117.

48. This is the plausible route proposed by Keen 1996, 116 (with map). It followed the coast or "as near to the coast as Alexander could practicably take his army" (cf. Diod. 17.27.7: ὁ δ' Ἀλέξανδρος τὴν παραθαλαττίαν πᾶσαν μέχρι Κιλικίας χειρωσάμενος πολλὰς πόλεις κατεκτήσ ατο καὶ φρουρία καρτερὰ φιλοτιμότερον πολιορκήσας τῇ βίᾳ κατεπόνησεν). Although Keen's suggested route is speculative, Stark's arguments for a march inland (1958a, 110–12) are equally so (Bosworth I 158: "an unverifiable guess").

49. Diod. 17.27.7 (see the note above) gives a different picture of resistance from that of Arr. 1.24.4-6 (where only Hyparna is mentioned as a fortress taken by force).

50. *Barr. Atlas* 65 C–D4 for Milyas. Arycandus Valley: Seibert 1985, 52. Bosworth I 158 thinks that Marmara lay in this region and may be the φρούριον ὀχυρὸν of Arr. 1.24.6. But Alexander came to this fortress on the road from Phaselis to Perge, and Diodorus' remark that the rock was on the border of Lycian territory implies that it was probably located also on the edge of Lycia, Pisidia, and Pamphylia (*Barr. Atlas* 65 D4; cf. Stark 1958a, 118, whose map places Marmara north of Phaselis and southeast of Termessus).

appointed to receive their submission. Nearchus was appointed satrap of Lycia, which was detached from Caria.[51] The move limited the powers of Alexander's adoptive mother, although the motives for the king's caution—if such it was—are not clear. The march from Phaselis took the invading army past Mount Climax into Pamphylia, with the mountainous regions of Pisidia inland and to the right. It was probably here that the Macedonians were attacked by the Marmares, an incident reported only by Diodorus:

> Near the frontiers of Lycia lies a large rocky outcrop of great firmness that a people called the Marmares inhabit; and as Alexander was marching by the place these people attacked the Macedonian rear, killing many and taking away numerous men and pack animals. Angered at this, the king mounted a siege and made every effort to take the place by force. The Marmares, being exceptionally brave, and confident in the strength of their position, stoutly withstood the siege. For two days there were continuous assaults, and it was clear that the king was not going to stop until he took the rock.
>
> The elders of the Marmares at first advised the young men to end the violence and make peace with the king on whatever terms they could. When these remained unconvinced and were instead all keen to die together for the freedom of their fatherland, they next encouraged them to kill their children, wives, and old people and (those with the strength to do so) save themselves at night, break through the midst of the enemy, and seek refuge on a mountain close by.
>
> The young men, agreeing to this, gave orders for each to go to his home and there await the terrible conclusion enjoying the best food and drink with his family; but some of these young men (about sixty in number) shied away from killing their kinsfolk and decided instead to set fire to their houses and, pouring out through the gates, to slip away to the mountain close by. (Diod. 17.28.1-4)

It is clear that what these people feared was not the transition from Persian to Macedonian supremacy but enslavement or some other abuse at the hands of the Conqueror as retribution for their predations against the farmers of Phaselis.[52]

---

51. Phaselis: Arr. 1.24.5-6. While Alexander was in Phaselis, he learned of the alleged conspiracy of Alexander Lyncestes, who was in Parmenion's camp at the time (Arr. 1.25). Nearchus' satrapy: Arr. 3.6.6. He remained there until 330/29.

52. Arr. 1.24.6: συνεξαιρεῖ αὐτοῖς φρούριον ὀχυρόν, ἐπιτετειχισμένον τῇ χώρᾳ πρὸς Πισιδῶν, ὅθεν ὁρμώμενοι οἱ βάρβαροι πολλὰ ἔβλαπτον τῶν Φασηλιτῶν τοὺς τὴν γῆν ἐργαζομένους. If these

In all likelihood, their allegiance to imperial authority was, and would continue to be, nominal.[53]

On the road to Perge, envoys from Aspendus arrived, offering to surrender their city but asking that it not receive a Macedonian garrison. Alexander granted their wish but demanded a payment of fifty talents and the tribute that they had paid in horses to the Persian king. The Aspendians formed their own estimate of the invader's strength (deceived by the size of the army,)[54] reneged on their promises, and repaired their fortifications in anticipation of an attack. Alexander had meanwhile occupied Side and moved against Syllium and its garrison of barbarian mercenaries. Faced with resistance there and the news of Aspendian treachery, the Conqueror turned back to deal with the latter:

> Most of Aspendus is built on a secure, sheer hilltop, and the River Eurymedon flows past the hill. Around it on the level ground they had not a few buildings encircled by a wall that was not large. When they learned that Alexander was approaching, those living there immediately left the wall and the houses built on the level ground, thinking it would be impossible to defend them, and sought refuge on the hilltop. When Alexander arrived with his troops, he passed beyond the now-abandoned wall and encamped in the houses left by the Aspendians. And when, contrary to their expectations, the Aspendians saw Alexander had come in person and also that his army was completely surrounding them, they sent emissaries and begged him for a treaty on the earlier terms. (Arr. 1.27.1-3)

Alexander now demanded one hundred (instead of fifty) talents, all the horses that had been promised, an annual tribute, and the submission of the Aspendians to an appointed satrap, presumably Nearchus, whose territory was enlarged to include Pamphylia.[55] He also required them to provide hostages.

---

barbaroi are the Marmares, this is probably how the incident was reported by Callisthenes. Hammond 1983, 51, attributes Diodorus' account to Cleitarchus.

53. Soon after Alexander's death, they offered stiff resistance to Perdiccas (Diod. 18.22; Justin 13.6.2).

54. The force, numbering about 15,000, comprised the *pezhetairoi* and the hypaspists, most of the Companion cavalry, the Agrianes, some archers, and Thracian *akonistai*. Some archers must have remained with Parmenion, who retained also a "hipparchy" (the term is anachronistic; see Bosworth I 155–56) of the Companions. From this group we must deduct the *neogamoi* who were sent back to Macedonia for the winter. These returned with an additional 3,000 infantry and 300 Macedonian cavalry, as well as 200 Thessalian horse and 150 Eleians, but the number of the *neogamoi* themselves is not recorded.

55. Arr. 1.27.4; Julien 1914, 17; Bosworth I 168.

Alexander moved north, with the aim of linking up with Parmenion's forces in Phrygia, thus entering the land of the Pisidians, warlike mountain men who were hostile to all, including some of their own people. Termessus was the first to offer resistance, and although the Macedonians gained access to a point below the city walls, Alexander soon considered a siege too difficult and time-consuming. He had received in friendship ambassadors from the Selgians, another Pisidian tribe, and may have relied on them to keep the Termessians in check.[56] He himself moved against the Sagalassians, allegedly motived by their reputation as "most warlike of the warlike Pisidians."[57] They occupied the heights near their city:

> When Alexander's men, climbing the hill held by the Pisidians, had already reached the steepest part of the ascent, the barbarians assaulted them on both wings, where attack was easiest for them and the climb most difficult for their enemy. The archers they drove back as they were not dangerously armed and were also the first to approach them, but the Agrianes stood their ground. For the phalanx of the Macedonians was already coming into proximity, and Alexander was to be seen at its head.
>
> As the fighting became hand-to-hand, the barbarians, with no body armor, met hoplites and fell wounded everywhere, finally giving way. About five hundred met their end. . . . For, nimble and familiar with the area, they had no difficulty in getting away, and the Macedonians, with their weighty weapons and lack of knowledge of the roads, were not reluctant to give up pursuit. (Arr. 1.28.5-7)

Alexander followed up this victory by mopping up the smaller villages and moving into Phrygia. At Celaenae, a garrison of a thousand Carians and a hundred Greek mercenaries protected the city for the satrap Atizyes. They agreed to surrender within a specified time if Darius' forces did not come to their aid. In the end, they submitted, and the city, along with its satrapy, was entrusted to Antigonus the One-Eyed.[58] Alexander then rejoined Parmenion at Gordium, where he was met by the *neogamoi*, who brought reinforcements from Macedonia and Greece. They were accompanied by envoys from Athens, seeking the return of their countrymen who

---

56. Termessus: Arr. 1.27.5–28.1. Selgians: Arr. 1.28.1. See also Kosmetatou 1997, 8–11, for Alexander and Pisidia.

57. Arr. 1.28.2: ἐδόκουν πάντων Πισιδῶν μαχίμων ὄντων αὐτοὶ εἶναι [οἱ] μαχιμώτατοι.

58. Celaenae: Arr. 1.29.1-2. Curt. 3.1.8 says that the specified period was sixty days. The activities of Antigonus the One-Eyed, the famous successor of Alexander and the father of Demetrius the Besieger, under Alexander were in fact limited. See Briant 1973; Billows 1990, 1–80; Heckel 32–34 s.v. "Antigonus [1]"; Berve II 42–44 no. 87.

had served as mercenaries and had been captured after the Battle of the Granicus.[59] When he reached Ancyra, the Conqueror received an embassy of the Paphlagonians, who offered to surrender and provide hostages in return for exemption from tribute ("which they had not paid even to the Persians").[60] They were added to the administrative sphere of Calas, the satrap of Hellespontine Phrygia. On the road to Cilicia, he sent Sabictas to take over control of Cappadocia. Without an adequate force to support his claim, Sabictas appears to have accomplished nothing.[61] In 322, the area was still under the control of King Ariarathes.[62]

The Persian colossus in the west had been staggered, with little hope of a reversal of fortune in the Aegean, especially when military resources were being withdrawn from the coast to strengthen the imperial army, now in northern Mesopotamia. Victory there, or perhaps in Cilicia, might yet turn the tide, but a chain of (relatively) minor defeats in Anatolia would prove both debilitating and demoralizing. Still there were those who believed that the Great King would fulfil his god-given role and restore the world order. Many were familiar with the proud boasts of previous Achaemenid rulers, as they pertained to the military realm, doubting neither their veracity nor the favor of Ahuramazda:

> I am trained with both hands and feet. As a horseman I am a good horseman. As a bowman I am a good bowman, both afoot and on horseback. As a spearman I am a good spearman, both afoot and on horseback. And the skills which Ahuramazda has bestowed upon me and I have had the strength to use them, by the favour of Ahuramazda, what has been done by me, I have done with these skills which Ahuramazda has bestowed upon me. (DNb, quoted by Kuhrt 1995, 681)

The time had come for the empire to strike back, to converge upon the invader in its midst.

---

59. Parmenion joins Alexander at Gordium: Arr. 1.29.3. Athenian envoys: Arr. 1.29.5. Curt. 3.1.9 says they met him at Celaenae. The Athenian concern for the captured mercenaries shows that some of them, at least, were not mere soldiers of fortune but prominent citizens.

60. Curt. 3.1.23-24. They nevertheless continued to exercise a fair measure of independence: from their territory, the generals who survived the battle of Issus recruited cavalry (see chapter 6); they were still unbowed in 323 (Diod. 18.3.1).

61. It was only when Alexander entered a small portion of Cappadocia that Sabictas was appointed as satrap (Arr. 2.4.1-2; cf. Curt. 3.1.22-24 for Calas and Paphlagonia; Curt. 3.4.1 for the appointment of Sabictas, whom Curtius calls Abistamenes).

62. Cappadocians at Gaugamela: Arr. 3.11.7. Cappadocia unsubdued in 323: Curt. 10.10.3; Plut. *Eum.* 3.4. Ariarathes: Diod. 18.16.1-3, 232.1; Justin 13.6.1; App. *Mithr.* 8 = *FGrH* 154 F3. For Ariarathes, see Heckel 44; Berve II 59–60.

5

Persian Countermeasures

THE WAR IN THE AEGEAN

THE EVENTS OF the war in the Aegean are treated superficially, in the form of digressions, by Arrian, Curtius, and Diodorus, and this is reflected in most modern accounts of Alexander's campaigns.[1] Diodorus alleges that Darius hoped Memnon would "transfer the entire war out of Asia and into Europe," a claim that finds support in Arrian.[2] Alexander was certainly alert to the danger: in late spring 333, he gave Amphoterus and Hegelochus 500 talents to defray the costs of defending coastal Asia Minor and freeing Lesbos, Chios, and Cos, all of which had been garrisoned by the Persians (*praesidiis hostium liberaturos*). Six hundred talents were sent to Antipater, who on the king's instructions reconstituted the allied fleet for the protection of Hellespontine waters,[3] placing it under the command of Proteas (a relative of Black Cleitus). Its task was also to guard against a possible attack on the western islands or Greece.

The number of ships at Proteas' disposal was hardly adequate to resist a full-scale invasion.[4] Nevertheless, if Darius had devised a grand strategy to turn the

---

1. Notable exceptions are Wirth 1989, a work that has escaped the attention of most modern historians/biographers of Alexander (listed in Carlsen 1993, 50, without discussion), and Ruzicka 1988 (also Ruzicka 1983); cf. Brunt I 453–56 (appendix II). Ancient accounts: Arr. 2.1-2; 3.2.3-7; Curt. 3.1.19-21; 4.1.36-40, 5.14-22; Diod. 17.29.1–30.1, 31.3.

2. Diod. 17.30.1: προσεδόκησε μὲν γὰρ ὁ βασιλεὺς μεταθήσεσθαι αὐτὸν τὸν πάντα πόλεμον ἐκ τῆς Ἀσίας εἰς τὴν Εὐρώπην. Arr. 2.1.1: ὡς ἐς Μακεδονίαν τε καὶ τὴν Ἑλλάδα ἀποστρέψων τὸν πόλεμον.

3. Curt. 3.1.19-20. The money given to Amphoterus and Hegelochus defrayed the costs of building and manning a new fleet in northwestern Asia Minor.

4. Numbers can only be guessed at. The only reference to naval action by Proteas is the attack on the ten ships of Datames at Siphnos, in which engagement the Macedonian commander had fifteen ships (Arr. 2.2.4-5). Since the ships collected by Proteas came from Euboea and the Peloponnese, it may be that these included ships and crews that had been disbanded at Miletus

In the Path of Conquest. Waldemar Heckel, Oxford University Press (2020). © Oxford University Press.
DOI: 10.1093/oso/9780190076689.001.0001

war back on Europe and thus call Alexander back to deal with the crisis, this grandiose scheme was, in all likelihood, beyond the capabilities of the Persian leadership.[5] The forces left behind with Antipater were sufficient, in the early years of
the campaign, to deal with an uprising, as Agis' war would demonstrate.[6] A system
of alliances, garrisons, and hostages, in the form of allied troops serving in the
Asiatic expedition, countered the threat of widespread resistance. Furthermore, a
shortage of soldiers (most of them mercenaries) and the unstable situation on the
offshore islands made a counter-invasion impractical. Despite Ruzicka's assertions
to the contrary, manpower was a limiting factor; whatever troops the Great King
had entrusted to Memnon—and the majority of these were mercenaries—many
were tied down in defensive positions (as at Halicarnassus and, later, Mitylene),
and others would be recalled by Darius to serve in Cilicia.[7]

Diodorus' claim that "Memnon, with three hundred triremes and a force of
infantry, was about to campaign against Macedonia, while the majority of the
Greeks were ready to rebel" misrepresents the historical situation in early 333[8]
but probably reflects the sources' inflated opinion of Memnon's role and competence.[9] The main and, indeed, the most practical purpose of the countermeasures
in the Aegean must have been to erode the Macedonian base in western Asia
Minor, disrupt the lines of communication, and draw the Conqueror's attention
away from the empire's heartland.[10] Financial aid for Sparta was also part of the

---

and had now returned home. The allied fleet in 334 was said to have numbered 160 (Arr. 1.11.6),
and of these some 20 Athenian transports remained with Alexander. The Persian numbers at
Miletus were reported as 300 (Diod. 17.29.2, 31.3) or even 400 (Arr. 1.18.5). Proteas: Berve II
328–29 nos. 664–65; Heckel 233.

5. Briant, *HPE* 821: "Diodorus credits him with plans . . . that were certainly not appropriate
at that date."

6. It is, of course, dangerous to judge the risk by the outcome. But we should not use the
Lamian War as a basis for comparison, since Antipater's forces had by then been depleted,
the Thessalians (who defected at that time) no longer had contingents serving in Asia, and
the Athenians were able to support—indeed, lead—the rebellion (on the shortage of manpower: Bosworth 1981). Alexander's derogatory comment about a "Battle of Mice," in reference
to Megalopolis, downplays the threat but does not alter the fact that the Spartan alliance was
inadequate for the task.

7. Ruzicka 1988, 133 n. 5, calculates that "when Memnon began operations in 333 he may have
commanded as many as 15,000 mercenary troops."

8. Diod. 17.31.3: τὸν Μέμνονα τριακοσίαις τριήρεσι καὶ πεζῇ δυνάμει μέλλοντα στρατεύειν ἐπὶ
Μακεδονίαν, τῶν δ᾽ Ἑλλήνων τοὺς πλείους ἑτοίμους εἶναι πρὸς ἀπόστασιν.

9. Briant, *HPE* 817–18, 820. Diod. 17.18.2: Μέμνων . . . ὁ Ῥόδιος, διαβεβοημένος ἐπὶ συνέσει στρ
ατηγικῇ.

10. Cf. Briant, *HPE* 826–27.

equation: 10,000 "Persian archers" had driven Agesilaus out of Asia in 394,[11] and Darius may have hoped to bring about a similar result.[12] But by the time Spartan preparations for war were set in motion, the Persian position had changed. Memnon was dead, mercenaries had been withdrawn from the Aegean to serve in Darius' army, and Alexander had prepared a new fleet, under the command of Amphoterus and Hegelochus. Whatever plans the Great King had for the West, they were outpaced by events in Anatolia.[13]

The ancient sources depict Memnon, brother of Mentor and son-in-law of Artabazus,[14] as the potential savior of Darius' cause. In 334, he commanded forces from his own lands in the Troad; the rejection of his advice to the Persian satraps at Zeleia is alleged to have contributed to their defeat at the Granicus. He escaped from the battle and, after the surrender of Sardis, moved to Miletus but was unable to prevent its capture. Darius III soon placed him in charge of the Persian forces on the Aegean littoral, possibly influenced by the presence of Artabazus at the Great King's court.[15] Thus, he conducted a valiant defense of Halicarnassus

---

11. Plut. *Ages.* 15.8. The reference is to the money—the crouching Persian archer was depicted on the Persian darics—distributed by Timocrates of Rhodes to hasten the outbreak of the so-called Corinthian War (cf. Hyland 2018, 149–51).

12. For the various measures used by Persia to undermine the Macedonian effort, see Kholod 2011. The alleged attempts to incite men in Alexander's camp to assassinate him (Curt. 4.1.12, 10.16, 11.18) are difficult to assess, since they were used by Alexander as effective propaganda; there was, of course, a long tradition linking the Persian king with the assassination of military leaders (including Jason of Pherae and Philip II).

13. Ruzicka 1988 presents various interpretations of Persian intentions in 333, and this reflects the difference between the ideal and the practical. "Persian commanders in the Aegean no longer had to play a cautious waiting game. Now they could initiate wide-ranging offensive actions. Even after the departure of many mercenaries and the ships needed to carry them, there remained in the Aegean several thousand mercenaries (to judge by the number of 'Persian' troops manning Aegean garrisons in 332) and a fleet of at least 250 ships" (137). This follows an account of the crippling setbacks suffered by the Persians in 333 (135). Still Darius was aiming "at nothing less than the quick destruction of the Macedonian threat everywhere, and such a strategy accords well with the assertive character Darius displayed repeatedly during his brief reign" (138). Next comes a belated recognition of the true situation: "Darius' Aegean strategy evidently proved too ambitious," and "[t]he problem was simply one of manpower"; "Pharnabazus could not . . . spare enough mercenaries to garrison captured sites properly" (140). Ruzicka is closest to the truth when he suggests that Memnon's aim was probably "encouragement of *rumors* about planned invasions rather than . . . *any actual invasion* of Greece and Macedonia" (136; emphasis added).

14. Mentor's career: Hofstetter 129–31 no. 220. Memnon: Heckel 162 s.v. "Memnon [1]"; Berve II 250–53 no. 497; Hofstetter 125–27 no. 215; Seibt 1977, 99–107.

15. Memnon himself may have petitioned Darius for the appointment, as Diod. 17.23.5-6 suggests, but his family connections must certainly have been a factor. Diodorus defines his position as ἡ τῶν ὅλων ἡγεμονία. Arr. 1.20.3: ἀποδεδειγμένος πρὸς Δαρείου τῆς τε κάτω Ἀσίας καὶ τοῦ ναυτικοῦ παντὸς ἡγεμών. Autophradates at that time must have answered to him. Plut. *Mor.*

together with the Carian satrap Orontopates, who would scarcely have relinquished supreme command unless ordered to do so by his master. Although he failed to hold the city, Alexander's disbanding of the Greco-Macedonian fleet gave Memnon an opportunity to launch a counterstrike by seizing islands that had gone over to the invaders and securing those that had remained untouched.[16] Some of these plans were effected, but Memnon's premature death from illness not only dealt a blow to Persian policy in the West but actually obscures what the precise aim of this policy was.

Matters began well with the capture of Chios, and Memnon moved on to re-assert Persian control over Antissa, Methymna, Pyrrha, and Eresus on Lesbos.[17] He was thwarted for some time by the defenders of Mitylene, but the city was taken, with heavy losses, after his death. His attempts to turn anti-Macedonian resentment into military action were supported by bribes,[18] but as he sailed to Euboea in the spring of 333, he died of illness.[19] This theater of operations was turned over, unofficially, for the time being to his kinsman Pharnabazus:[20]

> The Mitylenaeans were kept away from their lands and were under sur-
> veillance offshore by a large number of ships. They therefore contacted
> Pharnabazus and made an arrangement with him that they would send
> off the foreigners who had come to them from Alexander under the terms
> of the alliance, that the Mitylenaeans would destroy the stelae recording
> agreements they had made with Alexander, that they would be Darius'
> allies in accordance with the peace accord with the king made under the
> peace of Antalcidas, and that their exiles would return with half of what
> they had possessed when going into exile.

339e shows that he had been operating in the Aegean before 333. See Berve II 96 no. 188; Heckel 65 s.v. "Autophradates [1]."

16. For this purpose, he had 400 ships (Arr. 1.18.5; Diod. 17.29.2 mentions 300 ships in 333).

17. Diod. 17.29.2; cf. Arr. 2.1.1.

18. Diod. 17.29.3.

19. Death of Memnon: Diod. 17.29.3-4 (after the capture of Mitylene and as he planned to sail to Euboea with his fleet); Arr. 2.1.3 (during the siege of Mitylene); Curt. 3.1.21; 3.2.1. Memnon's death is usually dated to late spring 333 (Schachermeyr 1973, 196; but Bosworth I 183 assumes "late summer"). Curt. 3.1.21 says that Alexander, as he left Gordium, had not yet learned of Memnon's death. The new Persian command structure in the Aegean is unclear. The sources mention the activities of Datames (see above) and the defeat of a Persian fleet at the Hellespont under the command of Aristomenes, clearly a Greek in Persian service (Berve II 67). These were apparently subordinates of Autophradates, who in turn answered to Pharnabazus.

20. Curt. 3.3.1; Arr. 2.2.1.

Such were the terms of the agreement made between the Mytilenaeans and the Persians. However, as soon as they entered the city, Pharnabazus and Autophradates brought in a garrison with the Rhodian Lycomedes as its commander, and they also established one of the exiles, Diogenes, as tyrant in the city. In addition, they wrested money from the Mitylenaean citizens, extorting it from those who had some and levying a tax on the community at large. (Arr. 2.1.4-5)

After the fall of Mitylene, Pharnabazus sailed south, reasserting Persian control over Miletus and bringing a large mercenary force to Lycia, perhaps with the intention of winning back towns that had recently gone over to Alexander. But here he was met by his cousin Thymondas, whom Darius had sent (possibly on ships commanded by Aristomenes) with instructions to bring the Greek mercenaries to join the royal army and to confirm Pharnabazus as Memnon's successor.[21] The transfer of the Greek mercenaries marked the end of any hope—if it ever was a viable option—of turning the war back on Europe.[22]

Persian naval successes in the spring and summer of 333 proved ephemeral. For a time, they exercised control over the Hellespont, thus threatening to cut off the grain supply from the Black Sea. This position was strengthened by the capture of Tenedos, which was taken with relative ease.[23] By securing Siphnos and Andros, the Persians were dominant in the Aegean.[24] But once the new Macedonian naval power came into play, the tide turned against Pharnabazus and Autophradates. Datames' ships were taken by surprise at Siphnos, and Aristomenes' fleet, which guarded the Hellespont, was defeated as well.[25] In the following year, Amphoterus and Hegelochus ended Persian naval supremacy in the Aegean, recapturing the major islands off the coast and bringing Rhodes under Macedonian control.

---

21. Arr. 2.2.1. Bosworth I 183 says that "Pharnabazus moved to Lycia to transfer mercenaries to Thymondas" (thus also Ruzicka 1988, 132), but it is hard to imagine why this would occur in "occupied" territory. Arr. 2.13.3 says that the ships that brought the mercenaries to Darius came from Lesbos. Curt. 4.1.36 describes Aristomenes as *qui . . . a Dareo erat missus* (cf. Briant, *HPE* 831), which suggests that he was sent out at the time that the Great King was summoning reinforcements from the west. Pharnabazus: Berve II 379-80 no. 766; Heckel 206. Thymondas: Berve II 182 no. 380; Heckel 257; Hofstetter 182 no. 319; Seibt 1977, 110-13.

22. Thus Niese I 69: "es war ein Zeichen, daß der Angriff auf Griechenland und Makedonien aufgegeben war."

23. Capture of Tenedos: Arr. 2.2.2-3. The Persians stipulated that they abandon their treaty with Alexander and the Greeks and abide by the terms of the Peace of Antalcidas (see Bosworth I 181-82; Kholod 2011, 153-55).

24. Siphnos and Andros: Curt. 4.1.37.

25. Proteas' defeat of Datames: Arr. 2.2.4-5. Defeat of Aristomenes: Curt. 4.1.36.

Autophradates' fleet had disintegrated upon the news of Darius' defeat at Issus, which induced the Phoenicians (with the exception of the Tyrians) and the Cypriotes to defect. Pharnabazus himself was captured and, had he not escaped custody, would have been brought in chains to Alexander in Egypt.[26]

On the mainland, Orontopates' counterattack in Caria or, more likely, Lydia was rebuffed with heavy casualties on the Persian side by Asander, satrap of Lydia, and Ptolemy.[27] Finally, the political tinderbox in the Peloponnese, where Sparta sought to regain power at the expense of the absent Macedonian king, would erupt in flames sparked by subventions from Persia. But in the ashes of defeat and the death of King Agis III, Sparta found itself emasculated and, in all likelihood, forcibly enrolled in the Corinthian League it had earlier disdained to join.[28] This was yet to come, but these events marked the end of the attempt to divert the Conqueror from his march eastward.

---

26. Arr. 3.2.2-4, 7; Curt. 4.6.15-18.

27. Arr. 1.23.6; 2.5.7; Curt. 3.7.4. See also Ruzicka 1988, 135.

28. Agis' war: Curt. 6.1.1-21; Diod. 17.48.1-2; 17.62.6–63.4; Arr. 3.16.10; Plut. *Ages.* 15, *Agis* 3; cf. *Mor.* 219b; Paus. 1.13.4; Justin 12.1.4-11; Aes. 3.165; Din. 1.34. Modern literature cited in Heckel and Yardley 1997, 183.

6

The Great King and His Armies

NEWS OF THE debacle at the Granicus shifted the responsibility for the defense of the empire away from the satraps and onto the Great King himself. He wasted little time summoning the levies from the core and the satrapies of the Caspian region. To buy time for his own expedition, Darius had entrusted the campaign on the littoral of Asia Minor to Memnon of Rhodes, brother of Mentor. The latter had been an ambivalent supporter of Artaxerxes III, and Darius secured the loyalty of the younger brother by requiring him to send his wife and children to him as hostages. They remained with him when the army moved from Babylon to northern Mesopotamia, before they were sent with the other supernumeraries and the royal treasures to Damascus.[1]

I

Once Darius took up the campaign, there were the inevitable comparisons of the relative qualities of the opposing armies and their respective leaders. And even today, despite an awareness of the perils of Eurocentricity, the notion of "Western" superiority continues to find its way into otherwise sober accounts. In the Greco-Roman sources, the undertaking evoked memories of the great Persian war of 480. According to Curtius, Darius, while he was still at Babylon, enumerated his troops using the same method employed by Xerxes. Marking off

---

1. Damascus: Curt. 3.13; Diod. 17.32.3; Arr. 2.11.9-10; cf. Justin 11.10.1-3. Memnon's family: Diod. 17.23.5-6. The demand for hostages must have come from Darius. Diodorus says that "Memnon sent his wife and children to Darius, because he calculated that leaving them in the king's care was a good way to ensure their safety, while at the same time the king, now that he had good hostages, would be more willing to entrust Memnon with the supreme command. And so it turned out." This is surely an attempt to put a good face on Memnon's relations with the king. Cf. Badian 2000a, 80 n. 55.

In the Path of Conquest. Waldemar Heckel, Oxford University Press (2020). © Oxford University Press.
DOI: 10.1093/oso/9780190076689.001.0001

by means of a ditch an area that could hold 10,000 men, he marched his various units into the enclosure in order to be tallied.[2] The process lasted from sunrise to sunset, and the final total came to 312,200 men, a far cry from the numbers of his famous predecessor and small even in relation to the figures of 500,000 to 600,000 given by the other Alexander historians.[3] The dramatic touches of his account are clear, and there follow further allusions to Xerxes' campaign. The Athenian exile Charidemus assesses the relative strengths of the armies in the same way that Demaratus the banished Spartan did, but the difference is that Xerxes, though displeased with Demaratus, kept his temper, whereas Darius III had Charidemus executed for his outspokenness.[4] The main gist of that speech was that the Persian troops, though superior in numbers, were no match in training and fighting qualities for the Macedonians. And if he really did express such opinions, it is hard to imagine that Darius would not have been offended. Charidemus derides the Persian force as "gleaming with purple and gold," sufficient only to "strike terror into [its] neighbors." By contrast, the Macedonians were "coarse and inelegant" but a rough and ready fighting force, well disciplined and "schooled by poverty."[5] Then, with undisguised sarcasm, Charidemus mocks the primitive weapons ("slings and lances hardened in fire") of the barbarians, who are no match for the invincible Greeks (*invicta bello manus*), and urges Darius to use his wealth to hire real soldiers.[6]

Curtius' version is a literary fabrication that harks back to Xerxes' expedition—which Alexander ostensibly set out to avenge—and emphasizes another favorite theme, that numbers of men are no substitute for true soldiers. The harsh treatment of Charidemus is at odds with the otherwise kinder nature of Darius, as it is presented by Curtius. In a complete contradiction of the actions just described,

---

2. Curt. 3.2.2-3.

3. According to Curtius, there were 250,000 infantry and 62,500 cavalry; Diod. 17.31.2 and Justin 11.9.1 say there were 400,000 infantry and 100,000 horse; Plut. *Alex.* 18.6, Arr. 2.8.8, and an anonymous Alexander history (*FGrH* 148 F44) give Darius 600,000 men.

4. Xerxes and Demaratus: Hdt. 7.101-105; Darius and Charidemus: Curt. 3.2.10-19 (Blänsdorf 1971; the parallel was noted by Kaerst, *Hellenismus* I[3] 361 n. 1; but see also Atkinson I, 109–10; Heckel 1994, 68–69, 78). The Charidemus episode is a literary fabrication, and by placing the discussion in Babylon, Curtius has missed the importance of the Greek leader's advice for Darius' strategy at Issus. The important considerations are thus attributed to Thymondas (Thimodes: Curt. 3.8.1-6) or Amyntas son of Antiochus (Arr. 2.6.3-6).

5. Curt. 3.2.12-15.

6. Curt. 3.2.16: *argentum istud atque aurum ad conducendum militem mitte.*

Darius is called "a man of justice and clemency" (3.8.5) and is made to say that "nobody's life should be forfeit for making stupid recommendations" (3.8.6).[7]

Despite the inconsistencies of characterization, there was a tradition that depicted the Great King as vainglorious, cruel, and yet cowardly. For, as we shall see, his boast that he will root Alexander out of the lair in which is (supposedly) hiding[8] is followed by his own flight from the battlefield of Issus. Although propaganda was a far cry from truth, the ancients (contemporaries and those of subsequent centuries) were taken in, and several modern writers have followed suit, oblivious to the Alexander historians' deceit and to the complexities of Darius' situation.[9] Hence, any attempt to describe the confrontation from a Persian perspective must overcome the prejudices of not only the ancient sources but of many modern scholars as well.

The final months of 333 exposed the weakness of the Persian military—perhaps even flaws in its leadership—as the Great King himself took the field and set about stopping the Macedonian invaders who had made short work of the satraps of Asia Minor, some of whom now came to Darius with satrapal armies and hopes of redemption. By the time the engagement at Issus was over, Darius III was in flight, his army melting away (as barbarian armies usually did),[10] his womenfolk captured by Alexander, and his war chest in the hands of Parmenion. Those who read the history of Alexander backward from its conclusion view the whole course of events as inevitable. Darius' actions are thus regarded as ill advised and inept in execution—in short, the result of incompetence and cowardice. The fact that his family accompanied him to the battlefield is seen as a sign of Persian

---

7. On Curtius' depiction of Darius, see Rutz 1984.

8. Curt. 3.8.11: "But he, Darius, was not going to let him [Alexander] put off the fight any longer; he was going to crush the Macedonians as they hung back in that lair into which they had retreated in fear. But there was more show than truth in these boasts of his."

9. Despite the persuasive arguments of Seibert 1987, Nylander 1993, Badian 2000b, and especially Briant 2015, the view of Darius as the cowardly king persists in the writings of both laymen and scholars. Even Dandamaev 1989, 326, describing events from the Persian standpoint, remarks: "Darius, being a weak and cowardly man, fled from the battlefield." (Even more damning is Dandamaev 1989, 329: "For the cowardly ruler of a huge empire this was a well-deserved end.") The simplistic conclusion of Fawcett 2006, 10, that "Darius III lost two battles and the largest empire in the world because he was a coward" would not merit comment except for that fact that such drivel is influential with amateur military historians. There is certainly a strand of the Alexander tradition that gives some grudging credit to Darius. Diodorus (17.61.1) calls him a clever strategist: ὁ δὲ Δαρεῖος τῇ στρατηγίᾳ διαφέρων. But Curt. 4.14.25, knowing the outcome of Gaugamela, makes Darius say: "I will welcome it if you emulate my performance, whether my example be one of bravery or cowardice." Such a reference to (one's own) cowardice is inconceivable in the speech of an ancient military leader.

10. Cf. Hdt. 1.77.4.

decadence: the Great King could not be parted from his comforts even in a time of emergency.[11] His estimation of the campaign's success was unrealistic. Was he not aware of the superiority of Western forces? Did he really think that a Persian army could prevail against the Macedonian phalanx and Greek hoplites, who had given Persia plenty of opportunities to appreciate their merits? Of course, he had not read the Greek historians, heard the panegyrics of the Athenian orators, or witnessed a production of Aeschylus' *Persians*. How was he to know that he should think or act otherwise?

The size of Persian armies was routinely exaggerated by the ancients: the forces of Xerxes in 480 allegedly comprised millions, even when the camp followers were deducted from the total;[12] Artaxerxes II summoned four contingents of 300,000 each and, even though the one led by Abrocomas arrived too late to participate in the Battle of Cunaxa, was said to have marshaled an army of 900,000.[13] By comparison, the average number assigned to Darius III for his first meeting with Alexander amounted to a paltry half million. Clearly, the assumption was that there was safety in numbers—a sensible notion when the imperial forces fought against enemies armed and trained in a similar manner—and the king, who positioned himself in the center, could expect more than adequate protection. According to Xenophon:

> When they lead their troops into battle, all commanders of the barbarians keep to the center. They think that in this way they are in the safest position, as they have their forces on both sides of them, and if they want to pass along an order the army will receive it in half the time.[14]

Although it went a long way toward guaranteeing the king's security, the formation was not foolproof, and Artaxerxes II came dangerously close to being killed

---

11. Cf. the comments of Arr. 2.11.10 about "everything a Great King takes with him even on campaign for his extravagant way of living." Badian 2000a, 81, says that the bringing of the women and children "had not been the practice of Persian Kings"; but for the practice among barbarians, see Xen. *Cyr.* 3.3.67; 4.1.17, 2.2.

12. Herodotus' numbers for fighting men come to 2,100,000, excluding the naval forces (see De Souza 2003, 41). Although the figures must be reduced—particularly for logistical reasons—Maurice 1930 and Cuyler Young 1980 offer nothing more than intelligent guesses. Cf. Briant, *HPE* 796: "it is impossible to establish a numerical value that is certain."

13. Xen. *Anab.* 1.7.12-13. The number was allegedly supplied by deserters and captives from Artaxerxes' army.

14. Xen. *Anab.* 1.8.22. Cf. Arr. 2.8.11.

by his brother's javelin in the Battle of Cunaxa.[15] But the emphasis on the king's safety has often been unfairly regarded, even by modern writers, as an indicator of his timidity. This is, of course, nonsense, particularly when one considers the inordinate amount of security provided for a modern head of state, even in noncombat situations. Indeed, how many sitting heads of state since Napoleon have led their armies in person and exposed themselves to so much danger?

The composition of Darius' army in 333 is difficult to reconstruct. According to Curtius (3.2.4-9), the Persian army numbered 100,000 Persians, of whom 30,000 were cavalrymen; the Medes with 10,000 cavalry and 50,000 infantry; 2,000 Barcaean horse, accompanied by 10,000 foot; 47,000 Armenians, of whom 7,000 were horsemen. In addition to these, there were 6,000 Hyrcanians and 1,000 Tapurians, all cavalry; 40,000 infantry of the Debrices, along with 2,000 cavalry; 8,200 from the Caspian region; and another 6,000 men from the lesser-known tribes. To these were added 30,000 Greek mercenaries. Despite these numbers, this was only a partial mobilization of the imperial forces.

These contingents, levied in the traditional Persian manner from the various peoples of the empire (*kata ethne*), show that if Darius had taken the field in person against the rebels in Egypt, he had already returned to Babylon and demobilized the army. The setbacks in Asia Minor called for quick action and a hasty summoning of troops, which under the circumstances was limited to the core regions of the empire and satrapies bordering on the Caspian. Some Hyrcanians, Medes, and Bactrians had fought at the Granicus; perhaps they had been detached from the army sent to suppress the rebel pharaoh Khababash and had been placed under the authority of Spithridates.[16] The non-Anatolian cavalrymen who survived the Granicus battle, probably under the command of Rheomithres, appear to have joined Darius after he left Babylon.

In addition to the mustering of an army, the Great King took other measures to ensure his own security. That he had fears of a palace revolt in his absence is not unlikely. It had happened during Cambyses' Egyptian campaign, and he was more firmly established on the throne than Darius III. For this reason he took his

15. Xen. *Anab.* 1.8.26; Plut. *Artox.* 10. That it was Cyrus himself who wounded the king may be open to doubt.

16. Central Asian horsemen at the Granicus: Spithridates is named as the commander of the Hyrcanians, and Rheomithres led the Medes and Bactrians (Diod. 17.19.4). The Egyptian expedition is dated to various periods, and we cannot know with certainty whether it was the cause of Darius' apparent inability to send a naval expedition into the northern Aegean to contest the Macedonian crossing of the Hellespont. The timing and relevance of Khababash's rebellion have been the subject of some acrimonious debate, one of the lowlights of which is the deplorable comment by Badian 2000a, 78 n. 52, on the views and competence of F. K. Kienitz. For sober discussion, see Briant 2010, 43, and 2015, 49–54; also Burstein 2000.

immediate family—his mother, wife, two daughters, and son—with him on the campaign, keeping them in the royal tent even as the battle raged at Issus. Left unattended, they could become pawns in any bid for power by a potential usurper. In the event, they became bargaining chips in the hands of the very enemy Darius feared most. But there were also the family members of other magnates, who were kept with the army on the march but sent for safekeeping to Damascus. These were certainly hostages for the good behavior of their relatives. When Damascus was captured, the identities of many captives were made known, but the list of names is probably far from complete: three unmarried daughters of Artaxerxes III Ochus, as well as one of his wives; the daughter of Oxyathres (Amastris); the wife of Artabazus, along with her young son Ilioneus; the wife and son of Pharnabazus; three daughters of Mentor; and the wife (Barsine) and son of the recently deceased Memnon. Curtius adds that "scarcely any courtier's household was unaffected by the catastrophe," a clear indication that his list highlighted a select group, most of whom will figure in the events to follow.[17]

The presence of so many members of the royal house is not surprising, but the almost disproportionate number of relatives of Artabazus and Memnon is probably due to the bias and interests of the sources. But it is clear that the group of captives included many whose names were unknown or at least unrecorded. Their relatives who served in Darius' army or oversaw affairs in his absence remained loyal, and indeed, many were the commanders who sacrificed themselves on the field of battle. Along with these hostages, Darius deposited in Damascus a considerable treasure,[18] which shows that he was preparing for more than a single engagement. Were he to achieve the desired victory, he was prepared to drive the invader from his territories.

The imperial army marched northwest from Babylon and encamped at Sochi on the northern Mesopotamian plain,[19] an ideal spot for the deployment of the barbarian cavalry, which amounted by some estimates to 100,000 riders. It was

---

17. Curt. 3.13.12-14.

18. Curt. 3.13.16 adds that 2,600 talents in coin, as well as silver worth 500 talents, were captured. Arr. 2.11.10 says that in addition to the money sent to Damascus, Darius had about 3,000 talents in the camp. But it is clear that Arrian regards both the money and the womenfolk of the king as signs of addiction to luxury (τῶν τε χρημάτων τὰ πολλὰ καὶ ὅσα ἄλλα μεγάλῳ βασιλεῖ ἐς πολυτελῆ δίαιταν καὶ στρατευομένῳ). Athenaeus quotes from what he claims was a letter from Parmenion itemizing the goods captured at Damascus, and this, too, contributes to a picture of barbarian extravagance (Athen. 13.607f-608a). This list includes royal concubines, but it obscures the Great King's purpose in bringing the relatives of his most powerful nobles to the front.

19. Arr. 2.6.1 says it was two days' march from the "Assyrian Gates" (the Beilan Pass). Seibert 1985, 69: "Seine Lage ist ungewiß, doch dürfte sie in der Ebene des Karasu-Flusses zu suchen sein."

also ideally located to await the emergence of Alexander from Cilicia, whether he took the northerly or southerly route. Even the Greek mercenary leaders were convinced that the superior numbers of barbarian horsemen would tip the scales in the Great King's favor, if only he maintained his position on the plain. But Alexander was delayed in Cilicia, initially on account of illness but also because he needed to consolidate the satrapy. Arsames, the Persian satrap, had failed to hold the Cilician Gates against the invader and was now throwing the satrapy into turmoil, seeking to deprive the Macedonians of supplies. Darius, however, either misunderstood the reasons for Alexander's extended sojourn in Cilicia or chose to depict it as a sign of fear or cowardice. He was, of course, intent upon bringing the fight to Alexander; the earlier defeats suffered by his satraps had a detrimental effect on Persian morale. Hence, he decided to move into Cilicia and force the issue, showing in the process the confidence and leadership he hoped would inspire the troops. For us it is impossible to know whether Darius genuinely believed that Alexander was having second thoughts or whether this was just false bravado. It is hard not to think of Iraqi propaganda during the Gulf War, promising the "mother of all battles" and "death to America" before the collapse of resistance to a greater power.

Again the ancients depicted his actions as the result of bad judgment on the part of a vainglorious leader. Did he really believe that Alexander was avoiding battle? In retrospect, Darius' alleged boasts sound hollow and his flight from the battlefield all the more shameful because of them. But that is the victor's appraisal.[20]

---

20. There must have been a deliberate attempt to compare Darius with Xerxes. Cf. Justin 2.10.23: "Xerxes himself was always observed to be the first to flee and the last to fight, cowardly in the face of danger and arrogant once the danger was past."

7

The Campaign in Cilicia

WHEN ALEXANDER APPROACHED the Cilician Gates, the northern pass that separated the satrapy from Cappadocia, the defenders for reasons unstated and unclear abandoned a favorable defensive position, where "the road could barely accommodate four armed men abreast."[1] The satrap Arsames, who had participated in the unsuccessful engagement at the Granicus, had begun to destroy the crops in advance of the Macedonian invader.[2] But Alexander reached Tarsus before him and secured its treasures. Nevertheless, the city of Soli remained true to Persia, and many Cilicians held out in the hills. Perhaps they had already learned that Darius and his army were nearby, and they doubtless expected that the Macedonian invasion would be stopped in its tracks. In the days that followed, news that Alexander had succumbed to sickness after an ill-advised bath in the icy waters of the Cydnus River may have given encouragement to the resistance. If so, it was short-lived, for upon recovering, Alexander moved from Tarsus to western Cilicia. In Soli, he installed a garrison and fined the population 200 talents of silver for their unwavering support of Darius.[3] Resistance on the part of the hill tribes lasted no more than seven days. With Alexander back in Tarsus, the situation in Mallus was uncertain. The city, which claimed to have been founded by settlers from Argos, was engaged in factional strife—almost certainly between the pro-Persian party and those who favored collaboration with

---

1. Curt. 3.4.11.

2. The question of Arsames' position vis-à-vis Mazaeus need not detain us here, though it seems clear that Mazaeus had ceased to administer Cilicia during the reign of Darius III or at least by 334. See Erzen 1940, 125–29, and his critique of the views of Leuze 1935, 230–50. Description of Cilicia: Seibert 1985, 208–9.

3. Arr. 2.5.5; Curt. 3.7.2.

In the Path of Conquest. Waldemar Heckel, Oxford University Press (2020). © Oxford University Press.

DOI: 10.1093/oso/9780190076689.001.0001

the invader—and was rewarded for its surrender by a remission of the tribute due to Persia.[4]

Without support from the west, where Memnon had died and the forces of Orontopates were driven from Halicarnassus,[5] and before the arrival of Darius' army, opposition in Cilicia was easily crushed. But there remained some hope of eventual success: Darius' forces were nearby, and the Macedonian camp showed signs of intrigue and defection.[6] But for the moment, there was little to do but await the outcome of the first confrontation between Alexander and Darius. Arsames, for his part, fled to join the Great King's army.

I

The Alexander historians are unanimous in claiming that Darius' decision to move his camp from the vicinity of Sochi and meet the invader in Cilicia was opposed by mercenary leaders in his service. There is some disagreement, however, concerning the identity of the adviser: Arrian says that the Macedonian exile, Amyntas son of Antiochus, urged him to remain on the plains, where his numbers could be used to full advantage; Diodorus attributes this advice to Charidemus, who proposed that Darius hand over to him 100,000 men; Curtius substitutes the soldiers brought from the Aegean coast by Thymondas son of Mentor.[7] As noted above, Curtius inserts into his narrative a speech by Charidemus, strongly reminiscent of that given by the Spartan exile Demaratus to Xerxes in 480.

Darius, making a decision that in retrospect proved to be folly, marched through the Amanic Gates and entered Cilicia from the northeast. Persian troops had, in fact, guarded the gates by which the Macedonians would exit Cilicia, but these had been dislodged by an advance force led by Parmenion. This success was

---

4. Arr. 2.5.9, stressing their descent from Alexander's mythical ancestor Heracles.

5. Defeat of Orontopates: Arr. 2.5.7. The Persian fleet was certainly distracted at the time, but Thymondas had managed to bring 8,000 mercenaries by ship, landing his troops at Tripolis. Otherwise, there was little hope of reinforcement from the west.

6. Diod. 17.32.1-2 says that at this time Alexander learned of the treasonous activity of Alexander the Lyncestian, whose brothers (Heromenes and Arrhabaeus) had been executed for their alleged role in the murder of Philip II. Curt. 3.7.11-15 has a garbled story about Sisines, which suggests that he, too, was using a source that placed the Lyncestians' arrest at this point (see Heckel 1994). Furthermore, Harpalus fled from Alexander's camp (3.6.6-7), and it has been suggested (Bosworth 1988a, 57) that he was motivated in part by the belief that Alexander's chances in the upcoming battle with Darius were not good. See also Heckel, *Marshals*[2] 220-23, with earlier literature.

7. Amyntas son of Antiochus: Arr. 2.6.6. Charidemus: Diod. 17.30. Greek mercenaries: Curt. 3.8.1-6. All accounts emphasize the allegedly pernicious influence of Darius' courtiers.

reported to Alexander by the old general himself, who met the main army as it arrived in Castabalum from Mallus.[8] But as Alexander hurried south, the Persians were entering Cilicia via the Bahçe Pass. By the time they reached the town of Issus—where they allegedly tortured and mutilated those Macedonians who had been left behind on account of illness—Alexander's forces had advanced as far as Myriandrus. Darius caught the invaders by surprise, and they turned back to face the enemy, now positioned astride their lines of communication, in the narrows between the mountains and the Gulf of Issus.

The strategies of the two leaders are difficult to reconstruct with any certainty, since the sources disagree on their intentions. Arrian relates that Alexander, learning that Darius was at Sochi, was eager to bring him to battle there:

> Alexander then brought his companions together and told them of the reports on Darius and Darius' army. They urged him to march on from there right away. He thanked them for their support, terminated the meeting, and the next day marched on Darius and the Persians. On the second day he passed the gates and pitched camp close to the city of Myriandrus.[9] (Arr. 2.6.1-2)

But the version given by Curtius places Parmenion in the forefront and gives the impression that a battle in the narrows to the south of Issus, and presumably near Myriandrus, was actually what the Macedonians wanted, for here "the forces of both kings would be numerically equal."[10]

The only way to make sense of this is to assume that Alexander was preparing to confront the Persians as they attempted to enter Cilicia through the Beilan Pass.[11] Furthermore, in Arrian's account, the decision to march to where Darius was encamped was made at Mallus, but it is clear that the storm that kept Alexander's men in camp is meant to explain why he did not advance through the pass. It appears that Alexander was at the time prepared to fight a defensive

---

8. Castabalum is probably to be located on the coast to the west of Issus. See Bosworth I 198 and 1988a, 58–59, n. 105; Atkinson I 177, 470–71. Devine 1984 (cf. Devine 1985b, 30, 38) places it inland and supports this with reference to Diod. 17.32.4 (unrest in Cilicia), but Diodorus' account is compressed and confused and thus hardly compelling.

9. For the implausibility of a two-day march from Mallus to Myriandrus, see Devine 1985b, 30 n. 47.

10. Curt. 3.7.9.

11. Thus Devine 1985b, 28 n. 32: "Curtius' phraseology at 3.7.7 (*interior montium*) suggests the Beilan Pass rather than the Pillar of Jonah." For the pass(es) between Cilicia and Syria, see Hammond 1994b.

battle in the pass, as Parmenion had recommended; this decision, Curtius says, was adopted at Issus. Diodorus, as he does so often, only adds to the confusion:

> Alexander took Issus, a noteworthy city that he intimidated and overpowered.
>
> His scouts then reported to him that Darius was thirty stades away and approaching at an alarming rate with his troops ready for combat. Alexander took this as an opportunity granted him by the gods to overcome and crush Persian military dominance in a single battle, and he exhorted his men with fitting words to a fight for total power. He then formed up his infantry divisions and cavalry squadrons to fit the terrain, placing before his entire force the cavalry and, behind it in reserve, the phalanx of foot soldiers.
>
> Alexander himself went forward to meet the enemy at the head of the right wing, and he had with him the strongest of his cavalry. On the left wing were the Thessalian cavalry, who were far superior to the other cavalry in courage and experience. When the two forces came within spear-throwing range, the barbarians hurled at Alexander such a profusion of projectiles that they struck each other in the air because of their number and their impact was weakened. When the trumpeters on both sides then sounded the charge, the Macedonians were first to raise in unison an extraordinary war cry, and the Persians answered. (Diod. 17.32.4-33.4)

It is hard to imagine where Alexander is coming from—since Issus was north of the Pinarus—and it is possible that Diodorus wrongly attributed Darius' occupation of Issus to Alexander.

In any case, it is clear that the Macedonians did not know that Darius had marched north and entered the satrapy through the Amanic Gates (Bahçe Pass) and were taken by complete surprise. Quite possibly, the pro-Macedonian sources are correct in saying that Darius believed that Alexander's delay in Cilicia showed that he was reluctant to face him on the battlefield.[12] He would soon learn that his opponent was impetuous, although even this characteristic is probably

---

12. Curt. 3.8.10-11 ascribes this attitude to Darius himself; Arr. 2.6.4 says that the king's courtiers encouraged him to believe that "Alexander was no longer willing to advance further, but was hesitating on hearing of Darius' own approach."

exaggerated by the sources who chose to depict recklessness as a virtue, deliberately contrasting the caution and sluggishness of Parmenion.[13]

What, then, of Darius, who disregarded the advice of his mercenary leaders? The soundness of a decision is usually judged by its outcome. And if he had managed to bottle up and defeat Alexander at the Pinarus, the course of the war and Darius' reputation as a military leader would have been very different indeed. It did not turn out that way, of course, and since it is in the nature of historians to assign blame, one question remains unanswered: was it a failure of leadership or execution?[14]

II

The exact location of the battlefield is uncertain. We are told that Darius took up a position on the Pinarus River, but this could have been any one of three main rivers that flow into the sea between Issus and the Pillar of Jonah: the Deli Çay, the Payas, and the Sarisaki Su. The first of these exhibits many of the topographical features described by the ancient sources but is, in the opinion of some scholars, too far from Myriandrus to satisfy the chronology. For Alexander is said to have made a hurried march and to have reached the battlefield before sunset. The Sarisaki Su is too close to the Pillar of Jonah to merit consideration. Hence, the Payas has been a popular choice. But Freya Stark, who traveled in this area in 1954, remarked:

> The Deli Chay has been identified with the Pinarus, where the battle was fought; and I rather wondered why the more southerly Kuru Chay had not been chosen, giving as it does a ten- to fifteen-mile march between the start at dawn and the opening of the battle, and crossing the plain at a slightly narrower place, more like the fourteen hundred [*sic*] stadia of Polybius. This measurement, I take it, refers to the narrowest section of the plain, which widens with every torrent that pours out of its defile in the range. This opening and shutting of the ground explains Darius' maneuver. He stationed about twenty thousand men on the ridge "that opened here and there to some depth and had, in fact, bays like the sea;

---

13. See Bearzot 1987; Carney 2000a; and Heckel, *Marshals*[2] 49–50. Alexander's recklessness had already manifested itself at the Granicus (Plut. *Alex.* 16.4, where his behavior is described as μανικῶς and irrational; cf. Xen. *Cyr.* 1.4.24, on the actions of the young Cyrus the Great).

14. See, for example, the comments of English 2011, 103.

and, bending outwards again, brought those posted on the heights to the
rear of Alexander's wing." (Stark 1958b, 6)

Today the Kuru Çay (or Kurudere), located between the Deli Çay and the Payas,
is a mere trickle—hardly something that a Greek writer would dignify with the
word "river" (*potamos*)—but the hydrology of this area has changed over the
millennia. It is in fact an unstable region in which three tectonic plates overlap.
While the Deli Çay suits the ancient evidence better than the others, the Kuru
Çay remains attractive. It is a suitable distance from the Pillar of Jonah, and the
measurements of the battlefield approximate those described by Callisthenes.
That author was harshly criticized by Polybius, but certain features of his description may nevertheless be correct.[15] It is, however, difficult to imagine that Darius
would have abandoned the more spacious setting of the Deli Çay for a more restricted site farther south.[16]

    As the Persians had done at the Granicus, Darius positioned his troops with
the river on their front, without repeating the mistake of holding the infantry
in reserve,[17] making use of the rocky bed that would be treacherous for troops
attempting to cross in formation. Hence, the Macedonian phalangites, carrying
their eighteen-foot *sarissai*, would find it difficult to keep their footing and move
up the riverbank. The defensive position was strengthened by the construction of
an abatis near the middle of the Macedonian line. The effectiveness of this device
soon became clear, for here a gap occurred in the phalanx, which cost the lives of
many prominent infantrymen, including the phalanx commander, Ptolemy son
of Seleucus. Darius sent his best cavalry—allegedly 30,000, supported by 20,000
light-armed troops—across the river on the right, closest to the sea, where they
would confront the Greek allied cavalry. But before the engagement began, he
drew them back to the northern side of the river. He himself took up a position in

---

15. See Bosworth I 199: "It is generally accepted that Beloch was right to dismiss Polybius' detailed criticisms as petty and superficial (iii^2 2.355)."

16. The correct location of the battlefield will probably never be known, although scholars have
presented their arguments vehemently and often persuasively. The Deli Çay was the choice of
Bauer 1899 and Janke 1904, 53–74 (esp. 72–73) and also Janke 1910, followed by Fuller 1958,
154–57; Murison 1972, 403; and Seibert 1985, 67, with n. 42. Engels 1978a, 131–34, follows
Colonel Sir Charles Wilson (*Proceedings of the Royal Geographical Society* 6 [1884] 540–41) in
identifying the Pinarus with the Payas; Gruhn 1905; cf. Dittberner 1908; Devine 1980, 1985a,
and 1985b. More important, Engels rules out the possibility that Alexander could have advanced to the Deli Çay before sunset. Bosworth 1988a, 60, tentatively accepts Stark's identification with the Kuru Çay. See also Seibert 1972a, 98–102, 269–71.

17. For the battle, see Janke 1910; Fuller 1958, 154–62; Murison 1972; Devine 1985a and 1985b;
Hammond 1992a; English 2011, 71–109.

the center, supported by 30,000 Greek mercenaries, who faced the Macedonian phalanx and were flanked on each side by 60,000 Kardakes, experienced troops, armed in hoplite fashion.[18] To the Great King's left, 20,000 men extended to the hills, which some of them infiltrated in the hope of catching the Macedonian right in the flank.[19] Topography may have limited the freewheeling tactics of the horsemen—no matter where we locate the Pinarus River—but it allowed Darius to select a position that could be defended in depth.[20]

There is no doubt that there were advantages on the Persian side that offset the restriction of movement.[21] Darius' forces had time to reconnoiter the terrain, and indeed to adapt it to their needs. They were also confronting an army that had been on the march for the better part of the day. The terrain to the Macedonian right, where Alexander was inclined to lead his cavalry attack, was difficult to negotiate, on account of both the river and the mountains. And the banks of the river, more imposing than those at the Granicus, inhibited the forward thrust of the *pezhetairoi*. It appears that Darius had taken a defensive position in the center and left, hoping that his horsemen on the right could press down on the Macedonian left, where Parmenion was positioned with the allied horse.[22] One can hardly fault his battle plan, but Arrian (whose ultimate source was the propagandist Callisthenes) put this in a negative light: "This [the Persians' defensive stance] made it plain to Alexander and his staff that Darius was a beaten man" (2.10.1). Indeed, when he recognized that his cavalry would be of limited use on

---

18. Sekunda 1992, 51–53, believes that the Kardakes (or Kardaka) were non-Greek mercenary troops, perhaps from military settlements. Briant 1999, 120–24, postulates that they are barbarian troops not recruited by ethnic or territorial origin (*kata ethne*) but specially trained from youth (thus Strabo 15.3.18; cf. Cook 1983, 55: "young Persians under training"). This may have formed the basis upon which the recruitment of the 30,000 *epigonoi* in Alexander's time was built. Cf. Briant, *HPE* 1036–37. Charles 2012 regards them as infantrymen in the style of the Iphicratean *peltastai*; see also Atkinson I 102.

19. Arr. 2.8.7.

20. Arr. 2.8.8 sees no advantage in depth: "The main bulk of Darius' light and heavy troops, grouped in their national regiments, extended to a quite useless depth behind the Greek mercenaries and the front-line barbarian phalanx." Cawkwell 2005, 211, offers a different view: "It is also possible that Darius' army was not at all that large and the confined battle ground he actually fought on was thought well suited to a defensive battle."

21. Arrian (2.6.5) had the benefit of hindsight when he commented: "some divine power led Darius into the very position where his cavalry did not much help him, nor the number of his men and javelins and arrows, where he could make no display even of the splendor of his army, but delivered the victory easily to Alexander and his force."

22. Arr. 2.10.1: "once the barbarians had taken up their first positions, Darius made no further advance; he remained on the riverbank, which was in many places precipitous, in some parts building up a stockade, where it appeared more accessible."

his left wing, on account of the mountains, he sent many of them over to the right. Alexander saw this and transferred the Thessalians to that side.[23]

In some sectors, things went reasonably well for Darius. The gallant Persian horsemen, including his own brother Oxyathres, gave a good account of themselves in the fight beyond the Pinarus and along the shore. In fact, they suffered heavy casualties only when they learned that Darius had been beaten and they, too, turned in flight.[24] But the Macedonian phalanx had also broken, allowing Darius' mercenaries to knife into the gap, killing many, including the phalanx commander Ptolemy son of Seleucus. But it was in the center of the battle line that the Persians collapsed.

Alexander, with the Companion cavalry, easily overcame the forces on the Persian left, driving the defeated foe into the center, where Darius had positioned himself. The Kardakes had failed to hold off the charge, their position perhaps weakened by the forward surge of the mercenaries who exploited the gap in the Macedonian phalanx. Nor was Darius' personal guard able to prevent the collapse of the Persian line. The Great King turned his chariot, being (as the uncharitable Greek sources report) among the first to flee. Chares of Mitylene, one of Alexander's flattering contemporary historians, attempted to add drama to his account of the battle and said that Darius had inflicted a thigh wound on Alexander in hand-to-hand combat.[25] It was perhaps an allusion to the struggle between the younger Cyrus and his brother Artaxerxes II at Cunaxa,[26] but it is not corroborated by any other source and is virtually impossible if the other details of the battle are accepted.

As disgraceful as the commander's flight appears to modern readers, and indeed to the Greeks of the time, the survival of the empire depended on the Great King's personal safety and survival. Darius remained in his chariot as long as the terrain allowed, but he was eventually forced to mount a horse—some writers said the horse had accompanied his chariot for that very reason—and flee under the cover of darkness. That he discarded his royal insignia and his arms is plausible as well. The arms would do him no good in flight, and the abandoned insignia might even throw the pursuers off his track. He was doubtless not proud of his actions, but he did what the situation required, and the Persians had hopes of reversing the decision of fortune in a future engagement.

---

23. Arr. 2.9.1. The Thessalians rode behind the infantry lines in order to avoid detection.

24. Arr. 2.11.2-3.

25. Plut. *Alex.* 20.9 = *FGrH* 125 F6; cf. Hamilton, *PA* 52.

26. Xen. *Anab.* 1.8.24-27; Plut. *Artox.* 9, 11; Ctesias of Cnidus, *FGrH* 688 F19-20.

The dead were numerous, and among them were many of the best of Persia's leaders: Arsames the satrap of Cilicia, Rheomithres and Atizyes, as well as Sauaces, who had governed Egypt. That 100,000 of the troops died is a gross exaggeration, as was Ptolemy's claim that the fleeing king crossed a gully over the bodies of his own dead.[27] But there is no denying the extent of the disaster or its impact.

Not all contingents of the defeated army fled to the east. Some remained in Asia Minor, augmenting their forces with cavalrymen drawn from Cappadocia and Paphlagonia. But as they attempted to recapture Lydia, they were defeated by Antigonus the One-Eyed,[28] whom Alexander had appointed satrap of Greater Phrygia in 334. It was the only major contribution to the conquests of Alexander by a man destined to be a major player in the wars of the Successors. Of the 8,000 Greek mercenaries who escaped from Issus, half made their way to Egypt under the leadership of Amyntas son of Antiochus, only to perish there before Alexander's arrival.[29] The war in the west had not yet ended, nor had the attempt to promote countermeasures in the Greek mainland, but events in Phoenicia would be a serious setback to the undertakings of the Persian fleet and its support of the anti-Macedonian movement in the Peloponnese.

---

27. Arr. 2.11.8: 100,000 Persians killed, including 10,000 cavalry. Ptolemy says the Macedonian cavalry crossed a ravine on the bodies of the dead (2.11.8).According to Diod. 17.36.6, 100,000+ infantry were killed and at least 10,000 cavalry. There is no mention of captive numbers, but it is clear that captives were mistreated. Curt. 3.11.7 also gives 100,000 infantry dead and 10,000 cavalry. Plutarch and Arrian have similar numbers. Justin 11.9.10: 61,000 infantry and 10,000 cavalry, also 40,000 captives. For the fate of the women and noncombatants, see Curt. 3.11.21-22 in general and 3.11.23-26 for the family of Darius. For a discussion of casualties, see also Heckel and McLeod 2015; Hyland 2017, 78.

28. Curt. 4.1.34-35. Arrian's failure to mention Antigonus' achievement is perhaps due to Ptolemy's bias (on which see Errington 1969; Tarn II, 110; Burn 1952, 81–82).

29. Curt. 4.1.27-33; Arr. 2.13.2.

8

The Levant and Egypt

COLLABORATION AND RESISTANCE

THE STUNNING DEFEAT of Darius at Issus in November 333 left the Persian military in disarray. Rather than pursue his opponent, Alexander set his sights on Egypt, the biggest prize so far.[1] Nor could he afford to neglect the cities of the Levantine coast, where the rulers of Phoenicia faced a dangerous dilemma. Many of the kings were serving with their respective contingents in the Persian fleet, a force that dwindled with the loss of the coastal towns, exactly as Alexander is alleged to have predicted.[2] In many places, their sons remained at home as placeholders for the ruling father, as did, for example, Straton (Abd-ashtart, "Servant of Astarte") of Aradus (Arvad) on behalf of Gerostratus. In Sidon, another Straton was presumably represented by the aristocratic leadership during his absence—though this did not prevent the population from throwing open its gates upon the approach of the Macedonian conqueror.[3] Each town measured its chances and contemplated the consequences of defeat, mindful of lessons painfully learned in preceding generations.

---

1. Egypt as Alexander's ultimate destination at this time: Diod. 17.40.2. It is not my intention in this study to examine Alexander's motives for turning south, although I must register complete disagreement with the views of Bloedow 1998 and 2004, which downplay the importance of both Tyre and the need to control Egypt. It is absurd to think that the king would have allowed his desire to visit the oracle of Amun at Siwah to learn the secrets of his own paternity to override strategic and military concerns. See also Amitay 2008.

2. Arr. 1.20.1: "[Alexander] reflected that ... by capturing the cities on the coast he would break up the Persian fleet, since they would have nowhere to make up their crews from, and no place in Asia where they could put in."

3. No evidence for a legislative assembly (κοινόν) in Phoenician cities: Ameling 1990. The surrender of Sidon: Arr. 2.15.6 (adding that the citizens admitted Alexander on account of their hatred for the Persians: κατὰ ἔχθος τὸ Περσῶν); Curt. 4.1.15-16; Diod. 17.47.1 confuses Tyre and Sidon.

In the Path of Conquest. Waldemar Heckel, Oxford University Press (2020). © Oxford University Press.

DOI: 10.1093/oso/9780190076689.001.0001

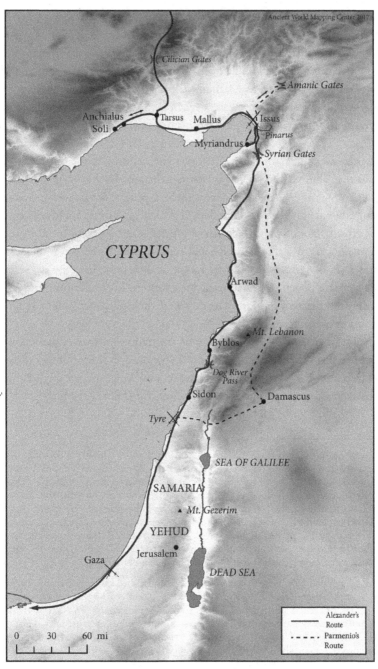

MAP 8.1 Map of the Levantine coast.

I

In the decades preceding Alexander's conquest, the Phoenician city-states dominated the Levantine coast from the lower end of the Gulf of Issus to a point just short of the entrance to Egypt, for the Phoenicians themselves, Canaanites in origin,[4] had extended their influence as far north as Myriandrus and controlled most of the coastline as far as Ascalum;[5] Citium on the island of Cyprus was also primarily Phoenician. In their early development they were both aided and restricted by the physical geography: five major centers—Aradus, Tripolis, Byblos, Sidon, and Tyre—dotted a coastline stretching some 200 miles and marked by small islands and promontories. These were backed by a fertile but narrow hinterland that abutted the range of Mount Lebanon. In this strip of mainland, smaller communities dependent upon their respective *metropoleis* provided an agricultural base for the coastal traders. But such agriculture could scarcely support a growing population, a fact that, as much as their maritime location, turned the Phoenicians to seafaring, trade, and colonization. By the seventh and sixth centuries (leading up to the incorporation of their cities into the Achaemenid Empire), these Phoenicians had settled the western Mediterranean, from Spain to Sicily and the coast of North Africa, where their settlements often replicated the features of the homeland.[6]

Byblos in ancient times was an important trading partner of the Egyptians, for it offered easy access to the cedars of Lebanon. Despite a military revival in the fifth century,[7] by the fourth, its glory days were long past, the city eclipsed by southern neighbors, especially Sidon and Tyre. The influence of these great cities

---

4. The ethnic identity of the Phoenicians remains a thorny problem. Rawlinson 2005, 20, regarded the Canaanites as Hamitic (akin to the Egyptians and Ethiopians) and the Phoenicians as Semites who came into the region and displaced them. The Semitic character of the Phoenicians is not in doubt—as is clear from their language—but they took their name from Greco-Roman sources (the name *Fnkhwu* appears in Egyptian sources: Kuhrt 1995, 1.318, 2.402), although the Phoenicians referred to themselves as Canaanites. They were certainly established in the region in the Late Bronze Age. See Culican, *CAH²* III 2.465; also Harden 1963, 22: "The Phoenicians as a people cannot be differentiated from the general mass of Canaanites until somewhere during the later half of the second millennium B.C."

5. Grainger 1991, 12: "The Phoenician cities had thus established a tight grip on the Palestinian coast, to such a degree that it is reasonable to include that coast as part of Phoenicia as it existed *c.* 350 BC." Myriandrus in Cilicia was described in the *Periplus* of Ps.-Skylax as ἐμπόριον καὶ λιμὴν Φοινίκων, but as Leuze 1935, 203, notes, this merely indicates that the population included Phoenicians and was perhaps founded by them (cf. Xen. *Anab.* 1.4.6), although it did not belong geographically or politically to Phoenicia.

6. For Phoenician settlements overseas, see Harden 1963, 30–43.

7. Elayi 2013, 259–61, based primarily on numismatic evidence.

extended along the coast of Palestine and was only partially restricted by the new Persian masters, who were content to limit the two cities' powers by a system of interspersed dependencies that left them economically prosperous but shackled by competing interests.[8] Nor were the Phoenician centers united in a meaningful political way.[9] Some had hereditary kings, others ruling oligarchies, and under Persian authority they exercised semi-independent rule, as long as they obeyed the orders of the satrap.[10] It was a familiar pattern that repeated the earlier relationship between Phoenicia and Neo-Assyria, as well as Babylon in the time of Nebuchadnezzar.[11]

Persia governed the region as part of the satrapy of Abarnahara (*ebir.nari*, "the land beyond the river"), and some control appears to have been exercised from Tripolis, a curious collection of three neighboring, but not contiguous, suburbs that represented Aradus, Sidon, and Tyre:

> There is in Phoenicia a notable city called Tripolis, and it has a name that accords with its features. For there are actually three cities, a stade apart from each other, within it, and their names are "the city of the Aradians," "the city of the Sidonians," and "the city of the Tyrians." It has the greatest reputation among the cities in Phoenicia; it was there the Phoenicians would convene their council and discuss their most important affairs. (Diod. 16.41.1)

Here the Achaemenids placed a satrapal palace and provided the Persian overlords with hunting parks (*paradeisoi*) for their leisure amusements.[12] The greatest

---

8. Grainger 1991, 11–12.

9. The council at Tripolis mentioned by Diod. 16.41.1 was a kind of *panphoinikion*, perhaps similar to the Panionium of the Greeks of Asia Minor (on which, see *OCD*[4] 1075). Cf. Wiesehöfer 2015, 101.

10. Cf. Maier, *CAH*[2] VI 320: "To respect existing political structures as long as they were compatible with Persian rule was a constant maxim of Achaemenid policy."

11. This was true in the early years of Assyrian domination, although under Sennacherib, Ashurbanipal, and Esarhaddon, their rule was far more direct and oppressive (on Assyria and Phoenicia, see Culican, *CAH*[2] III 2.467-70). After the collapse of Assyrian power, Nebuchadnezzar besieged Tyre from 598 to 585 (Elayi 2013, 213–16), and the Tyrians made submission on terms that permitted them control over their own internal politics. But the relationship with the Mesopotamian empires proved a valuable stimulus to Phoenician trade (Kuhrt 1995, 2.409-10).

12. For *paradeisoi*, see Tuplin 1996, 80–131; Dusinberre 2013, 54–56; cf. Wiesehöfer 2015, 104: "the park was considered to be a hated symbol of Persian control." There is an ongoing dispute concerning whether the *paradeisos* that was burned by the Sidonians was adjacent to their city or to their suburb in Tripolis (see Grainger 1991, 7–10, 24; Briant, *HPE* 683, 1004;

demand on manpower came from the needs of the Persian navy, of which the Phoenicians formed the most experienced and largest component.

One cannot separate the stormy relationship between Phoenicia and the Achaemenid rulers from events in Asia Minor, Cyprus, and Egypt.[13] It was clear from the start that any serious attempt at independence needed a coordinated effort. Indeed, many of the rebellions in these areas were supported as well by Greek politicians, condottieri, and mercenary armies. But safely beyond the Aegean, the Greeks found themselves isolated from the vicissitudes of war and the ebb and flow of Persian power on the western edges of the empire.

Despite its splendid natural defenses—the Sinai Desert, the Nile Delta, and adverse or unpredictable winds that limited naval support for an invading army[14]—Egypt was added to the Achaemenid Empire in 525, after Cambyses' successful campaign that apparently exploited internal divisions in the kingdom.[15] But the Persian yoke pressed heavily on the necks of the Egyptian subjects, and rebellions were frequent. In 486, Darius I died before he could subdue the first notable uprising, which was crushed by his son Xerxes.[16] The new Great King replaced Pherendates as satrap of Egypt with his own brother Achaemenes. But Persian power was challenged yet again, when a Libyan prince named Inarus son of Psammetichus, led a rebellion from 464/3 to 454, in the course of which Achaemenes was killed.[17] It appears that the attention Darius had lavished upon the Egyptians was starkly terminated after the suppression of the first rebellion,[18] and Inarus exploited the transition of power from Xerxes to Artaxerxes I and the

cf. Rawlinson 2005, 189). Elayi 2013, 286, notes that archaeological evidence shows habitation at Tripolis (that is, Atri) since the fourteenth century. Its importance administratively must, however, belong to the Achaemenid period.

13. The importance of Egypt in the history of the Persian Empire is rightly emphasized by Ruzicka 2012.

14. As demonstrated by the failure of Antigonus the One-Eyed's attack on Egypt in 306/5 (cf. Billows 1990, 162–64). Diod. 15.42.1 comments on the geographical difficulties when attacking Egypt: δυσπροσίτου παντελῶς οὔσης τῆς Αἰγύπτου.

15. See Lloyd 1982 for the Udjahorresnet inscription; also Kuhrt, *Corpus* 117 no. 11.

16. Whether this rebellion was in response to Darius' defeat at Marathon in 490, as Myśliwiec 2000, 155, suggests, is unclear. The cause may have been Darius' exactions for a renewed campaign against Greece (Hdt. 7.1.1, 4; Kuhrt, *Corpus* 236 no. 59; Kuhrt 1995, 2.663).

17. Hdt. 7.7; Kuhrt, *Corpus* 248 no. 6; cf. Hdt. 3.12.4. For the rebellion, see Thuc. 1.104, 109–10; discussion in Meiggs 1972, 93–94, 103–105; Kahn 2008.

18. Hdt. 7.7: τούτους μέν νυν καταστρεψάμενος καὶ Αἴγυπτον πᾶσαν πολλὸν δουλοτέρην ποιήσας ἢ ἐπὶ Δαρείου ἦν. Ruzicka 2012, 28.

support of the Athenian fleet in the eastern Mediterranean. But this attempt at liberation failed as well.[19]

Finally, during the course of the Peloponnesian War, a new uprising in 414 was led by a certain Amyrtaeus, supported this time by the Spartans.[20] By 404, the rebels had prevailed and remained relatively unmolested in the tension-fraught years that followed the transition from the reign of Darius II to that of his son Artaxerxes II. The death of Darius II precipitated the outbreak of a fraternal war, in which Cyrus the Younger, aided by the dowager queen Parysatis and her supporters at the court, challenged his brother's right to the throne. In the event, Cyrus died on the battlefield of Cunaxa in 401. But the diversion of Persian resources allowed the Egyptians much-needed respite. Artaxerxes had dispatched an army under Abrocomas—the figure 300,000 given by Xenophon is a gross exaggeration—to deal with the Egyptians, but he was summoned back to Babylonia on the news of Cyrus' invasion and, to add insult to injury, arrived too late to participate in the battle.[21] Not long after, Egypt was further aided by the arrival of a fleet commanded by Cyrus' former admiral, Tamos. An Egyptian himself, he was nevertheless put to death and his fleet confiscated by the rebels.[22] Amyrtaeus' reign thus inaugurated a new era and rulers who were classified by Manetho as Dynasties 28–30, spanning the years 404 to 343.

The first half of the fourth century attests to the tenacity of Egyptian resistance to Persia, but it also shows that the rulers who had set themselves up in opposition to their erstwhile masters were themselves divided and constantly in need of allies from abroad—Athens, Sparta, Cyprus, even Phoenicia.[23] Amyrtaeus was the only representative of the Twenty-eighth Dynasty. His support came from Saïs (located across the river from the Greek city of Naucratis). The recurrence of the name Psammetichus, whether the ruler's official name or his patronymic,

---

19. Thuc. 1.104.1.

20. Diod. 14.35.4-5 calls him Psammetichus, perhaps because he claimed to be a descendant of the pharaohs of that name (Twenty-sixth Dynasty). Since the last of these was defeated and executed by Cambyses, Amyrtaeus may have taken the name to recall that last era of true independence. But see Redford 2010, 146, who regards Psammetichus as a different person. Thuc. 1.104.1 gives Psammetichus as the name of Inarus' father.

21. Xen. *Anab.* 1.7.12; cf. Ruzicka 2012, 38–39.

22. Diod. 14.35.3-5. Tamos was a native of Memphis (Diod. 14.19.6), but as a satrap of Ionia and friend of Cyrus, he must have been regarded as a collaborator.

23. Out of necessity, the Egyptian rulers gravitated toward the Greek powers, Athens and Sparta, and also Evagoras of Cyprus, only to be left to their own devices when these made separate agreements with Artaxerxes II. This did not stop Chabrias and Agesilaus from coming to their aid, albeit with limited success.

suggests that these were the so-called Libyans, who traced their descent back to the ill-fated Inarus and farther into the past. Amyrtaeus' life and reign came to an abrupt end in 399, giving way to the Twenty-ninth Dynasty, two kings from Mendes named Nepherites and Achoris. In 380, the last independent dynasty of Egypt was founded by Nectanebo I (Nakhtnebef), whose descendants were the ephemeral Teos (Djedhor) and Nectanebo II (Nakhthoreb), the latter suffering defeat at the hands of Artaxerxes III and forced to flee to Nubia in 343. The reestablishment of Persian rule—Ochus now issued coins declaring himself pharaoh[24]—was, however, short-lived, and although the alleged atrocities of this king are surely exaggerated, the Egyptians were predisposed to jump ship once the Macedonian invader arrived.

The death of Artaxerxes II and the accession of his son Ochus brought renewed vigor to the Achaemenid Empire and threatened the survival of the Thirtieth Dynasty. And amid the death throes of pharaonic Egypt, the Phoenician rulers, particularly Straton of Sidon, were drawn into the vortex of Ochus' war of reconquest. In the end, Persia once more ruled in the Levant as well as in the Delta, but the harshness of the suppressors served only to minimize the resistance of this region to Alexander's invasion.

II

The island city of Aradus was the first to submit to Alexander, to whom Straton, son of the absent king, presented a golden crown and the allegiance of the dependent mainland towns of Marathus, Sigon, and Mariamme.[25] King Gerostratus was serving with the Persian fleet under the command of Autophradates, and the fact that the Aradians took so little account of the danger in which the town's surrender may have placed their king suggests that the Persian admiral himself must have been concerned about the numbers and the loyalty of his Phoenician allies. Indeed, it appears that there was little he could do to keep the Phoenicians from melting away once they learned of the affairs of their respective cities. This capitulation was soon followed by the surrender of Byblos (Ǧubail) and Sidon.[26] News reached the fleet, triggering full-scale defection, as some eighty ships returned to the eastern Mediterranean and entered Alexander's service at Sidon. This was

24. Mildenberg 1993, 73; Briant, *HPE* 1005, with additional literature. On Artaxerxes III Ochus, see also Lloyd 2011, 84–85.

25. Arr. 2.13.7-8. Curt. 4.1.5-6 wrongly says that Straton himself was king.

26. For Byblos, see Curt. 4.1.15. Arrian does not mention Byblos (or Tripolis) at this point but does mention the defection of King Enylus and the detachment from Byblos.

followed by the departure of the Cypriotes (some 120 ships), who also joined the Macedonian king and all but destroyed Persian naval power in the Aegean.[27]

About the actions of the Tripolitanians the sources are silent—except for Diodorus' general remark that Alexander "took the other cities of Phoenicia, since their inhabitants received him willingly"[28] —but it is clear that Persian authority collapsed with the defeat at Issus. In fact, some 8,000 Greek mercenaries, under the command of Amyntas son of Antiochus, had broken through the Macedonian line in that battle and made their way "through the hills" to Tripolis. There they found the ships that had brought them to the Persian host from Lesbos still beached on the shore. That they were able to seize as many of these as they needed and burn the rest shows that the Persians, such as might have remained in the city (along with pro-Persian sympathizers), were in no position to stop them. The Phoenician suburbs, with the exception of that of the Tyrians, one may assume, welcomed the invader, who followed closely on the heels of the mercenaries.[29] With the dissolution of Persian power, Tripolis may have lost its function as a political center, although it offered little or no military advantage to the Macedonians.[30]

The actions of the Sidonians, especially in contrast to those of the Tyrians, illustrate the impact of past events on the attitudes of the respective populations. The Sidonians not only surrendered but actually agreed to depose their king, also known as Straton, who owed his position to the Persian king.[31] Whether he returned to Sidon before or after his deposition—or if he returned at all—is unknown. Even his identity is uncertain.[32] Berve regarded him as possibly the

---

27. Alexander is said to have recognized that the Cypriotes and Phoenicians had joined the Persian fleet under compulsion and pardoned their earlier actions (Arr. 2.20.3). In truth, he could not have done otherwise without dooming his campaign in the Levant to failure, for the Tyrians, despite Alexander's grandiose attempt to besiege their city by means of a causeway, could only be defeated by an opponent who controlled the sea.

28. τὰς μὲν ἄλλας πόλεις παρέλαβεν, ἑτοίμως τῶν ἐγχωρίων προσδεξαμένων αὐτόν (17.40.2). The "other cities" are contrasted with Tyre, which did resist.

29. Amyntas and the mercenaries: Arr. 2.13.1-3; Curt. 4.1.27; Diod. 17.48.2-3. Other mercenary leaders included Bianor, Thymondas, and Aristomedes. Amyntas took 4,000 mercenaries and sailed for Egypt. See also Seibert 1985, 70–72.

30. It remained a shipbuilding center for Antigonus the One-Eyed (Diod. 19.58.4).

31. This may be seen as an indication that the Sidonians remained hostile to Persia, but Wiesehöfer 2015, 109, observes that Artaxerxes III's use of terror in suppressing the revolt had "convinced the Sidonians that insurgency was not worth the effort." Either way, Persian actions in the 340s impacted the Sidonian response to Alexander.

32. Arr. 2.20.1 says that Gerostratus of Aradus and Enylus of Byblos left Autophradates' fleet and joined Alexander, bringing with them the Sidonian ships. Hauben 1970, 7, assumes that Straton was already in Sidon when the city surrendered (based on Curt. 4.1.16) and then adds,

son of Tennes (Tabnit II),[33] but this seems unlikely in the light of Tennes' treacherous relationship with both the Persians and his fellow Sidonians. In 351, Tennes had rebelled against Artaxerxes III, but later (345) he sought to save himself by betraying the city to the Great King.[34] His machinations did not avail him, however, and he was executed on Ochus' instructions once Sidon had fallen into Persian hands.[35] It appears that Artaxerxes placed the Cypriote Evagoras II (son of Nicocles, who had been a friend of Abdashtart I) on the Sidonian throne, but upon his death he was replaced by Abdashtart (Straton) II. That this man was the son of the treacherous Tennes (Tabnit) seems unlikely. Straton II was probably the son or grandson of Straton I, the luxury-loving Sidonian king, mentioned by the historians Anaximenes and Theopompus. Straton I appears to have led a failed rebellion against Persia in 355 but remained in power until his death in 352. Not long afterward, the kingship passed to Tennes. After a brief interregnum, the rule of the city may have returned to the house of Straton.[36] The fate of Tennes seems to have been a lesson to the new king, who remained loyal to Persia,[37] even after Darius' defeat at Issus. Like Pixodarus in Asia Minor, he had little time to ponder his political course of action and, like the Carian dynast, found himself on the wrong side of history. Alexander, in concert with the leading Sidonians, placed a scion of the royal family, Abdalonymus, on the throne. The story of his elevation to the kingship from a humble station is undoubtedly historical fiction, just as the reputation he enjoys among modern scholars has little basis in fact. That he remained faithful to Alexander is virtually certain.

"Perhaps the Persian authorities ordered Straton to remain in the city because they were uncertain of the loyalty of the Sidonians who nursed a deep hatred of them since the revolt." On the other hand, Straton may simply have chosen not to return to Sidon when it submitted to Alexander.

33. Berve II 365 no. 728. I accepted this view until recently (see Heckel 257, s.v. "Straton [2]"). Elayi 2013, 292: "peut-être un petit-fils d'Abdashtart Ier, à en juger par son nom."

34. Rebellion: Diod. 16.43.1–45.4. Tennes' execution: Diod. 16.45.4. See Kuhrt, *Corpus* 409–11 no. 75. The Sidonian prisoners in Babylon and Susa in the fourteenth year of Ochus' reign and the date (Babylonian month Tashritu = October 11 to November 9): Kuhrt, *Corpus* 412–13 no. 76.

35. Full discussion in Wiesehöfer 2015.

36. The numismatic evidence suggests two rulers by the name of Straton (Abd-ashtart) between 345 and 333. See the discussion of events by Elayi 2013, 282–93.

37. Presumably, he remained under the watchful eye of Mazaeus, to whose satrapy of Cilicia Phoenicia had been added (Olmstead 1948, 437).

III

In stark contrast to their neighbors to the north, the Tyrians refused to submit to Macedonian authority. Diodorus, implausibly, states that the Tyrians "wanted to gratify Darius and keep unimpaired their loyalty to him, thinking they would receive great gifts from him in return." And he adds that a protracted siege would give Darius time to rearm. Furthermore, they hoped for aid from the Carthaginians.[38] It is hard to imagine that loyalty to Persia was a sufficient (even realistic) motive for Tyrian resistance. Although they sent envoys, including the son of the absent king, Azemilcus, to tell Alexander that they would follow his orders, they were in effect prepared to offer little more than their neutrality. For when Alexander demanded entry into the city in order to worship Melqart—whom the Greeks equated with Heracles and the Macedonian kings claimed as their ancestor[39] —the Tyrians told him that he could pay his respects to the god at Palaetyrus ("Old Tyre") on the mainland, adding that they would "not admit any Persian or Macedonian within the city."[40] Perhaps it is true that the Tyrians regarded it as the prerogative of their own king to conduct sacrifice at the temple in the city,[41] but they clearly recognized that Alexander meant to use his religious devotion—whether feigned or genuine[42]—as a ploy for gaining access to the city. The refusal, which incited the Conqueror to anger, came before

---

38. Diod. 17.40.3. A similar motive, but for surrender rather than resistance, is mentioned by Curt. 5.2.8: "Abulites sent his son to meet Alexander, promising that he would surrender the city—a step he may have taken independently or else on Darius' orders, so that Alexander would be delayed by taking plunder."

39. For Heracles and Melqart, see Will 1952; Brundage 1958; Bonnet 1988. For Arrian's excursus on Heracles and the Phoenician Melqart (2.16.1-6), see Bosworth I 235–38. Alexander's descent from Heracles: Plut. *Alex.* 1.1; cf. Curt. 4.2.3.

40. Arr. 2.16.7. The reference to Persians is a clear indication that they wished to remain neutral, but Arrian adds that the Tyrians were simply hedging their bets while the outcome of the war was in doubt. Curt. 4.2.2 says that they offered Alexander a golden crown and provisions for his campaign but notes that the city "seemed more likely to accept the status of an ally with Alexander than subjection to him" (*facilius societatem Alexandri acceptura videbatur quam imperium*). Diod. 17.40.3 claims that the Tyrians wanted to gratify Darius by barring Alexander from their city.

41. Welles, *Diodorus* 231 n. 2: "It was the time of the great annual festival of the god (Curtius, 4.2.10), and the Tyrians may have felt that to allow Alexander to sacrifice at that time would have meant acknowledging his sovereignty."

42. Whatever Alexander's true motive, there is no doubt that he treated with reverence and indeed emulated his mythical ancestor Heracles and that this was part of his political propaganda in a way that his alleged devotion to Achilles was not (Heckel 2015; Moloney 2015).

the Tyrians learned of the defection of their kinsmen from the Persian fleet.[43] The Assyrians and Babylonians had used the fleets of the other Phoenician cities to bring Tyre to its knees. But the lessons of the past, filtered through generations and centuries, were hardly compelling, and the Tyrians may have believed that their island location and their formidable defenses would deter or at least thwart any attempt to subjugate them. Alexander was, for them, an unknown quantity. Perhaps they had learned of the prolonged resistance of Halicarnassus.[44] And indeed, it was the capture of Tyre that did the most to enhance Alexander's reputation for invincibility. Furthermore, the defenders clung to the hope of assistance from their former colony, Carthage, which had a delegation in the city at the time,[45] although the evacuation of women and children reported by the historians must have involved only a small percentage of the population.[46]

Located about half a mile offshore, the island city seemed virtually impregnable.[47] Although the sea was shallow near the mainland, it increased in depth as one approached the island and the city walls, reaching three fathoms (eighteen feet). Here, too, the walls were higher and thicker than in other places. Despite the magnitude of the undertaking, Alexander's attempt to attack the city by means of a mole (now a permanent and much-enlarged feature of the topography)[48] was met with fierce resistance by the Tyrians, who at first sent triremes to attack the workmen and the Macedonian siege towers. When this proved to have only limited effect, they filled a transport ship with flammable material and towed it in the direction of the mole, where ship and contents were ignited with the aid of pitch and sulfur. The blazing vessel, pushed ahead by favorable winds,

---

43. Arr. 2.18.2, noting that Persia still had control of the sea; cf. 2.17.3, where Phoenician (Tyrian) sea power was a factor in Alexander's decision not to leave Tyre unsubdued. See also Curt. 4.2.15 for Alexander's deficiency in naval forces at the beginning of the siege. Cf. the comments of Rawlinson 2005, 218.

44. Reports of the fall of the citadel greeted Alexander just as the siege of Tyre began. The news would probably not yet have reached the defenders.

45. Curt. 4.2.10-11, who says that the Carthaginians actively urged them to resist.

46. Evacuation of women and children: Diod. 17.41.1; Curt. 4.3.20. But Diod. 17.46.4 speaks of women and children sold into slavery by Alexander. Curt. 4.4.14 says that "boys and girls filled the temples" when the city was captured. Diod. 17.41.2 contradicts 17.46.4, but it appears the former passage is correct. Justin 11.10.14 wrongly says that "they evacuated all who were not of age for fighting to Carthage."

47. The main ancient accounts of the siege: Arr. 2.16.1-24.5; Curt. 4.2-4; Diod. 17.40.2-46.5; Plut. *Alex.* 24–25. Modern discussions: Fuller 1958, 206–16; Romane 1987; Abramenko 1992b; Kern 1999, 209–19; Davis 2003, 17–20; English 2009, 56–84.

48. Rawlinson 2005, 171, rightly rejects Jerome's claim that Nebuchadnezzar had built a mole to attack the city.

crashed into the Macedonian causeway and engulfed the siege towers in flames. In the confusion, the Tyrians, sailing up in smaller boats, rushed to demolish the Macedonian palisade and torch the enemy's catapults, which the floating inferno had thus far left untouched.[49] But despite their efforts, the attack won them only a temporary respite.

In the course of the defense, the Tyrian resistance moved from tenacious to desperate, and the siege tested not only the resolve of the population but also the ingenuity of its engineers. As Curtius (4.3.24) remarks, "the urgency of the situation (more efficacious than any art) provided some novel means of defense beyond the conventional ones." Even in the spiritual (or rather superstitious) realm, extraordinary measures were contemplated. Only the restraint of the elders prevented them from attempting to placate the god with human sacrifice.[50]

The technological counterpunching of the opposing sides provides ample material for the history of warfare and technology, but in the end it was naval power that brought an end to the affair. Ultimately, it was not the mole (which has captured the imagination since its construction began) that determined the outcome of the siege but the inability of Tyrians to control the waters around their island. Paradoxically, the leader who had dismantled his fleet, with the intention of defeating the Persian navy "by land," was able to make use of the defectors from the Phoenician and Cypriote cities to capture the island. The Tyrians were clearly aware of the importance of naval power, for as Arrian tells us, "at the time they had some clear advantage by sea, as the Persians still dominated the sea and they themselves still had a good number of ships at their disposal" (2.18.2). Their decision to resist was based on reasonable calculations, and the Tyrians must have thought they could weather the storm and frustrate the besiegers. In fact, Arrian adds that "the siege seemed unlikely to succeed as long as the Tyrians were masters of the sea" (2.19.6). But they did not know—nor could they—the extent of Alexander's tenacity and determination.

The city possessed two of the best harbors in the eastern Mediterranean; the northern one faced in the direction of Sidon, the southern one toward Egypt. In the early stages of the siege, ships from the island could sail with relative impunity against the besiegers. But despite the efforts of the Tyrians, Alexander widened the mole so that it could accommodate more towers, and he himself marched back to Sidon with his hypaspists and Agrianes in order to collect ships

49. Arr. 2.19.1-5.

50. Curt. 4.3.23. The god the Romans called Saturn and the Greeks called Kronos was Ba'al Hammon. Human sacrifice: Garnand 2002 and 2006; in Carthage: Culican, *CAH²* III 2, 489; Lancel 1995, 248-56.

from the Phoenician leaders—including Gerostratus of Aradus and Enylus of Byblos—who had abandoned the Persian fleet. Their participation, along with that of the Cypriote kings, proved to be decisive.[51] The latter alone brought 120 ships to Sidon, and other ships were brought from Rhodes, Cilicia, and Lycia, so that the Macedonian force soon numbered more than 200.[52] This fleet advanced on the northern (Sidonian) harbor with Alexander commanding the right wing, while Craterus and Pnytagoras led the left. The Tyrians, who had prepared for a naval engagement, manned their eighty ships but pulled back when they saw the proportions of the opposing force.[53] Instead, forced into a defensive posture, even at sea, the Tyrians blocked the narrow entrance of the northern harbor with their triremes, bows pointing forward. Alexander, thus, decided against a direct attack to force his way into the harbor. The king's Phoenician allies did, however, attack head-on and sink three triremes anchored a little farther out; their crews managed to swim to safety.[54] Diodorus gives a different version, although his account is once again marred by compression and omissions. He does not mention Alexander's trip to Sidon and the acquisition of a large naval force. Nevertheless, he says that the Tyrians manned ships upon which they placed both light and heavy catapults, and with these they harassed the workers on the mole. But Alexander, "manning all his ships"—he does not say how many or where these came from—chased the Tyrians back to their harbor, picking off the ships at the tail of the column.[55] His account omits the story of the Tyrian fireship and the arrival of the fleet from Sidon but resumes with an episode that conflates an attack on the mole with that told of by Arrian on the Cypriote ships blockading the northern harbor.[56] A subsequent passage looks as if it, too, is a garbled version of Arrian's version of events:

---

51. But see Abramenko 1992b.

52. Curt. 4.3.11 says that Alexander had 190 ships; Arrian's figures (2.20.1-3) when added together come to 224. Plut. *Alex.* 24.5: 200 triremes.

53. The Tyrian fleet: Diod. 17.41.1.

54. Bosworth I 246 rightly notes that the Φοίνικες mentioned at 2.20.9 were not the Tyrians but other Phoenicians serving with Alexander.

55. Diod. 17.42.1-4.

56. Arr. 2.21.1–22.5; cf. Curt. 4.4.6-9. Arrian mentions that they sank the quinqueremes of Pnytagoras, Androcles of Amathus, and Pasicrates of Curium. Again, we are dealing with *three* ships, but whether this is coincidence or a sign of confusion in the sources is unclear.

As the Tyrians dared not put to sea again with their fleet but remained at anchor with three ships before the harbor, the king sailed up to them, destroyed all three, and then returned to his own army. (Diod. 17.43.3)

Hemmed in by the enemy fleet and helpless to stop the advance of the mole, the Tyrians could do little but assail the Macedonians from a distance, raining down missiles, arrows, and even hot sand and excrement on the attackers.[57] Divers did their best to cut the anchors of ships carrying siege engines that positioned themselves near the walls. But even here attackers and defenders took turns displaying their technical ingenuity.

In the end, although the mole had now advanced as far as the highest and thickest walls, battering rams, ballistic engines, and gangplanks were mounted on ships which took up positions at different points around the city walls. A storm disrupted the undertaking, but the Tyrians were no longer able to bring their own ships to bear against the attackers. Breaches in the wall were quickly repaired, but eventually the besiegers prevailed, and Alexander's crack troops, the hypaspists, and the battalion of Coenus son of Polemocrates,[58] gained the walls and poured into the city. Admetus, the commander of the Royal Hypaspists, fought gallantly against a determined enemy; he was felled by the blow of an axe, which split his skull.[59] The Tyrians resisted to the bitter end, knowing that they could expect no quarter from the besieging army, now determined to avenge their fallen comrades, for the Tyrians had captured a number of Macedonians and taken them up onto their walls, where they slit their throats in full view of the enemy camp.[60] With the perimeter breached, the blockading ships now forced their way into the two harbors, and the Tyrians, abandoning the walls, prepared to meet the invaders at the so-called Shrine of Agenor. Eight thousand defenders died in the slaughter.

The noncombatants—the women, children, and aged who had not been evacuated to Carthage—sought the protection of the altars, though even these were of no avail in some cases. The leading authorities, along with King Azemilcus, and the Carthaginian ambassadors took refuge in the Sanctuary of

---

57. Diod. 17.44.2-3; Curt. 4.3.25-26.

58. I do not subscribe to Griffith's theory (*HMac* II 712) that the performance of Coenus' battalion earned it the name of *asthetairoi* ("best Companions"). For this problem, see Heckel, *Marshals*² 266–68, with earlier literature.

59. Death of Admetus: Diod. 17.17.45.7 (killed by an ax); Arr. 2.23.5 (killed by a spear).

60. Arr. 2.24.3. Such atrocities—some would call them acts of defiance—are a commonplace in warfare, but it remains unclear whether the story is true or merely a justification of the victors' butchery.

Melqart. Alexander spared them.⁶¹ But the civilian population, numbering some 30,000, were sold into slavery, and 2,000 fighting men who had been captured were crucified along the beach.⁶² The siege lasted from January/February to August 332, a period of seven months. Despite his other shortcomings, Diodorus may be allowed the final word on the conflict: "So Tyre had undergone the siege bravely rather than wisely and come into such misfortune."⁶³ It was important for the conquerors to keep control of so vital a city and seaport, and Alexander ordered it repopulated and occupied by a Macedonian garrison.⁶⁴

IV

The Macedonian king had resorted to intimidation in the past, only to find his enemy more determined to resist. This had been his mistake at the Granicus, where he slaughtered the majority of the Greek mercenary force and sent the survivors to hard-labor camps in Macedonia. It only made the mercenaries in Persian service fight harder at Issus. Now, once again, the harsh measures against Tyre had a similar effect on the defenders of Gaza,⁶⁵ a town in Palestine near the entrance to Egypt. Those inhabitants of the region who had no easily defensible fortress did submit, but at Gaza, the local commander Batis, supported by an Arab garrison, remained true to his Persian masters.⁶⁶ The city was well suited

---

61. Curt. 4.4.18 says that although he spared the Carthaginian ambassadors, Alexander made a formal declaration of war against their state.

62. Arr. 2.24.5: 30,000 enslaved. Curt. 4.4.16 says that the Sidonians rescued some 15,000 Tyrians, spiriting them away in secret. That such a feat could be accomplished, with such numbers and limited means, seems unlikely, except with Alexander's approval. Curtius also says that 6,000 were killed in the fighting and 2,000 others were crucified, thus matching Arrian's total of 8,000. Diod. 17.46.3-4: more than 7,000 killed, 2,000 crucified, 13,000 captured.

63. Diod. 17.46.5. Curt. 4.4.19 says the siege ended in the seventh month (*septimo mense*). Arr. 2.24.6 does not give the length but adds that the city fell in the archonship of Nicetes (Develin, *AO* 387; Kirchner, *PA* 10753) and the month Hecatombaeon (August). Beloch III² 2.314-15; but see also Atkinson I 314; Bosworth I 255).

64. The Archelaus who was *phrourarchos* of Tyre in 321/0 may have been appointed by Alexander at this time (Heckel 42, s.v. "Archelaus [3]"; Berve II, 85 no. 149).

65. Slightly different is the remark of Kern 1999, 215: "The lesson of Tyre was not learned by Batis." Cartledge 2004, 185, suggests that "the capture of Gaza was not a military necessity and his treatment of its governor, the Arab eunuch Batis, was unnecessarily savage."

66. Heckel 71. For his loyalty to Darius, see Curt. 4.6.7 (*eximiae in regem suum fidei*). Arr. 2.25.4 says that Batis was a eunuch, but his ethnic origin is unknown. Josephus, *AJ* 11.320, calls him Babemesis. If Hegesias' description of him as black (see below) is correct, he may have been Ethiopian or Nubian. But Tarn II 267, commenting on the Hegesias passage, says that "modern historians . . . improve upon this rubbish by calling him a negro," adding in n. 5 that "μέλας

to withstand a siege: it stood twenty stades from a coast that offered no good harbor, was located on a mound (*tel*) some 250 feet high, and was surrounded by soft sand, which made it difficult to bring up siege equipment.[67] Furthermore, Alexander's lengthy delay in front of Tyre had given the population plenty of time to secure provisions.[68] By contrast, the Macedonians would have to deal with an extreme shortage of water, which had to be brought in from the ships on the coast.[69] But whether the resistance can be explained by the ethnic or economic concerns of the population (which found itself between the Phoenicians to the north and the Egyptians to the south, to say nothing of Judaea to the east) or by the pro-Persian, and perhaps oppressive, policy of its ruling party cannot be determined.[70]

Alexander, for his part, regarded the defiance of the city as a challenge to his reputation, just as Tyre had been: "the more impracticable it was, the more necessary was the capture; for the achievement would strike great terror into his enemies just because it was beyond calculation, while not to take it would be a blow to his prestige when reported to the Greeks and Darius" (Arr. 2.26.3). He built a wall to the south of the city and upon it he placed his siege engines.[71] It was in some respects a repeat of the Tyrian campaign, though the Macedonians constructed their works upon a sea of sand. The Arabs in turn made sorties against the builders, attempting to set fire to the siege engines, while the defenders on the walls directed missiles against the attackers. In the course of these skirmishes, a

---

means sunburnt." I find no comment on Hegesias' description and its implications in Snowden 1970 or 1983. Cartledge 2004, 185, calls him "the Arab eunuch Batis." His corpulence lends credence to the view that he was a eunuch. His official position is also unclear, and we cannot say whether he was a local dynast or merely the *phrourarchos* (garrison commander). Dionysius of Halicarnassus, introducing Hegesias' account of Batis' death, calls him "hegemon"; Curt. 4.6.7 says that he was in command of the city (*praeerat urbi Betis*; cf. Arr. 2.25.4: κρατῶν τῆς Γαζαίων πόλεως); Josephus calls him "*phrourarchos*." For Batis working on "instructions from Darius," see Briant, *HPE* 834; cf. 845: he "maintained his commitments to the Great King to the end."

67. Arr. 2.26.1 (twenty stades from the sea); Strabo 16.2.30 (seven stades); Pomponius Mela 1.64. For the city, see also Bezinger, *RE* VII, 880–86.

68. Arr. 2.25.4. Cf. Högemann 1985, 59 n. 10.

69. The difficulty of securing a water supply in this region was noted already by Herodotus (3.5-6). Engels 1978a, 58, estimates that Alexander's army would have consumed 6 million gallons of water during the two-month siege and that much of this must have been brought by sea from the Litani and other rivers to the north.

70. See Curt. 4.6.7 for Batis' devotion to Darius and for Gaza's defenses.

71. The siege of Gaza: Arr. 2.26–27 (*Itiner.* 45–47); Curt. 4.6.7-30; Plut. *Alex.* 25.4-5; cf. Diod. 17.48.7–49.1; Strabo 16.2.30 C759; Josephus, *AJ* 11.320, 325; Polyb. 16.22.5-6; Zonar. 4.10. Modern discussions: Fuller 1958, 216–18; Romane 1988; Kern 1999, 217–19; English 2009, 85–101.

catapult dart penetrated Alexander's shield and corselet, wounding him on the shoulder, perhaps even severing an artery. The wound was serious enough to limit the king's activities, and he called for siege engines—such as remained—to be brought by sea from Tyre. Once these were in place, the defenders sensed how dangerous their position had become, as the rams and *lithoboloi* battered the walls, which were at the same time being mined by the Macedonian sappers. They repelled three onslaughts before succumbing to the fourth. The Macedonian pha-lanx, inspired by the courage of Neoptolemus (a kinsman of the king), took pos-session of the city. As was the case in Tyre, the armed defenders fought to the bitter end, and the noncombatants were sold into slavery.[72] But the city itself was repopulated to serve as a Macedonian outpost in the future.

There is, however, one additional element to the story of the fall of Gaza that smacks of sensationalism and has been dismissed by some scholars as utter fic-tion.[73] Even those who believe it have expressed doubts about some of its details. We are told that Alexander, driven to anger by the stubbornness of the resistance and by the wound he suffered, had Batis captured and brought to him, that he decided to make an example of him in a manner worthy of his mythical ancestor Achilles.[74] Stripping him naked, he pierced the man's ankles and inserted bronze rings through the holes, attaching him by means of ropes to a chariot. Thus, like Achilles' enemy Hector, Batis was dragged around the city and died a most excru-ciating death.[75] Curtius tells the story but with a certain amount of disapproval, commenting on the king's excessive anger and the barbaric nature of his actions.[76]

---

72. Neoptolemus: Arr. 2.27.6. The fate of the defenders: Arr. 2.27.7, without casualty figures; Curt. 4.6.30 says 10,000 Persians and Arabs died. The number of enslaved is unknown. It was certainly no bloodless victory for the Macedonian forces. Curt. 4.6.31 notes the attrition that accompanied the campaigning and Alexander's need for reliable reinforcements.

73. Most notably by Tarn II 265–70, appendix 11: "The Death of Batis."

74. For Alexander's alleged imitation of Achilles, see Ameling 1988; Hornblower 2002, 290; Stewart 1993, 78–86; see also Atkinson I 341–43; contra Heckel 2015; but see now Bowden 2018. For the *Achillei imitatio* in Curtius, see Heckel 1994; also Vorhis 2017. That this was done in imitation of Thessalian practice (as Lane Fox 1973, 193, maintains) is doubtful. The Greco-Macedonians regarded such action as sacrilegious. Cf. Diod. 18.47.3 for Antigonus' maltreat-ment of the body of Alcetas. Green 1991, 267, makes the curious observation that Alexander, who "actively disliked ugly people (and was himself in a very ugly mood) seems to have lost control of himself."

75. In Homer's version, Hector was already dead. But see Sophocles, *Ajax* 1031; Euripides, *Androm.* 399 (both noted by Green 1991, 541 n. 58). It has been pointed out in online discussions that Homer, *Il.* 22.464-65 does not say that Hector was dragged *around* the city walls, but Curt. 4.6.29 (and perhaps Alexander himself) clearly thought so.

76. Curt. 4.6.26: Alexander as "elated with haughty satisfaction" (*insolent gaudio . . . elatus*); 4.6.29: "Alexander's anger turned to fury, his recent successes already suggesting to his mind

The claim that Alexander "generally admired courage, even in an enemy," is not supported by his actions, both past and future, with the exception of his treatment of the Indian king Porus. And in that case, his treatment was dictated by political necessity. The story appears to have been invented by Cleitarchus—and it forms part of a tradition that saw Alexander as a latter-day Achilles—but it was embellished to a degree unprecedented in the Alexander historians by the third-century sophist Hegesias, who described Batis in the most unflattering terms and mocked his death:[77]

> Baitis [*sic*] himself, however, was brought before the king alive by Leonnatus and Philotas. And Alexander seeing that he was corpulent and huge and most grim (for he was black in color too), was seized with loathing for his very looks as well as for his design upon his life, and ordered that a ring of bronze should be passed through his feet and that he should be dragged round a circular course, naked. Harrowed by pain, as his body passed over many a rough piece of ground, he began to scream. And it was just this detail which I now mention that brought people together. The torment racked him, and he kept uttering outlandish yells, asking mercy of Alexander as "my lord"; and his jargon made them laugh. His fat and his bulging corpulence suggested to them another creature, a huge-bodied Babylonian animal. So the multitude scoffed at him, mocking with the coarse mockery of the camp an enemy who was so repulsive of feature and so uncouth in his ways.[78]

Dead men tell no tales, and the defeated have no voice. What it was that Batis did to merit such punishment, if he did indeed end his life in this way, we cannot say. One is tempted to speculate that he oppressed the citizens of Gaza and that once he fell into the hands of his opponents, he was the victim of the kind of unrestrained vengeance that often accompanies the fall of such a man.[79] But the sources say nothing of factional strife. Instead, we are told that the entire

---

foreign modes of behavior (ira deinde vertit in rabiem, iam tum peregrinos ritus nova subeunte fortuna). In short, Curtius' portrayal is of a man who has abandoned normal modes of behavior in favor of barbaric ones.

77. Tarn II 268: "Hegesias' account is one of the most abominable things in Greek literature."

78. Hegesias, *FGrH* 142 F5. Translation by W. R. Roberts, in Robinson 1953, 1.254-55. Dionysius of Halicarnassus, who quotes this passage in a reproach of Hegesias' style and integrity, says that Batis was "a man held in honor on account of his fortune and his good looks" (ἄνδρα ἐν ἀξιώματι καὶ τύχης καὶ εἴδους).

79. Cf. Heckel 1997, 201.

population was enslaved. The argument from silence is never compelling, since the Alexander historians were not always interested in telling the whole story, especially from the standpoint of the losers. The truth cannot be known, and we must be careful not to replace an obvious fiction with a more plausible one. On the other hand, the story of Batis' death, intended to highlight the heroic nature of the king, does just the opposite and depicts a leader who was most cruel to his enemies whenever he suffered a serious wound.[80]

V

Gaza was the final impediment on Alexander's path to Egypt, a region that played no small part in his overall scheme of conquest. As noted above, the Egyptians had no love for Persia. Darius' satrap, Sauaces, who had brought a contingent to Issus, was among the prominent leaders who died on the battlefield. But soon after his flight, Darius appointed Mazaces as his replacement—he was in all likelihood Sauaces' second-in-command and entrusted with the administration in the satrap's absence—but his Persian forces were no doubt seriously depleted. His position was further weakened by the arrival of Amyntas son of Antiochus with a force of Greek mercenaries. These, originally 8,000 in number, had escaped from Issus and seized ships at Tripolis, whence they sailed to Cyprus. There it appears that the mercenary leaders—Amyntas, Thymondas, Aristomedes, and Bianor—divided their forces and parted ways. Amyntas, with 4,000, appeared in the Delta early in 331 with hopes of occupying the satrapy, which he knew to be in disarray.[81] He enjoyed success initially, capturing Pelusium and inciting the Egyptians to rise up against the Persian garrisons in the satrapy. That Amyntas hoped to hold Egypt with a force of 4,000 Greek mercenaries is difficult to believe; it would rival the audacity of the later conquistadors at Tenochtitlán and Cajamarca. But it is equally unlikely that this force was part of an orchestrated

---

80. On this aspect of Alexander's nature, see Heckel and McLeod 2015, 247–52. Curtius says that Alexander was injured twice during the siege and narrowly avoided a third blow to the neck: attempt to wound by an Arab soldier (4.6.15-16); arrow to the shoulder (4.6.17-20), struck on the leg by rock (4.623). He also speaks of Alexander "goaded also by his anger at having received two wounds in besieging this particular city" (*ira quoque accensus, quod duo in obsidione urbis eius vulnera acceperat*; 4.6.24). It has become fashionable to place the burden for such vengeance on the shoulders of the men. "Alexander had been wounded twice, and his army always took especially fierce vengeance on cities that gave him a wound" (Lane Fox 1973, 193). For the harsh treatment of the defeated after a wound, see the remarks of Justin 7.6.15 concerning Philip II's loss of an eye at Methone: "but the injury did not make him any less effective in combat or more savage in his treatment of his enemies."

81. Curt. 4.1.27-33; Diod. 17.48.1-5; Arr. 2.13.2-3. Curtius does not mention the other leaders or the larger force of 8,000.

counteroffensive against Alexander, one that extended from Egypt to Crete and ultimately the Peloponnese. If this were so, Amyntas' failure to cooperate with Mazaces is inexplicable. It is hard to avoid the conclusion that these were the actions of desperate men, intent upon plunder, for they did nothing to win the hearts of the Egyptians. Furthermore, unless they believed that Alexander would move to the east to pursue Darius—not entirely inconceivable at the time—they must have given little thought to the consequences of their actions.

Their arrival at Pelusium attracted supporters among the locals, who mistakenly regarded them as useful allies against the Persian garrison, firmly entrenched in Memphis under Mazaces. But if it was Egyptian support Amyntas was seeking, there was no point in making the false claim that "he had been sent as general [or governor] by Darius."[82] Diodorus says much the same thing, and it appears that the report of this fake appointment was addressed not to the Egyptians but to the Persian forces in the satrapy. Once Amyntas had seized Pelusium, he began his march on Memphis, generating enthusiasm among the native population, who saw this as the end of Persian domination. But the unruliness of the invaders proved to be their undoing; they turned to plundering the countryside, alienating the native population, and giving Mazaces an opportunity to destroy them. In the end, they accomplished little beyond the further destabilization of a divided satrapy.[83]

Diodorus claims that Amyntas' move to Egypt was in line with the actions of other leaders of Persian forces who escaped from Issus:

> Like him, a number of the other commanders and generals who escaped from the battle of Issus still clung to hope for the Persians. Some seized important cities and held on to them for Darius, and others brought peoples over to their side, provided themselves with troops, and carried out duties appropriate to the prevailing conditions. (Diod. 17.48.5-6)

---

82. Curt. 4.1.29 (*simulans a Dareo se esse praetorem missum*). *Praetor* is a leader of some kind, either military or administrative. J. C. Rolfe in the Loeb translates the word as "governor" (cf. Curt. 4.1.35: *Antigonus, praetor Alexandri, Lydiae praeerat*). I have opted for "general" on the basis of Diod. 17.48.3: ἀπέφαινε ἑαυτὸν ὑπὸ Δαρείου τοῦ βασιλέως ἀπεστάλθαι στρατηγὸν διὰ τὸ τὸν ἡγούμενον τῆς Αἰγύπτου σατράπην συναγωνιζόμενον ἐν Ἰσσῷ τῆς Κιλικίας πεπτωκέναι.

83. Curt. 4.1.33 says that Mazaces killed all the Greeks, including their leader (*ad unum omnes cum ipso duce occisi sunt*). Briant, *HPE* 845, suggests, plausibly, that the defeat of Amyntas strengthened Mazaces' position, "and he probably enrolled Amyntas' mercenaries in his service. The need to pay mercenaries is perhaps confirmed by the coins bearing his name that he issued in Egypt." Arr. 2.13.3 says that Amyntas was killed by the Egyptians (Ἀμύντας ἀποθνήσκει ὑπὸ τῶν ἐγχωρίων) but says nothing about the fate of his mercenaries. According to Diod. 17.48.4, the natives killed Amyntas and all those who came with him (τόν τε Ἀμύνταν ἀπέκτειναν καὶ τοὺς μετ᾽ αὐτοῦ πάντας ἄρδην ἀνεῖλον).

Clearly, the defeat at Issus did not crush the Persians' will to resist the invader.[84] The actions of the leaders were not, in fact, parallel; the difference between the forces of Amyntas and those who escaped to Asia Minor—particularly Cappadocia—is that the Persians themselves redoubled their efforts,[85] whereas the mercenaries, true to their nature, hoped to salvage some personal advantage from the plight of their former employers. And for Alexander, the unruly mercenaries only made his appearance in Egypt more palatable to the Egyptians, who received him without opposition.[86]

Six days after leaving Gaza, the Conqueror reached the mouth of the Nile, where his fleet awaited him, as well as a throng of Egyptians who welcomed him as a lib-erator.[87] The uprising that had accompanied Amyntas' arrival was a lesson to the Persian occupation force, and it appears that they did little more than hunker down in their garrisons awaiting instructions from their political masters. When Alexander arrived, having sailed up the Nile with a picked force, Mazaces surrendered the city and its treasure, amounting to some 800 talents of gold.[88]

What Curtius means when he writes that "they did not dare await Alexander's arrival" is surely that Mazaces anticipated the king's arrival and came out to make formal surrender.[89] For the garrison in Memphis, flight would have been far more dangerous than surrender to the Macedonians. There must have been a garrison in Pelusium, a town critical to the defense of Egypt. Still we hear nothing of reprisals by the Egyptian population against the occupation forces. It is not un-likely that "liberation" was accompanied, as it has been in modern times, by the settling of scores. In this respect, the accounts of the entry of the Macedonian army into Egypt are highly sanitized.[90] We know nothing about Alexander's

---

84. Noted by Briant, *HPE* 844–45.

85. Curt. 4.1.34.

86. Diod. 17.49.1: παρέλαβε πάσας τὰς ἐν αὐτῇ πόλεις χωρὶς κινδύνων. But see Ruzicka 2012, 205, who notes that the lack of an uprising in Egypt probably reflected "the absence of any dynastic leadership in the Delta." Briant, *HPE* 861: "when Alexander took Egypt, it was not because there was a general Egyptian uprising that supported him; more simply, it was because the Persian officials in charge of the satrapy had no military means of opposing him."

87. Curt. 4.7.2 says the place continued to be called Alexander's Camp (*Castra Alexandri*); cf. the similar designation of *Castra Cyri* at the entrance to Cilicia (Curt. 3.4.1). Six-day march from Gaza: Arr. 2.1.1; Curt. 4.7.2.

88. Curt. 4.7.3-4.

89. Thus Arr. 2.1.2.

90. Compare the account of the Egyptians' response to the arrival of Amyntas: "news of this [Amyntas' arrival in Memphis] brought all the Egyptians running from their various villages and cities to wipe out the Persian garrisons—for the Egyptians are a volatile people more

treatment of the Persians who surrendered, but a reference to Amminapes (a Persian who had been with Mazaces when he submitted to Alexander) suggests that Mazaces, too, may have remained in the king's entourage.[91] The fate of the common soldier is not recorded. Excessive generosity to the defeated might have caused the Egyptians to question his dedication to their cause, but other options were unappealing.[92]

In other respects, the lengthy sojourn in Egypt was a time of respite for the Macedonian troops, an opportunity to take stock of the campaign as a whole as well as the consolidation of the Conqueror's position (and image) in the land of the Nile. Egyptian gods were treated with marked respect—particularly Apis, the god most closely associated with Persian sacrilege in the times of Cambyses and Artaxerxes III.[93] That the stories of their conduct were invented or, at least, grossly distorted mattered little. The "truth" which shaped the thinking of the Egyptians had less to do with reality than with perception. Alexander was also recognized as a legitimate successor of the pharaohs, whether he was officially crowned in Memphis or not,[94] and his mission to the oracle of Amun at Siwah—whatever traditions and alleged motives came to be attached to the affair[95]—involved a

---

inclined to foment unrest than to get things done themselves" (Curt. 4.1.30). The characterization of the Egyptians probably reflects Roman prejudice and was influenced by the actions of the citizens of Alexandria, a city that had yet to be founded (cf. Atkinson I 285).

91. Arr. 3.22.1.

92. Certainly, there is no evidence that they were enslaved, incarcerated, or even executed, although any of these measures might have been taken.

93. Cambyses' mistreatment and killing of the Apis calf (Hdt. 3.27-29) is almost certainly a fiction (Asheri, Lloyd, and Corcella 2007, 427–28), although there are those who accept the story. For Artaxerxes III see Aelian, *VH* 6.8; cf. Diod. 16.51.3; cf. Lloyd 2011, 86. Even the successful trip to Siwah is contrasted with the alleged failure of Cambyses' expedition (Plut. *Alex.* 26.12; cf. Hdt. 3.25.3).

94. Burstein 1991 and 1994, 382. Kaerst, *Hellenismus* I[3] 381 notes what should be the obvious conclusion: "Indem er den Landesgottheiten in der alten Landeshauptstadt opferte, erschien er als der Nachfolger der Pharaonen und wurde von der Bevölkerung als solcher begrüßt." Cf. Schachermeyr 1973, 236. Also Lloyd 2011, 88: "It is, however, beyond dispute that he was treated by the Egyptian elite as a Pharaoh in the fullest sense."

95. I omit all discussion of Alexander's reception by the priest of Amun and the matter of Alexander's "divinity," which is relevant to the question of resistance only in that it, along with the apparent rejection of Philip II as the king's father (Hamilton 1953), was offensive to many Macedonians and formed one of the complaints against him. For Alexander's "divinity," the reader is directed to Badian 2012, 244–81 (= Badian 1981, the author's "do-over" of the paper in *Colloquies of the Center for Hermeneutical Studies* at Berkeley, 1976) and 365–85 (= Badian 1996).

confirmation of his position.[96] And of course, there was what was to become a feature of the campaign: the foundation of a city bearing the Conqueror's name. In this case, the settlement itself was to rival the king's own fame.[97] There were furthermore athletic and artistic competitions of the sort that accompanied successful ventures or, in the case of the ones at Dium in Macedonia, launched them.[98]

In the preceding year, the counteroffensive in the Aegean had gained initial success, but it faltered after the death of Memnon and the reconstitution of a Macedonian fleet. The report of the success of that fleet, by one of its authors when Hegelochus son of Hippostratus arrived in Egypt, is the story of further Persian failures.[99] Pharnabazus and Autophradates had assumed control of the war in the Aegean. During the autumn of 333, they had won over and garrisoned Chios.[100] As long as the fortress of Halicarnassus held out against Ptolemy, the harbor remained a base for the Persian fleet. Later in the year, the Spartan king,

---

96. This notion is rejected by Kaerst, *Hellenismus* 384–85, who sees "confirmation" by the oracle there as a necessary component of the Egyptian practice. The divinity of the pharaohs was one thing; confirmation of his status at Siwah, where the god Amun was equated by the Greeks with Zeus, greatly enhanced his position in the Greco-Macedonian world, though this had unwanted repercussions (see note above). I would now, somewhat reluctantly, recant my view that Cambyses' expeditionary force to "Oasis" (Hdt. 3.26.1; Asheri, Lloyd, and Corcella 2007, 425–26) was primarily an attempt to legitimize his rule in Egypt. Briant, *HPE* 54 (cf. Waters 2014, 55; Kuhrt 1995, II, 662) sees its purpose as "seizing strategic positions in the western oases." In the Alexander historians, there is not talk of military action in the west, though this may simply have been eclipsed by the story of Alexander's *Ammonsohnschaft*. But Edmunds 1971, 378, disagrees entirely: "The detour to Siwah was non-strategic and had nothing to do with Alexander's pharaohship. It was a personal matter."

97. Curt. 4.8.1-2; Diod. 17.52.1; Justin 11.11.13 (cf. Oros. 3.16.14); Arr. 3.1.5–2.2; Val. Max. 1.4 ext. 1; Ps.-Call. 1.32; Strabo 17.16 C792. For the foundation date: Jouguet 1940; Welles 1962; Borza 1967, 369; Brown 1978; Bagnall 1979. On Alexander's foundations, see Tarn II 232–59 and Fraser 1996. For Alexandria in Egypt, see the magisterial work of Fraser 1972.

98. For the practice, see Arr. 7.14.1: ὥσπερ αὐτῷ ἐπὶ ξυμφοραῖς ἀγαθαῖς νόμος. Adams 2007, 138: "He [Alexander] used them for practical purposes, to rest and entertain the army and even keep them in training. The games always served as religious functions for victory celebrations, thanksgiving celebrations, and funeral sacrifices. Alexander used them directly for propaganda purposes at Tyre and Memphis." Games in Memphis: Arr. 3.1.4 (they were held in the context of sacrifices to Apis).

99. Summarized by Arr. 3.2.3-7 (cf. Arr. 2.1.3–2.3); Curt. 4.5.13-22.

100. Arr. 3.2.3. Curtius' remark (4.1.37) that Pharnabazus exacted money from the Milesians for the campaign against Chios suggests that the city was recaptured after Alexander's disbanding of the fleet and his march into Lycia (cf. Atkinson I 289), and this is supported by Curt. 4.5.13, who remarks that Balacrus "recaptured" Miletus from a certain Idarnes (apparently Hydarnes son of Mazaeus: Heckel 141; Berve II 376 no. 759). Tenedos had also surrendered to Pharnabazus, since the fleet the Macedonians were building (Curt. 3.1.19-20) had not yet been brought up to strength (Arr. 2.2.2-3)

Agis III, met Pharnabazus and his colleague at Siphnos,[101] where they learned, to their obvious dismay, the unexpected news of Darius' defeat at Issus. Agis was given thirty talents of silver and ten triremes.[102] These the Spartan king ordered a certain Hippias to convey to his brother Agesilaus at Taenarum at the tip of the Peloponnese, giving him instructions to proceed to Crete and win over its cities to the Persian cause but in effect to secure Cretan mercenaries to be paid at Persian expense.[103]

In spite of these measures, the Persian counteroffensive in the Aegean began to collapse. A Macedonian fleet defeated Aristomenes off the Hellespontine coast,[104] and Hegelochus and Amphoterus recovered the islands, capturing at Chios both Aristonicus of Methymna and Pharnabazus. Also among the prisoners were Apollonides, Phesinus, and Megareus, who had fomented revolt on Chios and ruled by force. These men, with the exception of Pharnabazus, who evaded his captors and escaped at Cos,[105] were brought to Alexander in the Delta by Hegelochus, who also informed him of his capture of Mitylene. Amphoterus' success at Cos was probably reported by the victor himself, whom Alexander sent to the Peloponnese to quell the trouble that was brewing there and on Crete.[106] Of the prisoners, the tyrants were returned to their cities to be dealt with by their compatriots, and the Chians were sent under guard to a stronghold in Elephantine, deep in Upper Egypt.

Most of what we know about the counteroffensive in the period after Issus comes from a summary of events in Curtius, who tells us that several of Darius' generals who survived the battle at Issus had fled to Cappadocia, where they enlisted the natives of the region as well as Paphlagonians. With these, they made

---

101. Proteas' earlier victory over Datames off the island of Siphnos appears to have had minimal impact on Persian domination in the Aegean: Arr. 2.2.4-5; Heckel 105 s.v. "Datames"; 233 s.v. "Proteas."

102. Siphnos was noted for its silver mines (Atkinson I 290).

103. Arr. 2.13.5-6; Diod. 17.48.1-2 says that Agis took with him 8,000 mercenaries who had escaped from Issus (cf. Curt. 4.1.39) and won over the cities of Crete. If he did enroll 8,000 mercenaries, only half of these can have belonged to those who escaped to Tripolis and thence to Cyprus with Amyntas, Thymondas, Aristomedes, and Bianor. Cretan mercenaries: Badian 1967, 177: "The Persians would be glad to pay: 'Persian archers' for Cretan."

104. Aristomenes: the name is Greek and occurs frequently in the Aegean island region (*LGPN* I 73). He was probably a *nauarchos* in the service of Persia, but he is otherwise unknown; the battle is attested only in Curt. 4.1.36. The assumption that he was confused with Autophradates is both unlikely and unnecessary. See Atkinson I, 289. See also Heckel 48 s.v. "Aristomenes [1]"; Berve II, 67 no. 126; Seibt 1999, 107 and Hofstetter 28 no. 45.

105. Arr. 3.2.7.

106. Arr. 3.6.3; but cf. Curt. 4.8.15. Full discussion in Bosworth 1975.

an attempt to recapture Lydia, which was guarded by Antigonus the One-Eyed.
The Persians were defeated in three separate battles. Meanwhile, in the Aegean,
Aristomenes, whom Darius had sent to recapture the Hellespont, was defeated
by a newly formed Macedonian fleet. Pharnabazus, for his part, retook Miletus
and garrisoned Chios, Andros, and Siphnos. And on the Greek mainland, Agis
III began his war against Antipater, employing many of the mercenaries who
had escaped from Issus (excluding, of course, those who had gone to Egypt
with Amyntas), while encouraging anti-Macedonian activities on the island of
Crete.[107]

Cappadocia was divided into two parts, a southern region (Cappadocia-
Taurus) and the northern Pontic satrapy. Even the former had not been adequately subdued, as can be seen by the failure of Alexander's appointee Sabictas
to secure his post.[108] Together with its northern neighbor, it formed a staging
ground for a counteroffensive in Asia Minor. The leading role assigned to
Antigonus can be explained by the facts that he controlled the satrapy located
west of Cappadocia and south of Paphlagonia and that the Persian aim was to
bring their forces to the Aegean coast. Who the Persian generals were we are not
told, but Curtius says they were men who had fought at Issus. The assumption
that their leader was Nabarzanes has no support in the sources.[109] Most likely
they were the commanders of native levies from Cappadocia and Paphlagonia.
Alexander's general Ptolemy and the satraps Antigonus and Asander, along with
Calas and Balacrus, defeated the remaining Persian leaders in Asia Minor,[110] and

---

107. Curt. 4.1.34-40.

108. Cappadocia-Taurus and Cappadocia-Pontus: Strabo 12.1.4 C534. The division of the satrapy seems to have followed the Satraps' Revolt and was intended to limit satrapal power
(Michels 2017, 43). It was the southern satrapy that was entrusted to Sabictas. He may have been
killed attempting to annex the northern satrapy (presumably on Alexander's instructions) or
by the Persians who fled after the defeat at Issus (Curt. 4.1.34). See also Baumbach 1911, 59–60;
Julien 1914, 19; Briant, *HPE* 742–43. Berve II 348 no. 690 believes, implausibly, that Sabictas
was replaced by Abistamenes. The latter name is clearly corrupt (see Heckel 338 n. 661).

109. Briant 1973, 55, with n. 10. We are told very little about the Persian leaders who fought
at Issus. Curt. 3.9.1 mentions only Nabarzanes, and Diod. 17.34.2-3 notes the prowess of
Oxyathres, the brother of Darius, but he was clearly a member of the Great King's personal
guard (cf. Curt. 3.9.4, 11.8). Otherwise we know only the names of those who fell on the battlefield: Arsames, Rheomithres, Atizyes, Sauaces, and Bubaces (Arr. 2.11.8; cf. Diod. 17.34.5; Curt.
3.11.10). Nabarzanes is not attested at Gaugamela, but this may simply be an oversight (but see
Badian 2000a, 82).

110. Curt. 4.1.34-40. Tarn II 110 observes rightly that the failure of Arrian to mention any
of this can be ascribed to Ptolemy's unwillingness to shine light on his later rival Antigonus
the One-Eyed (cf. Burn 1952, 81–82). For the successes of Ptolemy and Asander (satrap
of Lydia), see Arr. 2.5.7 (with Bosworth I 195–97). These occurred in autumn 333, when
Alexander was in Cilicia (before the battle of Issus). Orontopates is described as having held

with the collapse of the Persian fleet, Rhodes submitted, accepting a Macedonian garrison.[111]

Curtius' description of Antigonus as commander of Lydia may be an error; he was satrap of Greater Phrygia, with his capital at Celaenae. But it may be that Lydia is used in the old sense of designating the lands ruled by the Lydians before their conquest by Cyrus the Great.[112] It has even been argued that the aim of the Persian generals was to push through to the Aegean coast and link up with the fleet in an effort to turn the war back on Europe.[113] But from a later passage of Curtius, it is clear that the Macedonians anticipated the Persian actions and that the "three battles in various places" were fought at or near their (temporary) bases: "Calas marched into Paphlagonia and Antigonus into Lycaonia; Balacrus defeated Darius' general Idarnes and recaptured Miletus" (4.5.13).

The news of these successes encouraged the Conqueror to push on into the heart of Asia.[114] It is doubtful that the Egyptians regarded themselves as liberated, as many modern scholars allege. Any hope of independence they had was quickly dispelled. Alexander's organization of the satrapy deviated very little from the Persian model.[115] As nomarchs, the king appointed Doloaspis and Petisis, preserving the ancient division of the country into Upper and Lower Egypt. Pantaleon of Pydna was installed as *phrourarchos* of Memphis, and the same office was held by Megacles of Pella in Pelusium. Greek mercenaries served as garrison troops, and an army of occupation remained, along with a fleet, all with Greek and Macedonian overseers and commanders. The areas adjacent

---

Halicarnassus, Myndus, Caunus, Thera, Callipolis, Cos, and Triopium (see *Barr. Atlas* 65 E-G3-4; cf. Briant, *HPE* 825). I see no evidence to support Ruzicka's assumption (1988, 135–36) that these cities had "submitted to Alexander as he moved eastward through Caria late in 334." Orontopates had been defeated with the loss of 700 infantry and 50 cavalry, as well as 1,000 who were taken prisoner. But the defeat resulted in the loss of many of Orontopates' territories (Curt. 3.7.4). Nevertheless, Halicarnassus and Cos remained in Persian hands well into 332.

111. Summarized by Justin 11.11.1 (cf. Oros. 3.16.12); Curt. 4.5.9, 8.12; Arr. 2.20.2. For Rhodes, see Berthold 1984, 34; Hauben 1977, 307–309.

112. Thus Briant 1973, 63–66; but see Billows 1990, 44.

113. Burn 1952, 82–84.

114. Alexander rewarded the Mitylenaeans and the Cypriotes for their support as he was returning from Egypt; but the Chians and Rhodians complained about their garrisons (Curt. 4.8.12-14). The garrisoning of Chios had been intended as a short-term measure. For Rhodes, see Hauben 1977, 309–10, who argues that Alexander did not remove the garrison but took measures to curb the indiscipline of the troops.

115. See Burstein 1994. Bosworth 1988a, 234, rightly observes that Alexander had every reason "to pay lip service . . . to the nationalistic aspirations of the Egyptians" (cf. Bosworth I 275: "the appointments seem primarily a public-relations exercise").

to Libya and Arabia were placed under Apollonius and Cleomenes,[116] and all parts of the country were subject to tribute payments. In truth, the only true native Egyptian in the administration was Petisis, who declined the office and was replaced by Doloaspis.[117] It was not long before the power in Egypt was effectively consolidated in the hands of Cleomenes of Naucratis.[118]

In Syria, local resistance delayed Alexander's march to the Euphrates. Parmenion had subjugated the area to the east of Mount Lebanon and secured the obedience of Sanballat II, who was allowed to retain his position in Samaria.[119] Northern Syria had been assigned to Menon son of Cerdimmas, and there is no indication of unrest there. But the stability that Sanballat's submission promised was overturned by political strife in Samaria that accompanied his death in late 332. Local insurgents then captured and burned alive the Macedonian general Andromachus. Alexander quickly crushed the rebellion and executed the perpetrators.[120] Arrian mentions a certain Arimmas, who was deposed for failing to make adequate provisions for the army as it marched inland. His removal appears to have nothing to do with events in Samaria, but the identity of Arimmas and his reasons for disobeying Alexander are unclear.[121] Judaea, despite the later

116. Administrative and military appointments: Arr. 3.5.2-5. Curt. 4.8.4-5 says that Aeschylus the Rhodian and Peucestas were placed in charge of 4,000 soldiers left in the satrapy, with the fleet assigned to Polemon. Cleomenes was placed in charge of the collection of tribute. On Alexander's conquest and administrative settlement of Egypt, Mahaffy's discussion (1899, IV 1–24) is still instructive.

117. Arr. 3.5.2 calls both Doloaspis and Petisis Egyptians (δύο μὲν νομάρχας Αἰγύπτου κατέστησε Αἰγυπτίους, Δολόασπιν καὶ Πέτισιν), but Doloaspis is a Persian name, and he could, at best, have been a naturalized Egyptian (Burstein 1994, 385). The reason for Petisis' resignation is not stated; perhaps there were personal reasons (health or age), but he may have feared being branded a collaborator.

118. The career of Cleomenes of Naucratis has been much discussed. For his life, see Heckel 88–89 s.v. "Cleomenes [1]"; Berve II 210–11 no. 431. For his activities in Egypt, see Seibert 1969, 39–51, and 1972b; Groningen 1925; Vogt 1971; Bosworth I 277; Höbl 2001, 12–14; Baynham 2015; Worthington 2016, 90–91.

119. Josephus, AJ 11.321-322.

120. Curt. 4.8.9-10, who says Andromachus was replaced by Menon (Memnon in the manuscripts), presumably the son of Cerdimmas (cf. Arr. 2.13.7). Andromachus' family and previous career are unknown. He was almost certainly Macedonian. Whether he was satrap of southern Syria, as Bosworth 1974, 50–51 suggests, is unclear. Since Sanballat submitted to Alexander at Tyre, at a point early in the siege, it is possible that Andromachus the nauarchos (Arr. 2.20.10) was sent to Samaria with a military force to act as strategos (Curt. 4.8.9: quem praefecerat Syriae). The territory may have been added to the administrative responsibilities of Menon son of Cerdimmas, who was later replaced by Asclepiodorus (see following note). See Heckel 166 s.v. "Menon [1]"; Berve II 259 no. 514. Full discussion of the administration of Syria: Bosworth 1974.

121. Arr. 3.6.8. Arimmas' inclusion in Justi (25) implies that he was a barbarian; Hoffmann 193 regards him as Macedonian (the name being a short form of Ἀρίμαχος); thus also Berve II 60

tradition, was bypassed by the Conqueror entirely.[122] New administrators were put in place, to whom Alexander, now called north by the news that Darius had marshaled a new army, left the task of securing peace and exacting revenues for the new master.[123]

VI

One final matter of concern for the Conqueror was the situation in the Peloponnese, where the Spartan king Agis III had made a bid to shake off the control exercised by Antipater and his supporters in Alexander's absence.[124] Preparations for this uprising had begun as early as 333/2 (after Issus), when Agis took money from the Persians and campaigned in Crete with his brother Agesilaus. In addition to the forces recruited there, Agis enlisted mercenaries who had escaped from Issus and sailed west from Cyprus. These were, however, only a portion of the group of 8,000; half of that force, as we have seen, went south to Egypt with Amyntas son of Antiochus.[125]

---

no. 114. I am inclined to follow Droysen in assuming a corruption of the patronymic of Menon son of Cerdimmas (Heckel 44, 166). But the sequence of events is hard to follow, since Arrian and Curtius (4.8.9-11) are not in agreement (discussion in Atkinson I 370–71). Nevertheless, since Arimmas was replaced by Asclepiodorus and the son of [Ce]r[d]immas disappears from our records, it likely that (i) southern Syria was added to Menon's administrative sphere after Andromachus' death but that (ii) the king soon found Menon negligent in the duties that pertained to northern Syria and therefore (iii) replaced him with Asclepiodorus. I do not subscribe to Bosworth's view (I 285; cf. Brunt I 241 n.) that Arimmas and the father of Menon were separate individuals.

122. Alexander's visit to Jerusalem and his meeting with the high priest is, of course, later fiction. Hence Bickerman 1988, 6: "the stories of Alexander in rabbinic tradition are drawn from the Greek Alexander Romance and testify only to the popularity of this fabulous work in Roman times." See Momigliano 1979; Delling 1981; Cohen 1982–83; and especially Klęczar 2012.

123. Bickerman 1988, 6: "Alexander's arrival did not change anything in Jerusalem except the name of the pagan sovereign. The rulers of the people, the tribute, the status of the Temple, all remained as they had been under the Persian king." Cf. Schäfer 2003, 6: Alexander's settlement of the region "suggest[s] a high degree of tolerance and indicates that Alexander had recourse to competent local officials and did not substantially alter the administrative structure of this very diverse country with its numerous more or less independent cities and provinces." Högemann 1985, 57–60, sees the administrative settlements in Syria as primarily military, allowing the movement of troops and treasure between the coast and Babylon and Susa.

124. Agis' war: Curt. 6.1.1-21; Diod. 17.48.1-2, 62.6–63.4; Justin 12.1.4-11 (cf. Oros. 3.18.1-2); Arr. 3.16.10; Aes. 3.165; Din. 1.34; Plut. *Ages.* 15, *Agis* 3; cf. Plut. *Mor.* 219b; Paus. 1.13.4. Cartledge in Cartledge and Spawforth 2002, 16–27. Badian 1967 = Badian 2012, 153–73.

125. Arr. 2.13.2 says the mercenaries who fled from Issus numbered 8,000, implying (2.13.3) that they all went to Egypt (ἐπὶ Κύπρου ἔφευγον καὶ ἐκεῖθεν εἰς Αἴγυπτον); there is no mention of a division of forces. Diod. 17.48.3, having mentioned 4,000 mercenaries with Amyntas, says

Hence, the combination of Persian money to recruit mercenaries on Crete and the flight of Darius' mercenaries from Issus placed Agis in a much stronger position, even if Athens refused to join his coalition. A disturbance in Thrace came at the most opportune time:

> An invitation for the Greeks to revolt was also offered by the uprising that was occurring in Thrace at this time; for Memnon, who had been appointed general [*strategos*] of Thrace,[126] who had an army, and who was a willful man, roused the barbarians and defected from Alexander. He swiftly acquired a large force and clearly revealed he was intent on war. Antipater, therefore, at the head of his entire army, marched through Macedonia into Thrace and fought it out with him. . . .When Antipater

---

he sailed to Cyprus and took on additional soldiers there (διαπλεύσας δ' εἰς τὴν Κύπρον καὶ προσλαβόμενος στρατιώτας καὶ ναῦς διέπλευσεν εἰς τὸ Πελούσιον). But at 17.48.1, he says that Agis enlisted 8,000 mercenaries who escaped from Issus (presumably the ones mentioned by Arr. 2.13.2). Anaximenes of Lampsacus (*FGrH* 72 F17) mentions the flight of Aristomedes of Pherae to Cyprus but says nothing of his continuing to Egypt, which appears to support the idea that he and perhaps also Bianor and Thymondas broke ranks with Amyntas. Perhaps other mercenaries joined them subsequently, but Diodorus treats the 8,000 and Amyntas' 4,000 as separate groups.

126. Berve II 254 no. 499 identifies Memnon as "vornehmer Makedone" and as the successor of Alexander Lyncestes. He is known only from this passage in Diodorus and a later reference in Curtius (9.3.21), where Memnon arrived at the Hydaspes with 5,000 Thracian cavalry and 7,000 infantry supplied by Harpalus. The name is otherwise unattested in Macedonia. Curt. 4.8.11 mistakenly calls Andromachus' replacement in Syria, Menon son of Cerdimmas, "Memnon," and it may be that the confusion of the names is common to the vulgate. Menon is certainly a genuine Macedonian name (Tataki 1998, 371–72 nos. 63–65, although she treats Memnon, *strategos* of Thrace, as Macedonian as well; 365 no. 29). Even if the man (whether his name was Memnon or Menon) was Macedonian, we are still forced to explain how a man who rebelled against Antipater in 331 could be trusted four years later to bring 5,000 cavalrymen of high quality to Alexander in India and to do so with impunity. Badian 1967, 179–80, identifies him as a member of the family of Artabazus and notes: "As it happens, another mysterious Memnon appears in our records just a little earlier [i.e., before 326]. He is a man honoured by the Athenians in the fourth prytany of 327/6: a man belonging to the family of the great Memnon of Rhodes, though we do not know precisely how he was attached to it and what was the occasion of the honour." Given the earlier connections of Artabazus' family (including his in-laws Mentor and Memnon) with Philip II, Badian considers it not impossible that a member of the family should have stayed in Macedonia and "continued to serve the King of Macedon—being left (prudently, in the circumstances) *in a fairly harmless post in Europe*, under Antipater's supervision, when Alexander crossed to Asia" (1967, 180; emphasis added). How one can describe the *strategia* of Thrace as "a fairly harmless post" at a time when the famous Memnon was conducting a counter-war in the northern Aegean is baffling. Perhaps his relationship to Barsine (now Alexander's mistress) sheltered him in 331, but by 326, Barsine and Artabazus were no longer in Alexander's entourage, possibly in disfavor (see Heckel 2018b) That was a bad time for a delinquent relative to arrive in the camp of the king, who may have been disgruntled for other reasons as well.

found out about the disturbance in Greece, he terminated his Thracian campaign as best he could and came into the Peloponnese with his entire force. (Diod. 17.62.4-5, 63.1)

In this context (331/0), Justin, who fails to mention Memnon, says that Zopyrion, whom Alexander had left as *strategos* of the Pontic region (12.2.16: *praefectus Ponti ab Alexandro Magno relictus*), was killed in a military disaster. Since the Pontic and Thracian regions formed part of the same administrative unit,[127] Zopyrion appears to have been trying to put down an uprising of Thracians. The words *ab Alexandro Magno relictus* ("left behind by Alexander the Great") suggest that Zopyrion was the predecessor of Memnon and not his successor, as is generally assumed.[128] Diodorus (or possibly his source) may have confused the events in Thrace. The disaster that saw the death of Zopyrion drew Antipater away from Macedon at a crucial time.[129] He settled affairs in the region by appointing Memnon as Zopyrion's successor and then moved south to deal with Agis.

News of the uprising in Greece reached Alexander on his second visit to Tyre in spring of 331.[130] Agis was the son of Archidamus III and grandson of the famous Agesilaus.[131] He had become king when Sparta received word that Archidamus had died fighting in Lucania. Ancient writers, who were fond of synchronisms,

---

127. Justin 13.4.16; cf. Arr. *Succ.* 1.7.

128. Thus Noethlichs 1987, 411. See Berve II 164: "Nachfolger Memnons"; cf. Velkov 1987, 260.

129. Justin 12.3.1 says that the news reached Alexander in Parthyaea in 330. In that case, Curtius' report on Zopyrion, whose unsuccessful expedition he dates to "while Alexander was engaged in the conquest of India," must be reported either out of context or as a prelude to the rebellion of Seuthes and the Odrysians (10.1.43-45). Cf. also Rüegg 1906, 76.

130. Arr. 3.6.3. The chronology is, however, confused. Curt. 6.1.21: "So ended the war. It had started suddenly, but it was concluded before Darius' defeat by Alexander at Arbela." What is important is the point at which news of the end of the revolt reached Alexander himself, for it had played no small part in determining his actions in Asia. From Susa in 331, he sent Menes to the coast with 3,000 talents intended for Antipater's use in the war (Arr. 3.16.10). Nevertheless, he must have known of the Macedonian victory before he dismissed the allies at Ecbatana or Hecatompylus. But Arr. 3.24.4 (cf. Curt. 6.5.6-7) says that Alexander kept in custody the Spartan ambassadors who fell into his hands after Darius' death, but there is no mention of Agis in this context. The entire war in the Peloponnese appears to have begun in the spring of 331 and concluded about a year later. The synchronism of Megalopolis and Gaugamela is probably contrived, but Aes. 3.165 is rhetorical hyperbole. Modern discussions: Cawkwell 1969; Borza 1971; Wirth 1971a; Lock 1972; McQueen 1978; Brunt I 482-85; Badian 1994; see also Yardley and Heckel 183-86.

131. Stemma in Clauss 1983, 126. Agis' career: Heckel 7-8 s.v. "Agis [1]"; Berve II 8-9 no. 15; Hofstetter 5-6 no. 5; Poralla 13 no. 27.

said his death occurred in the very hour of the battle at Chaeronea.[132] He had not committed Spartan troops to the coalition against Philip in that battle, although he resisted membership in the League of Corinth, something that unwittingly served Philip's purpose.[133] Spartan "autonomy" came at the cost of territorial losses.[134] But in the absence of Alexander, Agis worked against Macedonian interests in southern Greece. As we have seen, he recruited mercenaries, some from Crete, others escapees from the Great King's defeat at Issus. In 331, he organized a coalition of allies and struck at Megalopolis, where he defeated the Macedonian general Corrhagus.[135] The Spartan siege of Megalopolis resulted in a battle near the city in which Antipater, with some 40,000 men engaged a somewhat smaller Peloponnesian force (perhaps 30,000).[136]

Curtius is the only source to describe the battle in any detail, and even his account is abbreviated as a result of a lacuna in the text.[137] The struggle is depicted as one between the champions of liberty (the Spartans) and those who fought for power: *illi pro libertate, hi pro dominatione* (Curt. 6.1.8).[138] In truth, few of the Greeks would have agreed with this verdict. Sparta was once again Persia's agent, and in the end most Greeks preferred the domination of Macedon to the prospect of "liberty" under Spartan leadership. Agis III was seriously wounded on the battlefield and carried back to the camp—on his shield in true Spartan fashion.[139] Meanwhile the battle raged on, and the

---

132. Diod. 16.88.3.

133. See Badian 1967, 172. An "independent" Sparta remained a source of concern for the other Peloponnesian states and probably kept them loyal to the charter of the League.

134. Cf. Polyb. 9.33.8-12.

135. The Spartan alliance excluded the Messenians, of course, but included the Eleans, the Arcadians except Megalopolis, and the Achaeans with the exception of Pellene. In Pellene, Alexander had overthrown the democracy and installed the wrestler Chaeron as tyrant ([Dem.] 17.10; Paus. 7.27.7; cf. Heckel 82–83 s.v. "Chaeron [2]"). See McQueen 1978. Agis had at least 10,000 mercenaries (Din. 1.34), and Diod. 17.62.7 says the Spartans and their allies fielded a force of 20,000 infantry and 2,000 cavalry. This must exclude the mercenary force. Antipater's numbers: Diod. 17.63.1. Corrhagus: Aes. 3.165; Heckel 94 s.v. "Corrhagus [1]"; Berve II 219–20 no. 444. Whether he was identical with or a relative of Antigonus the One-Eyed's father-in-law (Plut. *Demetr.* 2.1) is unknown.

136. Badian 1967, 182, 184; Cartledge in Cartledge and Spawforth 2002, 22–23. Full discussion in Badian 1994, 259–68.

137. The last part of Book 5 and the beginning of Book 6 are lost in all the surviving manuscripts of Curtius.

138. See the discussion in Noethlichs 1987, 1.393.

139. Curtius and/or his source must have been mindful of the Spartan maxim "Come back with your shield or on it," since the abandonment of the shield was a sign of cowardice and

"Spartans, reflecting on their prestige of old," were nevertheless unable to hold off the Macedonian attack.[140]

Leuctra (371) had broken the back of the Spartan military, although it made a valiant attempt nine years later at Mantineia. Emasculated by a Theban invasion of the Peloponnese, the Spartans lost control of the Messenians, the helot serfs who lived to the west, and were kept in check by the founding of the new city of Megalopolis. At this very place, their bid to shake off Macedonian power and regain their traditional place in the Greek world was thwarted by a defeat scarcely less humiliating than that of Leuctra. Twice the Spartans had avoided confrontation with Macedon—they had not fought at Chaeronea, nor had Philip attacked them when he moved into the Peloponnese—but now they learned the futility of resistance. There were 5,300 Lacedaemonians who fell along with their king, compared with roughly 1,000 Macedonians.[141] The engagement that the Conqueror, resentful of Antipater's achievement, belittled as a "battle of mice"[142] left Sparta at the mercy of Alexander and the League of Corinth. Hostages were given, and in all likelihood the city was enrolled in the very League it had haughtily disdained at the time of its formation.[143] When the Lamian War broke out some eight years later, there was no fight left in the Spartans, neither the will nor the means.[144]

desertion; see, however, Kennell 2010, 157, who notes that the dictum "cannot have been from a Spartan source, since dead warriors were not brought home (Plut. *Mor.* 241f)." But Agis' experience is clearly in contrast to the *tresantes* ("tremblers"), who here, just as after Leuctra, presented a challenge to the Spartan military ethos.

140. Curt. 6.1.11-15. The text is preceded by a lacuna, and we do not get the full story of the battle of Megalopolis.

141. Curt. 6.1.16; Diod. 17.63.3 (but he gives 3,500 as the number of dead in Antipater's army).

142. Plut. *Ages.* 15.6; for Alexander's reaction, cf. Curt. 6.1.18: "he felt that anything redounding to another's credit detracted from his own."

143. Thus Clauss 1983, 75: "Sparta mußte doch dem korinthischen Bund beitreten." Contra Cartledge in Cartledge and Spawforth 2002, 24–25; more cautiously Noethlichs 1987, 1.404.

144. Clauss 1983, 75. To this we may add the complete lack of leadership (cf. Cartledge in Cartledge and Spawforth 2002, 24).

9

Darius' Last Stand and the Collapse of Persian Resistance

THE LENGTHY SIEGES of Tyre and Gaza and the organization of Egypt had given Darius time to levy his largest army to date and to select a battlefield on which his numerical advantage (as well as the makeup of his forces) could be used to maximum effect. He could, moreover, have greater confidence in the loyalty of his troops, for he was now placing his faith in the men from the very core of the empire. Those who lived on the eastern fringes had no previous experience of the Greco-Macedonian enemy or any exposure to their political institutions or philosophical ideas. Alexander himself announced to his men that "they were going to fight, not as before, for Hollow Syria or Phoenicia or Egypt: it was the sovereignty of all Asia that was there and then to be decided" (Arr. 3.9.6). The composition of the new Persian army is spelled out by Arrian and based, according to Aristobulus of Cassandrea, on a document captured from the enemy after the battle.[1] But the actual numbers of troops deployed by either side is, as always, difficult to determine. The Greek sources estimate the size of Darius' army at anywhere from 250,000 to a little more than a million.[2] Against this force, Alexander could marshal fewer than 50,000 men.

---

1. Aristobulus, *FGrH* 139 F17 = Arr. 3.11.3-7.

2. According to Diod. 17.39.4, Darius had assembled 800,000 infantry and 200,000 cavalry (conveniently totaling 1 million), along with scythed chariots. Plutarch (*Alex.* 31.1) agrees. But Justin (11.12.5) reduces the numbers of both infantry and cavalry by half. Arrian (3.8.6) speaks of 1 million infantry, 40,000 cavalry, and 200 scythed chariots. Only Curt. 4.12.13 offers conservative figures, 200,000 foot and 45,000 horse, but this is contradicted by his statement at 4.9.3 that Darius' army was "half as large again as it had been in Cilicia" (Curt. 3.2.4-9 gives the number there as 250,000 infantry and 62,200 cavalry). For discussion of numbers, see Marsden 1964, 31-7.

In the Path of Conquest. Waldemar Heckel, Oxford University Press (2020). © Oxford University Press.

DOI: 10.1093/oso/9780190076689.001.0001

I

Darius hoped to resolve the issue on the battlefield only after failing to reach a diplomatic solution. The first overture was made more than a year and a half earlier, when the Persian ambassadors, Meniscus and Arsimas, approached Alexander at Marathus in Phoenicia, bearing a letter that offered to initiate peace negotiations and speaking on behalf of their sovereign. Darius' primary concern was for the return of his wife and family, but he did not let personal (family) matters overcome his duty to the state.[3] Speeches and letters are, of course, not authentic in the vast majority of cases. But they should not be dismissed as worthless, since they are often attempts by ancient authors to represent the issues as they were viewed, or thought to have been viewed, by the respective leaders.[4] The words of Darius' letter were clearly not those of a man who regarded himself on the brink of defeat. The Persian Empire was nothing if not resilient. Instead, Darius found fault with Philip II for not observing the peace made with Artaxerxes III after that king's death and the accession of Arses. Furthermore, he blamed Alexander for not sending envoys to renew the "ancient friendship and alliance" with Persia and dismissed the Macedonian victory at Issus as the will of the gods.[5] It was not so much an excuse for his own failure as a reminder to the young king of the fickleness of fortune. This, at least, is the version given by Arrian. Despite its overall similarities, Curtius' version depicts Darius less favorably: the letter is described as arrogant (*quibus ut superbe scriptis vehementer offensus est*) and denying Alexander the title of king (*regis titulum*).[6] Unlike Arrian, Curtius alleges that Darius offered a large sum of money but again presented this offer in an offensive manner: "Alexander should accept as much money as the whole of Macedonia could hold in return for Darius' mother, wife, and children, and then fight for

---

3. There are, even in the international politics of today, leaders and their advisers who believe that conflicts should be resolved militarily and view diplomacy as a sign of weakness.

4. Cf. the famous comments of Thuc. 1.22.

5. The date and circumstances of a treaty between Philip and Artaxerxes are unknown. Arrian is the only writer who mentions it, but it is hard to imagine that the charge would be invented when it serves to justify Darius' position. Friendship and alliance: Arr. 2.14.2 (τῆς πάλαι οὔσης φιλίας τε καὶ ξυμμαχίας). The decision of the gods: Arr. 2.14.3 (τὴν μὲν δὴ μάχην ὡς θεῶν τῳ ἔδοξεν οὕτω κριθῆναι). Arrian and Curtius say nothing about concessions, but Diod. 17.54.1 claims that Darius offered Alexander the lands west of the Halys River and 20,000 talents of silver, which the Conqueror declined. Furthermore, this preceded the news that Darius' wife, Stateira, had died in the Macedonian camp.

6. Curt. 4.1.8. Cf. Alexander's response: "remember that you are writing not just to a king, but to *your* king" (Curt. 4.1.14). By contrast, in Arr. 2.14.3, Darius speaks "as one king to another" (βασιλεὺς παρὰ βασιλέως), although, as Bosworth I 230 rightly notes, this does not imply equality (cf. Diod. 15.9.2).

the kingdom on equal terms with Darius." The Macedonian's response, through
the agency of Thersippus, is essentially the same in both authors, who allege that
the Great King had orchestrated the assassination of Philip and itemize Persian
crimes against both Greece and Macedon. Finally, he demanded that Darius make
submission in person to the true "King of Asia."[7] There was posturing on both
sides, but it was clear at this point that the Persian was negotiating from a weaker
position. And thus Curtius' version emphasizes what Westerners regarded as the
natural haughtiness of Oriental kings.[8]

It appears that Darius' envoys were sent to establish a basis for further
negotiations. Thersippus, who carried Alexander's letter to the Persian ruler in
Babylon, returned at some point in 332, certainly no later than August, with a
more specific proposal. Darius now offered the Macedonian the hand of his
daughter Stateira, with all territory west of the Halys River as her dowry, and
probably a payment of 10,000 talents of silver.[9] Once more, Darius made reference to the fickleness of fortune,[10] claiming that he was afraid that "like the birds
wafted up to the sky by their natural lightness, Alexander would also be carried
away by the vanity of his youthful mind," adding that "nothing was more difficult
than keeping control of great fortune at his age."[11] That the Persian king was given
to such philosophical opining is doubtful, but it is clear that he did not feel that
the outcome of Issus had sealed his doom. And he reminded Alexander that he
still had extensive territories and resources to draw on for a second confrontation.

---

7. Arr. 2.14.9 (βασιλεὺς τῆς Ἀσίας). For the exchanges (Arr. 2.14; Curt. 4.1.7-14), see Kaerst,
Hellenismus I³ 374–79; Mikrojannakis 1970; Bernhardt 1988; and Bloedow 1995.

8. Cf. Schachermeyr 1973, 222.

9. The sources do not agree on the matter of chronology, and there is also confusion about the
terms. Curt. 4.5.1-6 says nothing about the ransom payment but dates the second contact to
after the fall of Tyre (Atkinson I 320 calls the chronology "vague, but Curtius means sometime
during the siege of Tyre"); Diod. 17.54.1, referring to an embassy sent *before* the fall of Tyre,
mentions 20,000 talents. But Arrian (2.25.1) gives 10,000 (a number corroborated by Plut.
Alex. 29.7-9, who says the offer came "during the siege" [ἔτι δὲ τῇ πολιορκίᾳ τῆς Τύρου]) and
that the concession included lands west of the Euphrates. Clearly, Arrian has conflated the two
offers received by Alexander at Tyre (one around the time of the siege and the other when the
Macedonians returned from Egypt). That Darius was willing to concede the territory west of
the Euphrates before the fall of Tyre and Egypt seems most unlikely.

10. See Baynham 1998, 118–23: "Alexander, *Fortunatus Rex*; Darius, *Infortunatus Rex*." Lane
Fox 2007, 270: "the king's 'glory' (*kvarneh*) or τύχη (fortune) was an important aspect of his
majesty."

11. Curt. 4.5.2-3. Cf. Diod. 17.39.1: Darius tells Alexander to bear his success as one who was
only human (ἀνθρωπίνως φέρειν τὴν εὐτυχίαν). The fictitious prebattle exhortation that Curtius
puts in the mouth of Darius before Gaugamela echoes these sentiments: "fortune's blessings are
never unmixed" (4.14.19). What was in the Persian ruler's mind we shall never know.

By the middle of 331, the situation had changed somewhat. Although Phoenicia, Coele-Syria, and Egypt had all fallen to the Macedonians, Darius had assembled a new army and was now in a position to challenge the invader on the plains of northern Mesopotamia. Perhaps hoping that Alexander would be intimidated by the size of his army, reports of which must have been reaching his camp on a near-daily basis, the Great King tried once more to apply diplomatic pressure. Persian envoys found the Macedonian once again in the vicinity of Tyre and offered him the territory west of the Euphrates, a large sum of money, and the hand of one of Darius' daughters. But the territories Darius was willing to concede were already in the Conqueror's possession, as indeed were the daughters of the Great King, and monetary considerations were no longer paramount, especially if, by accepting the payment, the Macedonian renounced further military action.[12] Alexander's position is summed up by Arrian:

> For he said he needed neither money nor part of the country, rather than the whole, from Darius since the money and the country were all his, anyway. And if he wanted to marry Darius' daughter, marry her he would— even if Darius did not betroth her. He then ordered the king to come to him if he wished to receive any benevolent treatment from him. On hearing this, Darius abandoned all hope of a treaty with Alexander and resumed preparations for the war. (Arr. 2.25.3)

But again, there is disagreement in our sources and, of course, no Persian account of the proceedings. Diodorus (17.54.1-2) says that this was the second attempt by Darius, that on the first occasion (in 333/2), he offered 20,000 talents of silver and the lands west of the Halys River, and that now (331) he raised the offer to 30,000 talents, the territory west of the Euphrates, and, as Darius' son-in-law, a share of the whole kingdom. Plutarch (*Alex.* 29.7-9) makes no mention of the embassy sent to Alexander at Marathus but says that Darius in 331 offered 10,000 talents, the lands beyond the Euphrates, and the position of friend and ally, sealed by marriage to one of his daughters. Now, this agrees in most respects with Arrian's version of a second embassy, except that Arrian places it anachronistically in the time of Alexander's siege of Tyre.[13]

---

12. Badian 2000b, 258: "[Alexander's] very success had made it impossible for him to stop."

13. Cf. Bosworth I 256: "It seems that Arrian misdated an offer actually made by Darius in 331, shortly before Gaugamela." Placing the final embassy in 331 creates problems with the interpretation of Alexander's relations with Darius' wife. If she died in childbirth in 331 (as Justin 11.12.6 maintains: *ex conlisione abiecti partus decessisse*), then it was clearly not Darius' child she

What did Darius hope to accomplish through negotiation? Was he actually prepared to cede a good portion of his kingdom for the return of his relatives? Or did he expect to recover the lost territory once he had blunted Macedonian military power by diplomacy? Certainly, the end of the Panhellenic War would put his opponent under pressure to demobilize his army, not only the allied troops but the Macedonian levies as well. And the end of a united purpose would doubtless weaken the bonds of the League of Corinth, eventually forcing Alexander to deal with his European base, which even now was scarcely secure. It is perhaps unreasonable to assume that had Alexander accepted the terms of the settlement, he would have remained in Asia. In the end, the agreement would have amounted to little more than an armistice, allowing the Persians to recover what they had lost in stages and over a period of time.[14] As we have seen, the empire had dealt with the loss of Egypt and the unruliness of the western satraps earlier in the century, and indeed the history of Near Eastern empires was one of expansion and contraction.

II

Failing to buy off the invader, the Persian ruler placed his faith in the numbers of his army and the advantages of the terrain. An apparently unsuccessful attempt by Mazaeus to block the Macedonian path at Thapsacus—with a force of 6,000 that was obviously insufficient for that purpose—was accompanied by a scorched-earth policy in the Euphrates valley and may have been intended to ensure that Alexander moved in the direction of the Tigris. Here Mazaeus' force once again threatened, but did not prevent, the Macedonian crossing, even though the swiftness of the river presented its own dangers.[15] Darius had at least lured his opponent—whom he, and even some of the Macedonian leadership, must have regarded as overconfident, if not downright reckless—to a battlefield of his own choosing. Historians, with the benefit of hindsight, have treated the Macedonian victory as all but preordained. But the comments of George Cawkwell are salutary and to the point:

---

was carrying, and the Alexander sources appear to protest too much when they speak of the Conqueror's restraint (see Yardley and Heckel 160–61).

14. Recognized by Badian 2000b, 257–58: "Whatever boundary Alexander accepted, he would have to hold it for the foreseeable future against the inevitable attack. He simply lacked the means to do so. He could not keep an adequate force along a line of vast length while leaving the initiative to Darius."

15. Euphrates: Curt. 4.9.7-8, 12; Arr. 3.7.1-2. Tigris: Diod. 17.55.1-3; Curt. 4.9.13; Seibert 1987, 452–53; cf. Marsden 1964, 13–20; Atkinson I 330.

Sober appraisal, however, makes one wonder whether Darius put Alexander in such a position by good luck or good management. There was perhaps more strategic talent in the Persian command than Alexander's adulators allow. At the battle of Gaugamela in 331, which was to decide the war, Darius prudently chose his ground. By letting Alexander come right into the heart of the Empire, Darius gave him the problems of supply on the long march and blocked the route to Babylon. If Alexander's army were defeated it could be the more easily destroyed. The strategy was sound.[16]

As in the previous battle, Darius had superior numbers, but at Issus he had squandered this advantage by fighting on terrain that limited his mobility, as mountains and sea gave protection to the Macedonian flanks. Far different was the ground selected for the second major engagement.[17] The extensive plain near the village of Gaugamela, located less than twenty miles from modern Mosul,[18] gave ample space to Darius' cavalry, the strongest element in his army, as well as to his 200 scythed chariots and a detachment of elephants,[19] something Greco-Macedonian armies had hitherto never experienced. The size of the cavalry force was increased by distributing horses to some of the infantry, and horsemen previously equipped with javelins were given shields and swords. That some of the infantrymen were rearmed in the Macedonian style with long thrusting spears is unlikely, since the lengthened lances (*xysta*) that Diodorus speaks of were weapons used by the cavalry.[20] Most of the front line was given over to horsemen,

16. Cawkwell 2005, 199.

17. Seibert 1987, 452, rightly comments: "Den nach persischer Auffassung entscheidenden Fehler von Issos wollte man dieses Mal vermeiden. Die numerische Überlegenheit sollte schlachtentscheidend sein."

18. The location: Sushko 1936; Stein 1942, rejected by Marsden 1964, 20–21 and Schachermeyr 1973, 270 n. 311; cf. Bosworth I 293–94; Atkinson I 381; Seibert 1985, 92–93.

19. For the elephants, to be used in tandem with the scythed chariots, see Charles 2008, esp. 17–19; Kistler 2007, 25–30. About Darius' use of scythed chariots, Fuller 1958, 167, comments: "His confidence in them is hard to understand, because at Cunaxa they had proved completely ineffective." They would prove equally so on the Persian left, where the light-armed infantry neutralized them. But for their effectiveness on the Persian right, see Heckel, Willekes, and Wrightson 2010.

20. See *LSJ* s.v. ξυστόν. Gaebel 2002, 162: "The two words used to identify this lance, *xyston* and *dory*, were applied rather indifferently by the historians and were commonly used for the infantry spear as well." This is certainly true of *dory*, but Gaebel's own footnote (162 n. 12) gives only two examples of the use of *xyston* (Arr. 1.16.1 and Diod. 17.20.3), both of which refer unequivocally to the spear of a cavalryman. Diod. 19.27.2 (battle of Paraetacene in 317) mentions "two *eilai* [= *ilai*] of select *xyston*-bearers" (εἴλας δύο ξυστοφόρων ἐπιλέκτων) in the army of Eumenes of Cardia. The word *ilai* or *eilai* is used only of cavalry squadrons; infantry units, by

with a core of infantry at the center, where Darius himself was located in accordance with the practice of Persian kings. Certain irregularities in the terrain
were leveled, and in an area to the Persian left, where Darius anticipated that
the Companion cavalry would direct their attack, spikes and traps were planted,
though marked so that the Persians themselves could avoid them.[21] These were,
however, revealed to Alexander by a deserter—presumably one of the mercenaries
in the Great King's service—and thus rendered ineffectual.[22]

Some scholars have observed that caltrops would have proved as great a
hindrance to the Persians as to their enemy and doubt their existence.[23] But
Darius, although he was commanding a large army for only the second time, had
learned from the tactics used by Alexander at Issus and (as reported to him) at
the Granicus, where the Companion cavalry was stationed on the right wing but
shifted in such a way as to knife into the Persian line and put pressure on the
center. Furthermore, the aim of the scythed chariots was to disrupt the striking
force, while the superior numbers of cavalry on both right and left executed a
double envelopment of the smaller Macedonian force. Bessus, with the horsemen
from the Upper Satrapies, was placed on the Persian left to catch Alexander's
cavalry in the flank when it began its patented maneuver, while Mazaeus sought
to outflank the Macedonian left under Parmenion, who was supported by the
Thessalians and the allied forces. Had these commanders managed to hem in the
Macedonian army, the outcome of the battle would have been far different. But

contrast, are *taxeis* or *phalanges*. At the Granicus, the Persian satrap, Spithridates (Σπιθροβάτ
ης in the manuscripts of Diodorus) hurled his lance (σαυνίον) at Alexander, who subsequently
thrust his spear (ξυστόν) into the enemy's chest (Diod. 17.20.3-4; Arr. 1.15.8: τοῦτον Ἀλέξανδρος
παίσας τῷ ξυστῷ; cf. Plut. *Alex.* 16.11, where Cleitus kills the man with his *xyston*; for the
Macedonians around Alexander using their *xysta* at Gaugamela, see Arr. 3.14.3). At Gaugamela,
Hephaestion, fighting on horseback, is wounded by a Persian *xyston* (Ἡφαιστίων μὲν εἰς τὸν
βραχίονα ξυστῷ βληθεὶς ἐτρώθη), showing the effectiveness of the new weapon in Persian hands.
Cavalry reform: Curt. 4.9.3-4. For the Persians armed with *sarissai* on the Alexander Mosaic,
see Badian 1999, 80–81, following the work of Nylander (cf. Badian 2000b, 258 n. 33; but see
the sensible comments of Briant 2015, 181–95). For full discussion, see Heckel 2017a.

21. On the extent of Darius' preparations and innovations, see Nylander 1993, 149, with n. 42.
Cf. Seibert 1987.

22. These are mentioned only by Curt. 4.13.36-37, 4.15.1, and Polyaenus, *Strat.* 4.3.17 (probably
from the same ultimate source). The deserter's name was Bion, clearly a Greek (Berve II 109–10
no. 217; Heckel 72; Hofstetter 38 no. 68). The fact that he is known by name is no guarantee
that he is a historical individual.

23. Their existence has been doubted by Marsden 1964, 41: "If the obstacles existed where
Curtius and Polyaenus would have us believe they did, Alexander would appear to have
envisaged a Persian thrust round his right wing and through their own mine-field. One
suspects, therefore, that Curtius and Polyaenus elaborated upon the theme of a mine-field
merely to explain the peculiar line which the Macedonian approach-march took."

although Darius had the numbers to inflict heavy casualties, Alexander was intent upon striking his enemy's nerve center.

The battle occurred on October 1, 331,[24] and the Persian army began the engagement with a serious disadvantage. Fear of a Macedonian night attack had caused Darius to keep his men under arms, leaving them in poor condition to face the rigors of the coming day. Immediately, the Scythians stationed on the Persian left were ordered to outflank the Macedonian right. Alexander sent Menidas, who commanded the mercenary cavalry, directly against them, but the Scythians overpowered and drove them back, forcing Alexander to throw the Paeonians under Ariston into the fray. The Scythians were, in turn, reinforced by Bessus and his Bactrians. Despite inflicting heavy casualties, the barbarians were eventually driven back.

At this point, Darius launched his first set of scythed chariots. But since they were directed against a mixed unit of cavalry, *hamippoi*, and other light-armed troops, they were easily evaded and their drivers picked off by the Agrianian javelin men. The tactics were the same as those used by Xenophon's mercenaries at Cunaxa, and it was not a case, as many scholars have maintained, of the chariots driving into the massed formation of the Macedonian phalanx. The driverless chariots were corralled by the grooms (*hippokomoi*) and the Royal Hypaspists, whose job it was to lend support to the Companion cavalry. Hence, a second attempt to stifle Alexander's attack on the Macedonian right came to naught.

Toward the center left, Darius now relied upon his Persian cavalry, which came under attack from the Companions, particularly the squadron led by Aretas. At the same time, the phalanx was surging forward, putting additional pressure on the troops in front of Darius. Once again, with the tide of battle turning against him, the Great King fled in an effort to preserve not only himself but the empire he represented.[25]

Thus, the battle was lost despite the gallant efforts of Mazaeus on the Persian right. Here the scythed chariots exploited a gap that had formed in the Macedonian phalanx when the battalion of Simmias son of Andromenes failed to keep pace with the battalion to its right:[26]

---

24. Archonship of Aristophanes, month of Pyanepsion, according to Arr. 3.15.7; but Plut. *Cam.* 19.3 dates the battle to Boëdromion 26 (= October 1). Beloch III² 2.315. Full discussions of the battle: Hackmann 1902; Griffith 1947; Fuller 1958, 163–80; Marsden 1964; Devine 1975, 1986a, and 1989; English 2011, 110–47, with figs. 14–23.

25. Arr. 3.14.3. That he was the "first to turn and run" (πρῶτος αὐτὸς ἐπιστρέψας ἔφευγεν) is certainly a lie, for it was only when the rout had begun and defeat was certain that he took what was the only practical measure.

26. For the gap, see Arr. 3.14.4-5. It was here that the scythed chariots enjoyed their only meaningful success (Heckel, Willekes, and Wrightson 2010). But most scholars continue to remark

First of all, the scythed chariots were driven out in a charge that instilled sheer panic and terror in the Macedonians, for the cavalry commander Mazaeus also supported the scythe-bearing chariots with his closely packed squadrons of horse, thus rendering the attack of the scythe bearers absolutely fearful. The phalanx, however, joined shields, and at the king's command, they all beat on them with their spears, producing a considerable noise. At this the horses panicked, and *most of the chariots* wheeled about and turned violently against their own people.

The others proceeded to attack the phalanx, but since the Macedonians created considerable gaps in their line, these went on through them. Some were, indeed, killed by javelins, but *others got through*, and some by their forceful impetus and effective employment of their weapons of iron brought to their enemy death in many cases and in different forms. Such was the edge and impact of these implements forged to bring destruction that they sliced off the arms of many together with their shields and severed the necks of not a few so that the heads fell to the ground with eyes still gazing and the facial expression maintained, and in some instances they cut through the ribs with deadly wounds and brought a swift death. (Diod. 17.58.2-5)

On this side of the battlefield, where Parmenion had been stationed with the allied troops and the Thessalian cavalry, Mazaeus wreaked havoc, causing the old general to send an urgent appeal for help to Alexander, who was already in hot pursuit of the fleeing king.[27] But Mazaeus' cavalry, comprising Indians, Persians, and Parthyaeans, was diverted from its purpose by the sight of the Macedonian baggage camp, now virtually unguarded. Had they not turned to premature plundering, the outcome on the Macedonian left might have been very different. But all that proved academic: at the news of Darius' flight on the Persian left, Mazaeus' troops were left with no choice but to disengage, only to be forced to fight their way through the waves of Macedonian cavalrymen returning from their pursuit of the Great King.[28]

---

upon the ineffectiveness of the scythed chariots on the Persian left and ignore the fact that on the Persian right, gaps in the Macedonian phalanx led to ghastly casualties.

27. Successes of Mazaeus: Diod. 17.59.3-8; Curt. 4.15.5-9, 16.1-2. The account of the Persian attempt to save Darius' mother, Sisygambis, is pure fiction (Curt. 4.15.10-11; Diod. 17.59.7). Parmenion's call for help: Diod. 17.60.7; Curt. 4.15.6, 16.2; Arr. 3.15.1; Plut. *Alex.* 33.9-10; Callisthenes, *FGrH* 124 F37. Arrian does not mention Mazaeus' role at Gaugamela.

28. Arr. 3.15.1-2.

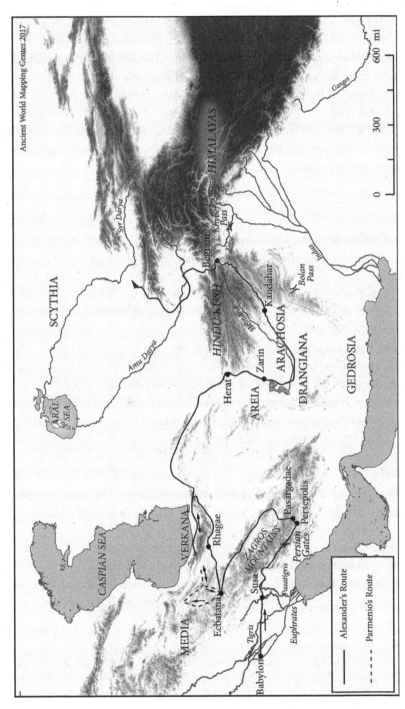

MAP 9.1 Map of Alexander's Expedition through Persia and Central Asia.

Some alleged that Darius, shamed by his second flight, contemplated suicide—a most unlikely scenario. To his credit, he refused to destroy the bridge across the Lycus River, unwilling to endanger the lives of more of his troops to facilitate his own escape.[29] But once the Persian lines had begun to crumble, flight was once more the only viable option. It saved not only the king but also the empire, though in both cases only for a short time. Darius' reputation suffered nonetheless. Gaugamela added one more chapter to the story of the "Cowardly King." Yet in truth, neither his strategy nor his tactics can be faulted. They failed in their execution and because the Persians were confronted by one of the greatest military leaders of all time.

III

As he raced for Arbela with the remnants of his army, Darius knew that 230 years of Achaemenid rule had all but come to an end. From Arbela, he moved quickly to Ecbatana in Media, placing his hopes in the troops of Central Asia and in the hard lands that produced them, but he knew also that the center had collapsed and many of his nobles were on the verge of making their own peace with the Conqueror.

Failure at Gaugamela opened the path to the very heart of the empire. The battlefield itself was in the old Assyrian territories, shadowlands of a once-great empire destroyed by a coalition of Babylonians and Medes. To the south lay Mesopotamia, the "land between the rivers" Tigris and Euphrates, and particularly the region the Arabs would later call the Sawad or al-'Irāq, extending from the point where the rivers were closest to each other down to the Persian Gulf. This had been the cradle of civilization, and it remained culturally relevant. Babylon retained its religion, language, and influence, forming one of the four capitals of the Persian Empire, all of which represented the contingent nations that made up its core. The locals continued to worship Bel-Marduk in an empire where the rulers gave primacy to Ahuramazda, Mithra, Fire, and (later) Anahita,[30] and their scribes kept records of business transactions in Akkadian cuneiform long after Aramaic had become the lingua franca of the Achaemenid Empire.

In the lands of Sumer and Akkad, Babylon, as a political center, was a relative latecomer, achieving prominence in the age of Hammurabi. But it was well sited

---

29. Lycus bridge: Justin 11.14.4 (wrongly calling the river the Cydnus); Curt. 4.16.8-9.

30. On Achaemenid religious practices, see Hdt. 1.131 (with Greek equivalents; see How and Wells I, 111–13); Briant, *HPE* 240–54; also Shahbazi 2012, 136–37; Wiesehöfer 1996, 94–101; Brosius 2006, 63–70. See also Naiden 2018, 160 and, on Anahita, 163, with 290 n. 17.

on the crossroads of trade, by land and sea, accumulating the wealth upon which political and military power are built. By Alexander's time, its name had become a byword for luxury and decadence. Greeks believed that it rose to splendor under the legendary queen Semiramis, even though she was in all likelihood an Assyrian of the late ninth century.[31] For the Persians, it was also a residence for the crown prince, who represented the Great King at the New Year's festival and underwent ritual humiliation at the hands of Marduk's priests.[32] One of the last of the great Eastern cities to fall to Cyrus the Great, it was the first to submit to Alexander.

Mazaeus (Mazday), who had served four Persian kings, ruled Cilicia and Abarnahara, and fought with distinction at Issus and Gaugamela, was the first to come to terms with the Conqueror.[33] He withdrew to southern Mesopotamia and occupied Babylon. Prudence dictated that he should seek terms, and together with the guardian of the city's treasure, Bagophanes, he came forth to make a formal surrender.[34] Meeting the Conqueror with gifts and ceremonies on a road strewn with flowers and fragrant with incense was undoubtedly a sign of both honor and submission—probably even the enactment of an ancient ritual[35]—but it also forestalled a more brutal transfer of power and property within the city.

Mazaeus, who made a virtue of necessity, was rewarded with the satrapy of Babylonia, albeit under the watchful eye of a Macedonian garrison and military

---

31. Hammurabi's accession is dated to 1792; for the first Babylonian dynasty, see Kuhrt 1995, 1.108–16. Semiramis: Hdt. 1.184. Her legend: Diod. 2.7.1–20.3 (text and notes in Llewellyn-Jones and Robson 2010, 119–30); Justin 1.1.10–2.10; cf. Capomacchia 1986. She is almost certainly the Sammuramat of the Assyrian annals (Kuhrt 1995, 2.491; Schramm 1972).

32. Kuhrt 1987, 40–52.

33. Mazaeus' career and background: Heckel 156–57; Berve II 243–45; Briant, *HPE* 848–50; Bing 1998.

34. Mazaeus appears to have assumed the responsibilities of Bupares, who brought the Babylonian troops to Gaugamela (Arr. 3.8.5) and presumably died there (cf. Briant, *HPE* 849). See Heckel 73; Berve II 110 no. 222. Bagophanes was probably a eunuch, as were many officials who served as *gazophylakes* (Heckel 68; Berve II 99 no. 197).

35. Ritual surrender: Kuhrt 1987, 48–49; but see Lane Fox 2007, 275: "for Curtius' Latin, the rhetorical patterns of Orientalism and descriptions of the 'arrival,' or *adventus*, of a Hellenistic king or Roman governor are more relevant." See also Collins 2013, who notes that Alexander did not undergo a ritual of accession in Babylon but fulfilled many of the functions of a Babylonian king: "Unlike the Persians, who had little experience with foreign kings, the Babylonians had a long history of non-native dynasties. This, along with Alexander's interest in the Babylonian temples (which was a fundamental part of the native ideology of kingship), allowed him to win over the priests and fulfil the local criteria for a legitimate king to some degree" (143).

overseers (*strategoi*).[36] A thirty-four-day sojourn in Babylon, which began as a welcome respite for the conquering army, soon corrupted discipline. Alexander took his men to Sittacene, which offered opportunities for hunting and military drill. It was probably on one occasion in this region that Alexander conducted a lion hunt in conjunction with Mazaeus, an unambiguous symbol of the harmony between victor and vanquished and probably a sign of his new role as King of Asia.[37]

Susa, to the east, was once the administrative center of the Elamites,[38] and beyond that was the city of Darius I and Xerxes, Persepolis. Only the old capital of the Medes, Ecbatana, lay off the main route that led to the east, a road that moved from the lowlands of Mesopotamia, into the higher elevations of the Zagros range—which bisected the land from the Persian Gulf to the Caspian at a roughly forty-five-degree angle as it moved from south to north—and eventually to the Iranian plateau. Nothing stood between the Macedonians and the ancestral capitals of Babylon and Susa, and Persepolis could do little more than buy time through the delaying tactics of forces who controlled the passes of the Zagros.

Without direction from the Great King, the ancient center of the empire submitted to Alexander. Diodorus claims, implausibly, that Abulites surrendered Susiane on the king's instructions, in order to preoccupy Alexander while Darius prepared to renew the war.[39] Given the financial resources of the city, which housed a substantial treasury, and the psychological impact of the loss of another

---

36. Mazaeus' appointment: Arr. 3.16.4; Curt. 5.1.44; cf. Diod. 17.64.5-6. He ruled as satrap until his death in late 328; Stamenes replaced him, but the name is not secure; Arr. 4.18.3; cf. Curt. 8.3.17 has "Ditamenes," even less likely. Macedonian officers: Agathon, Menes, and Apollodorus (Curt. 5.1.43; Diod. 17.64.5; cf. Arr. 3.16.4). It was, in fact, Achaemenid practice to temper the powers of satraps with imperial oversight (cf. Oates 1986, 136: "Their power was effectively restrained by holding the treasurer and garrison commander in each capital city responsible solely to the king, a system which had been tried with success in Babylonia as early as the 3rd millennium"). For the Persian practice of distributing such powers, see Olmstead 1948, 498.

37. This is how I interpret the lion-hunt scene on the so-called Alexander Sarcophagus from Sidon. Those who see the intended *Grabherr* as Abdalonymus would place the lion hunt in Syria, for which there is some literary evidence. But such hunts were common throughout the Achaemenid lands, and it defies the credulity of historians, if not art historians, that a Phoenician king should appear on a battle scene he did not participate in and on a hunting scene in which he dresses as a Persian notable. Indeed, depicting a Sidonian king (of this period) in Persian dress strikes me as absurd and as unlikely as the notion of a commemorative portrait of Chiang Kai-shek dressed as a Japanese soldier. See Heckel 2006 for full discussion. A negative Babylonian view of Alexander, written after the king's death but pretending to predict the overthrow of Alexander, is the *Dynastic Prophecy* (see discussion and translation in Sherwin-White 1987, 10–14). On Alexander as King of Asia, see Lane Fox 2007; Hammond 1986.

38. For the Elamites, see the convenient overview in Potts 2012.

39. Diod. 17.65.5 (cf. also Welles, *Diodorus* 305 n. 3).

of the empire's capitals, this seems most unlikely. Susa surrendered to Xenophilus, whom Alexander sent to the city after the victory at Gaugamela.[40] The news of Abulites' surrender was brought by a letter carrier (*epistoleus*), accompanied by the satrap's son, Oxathres, who acted also as guide.[41] Abulites himself made his official surrender to Alexander when the king arrived.[42] Like Mazaeus, Abulites was allowed to retain his satrapy, which probably included Uxians of the plain, who had served with the men of Susa at Gaugamela.[43] As *phrourarchos* of Susa, a certain Mazarus was replaced by Xenophilus himself, but Abulites remained as satrap.[44] Once again, the native ruler was fettered by Macedonian military occupation. At this time, anxiety about the outcome of Agis' war in the Peloponnese helped to buy time for Persia. The need to await news of events in the west kept Alexander in Babylonia and Elam longer than usual, a delay that allowed Ariobarzanes, satrap of Persis, to occupy the so-called Persian Gates with 25,000 men.[45] But his efforts, like those of the Uxians, served only to harass and delay the advancing army.

---

40. Arr. 3.16.6 calls Alexander's agent Philoxenus, but in the light of Xenophilus' appointment as commander of the citadel, it is likely that the component parts of the name were reversed either by Arrian or by his source. See Heckel 2002.

41. The *epistoleus*: Arr. 63.16.3. The role of Oxathres: Curt. 5.2.8-9.

42. Curt. 5.2.9-10: his gifts included dromedaries and twelve elephants sent to Darius from India.

43. Arr. 3.8.5. On that occasion, their commander was Abulites' son, Oxathres.

44. For Mazarus, see Arr. 3.16.9, with Bosworth I 319. Berve II 246 no. 486 (cf. Hoffmann 201) implausibly identifies him as Macedonian. See also Heckel 157. Curt. 5.2.16-17: Archelaus was entrusted with the administration of the city, and Callicrates was appointed treasurer. Alexander appointed Abulites' son Oxathres satrap of Paraetacene (Arr. 3.19.2), which he appears to have governed until 325, when he was executed along with his father for maladministration (Arr. 7.4.1; cf. Plut. *Alex.* 68.7).

45. For modern discussions of the battle, see especially Fuller 1958, 226-34; Atkinson II 83-102; Heckel 1980a; MacDermot and Schippmann 1999; but Speck 2002, 187, is right to find fault with others, myself included, noting that "a knowledge of the country is essential to any assessment of the sources. Without a clear idea of where something could, or could not, have happened, any interpretation of the sources is likely to prove misguided." See also Seibert 1985, 104 n. 14, with earlier literature. For the location, see Stein 1938; Bosworth 1988a, 90; rejected by Speck 2002; Moritani 2014. Speck 2002, 43-44, observes, plausibly, that Ariobarzanes did not take up his position at the Persian Gates until he knew the direction of Alexander's march (that is, once he was in the land of the mountain Uxians).

IV

The Uxians of the plain, a fruitful and peaceful region, made voluntary surrender and received remission of tribute.[46] Those of the hills were apparently under the authority of Medates. This man was a relative of Darius and the husband of the daughter of Sisygambis' sister. His exact title is unknown, but it appears that his family connections made him more determined to stand in the path of the invader.[47] But the Uxians, who had long made a living by exacting tribute from those traversing their lands and were accustomed to receiving payment even from the Great King, opposed Alexander for personal, material interests. Trusting in their mountain lairs, they were unafraid of the Macedonians; Arrian notes that they were prepared to allow the Macedonians safe passage if they made the requisite payment.[48] Hence, the motives of Medates and the Uxians

---

46. Arr. 3.17.1 The fertility of their land: Diod. 17.67.2. Geographical location of the Uxians: Strabo 15.3.4-5 C728-729; cf. 11.13.6 C524; cf. Seibert 1985, 101–3. Briant, *HPE* 728, believes that the Uxians of the plains were subject to Medates/Madates (cf. Bosworth I 321), but this is difficult to reconcile with the evidence. Arr. 3.17.1 says that they were subject "to the satrap of the Persians." The fact that they were brigaded with the Susians at Gaugamela suggests otherwise; the Persian tribes were under the command Orontobates, Ariobarzanes (satrap of Persis), and Orxines (Arr. 3.8.5). MacDermot and Schippmann 1999, 288, rightly note that "it is not understandable why the Uxii of the mountains, in spite of being under the rule of a Persian governor, could collect tolls from the Persian king." Arrian, who depicts the one group of Uxians as "subjects" and the other as "independent of Persia," may have meant that they obeyed "a Persian satrap" (not "the satrap of Persis"), unless he is simply mistaken. The "independence" of the latter is supported by Strabo 11.13.6 C524 (= Nearchus, *FGrH* 133 F1g), who lists the Uxians as one of four groups who lived on brigandage (τεττάρων ὄντων λῃστρικῶν ἐθνῶν). Atkinson II 78, recognizing that Curtius has omitted the Uxians of the plain altogether, suggests that "Medates seems to have held less than satrapal status, but exercised some authority for the Persian administration amongst the mountain Uxii. Thus we might style Medates a Native Commissioner." That both groups were geographically outside the satrapy of Persis is also demonstrated by Curt. 5.3.17, who says that after dealing with the Uxians (that is, those of the mountains), Alexander marched two days and then entered Persis, reaching the so-called Susidan Gates on the fifth day (*omni hac regione vastata, tertio die Persidem, quinto angustias quas illi Susidas Pylas vocant intrat*). Curt. 5.3.4 adds that Medates was determined to resist Alexander (*ultima pro fide experiri decreverat*), which is entirely at odds with Arrian's statement that the Uxians of the plains made voluntary surrender and received remission of tribute payments. Hence it must be the land of the mountain Uxians that leads to Persian territory (Curt. 5.3.3) and was subject to Medates.

47. Curt. 5.2.16. Medates was thus married to the niece of Darius' mother (Curt. 5.3.12; Diod. 17.67.4 calls him a cousin of the king).

48. Arr. 3.17.1: "they would only permit him to take the route toward Persia with his army if they received what they used to receive from the Persian king on his passage" (οὐκ ἄλλως παρήσειν ἔφασαν τὴν ἐπὶ Πέρσας ἰόντα ξὺν τῇ δυνάμει ἢ λαβεῖν ὅσα καὶ παρὰ τοῦ Περσῶν βασιλέως ἐπὶ τῇ παρόδῳ ἐλάμβανον).

themselves differed; the latter showed little concern for the fate of the Achaemenid Empire.[49]

It is clear that Medates and his men attempted to hold off the Macedonians in the narrows through which one had to pass in order to reach Persis. Henry Speck, who examined the terrain, concludes that "Alexander crossed the Kārūn near or at Shūshtar, where he received the submission of the Uxians of the plains," and that the encounter with the mountain Uxians "took place at narrows situated near the plains of Khūzistān, on what was the main road leading from Susa to Persepolis."[50] Details of the battle are confused, owing to the divergent accounts of the sources,[51] but it is clear that the Uxians were compelled to abandon their defensive position when Craterus' force,[52] which had been detached from the main column, appeared on the heights above them. Thereupon they retreated to a mountain stronghold, but even this proved insufficient to hold out against the enemy. Hence, they sought terms, and Alexander imposed tribute in kind (for they had no money): 100 horses per year, 500 pack animals, and 30,000 of their livestock.[53] After the Conqueror's departure, they returned to a life of brigandage.

Like Medates, the best Ariobarzanes could do was delay the Macedonians, or rather Alexander's select force, at the narrows known as the Persian Gates. At the same time, the wagon road to the south, which offered no significant natural barriers, led Parmenion, with the heavy infantry and the baggage train, toward

---

49. For Medates' motives, see also Seibert 1985, 102; cf. Speck 2002, 28: "Clearly he was not there to demand a 'fee.' The Macedonian advance on Persepolis had to be slowed, if it could not be halted. News of Alexander's move from Susa along a main road leading in the direction of the Kārūn and hence the territory governed by Medates (thus precluding a march on Ecbatana, which would have required a move in the direction of Andīmeshk . . .) would have preceded him."

50. Speck 2002, 37.

51. The accounts of Arr. 3.17.2-5 and Curt. 5.3.4-11 differ in virtually every aspect (see Howe 2015c), and Bosworth I 321–23 suspects that they described different events.

52. Arr. 3.17.4-5 names Craterus; Curt. 5.3.6-10 gives the command to Tauron. The latter was probably Craterus' subordinate, in charge of light-armed troops.

53. Arr. 3.17.6. Curtius (5.3.11-15) has a completely different story, saying that when Medates feared punishment if he surrendered, he appealed to Sisygambis, who intervened with Alexander on his behalf and gained a pardon and exemption from tribute. Clearly, there is some conflation of the terms given to the two groups of Uxians. Arr. 3.17.6 cites Ptolemy for the role of Sisygambis but says nothing about Medates. What became of him is uncertain (Berve II 243 does not speculate). Frye 1984, 140, assumes he was "either killed or at least removed from his rule."

the Persian capital.[54] Ariobarzanes was a formidable adversary, and he occupied a strong defensive position with a substantial military force.[55]

For Callisthenes, who had been hired to promulgate the deeds of the Panhellenic crusaders and, especially, their leader, this was Thermopylae in reverse.[56] Once again, the sources, who based their works (ultimately) on the work of Alexander's official historian, dredge up reminders of Xerxes' campaign. The hitherto irresistible advance of the Macedonian army is brought to a sudden, and unexpected, halt and the invader driven back by a shower of rocks and missiles hurled down from above. This precipitated a retreat of thirty stades, a distance of more than three miles.[57] The Thermopylae parallel is obvious. The Gates were the last obstacle to overcome before reaching the heart of the Persian Empire, the very city from which attacks against Greece had been launched. The existence of alternative routes, such as the wagon road along which Parmenion at that very point was advancing, is conveniently forgotten. And Alexander takes a page out of Xerxes' book, finding a Lycian herdsman who knew of a path that circumvented the Persian defensive position.[58] He was, of course, the equivalent of the traitor Ephialtes, who led the Persians around Thermopylae. History would indeed repeat itself, this time in the favor of the "Greeks."

One must, however, separate historical fiction and propaganda from the actual course of events. Ariobarzanes and his men certainly had no knowledge of

54. Parmenion's route: Arr. 3.18.1; cf. Speck 2002, 143–44; Moritani 2014, 142–45. Roads from Susa to Persepolis: Velásquez Muñoz 2013, 149–59. Accounts of the battle: Arr. 3.18.2-9; Polyaenus, *Strat.* 4.3.27; Curt. 5.3.17–4.34; Diod. 17.68 (virtually useless). Full discussion of battle and topography: Speck 2002; cf. Howe 2015c.

55. The size of the occupying force: Curt. 5.3.17 gives Ariobarzanes 25,000 infantry; Diod. 17.68.1 adds 300 cavalry. Arrian's figures are exaggerated: 40,000 infantry, 700 cavalry (3.18.2). Nor are the sources in agreement about the name of the pass: Arr. 3.18.2 calls them "the Persian Gates" (τὰς πύλας τὰς Περσίδας); Diod. 17.68.1 says "the so-called Susian Rocks" (τὰς Σουσιάδας καλουμένας πέτρας); Curt. 5.3.17: "which the Persians call the Susidan Gates" (*angustias quas illi Susidas Pylas vocant*). It has been suggested that there are two names (Persian and Susian or Susidan), which reflect the direction of the traveler, but Speck 2002, 49 remarks: "It is entirely possible that what we have is in fact an area, and that the "Susian" and the "Persian" Gates are separate passes situated at either end of it (i.e. the north-western and south-eastern ends, respectively) and so easily confused by the sources." But Diodorus and Curtius agree that Alexander reached the "Susian" Gates on the fifth day and that this is where the battle took place. This does not disprove Speck's theory but it does make two Gates less attractive. Curtius' remark "what the Persians call the Susidan Gates" may be a directional indicator, from the Persian standpoint.

56. For the Thermopylae motif: Burn 1973, 121; Heckel 1980a, 171; cf. Renault 1975, 128.

57. Curt. 5.3.18-23.

58. On the Lycian herdsman, see Zahrnt 1999.

Leonidas, and they did not see themselves in the role of the Spartans. The opposition at the Persian Gates could, as noted, be no more than a delaying action. Perhaps it was hoped that the treasures could be removed from Persepolis. But Tiridates, the *gazophylax* ("guardian of the treasury"),[59] may have doubted the wisdom of resistance, knowing full well that Mazaeus and Abulites had chosen surrender and prospered. There must have been many among the prominent Persians who weighed the relative merits of loyalty to Darius against collaboration with the invader.[60] Ariobarzanes' actions may have been considered honorable, but his reward was apparently death in defense of a noble, but lost, cause.[61] Tiridates had time to consider his options and chose to survive.

If those who favored delaying action hoped to facilitate the removal or even the destruction of the treasure in Persepolis, there is no indication that such measures were taken. Indeed, the process of transporting them was far too complicated to be effected in a short time.[62] Instead, attention was given to the destruction of the bridges on the Araxes River, which were easily rebuilt when the enemy arrived. Perhaps, too, there was the vain expectation that Darius with a refurbished army would come to save the city of his ancestors.

The repulse of the initial attack on Ariobarzanes' defenders placed the Macedonians in a difficult position. Although Speck mentions at least six passes through the mountains, a change of course would have involved backtracking and further delay, to say nothing of loss of face—something the Conqueror was particularly sensitive to.[63] Local informants brought knowledge of a path that circumvented the enemy position, and Alexander left the bulk of the force

---

59. Curt. 5.5.2 (*Tiridate, custode pecuniae regiae*); Diod. 17.69.1 calls him the ruler of the city (τοῦ κυριεύοντος τῆς πόλεως Τιριδάτου). See Heckel 268 s.v. "Tiridates [1]"; Berve II 374–75 no. 754.

60. Briant, *HPE* 850, rightly speaks of "dissension . . . among the high Persian officials, some (Ariobarzanes) wishing to defend the town, others (Tiridates) thinking that surrender was open to negotiation."

61. Berve II 60–61 no. 115 (cf. Kaerst, *RE* II 833; Frye 1984, 140) believes that Ariobarzanes was the son of Artabazus and assumes, contrary to the testimony of Curt. 4.5.33-34, that he escaped from the battle and joined his father, with whom he surrendered to Alexander after Darius' death (Arr. 3.23.7). This creates more problems than it solves, and it is likely that the satrap of Persis was a different person (see Bosworth I 325; Heckel 45 s.v. "Ariobarzanes [2]"). He must have been a man of considerable importance; Plut. *Alex.* 37.1 calls him "one of the most noble Persians" (γενναιοτάτων Περσῶν).

62. Logistical problems: Diod. 17.71.2-3, discussed below. Furthermore, there remained no safe haven for the imperial treasures.

63. As we have seen, Curtius depicted the setback at the Gates as a case of Alexander's fortune abandoning him.

under Craterus in the original camp. Taking with him the more nimble troops, Alexander followed a Lycian guide along treacherous paths leading to the rear of Ariobarzanes' position. En route he detached a force under Coenus, Amyntas, Philotas, and Polyperchon to move ahead in the direction of Persepolis and begin bridging the Araxes River, which the army would eventually have to cross. The Persians themselves were aware of the encircling route, but the men at the outposts (of which Arrian says there were three) could neither repel the Macedonian force nor alert Ariobarzanes. The first two outposts were overwhelmed before dawn, and the men of the third, although they managed to escape, fled to safety rather than warning the main defending force. Alexander achieved complete surprise, appearing at dawn and giving a trumpet signal for Craterus' men to attack from below. Those who attempted to evade both Craterus and the king's forces were cut down by the 3,000 infantry under the command of Ptolemy.[64]

It remains to say a few words about the location of the Persian Gates, which was identified by Sir Aurel Stein in the 1930s with what was known for a time as the Tang-i Mohammed Rezā (the valley of the Fahlian River). This remained the accepted location until it was challenged by Henry Speck, who surveyed the area in 1977–78 and determined that the pass was located farther north in the Mehrian valley.[65] Events in Iran prevented him from further examination, but his arguments and conclusions were investigated in a new topographical study conducted by Kimitoshi Moritani in 2011–12.[66] He confirmed both Speck's location of the Uxian pass and the Mehrian valley as the Persian Gates, adding that Alexander's route took him from Behbahan to Yasuj, and from there through the Persian Gates and on to Persepolis. Alexander thus left the winter road from Susa to Persepolis as he moved through Uxian territory but rejoined it north of Ramhormoz, then continued along the winter road to Behbahan before turning eastward. The Persian gates took him along the summer road to Persepolis.

64. Arr. 3.18.9. See Howe 2015c.

65. Tang-i Mohammad Reza, that is, the Tang-i Khās (on the problem of the name, see Speck 2002, 102 n. 86): Stein 1938, 316–17. Accepted by Engels 1978a, 73; Bosworth I 326 and 1988a, 90; Seibert 1985, 105; and, apparently, Wood 1997, 102–8. Against this identification, see Speck 2002, 107–35.

66. See Moritani 2014 (Japanese and English text, with exquisite color and black-and-white photos and 3-D maps). I am grateful to Professor Moritani for sending me the published results of his research.

V

The sequel to the desperate defense of the Gates was, once again, depicted by the sources who took their material from the propagandist Callisthenes in terms that emphasized the Panhellenic nature of Alexander's campaign. A band of Greek captives, the victims of atrocities at the hands of earlier Persian kings, greeted the Conqueror as he approached the "most hateful of cities to the Greeks."[67] They had been mutilated by their captors, and they rejoiced that Zeus, "the avenger of Greece" (*ultor Graeciae*), was at last giving them justice.[68] As drama, there could be nothing more powerful, but the absurdity of the situation is clear. Where did these victims come from? Which Great King had been responsible for their condition? In truth, they were little more than dramatic devices, intended to heighten the indignation of the reader and to justify the Macedonian treatment of Persepolis and its inhabitants.[69] Perhaps the whole episode was inspired by the existence of the Greeks who had been settled in the center of the empire after the invasion of Greece. They were indeed "mutilated," both culturally and linguistically.[70] But the image of Greeks whose noses, ears, and arms had been amputated by their cruel conquerors was invention pure and simple. If the plundering of Persepolis and the indignities imposed on its inhabitants needed justification, this was it.

With the defeat of Ariobarzanes, the organized resistance of Persian government officials all but came to an end. Tiridates, who had charge of the treasures in Persepolis, sent a message to Alexander offering to surrender them.[71] He was rewarded by retaining his position as *gazophylax*. But his surrender did not save the city or many of its inhabitants. Arrian passes over the destruction of

---

67. Curt. 5.6.1: "no city was more hateful to the Greeks than the seat of the ancient kings of Persia" (*nullam infestiorem urbem Graecis est quam regiam veterum Persidis regum*).

68. Curt. 5.5.8: *ut vero Iovem illi tandem, Graeciae ultorem, aperuisse oculos conclamavere.*

69. Recognized by Rüegg 1906, 9.

70. The Greeks encountered by the Macedonians at this point must have featured in Callisthenes' original. It certainly reinforces the negative stereotype of the Persians. It may be that Cleitarchus converted them into amputees (for his tendency to exaggerate, see *FGrH* 137 F14), but this is at best speculation. What is surprising is how reluctant modern scholars are to dismiss this obvious piece of fiction. Even Badian 1985, 443, calls it "a story that may or may not be true." Full discussion in Yardley and Heckel 174–75.

71. Tiridates' offer to betray the city: Diod. 17.69.1; Curt. 5.5.2; but Arr. 3.18.10 says nothing of the betrayal ("Alexander arrived there before the garrison had plundered the treasury"). His retention as *gazophylax*: Curt. 5.6.11; but Nicarchides was left as *phrourarchos*, with 3,000 Macedonian troops. Tiridates may have been responsible for shutting the gates against Ariobarzanes.

Persepolis and the treatment of its inhabitants, reluctant to criticize Alexander. Many modern scholars still engage in Alexander idolatry, and their arguments suffer accordingly. N. G. L. Hammond rationalizes Alexander's action and all but denies the atrocities:

> For at Persepolis, which had not resisted, the Macedonians were said in the Cleitarchan version to have killed all the men and abused the women until Alexander called a halt and tried to protect them from further violation (Curt. 5.6.8). In Asia the policy of Alexander was to win over the Asian people. To that end he had forbidden the army to ravage Asia (Just. 11.6.1). After the battle of Gaugamela he appointed Persians as satraps, took Persians into his entourage, and within a year formed a Persian Royal Guard of cavalry. With this policy in mind he would have been mad to let his army sack the city; for, if he had done so and atrocities had inevitably been committed, he would have wrecked his hopes of ever winning Persian support.[72]

What is not consistent with his views he dismisses as Cleitarchean invention,[73] and he concludes that his interpretation of events "fits the personality of Alexander,"[74] as if this is something we have even the slightest chance of knowing.[75]

Arrian is of little help for the understanding of events; he clearly found Alexander's behavior distasteful and claims that Parmenion had advised him "that it was not good to destroy what was now his own property, and that the Asians would not so readily adhere to him, but would suppose that even he had not decided to retain the Empire of Asia but only to conquer and pass on."[76] That his chief sources, Ptolemy and Aristobulus, gave credit to Parmenion seems unlikely,

---

72. Hammond 1992b, 363.

73. It has long been the practice to explain away what is unappealing in the history of Alexander by attributing the information to Cleitarchus, about whom far more has been written than understood. (I confess that I have myself fallen into the error on occasion.) The account of the treatment of Persepolis must almost certainly come from Callisthenes and forms a major part of the Panhellenic propaganda. But Hammond 1992b, 363 n. 30, says (most implausibly) that "it is likely that the work published by Callisthenes did not extend beyond the battle of Gaugamela, and *that in any case it did not cover the burning of the Palace*; for Alexander's official version of what he did at Persepolis would surely have been cited by the surviving Alexander-historians" (emphasis added). On Callisthenes, see Pearson 1960, 22–49; and Brown 1949a.

74. Hammond 1992b, 364.

75. Frye 1984, 140: "It is hardly possible, of course, to enter the mind of Alexander," but this has not stopped the many who attempt to do so.

76. Arr. 3.18.11. Alexander's response and Arrian's disapproval: 3.18.12.

since praise of the old general was tantamount to criticism of the king. When he called a meeting of his generals before entering Persepolis, it was not for the purpose of debating what action to take; the king was clearly bound by his own propaganda to make an example of the city.[77] Parmenion's advice, if he actually gave it, belongs to a later time. For it is clear that there were two separate outrages committed by the Macedonians: the first satisfied the lusts of the Macedonian and allied troops, as well as the ideology of the campaign; the second was the treatment of the palace itself, and this did not occur immediately. Both were symbolic acts yet different in execution and long-term impact. The city endured, but so did the stain on Alexander's reputation.[78]

It appears, however, that there was a lengthy hiatus between the plundering on the part of the troops and the firing of the palace. The troops were given free rein in the city, apart from the palace area,[79] though clearly there were wealthy districts that offered booty on a scale hitherto unseen. The fires must have been limited; Persepolis continued as a functioning center after the event. To underscore his orders, Alexander must have posted guards around the treasure house to secure the 120,000 talents of accumulated Persian wealth in the form of coin and bullion. By comparison, a paltry 6,000 talents were captured at Parsagadae.[80]

The Alexander historians are, however, most unhelpful when it comes to the chronology of the Macedonians' stay in Persis. We may place his progress from Susa to Persepolis at the end of 331 and the beginning of 330, with his arrival at the gates of the city at the end of January. Curtius dates the subjugation of Persis, Alexander's month-long campaign against recalcitrant tribes, to the time of the setting of the Pleiades, roughly April 330.[81] The campaign itself, an arduous task on account of both the resisting tribes (particularly the Mardi)[82] and the inclement weather, is also poorly documented, and we know little about Alexander's opponents, their specific grievances, or even the measures they took.

---

77. Cf. Strabo 15.3.6 C730.

78. Curt. 5.6.1-8.

79. Diod. 17.70.1 (τὴν δὲ Περσέπολιν . . . τοῖς στρατιώταις ἔδωκεν εἰς διαρπαγὴν χωρὶς τῶν βασιλείων). Diodorus contradicts himself at 17.70.3, when he says that "the enormous palaces, famed throughout the whole civilized world, fell victim to insult and utter destruction" (τὰ δὲ μεγάλα καὶ κατὰ πᾶσαν τὴν οἰκουμένην περιβόητα βασίλεια πρὸς ὕβριν καὶ παντελῆ φθορὰν ἀπεδέδεικτο). This is probably just carelessness on his part. On the Persepolis treasury, see Cahill 1985; cf. Sancisi-Weerdenburg 1993.

80. Curt. 5.6.9-10.

81. Curt. 5.6.12: *ipse cum mille equitibus peditumque expedita manu interiorem Persidis regionem sub ipsum Vergiliarum sidus petiit.*

82. Not the Mardians who lived near the Caspian and stole Bucephalas (on which see below).

We are told of "fields devastated and many villages reduced" [83] but not much more. Perhaps it was when he returned that Alexander appointed Phrasaortes as satrap of Persis.[84] He was now ready for his final act of "vengeance," which must have occurred just before his departure from the city in May.

The sack of Persepolis was but a part of the Conqueror's program. Virtually spontaneous, it satisfied the troops' need for gratification at the end of a long campaign. In fact, it was not more than four months since the great battle at Gaugamela. A month's rest in Babylon had been welcome, but there had been no rewards in terms of plunder in that city or at Susa. Nevertheless, the grand display of Panhellenic victory was still to come. Persepolis had come to symbolize the greatness and wealth of the empire and had been built in the late sixth century to assert the power of the Achaemenid rulers. Diodorus considered it worthy of description:

> I do not think it inappropriate to give a brief account of the palace area in this city in view of the magnificence of its architecture. Its remarkable citadel is encompassed by a triple wall, the first part of which was built on an elaborate substructure and is sixteen cubits high with battlements. The second is just like the one just described but twice its height. The third wall around it is four-sided in shape, sixty cubits high, and built of stone that is solid and by its nature long-lasting. Each one of its sides has bronze gates and beside them bronze stakes twenty cubits in height—these are fashioned to attract attention, while the gates are for ensuring safety.
>
> In the area four plethra east of the citadel lies the so-called Royal Hill, in which the kings' graves were to be found. This was a hollowed-out rock with numerous chambers in its center in which lay the sepulchers of the dead kings. There is no way that this can be effected by hand; they receive their burials when the corpses are lifted by some mechanical implements.[85] Around this palace area were many rich quarters for the royal family and for military commanders, and storehouses well constructed for safeguarding the royal treasure. (Diod. 17.71.3-8)

---

83. Curt. 5.6.17: *vastatis inde agris Persidis vicisque compluribus redactis.*

84. Perhaps the son of that Rheomithres who fought at the Granicus and died at Issus (Diod. 17.19.4, 34.5; Arr. 1.12.8; 2.11.8; Curt. 3.11.10). For his appointment as satrap: Arr. 3.18.11. Polyaenus, *Strat.* 4.3.27, mistakenly places him in charge of the defenders at the Persian Gates.

85. The Greek here is very obscure and the translation by no means certain.

But his observations fall far short of capturing the true splendor and the visual imagery that impressed local and foreigner alike. Access to the great hall (*apadana*), which could hold up to 10,000 people, was facilitated by a double stairway, leading to the hall built in the reign of Xerxes. This led to the "Gate of All Nations," where the various subject peoples of the empire brought tribute to the Great King. The entrance was guarded by giant bulls (or bull-like creatures) modeled on those of the Assyrian palaces. To the left of the *apadana* was the "Hall of 100 Columns" (the Throne Hall) and behind that the treasury. Directly behind the *apadana* were the palaces of Darius, Xerxes, and Artaxerxes I—three separate structures—and to their left the quarters of the royal harem. Ceilings and doors were made of cedar, fitted with bronze hardware, and walls were decorated with paintings and luxurious curtains. But these were the areas most susceptible to fire and vandalism. The symbols of power and the luxury (some would say decadence) of the structure invited desecration in retribution for the crimes of previous kings.

In the interval between unleashing the troops on the city and his return from the campaign in the interior of Persis, Alexander put his men to work on the task of preparing for the transport of the city's treasures to Susa:

> Wishing to take some of the money with him for war expenditures, and to deposit some in Susa and have it guarded in that city, Alexander sent for a number of mules from Babylon and Mesopotamia, and also from Susa (some pack animals and some yoked in pairs, plus 3,000 pack camels), and with these transported everything to the places of his choosing. He was very annoyed with the inhabitants and mistrusted them, and he was intent on destroying Persepolis entirely. (Diod. 17.71.2-3)

This process would have required laborers of various sorts, supervisors, drivers, and, most of all, guards—for there was risk of looting from both the native population and soldiers themselves. And there was further delay as they awaited the camels and other pack animals. When this process was complete and the convoy had been dispatched, the Conqueror turned his attention to the victory ceremony. In Babylon, this had taken the form of a grand procession, but there the city had been spared the outrages of the troops. Here there were games to celebrate the success of the campaign, with banquets and public sacrifices. And in the course of one of these banquets, a seemingly spontaneous—though almost certainly rehearsed—call for "vengeance" was answered and acted out in dramatic fashion:

> While his companions were being well entertained, with the carousing in full swing and drunkenness well advanced, madness took hold of the inebriates' minds. One of the women present—her name was Thaïs, and she was of Attic stock—said to Alexander that if he conducted a *komos* with them and set fire to the palace, and if it were women's hands that in a brief moment blotted out the famed achievements of the Persians, that would be for Alexander the finest of his achievements in Asia. This being said to young men who were high with drunkenness, somebody, as could be expected, shouted out that they should hold the *komos* and light torches, and he encouraged them to exact vengeance for the unconscionable action taken against the temples of the Greeks. Others raised a chorus of applause and declared that this act was the prerogative of Alexander, and when the king was also excited by the declaration they all jumped up from their drinking and cried out for the victory *komos* in honor of Dionysus.
>
> A number of torches were swiftly gathered, and as there had been singing girls invited to the drinking party, the king led them out for the *komos* accompanied by singing and the music of flutes and panpipes, with the hetaira Thaïs leading the event. After the king, she was the first to hurl her blazing torch into the palace. When the others did the same the entire area around the palace went up in flames because of the intensity of the fire. The most amazing thing of all was that the sacrilegious act of the Persian king Darius at the acropolis of Athens was, many years after that event, avenged with the same agonies—and in fun—by one woman, a fellow citizen of those who had suffered it. (Diod. 17.72)

The role of the Athenian courtesan was, of course, a double insult—and so it was intended to be. Not only were the Persian palaces reduced to rubble by an Athenian, in return for Xerxes' destruction of the temples on the acropolis, but by a woman—a woman of ill repute, for that matter.[86] But since the woman in question was—or was to become—the mistress of the later king of Egypt, Ptolemy, many scholars have believed that he was responsible for omitting her role in the affair from his own history.[87] What was regarded by Callisthenes as a just conclusion to the Panhellenic War was viewed by one of Alexander's closest

---

86. Diod. 17.72.6; Rehork 1969.

87. The other side of the argument is that Cleitarchus, writing in Alexandria, would have given offense by including the story of Thaïs. But it is not at all certain that Cleitarchus wrote in

companions as a personal embarrassment. Her role in the affair was not invented. Rather, it was deliberately suppressed. And we must bear in mind that no matter how sensational the "official" account was, it represented what the victor wanted the Greek world to believe. For reasons of propaganda, the role of Thaïs suited the Conqueror and his historian, even if Ptolemy chose to deny it for personal reasons.

The position of the Persians is hard to recover, owing to the bias of the sources. But it is impossible to give honor to the defenders who had no recourse but to accept the indignities of the conquerors. Hostility must surely have existed—both before and after the sack of Persepolis—and anti-Macedonian traditions developed after the fact, primarily in the age of the Sassanid Persians who saw themselves as the heirs of the Achaemenids.[88] But in truth, we can say little about organized resistance, which did not manifest itself—at least, not in any way that caught the attention of the Greek historians—at this time.

The burning of the palace was deliberate, though it was meant to seem like a spontaneous act. That the king regretted his actions later is not unlikely. If it was a battle for hearts and souls, it was one he could not win. He was unable to please the Greeks without offending the Persians, and to spare the latter would be to deny the legitimacy of the League of Corinth and his campaign. Diodorus' comments about Alexander's intention to destroy the city utterly are at odds with his comment about the burning of the palace being done "in fun." Curtius ends his account with a reminder that Persepolis was "the birthplace of so many kings, once the special terror of Greece, a city that built a fleet of a thousand ships, and armies by which Europe was flooded."[89] The play had been acted out, and what seemed to be its final act was the great spectacle at Persepolis. Legend maintained that the Pythian priestess (of Delphi) had prophesied that the Conqueror would

---

Ptolemy's lifetime or that Ptolemy was troubled by the role of his mistress. Thaïs was the mother of three children by Ptolemy: Lagus, Leontiscus and Eirene. She lived with him in Egypt, but there is no record of what became of her. She may even have been Alexander's mistress at the time of the burning of the palace. We cannot be certain. Thaïs: Heckel 262; Ager 2018, 39–40.

88. See Balcer 1978. On attitudes toward Alexander in the Sassanid period and onward, see Stoneman 2008, 43. Venetis 2012, 149, writes: "It must not be considered a coincidence that many centuries later (ninth century CE), the Pahlavi sources, reflecting fully the Zoroastrian tradition, also created a negative profile for Alexander. As these sources were compiled much later and had a strong element of fable, they cannot be considered historically reliable. Nevertheless, they probably reflect the beginnings of an older tradition, literary or oral, dealing with Alexander's policy toward Zoroastrianism." Venetis does not, however, even hint at what this policy might have been.

89. Curt. 5.7.8.

be led into Persia by a wolf (*lykos*); more prosaic was the role of the Lycian guide, who received a reward of thirty talents.[90] But by now, the melting of the winter snows opened the roads to the north, where the elusive Darius threatened to bring his enemy to battle one more time.

90. Lycian guide: Curt. 5.7.12. The Delphic prophecy: Plut. *Alex.* 37.1-2.

10

The End of Darius III

OF THE GREAT host that accompanied Darius to Gaugamela, only a fraction remained with him at Ecbatana, where he attempted to assemble an army once again. There were many who had been killed and captured, even if the excessive numbers given by the Alexander historians do not inspire confidence.[1] Some contingents melted away as their satrapies were annexed by the Macedonian conqueror; demoralized and concerned for their families and property, they laid down their arms as their leaders made peace. But those from territories as yet unconquered either fled homeward or remained with their satrapal units determined to fight again. Virtually all, the Great King included, knew that the end was near, and it was now a struggle for survival. They might hope that fortune, which had hitherto abandoned them, would finally show favor, but the bravest longed for an honorable death in a noble cause.

I

In an empire where the king's word was law and even the voicing of an opposing opinion was perilous,[2] the military leadership was divided on the future course of action. Failure tarnished the most powerful leader, especially the one chosen by their god as protector of his people. And of those who remained in the Persian camp, Artabazus and his sons, scions of the royal house, were among the most faithful, as concerned for the future of the empire as for their own advantage. The only account of the debates and decisions at Darius' court comes from Curtius, and it is heavily dramatized and colored by Roman imperial intrigue. Hence, it

---

1. Casualties: 300,000 dead and more captured (Arr. 3.15.6); 90,000 dead (Diod. 17.61.3); 40,000 dead (Curt. 4.16.26); 53,000 dead (*P.Oxy.* 1798).

2. Cf. the case of Charidemus, discussed in chapter 5.

In the Path of Conquest. Waldemar Heckel, Oxford University Press (2020). © Oxford University Press.
DOI: 10.1093/oso/9780190076689.001.0001

is hard to draw the line between truth and imagination, even though the historical background (and, indeed, the military dilemma) against which the events
unfolded is depicted in a way that strikes us as plausible. In the final days, Darius
was challenged by his kinsman Bessus and a cabal of accomplices. Bessus was to
become the villain of the story, and as a result, a more sympathetic view of Darius
emerges.[3]

The question was simple: should the Persians make a last stand in Media,
hopeful that they could yet augment their numbers with reinforcements from
the east? The true size of Darius' forces is uncertain: Curtius says he had 30,000
infantry (of whom 4,000 were Greek mercenaries), 4,000 slingers, and 3,300 cavalry, the last under the command of Bessus; Arrian claims that there were only
6,000 infantry and 3,000 cavalry,[4] thus explaining the Great King's apprehension
concerning what Alexander would do next. Darius was apparently intent on remaining closer to the center of the empire (a sensible approach), and therefore
he waited in Ecbatana, uncertain whether Alexander would stay in Persepolis
or move north. His opponents had no faith in the strategy, the numbers, or the
king's leadership. Hence, it was with reluctance that he made the decision to
withdraw into Central Asia. When he learned that the invader was on the move,
Darius sent ahead in the direction of the Caspian Gates (Sar-i-Darreh Pass) the
harmamaxai, the covered wagons that carried the women, and the other royal
impedimenta. But even the decision to move eastward was regarded as insufficient, at least, as long as Darius remained as commander-in-chief. As the enemy
approached, Darius himself abandoned the Median capital. When Alexander was
three days from that city, he was met by Bisthanes, a son of Artaxerxes III Ochus,
who told him that Darius had left four days earlier.[5] The Conqueror pushed on to
Ecbatana, where he dismissed the Thessalian cavalry and the Greek allies. Most
of these regarded the Panhellenic crusade as concluded after the fall of Persepolis.
The attitude of the troops toward the war would become a problem in the coming

---

3. See Heckel 2018b, 100–101; cf. Rzepka 2009.

4. Numbers: Curt. 5.8.3-4 (cf. Diod. 17.73.2); 3.19.5. Curt. 5.8.4 says that Bessus' cavalry were
primarily Parthyaeans (*maxime Parthienorum*). This, at least, is the manuscript reading, which
Froben emended to *Bactrianorum*, and the emendation has been generally accepted (see
Atkinson II 137). Whatever the value of the paleographical arguments, the emendation draws
attention away from Arrian's interesting (but equally mistaken) remark that Darius' death in
Parthyaea was in Bessus' satrapy (3.21.5).

5. Arr. 3.19.4-5. Bisthanes was probably the son of a concubine, since Arses was said to have been
the only son of Ochus to survive Bagoas' purge. At any rate, his failure to challenge Darius' legitimacy, even in his final days, suggests that his own claim was not a strong one. Heckel 72;
Berve II 109 no. 215; Bosworth I 335.

month. But for the moment, it was not in the forefront of Alexander's mind, since the pursuit of Darius required a smaller, more mobile force.[6]

The fleeing king's route took him south of the Caspian Sea along the road that led between the Great Salt Desert on the south and the Elburz Mountains to the north. On the other side, these mountains sloped to the Caspian, forming the region of Hyrcania; its satrap continued on in the company of Darius.[7] The path led through the Caspian Gates and into Parthyaea. Any thoughts that Darius had of torching the land as he fled were abandoned under the relentless pressure of Alexander's pursuit.[8] To secure the territory behind him, Alexander assigned Paraetacene to Oxathres son of Abulites and instructed the bulk of his army to proceed at a slower pace, subduing those who continued to hold out and foraging for provisions.[9]

II

Having abandoned all hope of marshaling an army in Media, Darius was forced to flee to the satrapies of the very men who had become disillusioned with his military leadership and aspired to the kingship. In order to understand the Great King's predicament in the last months of his life, we must consider once again the origins of his power, as well as the relationship he had (or had developed) with the Persian aristocracy.

It is regularly noted that Darius' legitimacy was called into question; he was not in the direct line of descent from Artaxerxes III, being instead a grandson of Ostanes, a brother of Artaxerxes II. The bloodline of their parents, Darius II and Parysatis, was itself less than impressive, for both husband and wife were children of Babylonian concubines, if the evidence of Ctesias is credible.[10] But Artaxerxes II strengthened his position by marriage to Stateira, a member of the Hydarnid family and thus descended from the Seven. In comparison, the credentials of

---

6. Curt. 5.13.1-2 says that Alexander, on learning the news, changed his line of march, apparently bypassing Ecbatana. This seems highly unlikely. See Arr. 3.19.5 for the dismissal of the allied troops. Cf. Brunt I 529: "Media lay on the most direct route to the Mediterranean, via Babylon but bypassing Susa and Persepolis." For the vexed question of march rates by Alexander's army, see Milns 1966; Neumann 1971. Comparative data are useful but can also be misleading, since not all geographical and climatic factors are the same. Thessalian cavalry: Strootman 2010/2011.

7. Seibert 1985, 114: "die einzige Landbrücke nach Osten."

8. Darius' plan to devastate Hyrcania and Parthyaea as he fled: Arr. 3.19.1.

9. Oxathres' appointment: Arr. 3.19.2. Parmenion was sent to Hyrcania, moving past the country of the Cadusians (3.19.7); Cleitus was to follow on into Parthyaea (3.19.8).

10. Ctesias, *FGrH* 688 F15.

Ostanes and his children were weak.[11] Furthermore, Darius III had been placed on the throne through the machinations of Bagoas. Stories of his single combat with a Cadusian champion—we cannot say whether they are true—were thus intended to give luster to an otherwise unaccomplished ruler. Nevertheless, legitimacy in this case was relative—the pun is unavoidable. Who, we must ask, had a better claim to the throne? Bisthanes, a son of Ochus, was probably the son of a concubine and even less acceptable to the Persians. And certainly, neither Darius nor Alexander felt in any way threatened by his lineage.[12]

Bessus, the satrap of Bactria, was apparently an Achaemenid,[13] but the limited support he received after Darius' death suggests that he was not acceptable to most of the Iranian nobles. Curtius' claim that Darius feared him, since he was thought to aspire to the kingship, merely retrojects later events into the past.[14] Those who remained with him, even before he assumed the upright tiara, belonged for the most part to the eastern satrapies, and their primary concern was for their own territories, thus far untouched by the conquest. These included the very men who were directly involved in Darius' murder: Satibarzanes, who governed Aria and thus the approaches to Gandhāra, and Barsaentes, whose satrapy of Drangiana gave access to India via the Bolan and Mullah passes. Others who supported him, at least temporarily, were the barons of Bactria and Sogdiana. If Diodorus may be taken literally, Bessus had been made satrap of Bactria by Darius himself, perhaps

---

11. Arsanes appears to have married his sister Sisygambis (although we do not know if they had the same mother; cf. the case of Darius and his sister-wife Stateira). For the family, see Neuhaus 1902.

12. Arr. 3.19.4; Berve II 109 no. 215; Heckel 72; Bosworth I 335. Arr. 1.16.3 records the death of Arbupales, a grandson of Artaxerxes II. His father was Darius, who had been Artaxerxes' designated heir (Plut. *Artox.* 26–29); since Arbupales posed no threat to Darius III, we may assume that he, too, was illegitimate.

13. Satrap of Bactria: Arr. 3.8.3; Curt. 4.6.2; Diod. 17.73.2; but Arr. 3.21.5 wrongly says that the arrest of Darius in Parthyaea occurred in Bessus' satrapy. Arr. 3.21.5 speaks of his kinship (οἰκειότης) with Darius; he was not simply a member of the group known as the συγγενεῖς. But see Briant, *HPE* 781: "Bessus had family ties (*oikeiotēs*) to Darius—though even this word can mean 'ties of familiarity'." (On *syggeneis* see also Briant, *HPE* 309–10). On the other hand, Bosworth I, 343 notes that his kinship with Darius probably explains the fact that his leadership appears uncontested. For Bessus' career see Heckel 71–72; Berve II, 105–108 no. 212.

14. Curt. 4.6.4 says that when Darius summoned troops before the battle of Gaugamela, "Bessus alarmed the king: his loyalty was suspect, and he was restless in his position as second-in-command; he had regal ambitions, and treason was feared on his part since it was his only way to fulfill them" (*Sed Bessus, suspecta perfidia haud sane aequo animo in secundo se continens gradu, regem terrebat; nam cum regnum affectaret, proditio, qua sola id adsequi poterat, timebatur*). Holt 1988, 45 n. 137, rightly notes that this may be a "rhetorical device to set the stage for Bessus' later treachery."

as part of an administrative shuffle that accompanied his accession.[15] Ironically, his authority and legitimacy were based on the very king whose title he usurped.

Darius appears to have made his peace with certain powerful families in the west and center of the empire. Among these were satraps of Asia Minor and Syria, along with the former ruler of the Dascyleum satrapy (Hellespontine Phrygia), Artabazus. Of the rulers of Asia Minor, most had perished at the Granicus or Issus. Mazaeus, who had long been associated with Cilicia and Syria, stayed with the king and served with distinction at Gaugamela. But in the aftermath of that defeat, he surrendered himself and Babylon to the Conqueror. Artabazus, although removed from his ancestral lands, remained faithful, despite Darius' precautions against him rather than on account of them. The rulers of the Caspian area— Phrataphernes and Autophradates—also continued to support their sovereign after Gaugamela.

Once he left Ecbatana, Darius was virtually a king in exile. He still controlled vast expanses of territory in the east, but he had abandoned his palaces, the bulk of his treasures, and the Iranian heartland. Twice he had suffered defeat; twice he had fled from the battlefield. His military options were limited, and although there was ample manpower to draw on in Central Asia, he was now a desperate man who had failed in his primary duty to his people. Whatever the true motives were of those who arrested and eventually killed him, it is clear that they were driven as much by desperation and the will to survive as by prospects of personal gain. They were, however, branded as traitors by the Conqueror who was laying claim to the kingship of Asia and, no longer the avenger of Greece (*ultor Graeciae*), the champion of the institution of kingship.

Most prominent among the "traitors," after Bessus, were the chiliarch Nabarzanes and Barsaentes (satrap of Arachosia and Drangiana). Meeting with Darius and his advisers, Nabarzanes is alleged to have made a speech in which he recommended that Darius temporarily turn over his authority to another. The obvious candidate, he claimed, was Bessus, since Bactria was still intact and the neighboring Indians and Sacae could be relied on to support them: "Let us appoint Bessus, the satrap of the area, as temporary king, and when the issue is settled he will return to you, the legitimate king, the command he has held in trust."[16] The Roman reader would have understood the logic of such a plan, familiar with the practice of appointing a dictator in a time of crisis. To the Persians such a proposal would have been unheard of and its mere utterance an act of

---

15. Diod. 17.73.1: ἀποδεδειγμένος δὲ ταύτης σατράπης ὑπὸ Δαρείου.

16. Curt. 5.9.8.

treason.[17] That Bessus and Nabarzanes announced their plan, contriving to veil treachery with pragmatism, defies credulity. But the reader is, at least, given an insight into the breakdown of Persian authority and the desperate nature of the situation.

III

Rejecting the substance of the debates among the Persian nobles as reported by the vulgate sources on the grounds that "what was actually said within the small circle of nobles around him [i.e., Darius] could never be known,"[18] one historian offers a novel "suggestion" concerning the conspiracy, which he immodestly asserts "covers all the known facts as no other does."[19] He believes that "the conspiracy had begun at Ecbatana and that Darius, who did not want to continue the hopeless war (there is no explanation for his inaction during seven months at Ecbatana) was already virtually a prisoner of those who did when they left Ecbatana."[20] In short, and in defiance of all credulity, the Great King planned to surrender to Alexander, and this the conspirators were anxious to prevent. They placed him in chains because "there was a danger that Darius might escape in order to surrender."[21] Now, despite the fact that such fantasies cry out to be ignored, they do nonetheless raise issues that are illuminated by the obvious counterarguments. First of all, if it was Darius' intention to surrender

---

17. It has, however, been construed as a "substitute king" ritual (Nylander 1993, 152 and 159 n. 80; cf. Müller 2014, 224, who adds, "Danach sah das Ritual traditionell vor, dass der Ersatzkönig zur Neutralisierung des Unheils getötet wurde und die eigentliche Herrscher wieder die Regierung übernahm"). Such altruism seems uncharacteristic of Bessus, who was in other respects ruthless and ambitious. For the ritual, see Bottéro 1992, 138–55; Huber 2005, 157–59, 164. Hdt. 7.12-18 is similar but without dire consequences for the impersonator.

18. Badian 2000b, 262. Whatever information had "come (*demonstrably*) from the leader of the Greek mercenaries" (emphasis added) was indeed of little value, since he (that is, Patron) would have had no knowledge of these private discussions. But the most obvious person to inform Alexander and his official historian was Artabazus, who surrendered to the king soon after the events.

19. Badian 2000a, 85. I do not see how Badian's theory "covers the fact" that Arr. 3.19.3 says that Darius had decided to fight it out (presumably at Ecbatana) with the help of his Scythian and Cadusian allies. These allies did not arrive (3.19.4).

20. Badian 2000b, 262. The idea goes back, at least, to Rüegg 1906, 80: "Alle diese Ereignisse lassen sich nur so erklären, dass Dareios, des Kampfes müde, sich Alexander ergeben wollte."

21. Badian 2000b, 262. Arr. 3.21.5 says that "those who had seized Darius had decided, if they learned that Alexander was pursuing them, to give him up to Alexander and make good terms for themselves." But an accommodation with Alexander (i.e., surrender) is precisely what Badian claims the conspirators wanted to avoid.

that cost him his life, would it not have been to the Conqueror's advantage to have his historians report that Darius was set to recognize the superiority and the authority of his adversary, that he was prepared to bring the campaign to a peaceful conclusion and allow Alexander to make a display of magnanimity? Second, the conspirators themselves stood to gain from such an outcome, especially since it was already clear that the Conqueror was prepared to allow local governors to retain their positions. By arresting and killing Darius, they were not only committing themselves to a lost cause but were also putting themselves on the wrong side of the legal and moral debate, and thus they squandered their prospects, turning a determined enemy into a ruthless avenger.

The fallout from their actions was not long in coming. Some of the "loyalists"— Bagisthanes the Babylonian and Antibelus, one of the sons of Mazaeus, along with the interpreter Melon[22]—defected as they were being overtaken by their pursuers. Even the most faithful of the Great King's supporters were powerless to prevent his fall—unless it proved expedient to deny participation in the coup after the fact.[23] Artabazus and his sons had been staunch supporters of Darius, and the old man did what he could to defuse the uprising in the camp. Unable to prevent Darius' arrest, he and his people took refuge in the Elburz Mountains and finally made submission to Alexander, who had reasons to treat them with leniency. During the early years of Artaxerxes III Ochus, Artabazus and his family—eleven sons and ten daughters, all born to the same mother—found refuge at the court of Philip II. His daughter, Barsine, widow of both Mentor and Memnon, was already Alexander's mistress when her father and brothers made their submission.[24]

---

22. Bagisthenes and the son of Mazaeus brought news of Darius' arrest: Arr. 3.21.1 (Bagisthanes and Antibelus); Curt. 5.13.3 (Bagisthanes), 13.7 (Melon), 13.11 (Brochubelus instead of Antibelus; for the problem of the name, see Bosworth I 341; Heckel 73 s.v. "Brochubelus"; Berve II 40 no. 82 s.v. Ἀντίβηλος). The presence of Mazaeus' son in Darius' camp long after the surrender of Babylon may indicate that the father was not burning any bridges. Curt. 5.13.9 mentions also Mithrazenes and Orsillos as supporters of Darius who defected from Bessus' camp. Melon had been left behind at Thara on account of illness (Curt. 5.13.7). See Heckel 161; Berve II 250 no. 496; Hofstetter 125 no. 214; Franke 1992, 91.

23. Thus, again, Badian 2000b, 262, remarks that "the Persian nobles, who joined Alexander after Darius' death . . . had their own, far from disinterested, stories to tell."

24. Supporter of Darius: Curt. 5.9.1; 5.9.12-13, 17; 5.10.10-11; 6.5.1. Flight of Artabazus: Curt. 5.12.18; Arr. 3.21.4. He surrendered in Hyrcania along with nine of his sons: Curt. 6.5.2-6; Arr. 3.23.7. Artabazus at Philip II's court: Diod. 16.52.4; he may have been one of the Persians "interrogated" by Alexander when he was a child (Plut. *Alex.* 5.1-3). Barsine: Curt. 3.13.14 (captured at Damascus by Parmenion); Justin 11.10.2-3 (Alexander's mistress); see also Brunt 1975 (against Tarn 1921) and Heckel 70. For her position at Alexander's court, see Carney 1996a, 572-76. Artabazos' relations with Alexander: Heckel 2018b.

Bessus led the fleeing rebels, though he had not yet laid claim to the king-ship.[25] Darius, in a miserable state, was conveyed in a covered wagon, some said in golden chains, as if this could mitigate the crime.[26] If the rebels truly believed they could exchange Darius for the Conqueror's mercy, they were sadly mistaken. Their crime had given Alexander the pretext he needed; having betrayed and arrested Darius, Bessus now allowed the Conqueror to play the role of avenger and defender of the dignity of kings.[27] That the Great King recognized and welcomed this is, of course, Greek fiction.[28]

Unable to shake off their pursuers, Bessus and his accomplices murdered Darius and left him by the roadside. This at least bought time for their escape.[29] That either Alexander or one of his men found him still breathing concludes the fiction of the changing relationship between the two men.[30] One of Alexander's men, who had stopped at a nearby spring, found the Persian king in his carriage, mortally wounded but still breathing. A captive of the Macedonians, who was a countryman of Darius, was brought onto the scene in order to translate the king's last words. The implausible set of circumstances—the presence of a captive "Persian" who just happened to know enough Greek to serve as an interpreter—provides us with good "theater," even if it defies credulity, and it allows Darius to note that his captured family received better treatment at the hands of an enemy

---

25. Arr. 3.21.4: Βήσσῳ δὲ ἀντὶ Δαρείου εἶναι τὸ κράτος καὶ ἡγεμόνα ὠνομάσθαι Βῆσσον. It is doubtful that he could have done so while Darius lived, and he still considered the possibility of handing the king over to Alexander (Arr. 3.21.5).

26. Curt. 5.12.20, with Atkinson II 153.

27. Justin 11.15.12. The importance of punishing the usurper as opposed to the regicide is spelled out in Justin 11.15.12: "As for revenge, the reason for exacting it was no longer just Darius; now it was a question of precedent and the common cause of all kings—and for Alexander to ignore this would be dishonorable as well as dangerous." Cf. Kaerst, *Hellenismus* I³ 416. Cf. King 2018, 162: "Bessus' mutiny and usurpation of the royal title . . . was a stroke of luck for Alexander, and quickly seizing the opportunity, by the act of throwing his own cloak over the murdered king's corpse, he metamorphosed from Darius' unrelenting foe into his lawful avenger."

28. Curt. 5.12.5: "none would be a more severe avenger or punisher of treason than Alexander" (*violatae fidei neminem acriorem fore vindicem ultoremque*).

29. Arr. 3.21.10 says that the murder was committed by Satibarzanes and Barsaentes and that they escaped with 600 horsemen. Since Bessus was later punished for the crime—and certainly for usurping royal power (Arr. 4.7.3: the charge was *prodosia*; Bosworth I 345 comments that perhaps "the actual assassination was not in Alexander's eyes an unpardonable crime")—the omission of his name is curious. It is possible that Satibarzanes is an error for Nabarzanes, but *Metz Epit.* 3 says that *Ario*barzanes "had joined Bessus to murder Darius." This would seem to support Arr. 3.21.10, but the epitomator also confuses Satibarzanes with Barsaentes.

30. Justin 12.5.11: "Alexander felt that Darius had been less his enemy than the 'friend' by whom the king had been assassinated."

than he had obtained from kinsmen and subjects. He now recognized Alexander as a worthy successor and avenger, speaking of "the common cause of all kings" and saying that "for Alexander to ignore this would be dishonorable as well as dangerous," since it was a matter of both justice and expediency.[31] At a time when the Panhellenic crusade had come to an end, he found new purpose and a claim to legitimacy, by posing as the avenger of his predecessor and the defender of the rights of kings.

IV

The murder of the Great King finalized the rift between those loyal to the crown and the supporters of Bessus. The political (perhaps even ideological) differences between them were already manifest in the separation of the army into two camps. For the one side, vengeance was impractical (if not impossible) for want of numbers; for the other, the flight left no time for coercion. The settlements made by Alexander with the remaining satraps deserve closer attention.

Atropates had commanded the Medes at Gaugamela and after the defeat remained with his king. Whether he surrendered to Alexander or continued on with the supporters of the regicides is unclear. He was not reinstated as satrap of Media until 328/7. In his place, Alexander appointed Oxydates, an enemy of Darius, who had imprisoned him in Susa.[32] It was a move he soon came to regret, for Oxydates proved to be rebellious or at least neglectful of his duties.[33]

Phrataphernes and Autophradates also made prompt surrender to the Conqueror, although in the case of the former, it may not have been prompt enough. Autophradates was retained as ruler of the Tapurians, probably on the basis of connections (either by family or *philia*) at the divided court of Darius.[34]

---

31. Justin 11.15.5-15.

32. Atropates: Heckel 61–62; Berve II 91–92 no. 180. His command at Gaugamela: Arr. 3.8.4. Oxydates installed as satrap: Arr. 3.20.3 (before Darius' death); Curt. 6.2.11 (afterward). Atropates' reinstatement: Arr. 4.18.1. The treatment of Mazaeus, Abulites, and Oxathres suggests that Alexander would not have replaced Atropates with Oxydates if he had surrendered earlier. Curiously, Arr. 3.20.3 says that Alexander trusted Oxydates on account of his opposition to Darius but later says he trusted Artabazus and his sons on account of their loyalty to the Great King (3.23.8); Brunt I 206 n. 5 rightly notes: "Al. rewards or punishes men for their conduct to Darius as it suits him." For Oxydates' brief administrative career, see Heckel 188; Berve II 293 no. 588; also Bosworth 1981 21. On the satraps of Media, see Hyland 2013.

33. See Bosworth 1981, 20–21, for the meaning of ἐθελοκακεῖν.

34. Curt. 5.4.24-25, 5.21. Autophradates surrendered at Zadracarta, the capital of Hyrcania (Arr. 3.23.7; Curt. 6.4.24-25 says Craterus and Erigyius arrested him). At Gaugamela, he had commanded the "Caspians" (thus Curt. 4.12.9; presumably the Tapurians). Alexander

Phrataphernes' reinstatement to full powers—he had been satrap of Hyrcania and Parthyaea—was delayed[35] as the king placed his trust in Amminapes, who had been in his entourage since the Egyptian campaign, where he had surrendered along with Mazaces.[36] The decision not to restore Phrataphernes immediately may have something to do with that man's relationship with Bessus, which was reported to Alexander by Artabazus. At best, Phrataphernes governed only Parthyaea until 328/7, when he was instructed to arrest Autophradates and assume control of the Mardians and the Tapurians. Since Phrataphernes was also awarded Hyrcania, we must assume that Amminapes had either died or incurred the king's disfavor—though possibly Autophradates, in his bid for greater power, had deposed (or even killed) him.[37]

We are told that when Arsaces—who, as we shall see, replaced Satibarzanes as satrap of Aria—was brought to Alexander at his winter quarters in central Asia, it was "along with Brazanes, whom Bessus had made satrap of Parthyaea,

later enlarged his administrative sphere to include the Mardians (3.24.3). He may have been a relative of his namesake of the 360s (cf. Weiskopf 1989, 43, speculative but sensible). The Phradates named by Curt. 4.12.9 as commander of Caspian troops is probably Autophradates, who appears at Curt. 8.3.17 as Phradates (cf. Arr. 4.18.2: <Αὐτο>φραδάτην). This rules out the assumption of Julien 1914, 34, that Autophradates ruled the satrapy in Phrataphernes' absence: "Da deren [i.e., the Tapurians] Satrap Autophradates nicht genannt wird, so kann man vielleicht vermuten, er habe auf die Dauer des Feldzuges dessen Vertretung in Parthien und Hyrkanien mit übernommen."

35. Phrataphernes commanded the Parthyaeans, Hyrcanians, and Tapurians at Gaugamela (Arr. 3.8.4; cf. Curt. 4.12.11).

36. Curt. 6.4.25.

37. Arrian (3.22.1) makes Amminapes satrap of both Hyrcania and Parthyaea, indicating that this occurred before Phrataphernes' surrender (3.23.4). Arrian may be wrong in assigning both Parthyaea and Hyrcania to Amminapes; possibly his jurisdiction was limited to Hyrcania soon afterward when Phrataphernes was allowed to resume control over Parthyaea (although this seems odd in view of the fact that Amminapes was himself a Parthyaean); or else Arrian refers to Phrataphernes as satrap of Parthyaea prematurely. Phrataphernes appears in 330 in the company of Erigyius, Caranus, and Artabazus in Aria, and at that time he is called "satrap of Parthyaea" (Arr. 3.28.3: Φραταφέρνην τὸν τῶν Παρθυαίων σατράπην). He next appears at Bactra (Zariaspa), along with Stasanor, in the winter of 329/8, bringing in chains Barzanes (Brazanes), "whom Bessus had made satrap of Parthyaea" (Arr. 4.7.1); once again, he is described as "satrap of Parthyaea." Arrian (4.18.1) then says that when Alexander was wintering in Nautaca (328/7), Phrataphernes, "satrap of Parthyaea," came with Stasanor "after carrying out all Alexander's orders." From there he was sent to the Mardians and Tapurians to arrest Autophradates, who had refused to come when he was summoned by Alexander (Arr. 4.18.2). Curtius (7.10.11-12) mentions those who joined Alexander over the winter (329/8) in Bactra and names only Ptolemy and Melanidas (Melamnidas), as well as Asander from Lycia (i.e., Lydia) and Asclepiodorus from Syria. Full discussion in Heckel 2018b.

and others who had revolted with Bessus."[38] This Brazanes (or Barzanes) is otherwise unknown, and it appears that Arrian's text is corrupt.[39] The prisoner in question is almost certainly Nabarzanes. That man was one of Darius' highest officials, the "chiliarch of the cavalry."[40] He betrayed his king, along with Bessus and Barsaentes, and was involved in his arrest and (apparently) his murder.[41] When Bessus fled in the direction of Bactria, he turned over the satrapies of Hyrcania and Parthyaea (which were linked administratively) to Nabarzanes;[42] its rightful governor, Phrataphernes, as we have seen, did not recover his territories immediately. The resistance of the Hyrcanians was sufficient, at least, to warrant a Macedonian move in the direction of the Caspian; that of the Mardians, who could melt away into the mountains, was more determined.[43] These people, like the Cossaeans and Uxians, lived by brigandage, more concerned with personal gain than the fate of the empire. It was their misfortune that they unwittingly stole Alexander's horse Bucephalas. Nabarzanes himself, recognizing the hopelessness of his position, sought Alexander's forgiveness, claiming that he had acted in the Persians' best interests and, even then, was swept up in the actions of another. Trusting in the king's clemency, he brought with him the eunuch Bagoas, a favorite of the Great King. He not only won over the Macedonian king with his charms but also secured a reprieve for Nabarzanes.[44]

---

38. Arr. 4.7.1. But see also Arr. 4.18.1; Curt. 8.3.17 says Phrataphernes brought "Phradates" in chains to Alexander, meaning Autophradates the satrap of the Tapurians.

39. This is often the case when he summarizes material. See, for example, 1.14.2-3; 3.5.5-6; 4.7.2 "Bessus, satrap of Syria"; 6.27.1-3; *Ind.* 18.3.

40. Arr. 3.21.1: χιλίαρχος τῶν ἱππέων.

41. As noted above, Arr. 3.21.10, naming the regicides, speaks of Satibarzanes rather than Nabarzanes.

42. Hyrcania and Parthyaea linked administratively: Strabo 11.9.1-2 C514; Julien 1914, 34–36. Nabarzanes' position under Bessus: Curt. 5.13.8; cf. 6.3.9. Arrian's remark Βραζάνην, ὅντινα Βῆσσος τῆς Παρθυαίων σατράπην κατέστησε (4.7.1) shows that we are most likely dealing with <Na>barzanes. Bosworth 1981, 21, speaks of Parthyaea as "menaced by the enemy in Bactria," as if "Barzanes"—whom he regards as a separate individual (cf. *CE* 238)—had been sent from there by Bessus. Diod. 17.74.1 does say that "Bessus . . . with Nabarnes [*sic*] and Barxaës [*sic*] and many others eluded the hands of Alexander and got through to Bactriana" (Βῆσσος . . . μετὰ Ναβάρνου καὶ Βαρξάεντος καὶ πολλῶν ἄλλων διαφυγὼν τὰς Ἀλεξάνδρου χεῖρας διήνυσε μὲν εἰς τὴν Βακτριανήν). But this is probably an inaccurate generalization.

43. Alexander's dealings with the Mardians: Arr. 3.24.1-3. Alexander showed too much trust in Autophradates, who was given the Mardians in addition to the Tapurians as his administrative unit (Arr. 3.24.3; Curt. 6.5.21). Arrian says nothing about the Mardian theft of Bucephalas. See Curt. 6.5.11-21; Diod. 17.76.3-8; Plut. *Alex.* 44.3-5.

44. Curt. 6.6.22-23. On this episode, see Badian 1958, 144–46.

But Nabarzanes found himself without political or military office. He might have been content with the sparing of his life were it not for the honors he saw heaped upon other nobles who had surrendered. In the end, when the invader advanced into central Asia, he rebelled once again and thus came to be arrested by Phrataphernes.[45] Although it is not specifically stated, there is reason to believe that Nabarzanes was executed in Bactria.

How and why certain Persian nobles were treated as they were by the Conqueror is a question that is seldom considered—though there are those who regard Alexander's orientalizing policies as a sham, motivated by expediency but hardly sincere. To understand the Conqueror's true—as opposed to stated—motives, we would have to know what was in his mind. And this we cannot do. Nevertheless, we can get some insight into some of the decisions made by Alexander as he established his new order. Why was there a hiccup in the career of Phrataphernes, a man who proved himself so loyal to his successive masters that he still held office in the early age of the Successors? Why did Nabarzanes transition from conspirator to suppliant to rebel in a short period of time? And what was behind the rebellion and the deposing of Autophradates? The answers to the question *why* may be found if we ask ourselves *who* might have been behind all this. The explanations are sure to follow.

The sources are not entirely in agreement concerning the exact point at which each of the former supporters of Darius submitted to Alexander.[46] But we do know that Phrataphernes, Autophradates, and Artabazus surrendered to the Conqueror in or near Hyrcania at roughly the same time. Hence, the new satrapal appointments must reflect not so much the order of surrender as Alexander's attitude toward these individuals. The same must apply to the appointment of Amminapes. This man, if it is permissible to create a composite

---

45. Phrataphernes: see Heckel 223; Berve II 400–401 no. 814. Arr. 4.7.1 and 4.18.1 could be clumsy doublets, but they describe the events of different years. It appears that in 329, Phrataphernes arrested Nabarzanes and that in 328, he was sent to arrest Autophradates and assume his administrative functions, as well as those of Amminapes.

46. Curtius and Arrian disagree about the order in which the satraps surrendered. Curtius reports that Alexander was met by Phrataphernes, who submitted to the king's authority (Curt. 6.4.23) and that Craterus and Erigyius brought in Phradates (that is, Autophradates: Curt. 6.4.24, *praefectus Tapurorum gentis*); after that, the satrapy of Hyrcania was given to Amminapes, and the rule of the Tapurians was restored to Autophradates (Curt. 6.4.25). Arrian reports the appointment of Amminapes as satrap of the Parthyaeans and Hyrcanians (Arr. 3.22.1, appointment of Amminapes: σατράπην δὲ ἀπέδειξε Παρθυαίων καὶ Ὑρκανίων Ἀμμινάπην Παρθυαῖον), followed by the surrender of Nabarzanes and Phrataphernes, adding nothing further about their positions (i.e., as far as we know, they were given no rewards at the time; Arr. 3.23.4); Autophradates surrendered together with Artabazus and his sons and was allowed to retain his satrapy (Arr. 3.23.7), to which the Mardians were added (Arr. 3.24.3).

picture from the evidence of Arrian and Curtius,[47] was himself a Parthyaean. He had been an exile at Philip's court during the reign of Artaxerxes III Ochus, and he, along with Mazaces, had surrendered Egypt to Alexander. Hence, it is very likely that Amminapes was known to, and on friendly terms with, Artabazus.[48] Autophradates too appears to have belonged to a family that had associations with Artabazus in the middle of the fourth century.[49] He was reinstated as satrap of the Tapurians immediately after his surrender, and the Mardians were placed under his rule not much later.[50] By contrast, Phrataphernes, despite the fact that he had not betrayed Darius,[51] remained in Alexander's entourage and without an administrative post. Interestingly, Autophradates is said to have joined Alexander in the company of Artabazus and his sons, whereas Phrataphernes arrived only slightly earlier, along with Nabarzanes. Neither was rewarded at the time.[52] Alexander can have known little about them except from someone with knowledge of their actions.[53] That person was undoubtedly Artabazus, who continued to wield influence with the Conqueror, holding military commands in Aria and

47. The details are not mutually exclusive. Arr. 3.22.1: he surrendered Egypt and was assigned both Hyrcania and Parthyaea. Curt. 6.4.25 (calling him Manapis): he had been in exile and received Hyrcania. Whether the omission of Parthyaea is deliberate or an oversight we cannot say.

48. Despite his apparent trustworthiness, his actions were supervised by the Macedonian Tlepolemus (Arr. 3.22.1: Τληπόλεμος . . . ξυνετάχθη αὐτῷ σκοπεῖν τὰ ἐν Παρθυαίοις τε καὶ Ὑρκανίοις).

49. In fact, both attested men of that name (the other was the admiral, who was clearly acquainted with Artabazus' family; see Heckel 65 s.v. "Autophradates [1]") may have been related to the Autophradates of the so-called Satraps' Revolt.

50. Arr. 3.23.7; Curt. 6.4.25. Mardians: Arr. 3.24.3.

51. Arr. 3.23.7 says that Alexander honored Artabazus and his sons for reasons that included their loyalty to Darius (Ἀρτάβαζον δὲ καὶ τοὺς παῖδας ἅμα οἱ ἐν τιμῇ ἦγε, τά τε ἄλλα ἐν τοῖς πρώτοις Περσῶν ὄντας καὶ τῆς ἐς Δαρεῖον πίστεως ἕνεκα). Brunt I 306 n. 5 calls this "naïve," but Curtius also goes to great lengths to emphasize Artabazus' loyalty; cf. also Arr. 3.21.4. Badian 2000a, 82–83, has doubts about his reliability and says that the presence of so many members of Artabazus' family who appear to have been hostages at the time of Issus "strongly suggests that Artabazus, one of the most distinguished Persian nobles, had been left behind in charge of affairs at the centre, and that his loyalty consequently had to be ensured at whatever cost in delay to the expedition."

52. Phrataphernes, Nabarzanes, and other prominent Persians: Arr. 3.23.4. Artabazus and his sons, along with Autophradates: Arr. 3.23.7. Curtius has them arriving separately (6.4.8-14, 5.22-23: Nabarzanes; 6.4.23: Phrataphernes).

53. Badian 2000a, 83–84, believes that Artabazus had remained "in charge of affairs at the centre" at the time of Issus but was replaced by Nabarzanes during the Gaugamela campaign. This might suggest some animosity between the two men—although this is not needed if there is any truth to their relative positions during Darius' last days (Curt. 5.9-10, 5.12.7-15)—but Nabarzanes' presence in Ecbatana and beyond points to the fact that he was at Gaugamela, even though the sources fail to name him.

Bactria and ruling the latter as satrap of Bactria.[54] His daughter was already in favor, and his sons appear to have shared Alexander's goodwill.[55] But it is curious, and surely significant, that the decline of Artabazus and his family coincides very closely with Amminapes' disappearance, the arrest of Autophradates, and the restoration of Phrataphernes' full powers.

The drama that concluded with the death of Darius and the discovery of his body appeared to signal "mission accomplished"[56] to many of those who served Alexander in the Panhellenic crusade—Greeks and Macedonians alike. If they had been wrong to see Persepolis as the conclusion of the war, surely now that Darius was dead, there could be little doubt. In truth, the struggle against the invader was far from over.

---

54. Military commands: Curt. 7.3.2; 8.1.10; Arr. 3.23.9, 28.2-3; 4.16.2-3. Satrap of Bactria: Arr. 3.29.1; 4.15.5; Curt. 7.5.1, 11.29. Artabazus was able to influence not only the king but his historians as well, and the claim that he relinquished his satrapy voluntarily may be intended to put a good face on a bad situation: Curt. 8.1.19; Arr. 4.17.3. I can make no sense of Curtius' remark (6.5.22) that after the Mardian campaign, Alexander "sent home Artabazus, doubling the honors Darius had conferred upon him" (*Artabazum deinde, geminato honore quem Dareus habuerat ei, remittit domum*).

55. Cophen conducted negotiations with Ariamazes: Curt. 7.11.5, 22 (Cophes). If Curt. 8.3.17 is not mistaken about Arsames, satrap of the Drangians, being replaced by Stasanor (*Arsami, Drangarum praefecto, substitutus est Stasanor*), this could possibly be Artabazus' son. His removal from office coincided very closely with his father's. Barsine, Alexander's (now-pregnant) mistress was sent back to western Asia Minor (Pergamum) at roughly the same time.

56. The famous and ill-advised slogan on a banner aboard the aircraft carrier USS *Abraham Lincoln*, where on May 1, 2003, US president George W. Bush prematurely celebrated victory in the Iraq war.

The War in Central Asia

BESSUS' USURPATION AND the stiffening of resistance in Central Asia gave new urgency to the Macedonian cause. Failure to challenge the usurper could only be interpreted as recognition of regime change, and Darius' death would thus represent no more than the end of another chapter in the history of an empire that had weathered many storms. Now, more than ever, the task needed to be brought quickly to its desired conclusion, with the Conqueror securely, and without rival, on the Achaemenid throne.[1]

But despite the need for prompt and sustained military action, Alexander did his best to confirm his conquests through negotiation and displays of reconciliation.[2] Many of Darius' officials made their peace with the Conqueror, hoping to retain old positions of power or gain new ones. And indeed, the Macedonian king showed clemency, placing a cautious faith in the Persian aristocracy. Over a three-year period, he appointed a string of barbarian rulers, though not all repaid his trust with loyalty.[3] What motivated those who continued to resist deserves closer attention. Unfortunately, we know too little about Persian factions or

---

1. See Curt. 6.3.8, where Alexander is alleged to have remarked to his troops: "It is your military strength that checks them: fearing us while we are here, they will be our enemies when we are gone." Curtius here, and elsewhere (8.2.35), compares the inhabitants of Central Asia with "wild animals" (*ferae bestiae*).

2. The conciliatory policy had a personal aspect, which drew the ire and resentment of his own troops. That was the adoption of Persian dress and practices. The resistance of the Macedonians to this—no less dangerous than the actions of the enemy—is discussed in chapter 12.

3. One significant exception is Barsaentes, who fled from his satrapy in 329 upon Alexander's approach (Curt. 6.6.36). He took refuge with Samaxus (probably Sambus), a dynast of the neighboring Indian hill tribes, who later surrendered him to Alexander for execution (Curt. 8.13.3-4; Arr. 3.25.8). Grainger 2007, 190, sees his flight as an indication of the failure of Alexander's policies: "There is some evidence, indeed, that numbers of Iranians left Iran, particularly for India, rather than accept Alexander's rule." Barsaentes as a regicide and co-conspirator with Bessus was a marked man, and he knew it. In Arachosia, Alexander deviated from his practice

In the Path of Conquest. Waldemar Heckel, Oxford University Press (2020). © Oxford University Press.

DOI: 10.1093/oso/9780190076689.001.0001

family groupings to judge the actions—whether these involved cooperation or rivalry—of these individuals. What is clear is that those who remained belligerent were the ones into whose territories the Macedonian army was now advancing. Their troops had been in the field since they were levied for the confrontation at Gaugamela, and their political structures were still intact. In short, they still had something to fight for and the means with which to do so. Some of them—Satibarzanes, Nabarzanes, Autophradates (and there were doubtless other hyparchs of lesser rank)—made little more than token surrender.

The defenders were now concentrated on the northeastern edge of the empire, beyond the Iranian plateau. Strabo describes the country that lay ahead of Alexander:

> Beyond them [the Hyrcanians] is the tribe of the Parthians, then that of the Margianians and the Arians, and after that comes the desert which, as one travels east toward the River Ochus, the River Sarnius separates from Hyrcania. The name of the mountain that stretches from Armenia to this point (or just short of it) is Parachoathras. From the Hyrcanian Sea to the Arians the distance is some six thousand stades, and Bactriana, Sogdiana, and, finally, the nomadic Scythians come next.
>
> The Macedonians called all the mountains that stretch in a row from the Arians the Caucasus. (Strabo 11.8.1 C510-511)

Aria thus represented the last easily accessible region before the Hindu Kush, unless one moved in a northeasterly direction toward Margiana and the Merv Oasis. Satibarzanes diverted the Macedonians from their path, buying time for Bessus and eventually drawing the enemy toward more strenuous roads and harsher climes. Whether Satibarzanes was actually one of the regicides is unclear, but he surrendered to Alexander at Susia (Tūs) in Aria and was confirmed in his satrapy.[4] From Susia, Alexander marched in the direction of the Merv Oasis, sending Satibarzanes back to his capital at Artacoana (probably in the vicinity of modern Herat) accompanied by Anaxippus and forty mounted javelin men

---

and appointed a Macedonian, Menon, as satrap (Curt. 7.3.5; Arr. 3.28.1). For the importance of Arachosia as a gateway to India, see Vogelsang 1985, 77–82.

4. Curt. 6.6.20 says he brought news that Bessus had assumed the upright tiara and was styling himself as Artaxerxes (V); he was also mobilizing the Scythians (Curt. 6.6.13). Arr. 3.25.1 mentions Satibarzanes' surrender to Alexander and at 3.25.3 says that some Persians (Περσῶν τινες) came to inform him of Bessus' assumption of kingship. Cf. *Metz Epit.* 3; Diod. 17.74.2. Diod. 17.83.3 implies that Alexander learned of Bessus' usurpation later, but he is merely resuming his earlier narrative.

(*hippakontistai*).[5] Satibarzanes promptly butchered his escort, perhaps believing that Alexander would become embroiled in guerrilla warfare in Bactria and even suffer defeat there. Within two days of receiving news of the treachery, Alexander had turned back and arrived at Artacoana, from which the satrap fled to Bactria.[6] Aria was entrusted to a Persian named Arsaces, and Alexander marched in the direction of Parapamisus, following the bend of the Helmand River valley. As he moved out of Aria, he learned that the rebel had returned. Erigyius, Caranus, Artabazus, and Andronicus were sent to deal with him;[7] Alexander himself led the main force against Bessus.

Satibarzanes' second attempt at rebellion proved less successful than the first. In one of many scenes of single combat (*monomachia*) in the Alexander historians, Satibarzanes challenged one of the Macedonian leaders to a duel. Erigyius, an old friend of the king and now advanced in years,[8] accepted the challenge and dispatched the arrogant barbarian by driving his lance through his throat and throwing him from his horse. In triumph, he withdrew the lance and drove it into Satibarzanes' face. At that point, the barbarians, according to Curtius, willingly surrendered to Erigyius, "remembering Alexander's past kindness to them."[9] Arrian, in contrast, says that the barbarians fled after the death of their leader.[10] Arsaces, it appears, returned to his duties as satrap of Aria and,

---

5. Artacoana: Arr. 3.25.5; Curt. 6.6.20; Diod. 17.78.1 (Chortakana). For its location, see Olmstead 1948, 46 n. 55; Seibert 1985, 120; cf. Bosworth I 356–57; *Barr. Atl.* 6 A3. Against the view of Engels 1978a, 89–90, who puts Artacoana north and east of Kalat-i-Nadiri, see Heckel, *Marshals*[2] 292–93; and Atkinson II 207–9.

6. This does not mean that his earlier action was coordinated with Bessus, although one cannot rule it out.

7. Curt. 7.3.2: they had 6,000 Greek infantry and 600 cavalry. Arr. 3.28.2-3: Satibarzanes had 2,000 cavalry. Also fighting with Alexander's forces was Phrataphernes. Diod. 17.81.3 says that Erigyius was accompanied by Stasanor. This is probably a careless compression of events. It is doubtful that Stasanor, although he was enrolled in the *hetairoi*, had the requisite military skills that would warrant such a command. Later he was sent to Aria as its designated satrap.

8. Curt. 7.4.34: "Though well advanced in age, Erigyius was not to be ranked second to any of the younger men in courage or agility. He took off his helmet and revealed his white hair." Despite Curtius' evidence and other arguments to the contrary (Heckel 1992, 205–8), many scholars still persist in regarding the *hetairoi* of Alexander who were exiled for their role in the Pixodarus affair as coeval with the king.

9. Curt. 7.4.33-38; cf. Diod. 17.83.4-6; Arr. 3.28.2-3.

10. Arr. 3.28.3. Satibarzanes' surrender: Arr. 3.25.1; Curt. 6.6.13. Anaxippus' force: Arr. 3.25.2; cf. Diod. 17.78.1. Murder of Anaxippus: Arr. 3.25.5; Diod. 17.78.1, 81.3; Curt. 6.6.20. Heckel 27–28; Berve II 37 n. 3 is probably correct in seeing him as the *episkopos* in Satibarzanes' territory. Flight to Bactria: Curt. 6.6.22; cf. Arr. 3.25.6-7. Replaced by Arsaces: Arr. 3.25.7. Satibarzanes' rebellion: Curt. 7.3.2; Arr. 3.28.2; Diod. 17.81.3. See Heckel 245; Berve II 350–51 no. 697.

possibly, Drangiana.[11] A year later, he was brought in chains to Bactra. The exact
nature of his crime is not recorded.[12]

III

With the death of Satibarzanes, the Helmand River valley, in what is today
western Afghanistan, was firmly under Macedonian control. Near Lake Sistan,
the Ariaspians, who had earned the sobriquet "Benefactors" (*euergetai*) for their
support of Cyrus the Great in the 530s, supplied the invaders.[13] As the army
moved up the river valley, Kandahar was founded under the name Alexandria-
in-Arachosia,[14] and only the physical obstacles of the Khawak Pass stood between the Conqueror and the fertile satrapy of Bactria, which "supports large
populations of humans and horses" and could field as many as 30,000 cavalry.[15]
Making the difficult crossing in deep snow and without adequate provisions,
Alexander emerged from the Khawak Pass near Drapsaca (Kunduz), whence
he moved to Aornus[16] and then Bactra (Bahlk), which lay at the foot of Mount
Parapamisus and by the Bactrus River. The much easier approach through the
Sibar Pass and Bamian was guarded by Bessus' supporters.

Here the pretender to the Achaemenid throne prepared to make his stand.[17]
And here Bessus squandered an opportunity to deal a serious, if not lethal, blow
to the invaders. Had he attacked them as they emerged from the Hindu Kush
physically spent and with their resources depleted, he might have won a stunning

---

11. There is, however, a chronological problem or at least the possibility that Arr. 4.7.1 and 4.18.1
refer to the same event.

12. Arr. 4.7.1; but Curt. 8.3.17 is problematical. Howe 2015a, 170, believes that the "insurgency"
in Aria ended with the death of Satibarzanes. But the force sent to arrest Arsaces suggests that
his crime may have been rebellion rather than malfeasance.

13. Ariaspians (*Metz Epit.* 4: Arimaspi). They were nevertheless assigned a satrap (or hyparch)
named Amedines, a former secretary of Darius III (*scriba regis*): Curt. 7.3.4. Diod. 17.81.2 says
that Tiridates was entrusted with the *strategia* of the Gedrosians and Euergetae.

14. See the discussion in Fraser 1996, 132–40, against Tarn II 234, 241.

15. Curt. 7.4.30-31.

16. Chulum, according to Schwarz, *Feldzüge* 27–28; Engels 1978a, 97 n. 111: "Sharhr-i-Banu,
near Khulm"; see also Seibert 1985, 127 n. 10.

17. Bessus' assumption of the royal title is supported by a fourth-century document from the so-
called Khalili Archive (Document IA). Here we have a reference to both "year 1 of Arta[xerxes]
the King" and to Bayasa (apparently Bessus). See Mairs 2014, 43.

victory and inspired the barbarians of the northeast.[18] Yet Bessus appears to have abandoned any attempt to protect Bactria. If Diodorus can be trusted, he had made plans and promised—at least, by the manner of his preparations—to defend Bactria from invasion:

> As Bessus had been appointed satrap of the region by Darius and become well known to the masses through his governance, he exhorted them to defend their independence. He pointed out to them the topography of their region, which would greatly assist them as it was difficult of access and possessed a sufficient male population to maintain its autonomy. He announced that he would take command in the war and, after persuading the people, appointed himself king. He then proceeded to enlist soldiers, stockpile weapons, and strenuously make all other preparations for future needs. (Diod. 17.74.1-2)

Bessus' satrapal levies numbered 8,000 Bactrians,[19] but these began to waver in their support of the usurper and melted away when it became clear that Alexander had crossed the Hindu Kush, intent upon bringing Bessus to justice.[20] Instead of defending the satrapy, Bessus crossed the Oxus (Amu-darya) with reduced forces, burning the boats when he reached the opposite shore and making for Nautaca.[21]

---

18. Schachermeyr 1973, 339; cf. Lane Fox 1973, 297. The reader is also directed to Klaus Fischer's account of his archaeological journey in this area in 1960 (Fischer 1987, with photographs).

19. Curt. 7.4.20. These were presumably the same men who accompanied him to Gaugamela (Curt. 4.12.6); the figure is nominal, and we must allow for losses in battle; at the time of Darius' flight from Ecbatana, he was in charge of 3,300 cavalrymen whom Curt. 5.8.4 calls "Parthieni." Arr. 3.25.3 gives no precise figures but says that "he had with him the Persians who had escaped to Bactra and a good number of the Bactrians themselves and was expecting the arrival of Scythian support as well." He subsequently lent 2,000 horsemen to Satibarzanes (Arr. 3.28.2).

20. Arr. 3.28.10; cf. Curt. 7.4.20.

21. Curt. 7.4.20-21. Bessus to Nautaca: Arr. 3.28.10. He was accompanied by Spitamenes and Oxyartes and by horsemen of the Dahae (the last had been with him at Gaugamela: 3.11.3). The location of Nautaca: Schwarz, *Feldzüge* 74–75, identifies it with Shakhrisyabz; but see the objections of Geiger, *Feldzüge* 10–12; Engels 1978a, 102, places it on the Kashka River but at 102 n. 12 wrongly attributes to Schwarz the identification of Nautaca with "Karshi (the ancient Nakhshab)." Geiger, *Feldzüge* 10, attributes this argument to Menn (*Meletematum historicorum specimen duplex. I. De Alexandri expeditionibus Oxianis*, 58, *non vidi*) and rejects on both geographical and linguistic grounds. Seibert 1985, 126–27 n. 8, rightly objects to Engels' dismissive approach to Schwarz's work (see esp. Engels 1978a, 99, with n. 2): "Immerhin besaß v. Schwarz—ganz im Gegensatz zu Engels—vorzügliche Lokalkenntnisse."

The earlier flight of Barsaentes from Drangiana to India[22] left him with only a small number of Bactrians and the tribesmen of Margiana and Sogdiana, as well as the allied Scythian Dahae and Massagetae. These were all peoples of similar background who differed primarily in their mode of life.[23] Why Bessus failed to make a stand in Bactria is perplexing. Certainly, he lacked the numbers to fight the larger army of the invader, but the enemy was debilitated by the harsh crossing of the Hindu Kush. For the Macedonians, horses were in short supply, and those that survived the crossing were in poor condition. Nevertheless, Bessus fled into Sogdiana, losing in the process many of the Bactrians who saw their homeland abandoned by the self-styled Artaxerxes V. It soon became clear that the usurper's actions fell short of his bluster. One of his advisers correctly but unwisely noted that "the frightened dog barks more fiercely than it bites."[24] Perhaps his supporters had never been numerous, and the most influential of these were now either dead or in flight. Furthermore, his high-handed style of leadership—as displayed in his dealings with Gobares—caused his erstwhile followers to abandon him.[25] His only hope, it seemed, was to wage a war of attrition, drawing the enemy into the wastelands north of the Oxus, where they could be denied supplies and harassed by the Scythian allies.

Bessus was losing the propaganda war. The hyparchs and local dynasts of Bactria-Sogdiana saw that they were isolated, that a reversal of fortunes—at least on a large scale—was not in the cards. Alexander had assumed the trappings of royalty and been recognized as "King of Asia" in stages since his victory at Gaugamela. But he also showed signs of maintaining the structures of the Achaemenid Empire.[26] The patterns of life in Central Asia would remain as they

---

22. Flight of Barsaentes: Arr. 3.25.8; *Metz Epit.* 3 (wrongly calling him Ariobarzanes); Curt. 6.6.36. Diod. 17.74.1 says that Barxaës (*sic*) accompanied Bessus to Bactria, which is probably a mistake.

23. Schwarz, *Feldzüge* 24: "Die Bewohner der Städte und Dörfer von Baktrien und Sogdiana waren zur Zeit Alexanders Indogermanen und Stammverwandte der Skythen, von denen sie sich nur durch ihre ansässige Lebensweise unterschieden." Those who dwelt south of the Amu-darya were engaged in agriculture, those to the north in animal husbandry (Vogelsang 2002, 122).

24. Curt. 7.4.13: *canem timidum vehementius latrare quam mordere.*

25. If there is any truth to the story of Bessus' treatment of Gobares (reminiscent in some ways of Alexander's later clash with Cleitus the Black), it appears that Bessus' usurpation and arrogance did not sit well with his subjects. See Curt. 7.4.1-19; cf. Diod. 17.83.7-8, who calls him Bagodaras and says that his favorable reception by Alexander induced other prominent barbarians to surrender, leading to the arrest of Bessus himself.

26. It is telling that in Persis alone, Alexander did not make any clear display of assuming the kingship. Perhaps this is because of the Zoroastrian aspects of Achaemenid kingship. On the other hand, Darius was still alive, and Alexander's legitimacy depended to a great extent on

were before his arrival, and the political and economic headmen could expect to continue exercising their authority, even if the identity of the satrap changed. So much was clear from Alexander's careful policy of clemency, as he not only pardoned his former enemies but also reinstated many of them as satraps. It was Bessus who now seemed to pose the greater threat to their security. And indeed, it proved difficult to bend the knee to a man who had until recently been an equal. Once again, the barbarians sought reprieve by surrendering the author of the mischief. Like Darius before him, Bessus was arrested by his own men and handed over to Alexander, who rewarded them with freedom and gifts.[27] The extradition of Bessus indicated, at least to Alexander, that the local barons were prepared to accept not only his overlordship but also its legitimacy. Continued resistance must therefore have come as an unwelcome surprise to the Conqueror.[28]

The role played by Ptolemy son of Lagus in the extradition of Bessus appears only in Arrian, who followed Ptolemy's own account of the affair that the mission was entrusted to him:

> It was there that Ptolemy was told that Spitamenes' and Dataphernes' minds were not entirely made up about surrendering Bessus. He then left the infantry behind, commanding them to follow in battle order, and he himself rode ahead with the cavalry and came to the village, where Bessus

defeating him (cf. Naiden 2019, 144–45). Whether he would have allowed Darius to live on, as he allegedly promised, is uncertain. Furthermore, in 330, when the Panhellenic aspect of the war was in the forefront, it would have been difficult for Alexander to cast himself in the role of Great King. By contrast, "King of Asia" was an all-embracing term that also reflected his position as Conqueror.

27. Those who arrested Bessus brought him to Alexander in person: Curt. 7.5.26, 36–39; cf. Diod. 17.84.8. Catanes remained with Darius' brother Oxyathres, to whom Bessus was entrusted: Curt. 7.5.40-43. Alexander's treatment of Spitamenes, Catanes, and Dataphernes: *Metz Epit.* 6; Curt. 7.5.43. But all this occurred before the general uprising in Sogdiana.

28. Anson 2015c, 226: "These lands revolted from Alexander's authority after their relatively peaceful acquisition." Did the actions of the local barons constitute "rebellion" (that is, "insurrection") or simply a continuation of resistance to the invader? For different views on the value of the war in Bactria-Sogdiana for students of insurgency and counterinsurgency (COIN), see Lonsdale 2007, 94–97; Anson 2015b and 2015c; Howe 2015a; and, of course, Holt 2005. Howe 2015a, 160, is right to note that the activities of Bessus and his Bactrians in the Upper Satrapies were not insurgency against a legitimate government but rather a continuation on the part of "loyalists, not rebels," of the resistance against an invader. But later, when Spitamenes, Catanes, and Dataphernes handed Bessus over to Alexander, they were in effect recognizing Alexander's authority. By this very fact, they transformed themselves from resisters into insurgents. If Spitamenes, or one of his followers, had hopes of replacing Bessus as a pretender to the throne (Howe 2015a, 172), their implicit recognition of Alexander makes little sense. Perhaps it is just a matter of semantics, but the implications of these actions must be considered. I do, however, agree with Howe that modern terminology applied to ancient history can be misleading.

was to be found with a few soldiers. For Spitamenes and his men had already left the place, ashamed as they were to hand over Bessus themselves.

Ptolemy had the cavalry surround the village (it had around it a kind of wall with gates) and announced to the barbarians in the village that they would be released without harm if they surrendered Bessus. They then let Ptolemy and his men into the village, and Ptolemy arrested Bessus and left. Sending a messenger ahead to Alexander, he asked him how he should bring Bessus into his sight; and Alexander instructed him to bring him naked, tied up, and with a wooden collar, and to put him down on the right side of the road on which he and his army were going to pass. And this Ptolemy did. (Arr. 3.30.1-3 = *FGrH* 138 F14)

What followed was political theater. Alexander, standing tall in his chariot, drove past the prisoner. Hardly the vehicle of choice in the rugged terrain of Central Asia, for his barbarian audience the chariot was a symbol of his status as rightful king.[29] Thus he staged a meeting between conqueror and usurper, a spectacle of humiliation and retribution. Asked to defend his behavior, Bessus noted that he had acted in concert with those who attended on Darius in the hope of gaining immunity from Alexander. Clearly, he was not prepared to shoulder all of the blame.[30] In Curtius' version, he could offer only the most implausible excuses, absurd even by the standards of the writer who invented the dialogue: "Bessus, not daring to deny his crime, said that he had used the title of king in order that he might be able to hand over his nation to him; for if he had delayed another would have seized the rule."[31] As the regicide was publicly flogged, his crimes against his former master were recited between lashes. Later he was mutilated in the Persian fashion—his nose and ears were cut off—and sent to Ecbatana for execution in front of Darius' kinsmen. Nevertheless, the manner of his death is disputed by

---

29. Arr. 3.30.4. Milns 1968, 170, misses the point when he says of this episode that "Alexander . . . stopped the chariot in which he had taken to riding." Seibert 1985, 129–30, bases at least one of his arguments for Alexander's route on its suitability for wagons (chariots): "Der Weg des Hauptheeres ging wohl kaum durchs Gebirge über Saumpfade, sondern auf einer Fahrstraße in Richtung Marakanda, da Alexander in einem Wagen reiste." This is not to say that Alexander did not make use of the chariot on other occasions (e.g., in his triumphal entry into Babylon, Curt. 5.1.23, immortalized in Charles Le Brun's painting), including his imitation of the Persian king in the hunt (Spawforth 2012, 183–84; and Ephippus, *FGrH* 126 F5). For the Persian royal chariot, see Curt. 3.3.15. Compare also the later Roman use of the chariot in the triumph. For Ptolemy's account of the arrest of Bessus, see Heckel 2018a, 9–10.

30. Arr. 3.30.4. This shared guilt may explain the actions of Spitamenes and others: οὐ μόνῳ οἱ ταῦτα δόξαντα πρᾶξαι . . . ἀλλὰ ξὺν τοῖς τότε ἀμφὶ Δαρεῖον οὖσιν.

31. Curt. 7.5.39. At least the very last statement approximates the truth.

the sources; crucifixion is mentioned, as is dismemberment.[32] If the aim of all this was to discourage opposition or satisfy the nobles who had been steadfast in their support of the crown, it appears not to have had the desired effect. Not for the first time did Alexander misjudge the effects of his brutality; the continued resistance in Central Asia caused the king to revert to terror, a policy that had not served him well in the past.

The warlords of Bactria and Sogdiana remained distrustful of the enemy and confident in the ability of their horsemen to resist; as a last resort, they could retreat to the mountain fortresses that experience had shown to be impregnable. When summoned, they refused to attend a parlay with Alexander, for "they found Alexander's brutality just as intolerable as Bessus' treason."[33] Some had been with Bessus when he deposed and killed Darius, and they no doubt feared punishment. The subtle difference between regicide and usurpation stressed by some modern scholars—and perhaps even formulated in Alexander's own mind—would have escaped them. Darius still had several relatives and close friends who were influential with Alexander, a dangerous situation for those who understood Oriental court intrigue. In this respect, the appointment of Artabazus as satrap was ominous rather than reassuring. He was viewed with suspicion by many—an outsider, a traitor and collaborator, possibly even an avenger.[34]

---

32. Arr. 3.30.5 says Bessus was whipped and sent to Bactra for execution, but at 4.7.3, he claims that he was mutilated and sent to Ecbatana (cf. Curt. 7.10.10). Diod. 17.83.9 has Bessus turned over to Darius' brother Oxyathres (cf. Justin 12.5.10-11), mutilated, killed, and dismembered, though it is not clear if this occurred at the time of his arrest or later; *Metz Epit.* 14 claims he was killed by slingers and Plut. *Alex.* 43.6 by recoiling trees (see Heckel 1994, 70). See also Curt. 7.5.19-43, who says that he was crucified and pierced with arrows but that he was later sent to Ecbatana for execution. That Catanes was assigned the task of shooting down carrion birds (7.5.40-42) is a sign that Bessus adhered to the Zoroastrian faith (Jacobs 1992, 183). The discrepancies are clearly attributable to the use of different sources and virtually impossible to reconcile. This is not the only time that the Alexander historians disagree on the manner of someone's death; compare the accounts of the death of Callisthenes (Arr. 4.14.3; Plut. *Alex.* 55.9).

33. Curt. 7.6.13-15; cf. Arr. 4.1.5.

34. Appointment of Artabazus: Arr. 3.29.1; Curt. 7.5.1; 8.1.19. This occurred before Alexander left Bactra and marched toward the Oxus. The attempt to establish Mithrenes as satrap of Armenia seems to have been equally ineffective (Arr. 3.16.5; Curt. 5.1.44; Diod. 17.64.6; cf. also Sabictas in Cappadocia: Arr. 2.4.2; Curt. 3.4.1, "Abistamenes"); lack of local support may explain also the brief tenure of Amminapes in Hyrcania and Parthyaea. Bosworth II 18 notes that Artabazus was viewed as an outsider; cf. Vacante 2012, 88; Smith 2009–10, 66; Heckel 2018b. Curtius stresses Artabazus' loyalty to Darius (5.9.1; 6.5.1-2), his opposition to the conspirators (5.12.7-8), and his defection from what was now Bessus' camp (5.12.18).

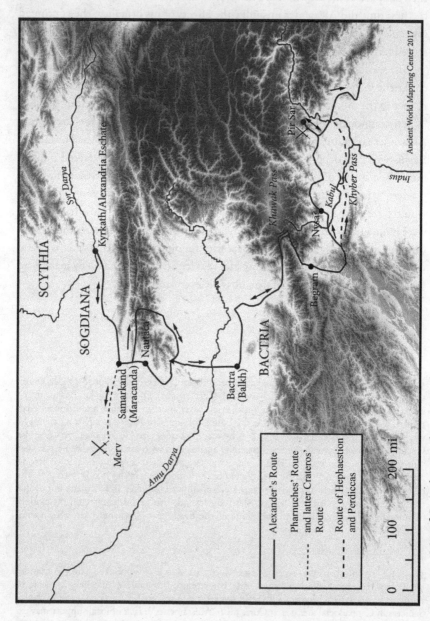

MAP II.I Map of Central Asia and route to Indus.

IV

Sogdiana, situated between the Oxus River (Amu-darya) in the south and the Iaxartes (Syr-darya) to the north, presented in comparison with Bactria a desolate landscape, although even the road from Bactra to the Oxus had tested the endurance of the invading army. The land was ideal for guerrilla warfare,[35] offering easy paths of escape and secure fortresses that could easily provisioned. Alexander advanced to the Iaxartes, where a native force confronted the Macedonian foragers, precipitating a larger military engagement in which the king was seriously wounded. The Macedonians had supplied the cavalry with mounts from Sogdiana—replenishing the losses incurred in the crossing of the Hindu Kush and the Oxus—and this may account for the sudden uprising.[36] There appear to have been other factors as well: the massacre of the so-called Branchidae[37] and the imposition of Macedonian garrisons in local towns. Seven settlements of varying size existed along or near the Iaxartes, at least three of them dating to the time of the Persian conquest;[38] whether all were established for military or economic purposes is impossible to say. They were now in open rebellion, having massacred the garrisons.[39] Their subjugation came at considerable cost, to the Macedonians and even more so to the inhabitants, who were either slaughtered

---

35. Curt. 7.10.1. Cf. Geiger, *Feldzüge* 6, who says of Bessus: "Jedenfalls konnte er in Sogdiana leichter als anderswo einen Volkskrieg organisieren."

36. Holt 1988, 53, calls them "a large force of local 'brigands,'" which not only obscures the underlying problems but hardly suits the numbers involved. Curt. 7.6.2 says there were 20,000, Arr. 3.30.10 "about 30,000." Holt (53 n. 7) believes that 30,000 is merely a figure intended to indicate "a great number" (cf. Holt 2016, 13–14), but according to Arr. 3.30.11, some 22,000 perished in the engagement. Curt. 7.6.1-7 gives a very different story, in which the natives are allegedly distressed by Alexander's injury and willingly surrender. For the problem created by the requisitioning of horses, see Bloedow 1991 (contra Bosworth II 18). Alexander received an arrow wound that broke his fibula (Arr. 3.30.11; according to Plut. *Alex.* 45.5, cf. *Mor.* 341b, 327a, it was the tibia; Curt. 7.6.3: *in medio crure*).

37. Curt. 7.5.27-35. Not mentioned by Arrian. They were reputedly descended from Milesians who had plundered the oracle of Apollo and were transplanted by Xerxes. For this there is no contemporary (or near-contemporary) evidence. Full discussion of the event and Alexander's motives: Parke 1985; cf. Nudell 2018, 48. Tarn II 272–75 dismissed the massacre as fiction, as he dismissed virtually everything unfavorable to Alexander. The incident is almost certainly true (Bosworth 1988a, 108; cf. Holt 2005, 184)—an overt act of terror. The identity of the "Branchidae" is less certain. But see Hammond 1998; Bettenworth 2016.

38. Justin 12.5.12.

39. Arr. 4.1.4. Of the seven cities, the largest was Cyropolis; only one other, Gaza, is known by name. Curtius speaks of people called Memaceni, but little is known about them.

or enslaved.[40] Those who survived were resettled in the Conqueror's new city, Alexandria-Eschate (Alexandria the Farthest), which was designed to replace the old outpost of Cyropolis, a foundation of Cyrus the Great.[41] But this heightened tensions in the northeast, as it threatened the old patterns of life in Sogdiana and placed new restrictions on an otherwise porous border.[42]

The leaders of Bactria and Sogdiana did not stand alone in opposition to the securing of the Iaxartes boundary; the Scythians (in this case, the Sacae) sought to reassert their right of movement to the south, forcing the Macedonians to conduct a preemptive strike, not unlike Alexander's campaign against the Getae beyond the Danube at the beginning of his reign.[43] It appears that the barbarians

40. At Cyropolis, where he was again wounded (Arr. 4.3.3: he was struck on the head and neck by a stone), the reprisals were just as fierce: "in the first phase of the city's capture about 8,000 of the enemy were killed. The rest, out of the total number of 15,000 fighting men, gathered and took refuge in the citadel" (Arr. 4.3.4). These were forced to surrender, and in another of the seven cities no one was spared. Arr. 4.35. Curt. 7.6.16: "Alexander gave the signal for the execution of all adult males, the other inhabitants becoming the booty of the victor. The city [one of the cities near Cyropolis] was demolished so that its destruction could serve as an example to keep the others in line." Cyropolis itself was sacked because of its stubborn resistance. At the city of the Memaceni, Alexander was wounded on the neck (Curt. 7.6.22), and the city was destroyed upon capture (7.6.23). Casualty figures for the entire war in Bactria and Sogdiana, from Holt 2005, 107: "Estimates of men, women and children killed begin at 120,000 and climb considerably higher. The king's known losses (up to 7,000 soldiers) seem small by comparison." Holt does not, however, indicate the source of these "estimates." The sources attest at least 35,170 (in some cases, the figures include civilians), but there must have been considerably more (see Heckel and McLeod 2015, 244–45).

41. See Olbrycht 2011 on these settlers, especially the Iranian ones, who appear to have had equal rights with the Macedonians and Greeks. Cyropolis, Ura-Tübe, was not located on the river.

42. Holt 1988, 57 (following Briant 1976, 185–94): Alexander "wished to avoid . . . a hostile confederacy of Sogdians and Scythians on the north-eastern frontier of his new empire." For the full discussion, see Holt 1988, 54–59. I do not see how Alexandria-Eschate could effectively prevent a Sogdianian-Scythian coalition, since many Scythian allies came from the west, from the Kyzyl Kum area.

43. On the boundaries of Alexander's empire, normally demarcated by rivers and deserts, and the limits set by the Macedonian king on his conquests, see Heckel 2003a. Campaign against the Getae: Arr. 1.3.1–4.5; see chapter 2. The Scythians north of the Iaxartes—the ancients called it the Tanais and believed it formed the boundary between Europe and Asia (Hamilton 1971; Brunt I 522–25)—had come with the intention of destroying Alexandria-Eschate (Curt. 7.7.1); *Metz Epit.* 8 says they intended to prevent Alexander's crossing of the river. In either case, it was in Alexander's interests to attack them before they could join with the rebels. Arr. 4.3.6 calls them a contingent of Scythians from Asia (τῶν ἐκ τῆς Ἀσίας Σκυθῶν), which makes little sense (Bosworth II 22 provides an unsatisfactory explanation), since Arrian has earlier spoken of those living beyond the Tanais as "European Scythians" (4.1.1-2). To postulate confusion of the "Asian" and "Abian" Scythians does not help matters, since Arr. 4.1.1 said the Abii lived in Asia. Nevertheless, it is clear that the Scythians to whom ambassadors (πρέσβεις: Arr. 4.1.1) were sent (Curt. 7.6.12 says Alexander sent Derdas, *quondam . . . ex amicis*, but he may simply have been

occupied the far bank of the river while Alexander was supervising the construction of Alexandria-Eschate, a process that took some twenty days, and fired
arrows in the direction of the Macedonians, taunting them all the while. For the
Scythians, the perils of defiance were limited, for they placed their trust in the
mobility of their forces and in the solitudes of the desert. Alexander, on the other
hand, could do little more than make a demonstration, which entailed a dangerous river crossing unless the enemy could be driven from the opposite bank.
The military results were, in truth, minimal—and the seer Aristander claimed
that even the gods opposed the campaign[44]—but as propaganda it reinforced
the determination of the king to overcome any obstacle.[45] The crossing was made
with efficiency, just as at the Danube, and skirmishing quickly turned to pursuit.
The Scythians lacked infantry and artillery support. Alexander's catapults drove
them back from the shore, whereupon the army crossed on skins (*diphtherai*),
first disembarking the slingers and archers and finally bringing up infantry
and cavalry.[46] Skirmishing—in which the Scythians rode in circles around the
Macedonians, peppering them with arrows—turned into flight once the entire
enemy force had crossed and assumed more effective formations. The conclusion
was hardly glamorous for either side. The Scythians were said to have lost a thousand horsemen, including one of their leaders,[47] but a bout of diarrhea forced

---

the leader of a delegation) were those who lived farther to the west—in the area bordering on
Chorasmia—and not the Sacae who threatened the Macedonians on the Iaxartes, with a force
led by the Scythian king's brother Carthasis (Heckel 78–79; cf. 245 s.v. "Satraces").

44. Arr. 4.4.3, 9; Curt. 7.7.26-29 (but the authors disagree about whether Aristander eventually
told Alexander what he wanted to hear). It is unclear whether Aristander was a historical individual. Robinson 1929 has demonstrated that he vanishes from the accounts at about the same
point where Callisthenes ended his history (but see Heckel 45–46; Greenwalt 1982).

45. As Alexander predicted: "If we ignore the Scythians, who are actually on the offensive, we
shall have no respect from the rebels when we return to them. But suppose we cross the Tanais
and with a bloody slaughter of the Scythians demonstrate that we are universally invincible—
who then will hesitate to submit to us . . .?" (Curt. 7.7.11-12). See, however, the very positive
assessment of Fuller 1958, 238–41.

46. On *diphtherai*, see Bloedow 2002. I see no evidence in Arrian for artillery mounted on
them, and Curtius' account (7.9.2-9) has some very distinct Roman coloration. Arr. 4.4.4-5
shows that the catapult darts were launched from the shore, and once the barbarians had been
pushed back, Alexander gave the signal for the men to cross. Curt. 7.8.7 says that 12,000 boats
were constructed in three days but that some men crossed on hides and others on more elaborate rafts (7.8.6).

47. Curt. 7.9.15: the Macedonians "killed many of Scythians, capturing more, and driving off
1,800 horses. Of the Macedonians 60 horsemen fell and about 100 infantrymen. A thousand
were wounded."

the king to end the chase.[48] Once again, his adulators put a fine spin on the campaign: "This campaign by the fame of so opportune a victory completely subdued Asia, which in great part was revolting."[49] In truth, the war of resistance had only begun.

IV

The fiercely independent local dynasts—Spitamenes, Catanes, and Dataphernes—believed that the yoke of Macedonian authority would weigh more heavily on their necks than that of the Achaemenids and took flight, triggering two years of guerrilla warfare.[50] Families and movable possessions were deposited in the secure mountain stronghold of Ariamazes. In fact, Spitamenes had joined forces with Scythian allies from south of the Iaxartes and, while Alexander was dealing with the ones from the north, attacked the Macedonian garrison left behind at Maracanda (Samarkand). Learning of this, Alexander sent what he regarded as a sufficient force against them under the leadership of Andromachus, Caranus, and Menedemus; inexplicably, a Lycian named Pharnuches was placed at the head of the force.

After being defeated by the garrison troops who made a sortie from the city, Spitamenes learned of the approach of the relief force and retreated from Maracanda to the lands of the nomadic Scythians at the edge of the desert.[51] Here

---

48. Curt. 7.9.13 does not specify Alexander's condition (although he had been injured in campaigns south of the river): "The king, although he was unable to endure the tossing of his ailing body, yet persisted in pursuing them for eight stades." Plut. *Alex.* 45.6: "[Alexander] pursued them for a hundred stades, although he was suffering all the while from diarrhea."

49. Curt. 7.9.17. J. C. Rolfe, in the Loeb edition (II 210 n. *a*), rightly comments: "The influence of the report of the victory is greatly exaggerated." Similarly, Arr. 4.4.9 says that Alexander had to call off the pursuit on account of illness and that "otherwise . . . the Scythians would all have perished in their flight." Lonsdale 2007, 93: "One decisive battle was sufficient to subdue this dangerous enemy." These Scythians did, however, sue for peace, and Alexander sent a certain Euxenippus to them to discuss the terms (Curt. 7.9.17-19).

50. For an overview of the failure of Alexander's heavy-handed approach to the administration of Bactria-Sogdiana, see Smith 2009–10.

51. Curtius' account is different at this point. He claims that Spitamenes captured Maracanda, driving out the Macedonian garrison, and occupied the city (7.6.24). His source may have mentioned that he took possession of the citadel, perhaps the same source used by Arr. 4.5.3, who has a curious comment about Spitamenes going to the royal residence of Sogdiana (αὐτὸς δὲ ὡς ἐς τὰ βασίλεια τῆς Σογδιανῆς ἀνεχώρει); on the possible textual problem, see Bosworth II 32–33; Brunt I 505. It has been suggested that there was a second royal residence at Bokhara. Curtius then says that Spitamenes left the city to set an ambush for the approaching Macedonian force (7.7.31). For an attempt at *Quellenforschung* with respect to this episode, see Hammond 1991a and 1983, 143, with some unsatisfactory arguments that cannot be discussed here.

he added about 600 Scythian horsemen, and on the arrival of the Macedonian force, Spitamenes attacked them in typical Scythian fashion, riding around the enemy and firing arrows into the ranks of the infantrymen. When the Macedonians attacked, Spitamenes' forces withdrew, only to attack once again and inflict further casualties with their arrows when the enemy stopped and reverted to a defensive formation. Thus, he forced the Macedonians to form up in a square and withdraw in the direction of the Polytimetus River (Zeravshan). Here they were shot down by the Scythian horsemen as they attempted to cross the river.

This is apparently the account given by Ptolemy. The alternative version of Aristobulus claimed that the Macedonian forces were ambushed and that their actions were hampered by a crisis in leadership when Pharnuches[52] attempted to relinquish his command. The experienced military commanders (Andromachus, Caranus, Menedemus) declined the leadership, claiming that this would be contrary to Alexander's orders, but in fact "they were reluctant to accept responsibility even for their individual roles in any bungled operation."[53] Only 40 cavalrymen and 300 infantry escaped the slaughter. Menedemus, it is said, died an honorable death.[54] Spitamenes himself briefly returned to besiege Maracanda but moved south toward Bactra before Alexander brought up the rest of the army.[55]

Some kind of punitive action was directed against the natives of the region between Maracanda and the Polytimetus River, where the military disaster occurred, and it appears that Alexander conducted reprisals against local villages thought to harbor rebels. Curtius tells us that after Alexander had attended to the

---

52. The name Pharnuches suggests very strongly that he was Iranian (Justi 94). His designation as Lycian is difficult to explain. His main function seems to have been to serve as guide and interpreter and to negotiate with the enemy. That he was placed in charge of a Macedonian military force is hardly credible. It appears that after the disaster, Pharnuches became a convenient scapegoat. His identity is uncertain, but it seems likely that he was the father of the trierarch at the Hydaspes named Bagoas (Arr. *Ind.* 18.8). His son may have been the famous eunuch (Heckel 298 n. 166; noted also by Lane Fox 2007, 284; on eunuchs in general, see Tougher 2008, 7–38). Pharnuches: Heckel 207; Berve II 380–81 no. 768. Berve's suggestion (II 380) that Pharnuches may have participated in Alexander's expedition since 334/3 (cf. Bosworth II 24) strikes me as implausible.

53. Arr. 4.6.2.

54. Numbers: Arr. 4.3.7 says the Macedonian force numbered 60 Companions and 800 mercenary cavalry, along with 1,500 mercenary infantry. For the number of survivors, see Arr. 4.6.2. Curt. 7.6.24 says there were 3,000 infantry and 800 cavalry, all under the command of Menedemus; the dead are given as 2,000 infantry and 300 horse (7.7.39, 9.21). The gallant death of Menedemus and his friend Hypsicles (Hypsides): Curt. 7.7.34-37. Alexander gave him an honorable burial: Curt. 7.9.21; *Metz Epit.* 13.

55. Second siege of Maracanda: Arr. 4.6.3-4. Flight to Bactra: Curt. 7.9.20.

burial of the dead, "he divided his forces and ordered the burning of the country-side and the execution of men of military age."[56] Those who were judged to be ringleaders of the rebellion appear to have been taken to Bactra, where over the winter of 329/8, or at least at the start of the campaigning season, they were publicly executed.[57] It was becoming clear to all that the king did not take defeat or personal injury with good grace.

Where the leaders of the resistance went and what they did over the winter of 329/8 are unknown, but it is likely that they found themselves dispersed in Sogdiana. Spitamenes alone is mentioned by name, and he appears to have wintered with the Scythians (probably the Massagetae) on the western reaches of the Oxus. They prepared to move in the direction of Bactra as soon as Alexander crossed back into Sogdiana. Dataphernes and Catanes are later found in the company of the Dahae; presumably, they wintered in their lands. Alexander had left garrisons in several towns in Sogdiana, and we are told that a certain Peucolaus remained there with 3,000 men.[58] Possibly he was placed in charge of Maracanda, which after Spitamenes' attack in 329 needed to be reinforced. Peucolaus' troops were foot soldiers, which suggests that their role was primarily defensive. The beginning of the campaigning season saw the invaders making a determined effort to subdue Sogdiana by means of a sweep program. Dividing the army into three or five contingents, the Macedonians hoped to root out the enemy. In the process, they planted military colonies that were close enough to one another to render mutual assistance.[59]

The exact routes taken by these military detachments is a matter of conjecture, but it appears that the main efforts of the campaign of 328 were concentrated on the eastern portion of the satrapy. Hence, they probably followed the river valleys of the Pamir region.[60] When Alexander left Bactra in the spring of 328, he first

56. Curt. 7.9.22.

57. Curtius 7.10.4-9 tells a (seemingly) implausible story of thirty fine soldiers who were captured and rejoiced because they would have the honor of being executed by a man as great as Alexander. But this may reflect some local ritual or a means of facing death with courage and anticipating the rewards of the afterlife. It won them a reprieve, and four were taken into the Macedonian king's service. It is not clear if Curt. 7.10.13 refers to the same insurrection or to a later one, for it seems to occur when Alexander begins a new campaign. The story was told by Diodorus, as we learn from his list of contents (ὡς οἱ πρωτεύοντες Σογδιανῶν ἀπαγόμενοι πρὸς τὸν θάνατον παραδόξως ἐσώθησαν), but this section of the actual text is lost.

58. Peucolaus: Curt. 7.10.10.

59. Military colonies: Curt. 7.10.15 (six); cf. Justin 12.5.13 (twelve).

60. Bosworth 1981, 28; Seibert 1985, 139; Holt 1994, 55.

crossed the Ochus River and then the Oxus.[61] This makes geographic sense only if we identify the Ochus with the Kokcha River, located just east of Drapsaca (Kunduz). Although the sweep campaign was making progress, many insurgents sought refuge in the mountain fortresses. One such was that of Ariamazes, a place also known as the Rock of Sogdiana or the Rock of the Oxus. The exact location of this stronghold has been much debated, but it is generally assumed to be in the Derbent region southeast of Nautaca. It may, however, have been located in the Pamirs, probably not very far from the Oxus and its tributary, the modern Wakhsh (as is suggested by the alternative name given by Strabo).[62]

The Rock of Sogdiana presented Alexander with yet another of those challenges he could not resist, at least as far as the literary tradition about the king was concerned. Arrian has confused the chronology in a way that makes the king's capture of the Rock more effective.[63] The so-called Sogdian Rock was occupied by 30,000 men under the command of Ariamazes, and it was stocked with provisions to support this force for up to two years. The rock is described as 30 stades in height and 150 in circumference, steep on every side, and accessible by a narrow path.[64] The story of its capture is famous because of the foolish arrogance of its defender, who told Alexander that he would come to terms when the Macedonian king found "soldiers with wings," for this was the

---

61. Thus both Curt. 7.10.15 (the reference to "Margiana" is misleading; for the problem, see Bosworth 1981, 24–29) and *Metz Epit.* 14. Alexander experienced none of the difficulties of the previous advance to the Oxus, which he crossed near Khelif.

62. See Strabo 11.11.4 C517. Curt. 7.11, calling him Arimazes. *Metz Epit.* 17: "Ariomazes." Curtius' account makes it clear that the siege of the Rock belonged to the beginning of the campaigning season (which could mean late winter 329/8) and preceded the Cleitus affair (summer 328). It was almost a year before the capture of the Rock of Chorienes (Sisimithres) and the marriage to Roxane. Arrian, however, places the attack on the Rock of Sogdiana in the spring of 327. I am not convinced by the arguments of Bosworth 1981; see Heckel 1986. For the chronological difficulty, see also Holt 1988, 61 n. 47. The location: Geiger, *Feldzüge* 46 ("beim Pass von Derbend"; but Geiger wrongly accepts this as the occasion of the marriage to Roxane); Schwarz, *Feldzüge* 75–82; cf. Hammond 1981, 173.

63. Arr. 4.18.4 dates the attack on the Rock of Sogdiana (Ariamazes) to the beginning of spring 327 (ἅμα δὲ τῷ ἦρι ὑποφαίνοντι). Arrian provides no details on the size or height of the fortress, saying only that it was sheer on all sides, well provisioned, and with abundant water (4.18.5).

64. Curt. 7.11.1-2. Very different is the description of the Rock of Chorienes (Sisimithres) given in Strabo 11.11.4 C517: "that [Rock] of Sisimithres is fifteen stades in height and eighty in circuit, and . . . on top it is level and has a fertile soil which can support five hundred men" (τὴν μὲν οὖν Σισιμίθρου πεντεκαίδεκα σταδίων . . . τὸ ὕψος, ὀγδοήκοντα δὲ τὸν κύκλον. ἄνω δ᾽ ἐπίπεδον καὶ εὔγεων, ὅσον πεντακοσίους ἄνδρας τρέφειν δυναμένην). Strabo adds that the Rock of Sogdiana was twice as high, which supports Curtius' estimate of thirty stades. Arr. 4.21.1 says the Rock of Chorienes was twenty stades high and sixty stades in circumference, but this merely indicates disagreement in the underlying sources.

only way, Ariamazes thought, that the Rock could be taken.[65] When climbers
did indeed ascend to a point above his position, Ariamazes believed himself to
be outflanked, but his premature capitulation—there was actually very little
the climbers could do to coerce him[66]—came too late to save him. Although
Ariamazes surrendered, he did not gain favorable terms. Instead, he, his family,
and his leading nobles were scourged and crucified.[67] Others who surrendered
were distributed as slaves (probably as agricultural laborers), along with their
property, among the new military outposts.[68] It was a clear sign that Alexander did
not yet consider Central Asia fully subdued. Arrian's remark that among those
who had sought refuge on the Rock were the wife and family—particularly the
daughter—of Oxyartes is surely mistaken. The circumstances do not allow for
both the brutal punishment of the defenders and the conciliatory banquet and
marriage of the Conqueror to the native girl. Curtius says that the attempted
negotiation with the defender was conducted by Cophen (Curtius calls him
Cophes), the son of Artabazus, and that the Rock was subsequently entrusted to
Artabazus himself. This appointment rules out Arrian's date (winter 328/7) for
the campaign, since Artabazus relinquished his office as satrap before the Cleitus
affair in the summer of 328.[69] Furthermore, if Artabazus was given authority over

---

65. Arr. 4.18.6: πτηνοὺς ἐκέλευον ζητεῖν στρατιώτας Ἀλέξανδρον. Curt. 7.11.5: *Arimazes loco fretus,
superbe multa respondit, ad ultimum, an Alexander etiam volare posset interrogat.* Somewhat
different is *Metz Epit.* 18. The number of defenders (30,000) is suspect (cf. Holt 1988, 61 n. 46,
citing Briant 1984, 81–82, who accepts it).

66. Schwarz, *Feldzüge* 81: "Hätte sich Arimazes nicht durch die wenigen Makedonier verblüffen
lassen, die den Rand der Schlucht erklettert hatten, ihm aber in Wirklichkeit absolut nichts
anhaben konnten, weil es für sie unmöglich war, an den senkrechten Felswänden zu ihm in
der Schlucht hinabzusteigen, so hätte wohl Alexander unverrichteter Dinge wieder abziehen
müssen." On the feat of mountaineering, see the doubts of Vacante 2012, 92–95.

67. Curt. 7.11.28: Ariamazes and all his noble supporters were whipped and crucified (*quos
omnis verberibus affectos sub ipsis radicibus petrae crucibus iussit affigi*). If Oxyartes and his
family were among the nobles, it is hard to imagine how and why they were spared. *Metz Epit.*
18 claims that Ariamazes was murdered by his own men and that Alexander spared everyone
else. Where the *Metz Epitome* got this alternative version is unknown. It is more likely that
if Ariamazes was murdered by his own men, this would explain Alexander's treatment of the
captives—particularly the crucifixion of the nobles.

68. Curt. 7.11.29: *multitudo deditorum incolis novarum urbium cum pecunia capta dono data est.*

69. Curt. 8.1.19. Plut. *Alex.* 47.7 is of no help for the chronology, since he discusses the affair
of Roxane (τὰ περὶ Ῥωξάνην ἔρωτι μὲν ἐπράχθη) before the Philotas affair (i.e., 330). Hamilton,
PA 129, is wrong in attributing the confusion of the Rocks of Ariamazes and Chorienes to
Strabo. In fact, Strabo merely helps to confirm the correctness of Curtius' version. For the
relinquishing of the satrap by Artabazus (on the grounds of old age), see Curt. 8.1.19 (summer
328); cf. Heckel 2018b.

the region, this would not have been acceptable to the warlords and would thus explain their continued resistance.[70]

Gains in Sogdiana were offset by the renewed attacks of Spitamenes and the Massagetae, reminding Alexander that the capture of one fortress and the brutal treatment of its commander had failed to intimidate. As Alexander's army toiled north of the Oxus, Spitamenes and the Massagetae, along with some Sogdianians and disaffected Bactrians, invaded Bactria from the west, taking the enemy by surprise and, in a manner worthy of General George S. Patton, "hitting them where they ain't." Attinas, the *phrourarchos* of one of the military outposts near the satrapal capital, was lured from his base, ambushed, and killed.[71] From here, Spitamenes proceeded to Bactra (Zariaspa) itself, which his forces surrounded, plundering the countryside. The campaign amounted to a large-scale "cattle-rustling" expedition, intended to deprive the Macedonians of an important part of their food supply;[72] it also appealed to the Scythian allies who made their living in this manner. Peithon son of Sosicles had been left here with some of the Companions who were suffering from illness, along with several of the *paides basilikoi*. In response to the aggression, these mustered a force that included eighty mercenary horsemen and engaged Spitamenes, but they were caught by the Scythians and driven off with heavy casualties. Seven Companions and sixty mercenary horsemen were lost, along with the harpist Aristonicus, who fought

---

70. Cophen as negotiator: Curt. 7.11.5, 23–26. Artabazus: *Artabazus in petrae regionisque quae apposita esset ei tutelam relictus* (7.11.29). Since Curt. 7.5.1 says *Bactrianorum regione Artabazo tradito*, this can only mean that Alexander added Sogdiana to his administrative responsibilities. Lane Fox's view (1973, 318) that Artabazus "was retired to the governorship of the first Sogdian rock in place of the baron Ariamazes who had been crucified" (cf. also 1973, 410) must be rejected not only on the basis of the chronology but also because it demeans Artabazus without solving the political problem in Sogdiana. Oxyartes may also have objected to Artabazus' appointment. Certainly, there would have been rivalry if after the marriage to Roxane, Alexander had kept Artabazus' daughter Barsine as his mistress when she was either pregnant or had already given birth to his child. Her dismissal from the court and her return to Asia Minor in 327 were surely significant, and it must have impacted both families.

71. Curt. 8.1.3-5. He is called *regionis eius praefectus*, but the area he "governed" is not stated (Arr. 4.16.4 calls it τι φρούριον). See Heckel 64; Berve II 95 no. 185. The incident is described by Arr. 4.16.5 (without naming the commander). If Attinas was captured, as Arrian says, he was presumably executed afterward. Curt. 8.1.3 mentions a Bactrian contingent, which he calls *exsules*. We may assume they were those who did not come to terms with the invader when he arrived or perhaps those of Bessus' cavalry who did not abandon him when he crossed the Oxus. There were certainly Bactrians in the company of Spitamenes, as is clear from Arr. 4.17.7 (οἵ τε Μασσαγέται οἱ Σκύθαι κακῶς πεπραγότες τὰ μὲν σκευοφόρα τῶν ξυνπαραταξαμένων σφίσι Βακτίων τε καὶ Σογδιανῶν διήρπασαν). The Scythians numbered 900 (Curt. 8.1.3).

72. Holt 1994 notes the importance of herds to the Macedonian army, rightly faulting Engels's arguments that the army was dependent upon a grain diet (1978a, 18–25, 124–25, 144–45).

valiantly.[73] The Macedonian conqueror had not yet learned that the solution to his problem was not to be found in military action. The resistance in Sogdiana showed no signs of lessening. And the Bactrians, too, were at best ambivalent, caught, as Bosworth rightly notes, "between the hammer of nomadic incursion and the anvil of the Macedonian occupation."[74]

V

The three- or five-pronged Macedonian campaign across the breadth of Sogdiana, along with the capture of Ariamazes' Rock, had all but crushed the resistance north of the Oxus. Alexander moved his summer quarters to Maracanda, where he accepted Artabazus' resignation from the satrapy, allegedly on the grounds of old age. Curtius (6.5.3) says that he was in his ninety-fifth year in 330—hence, at the time of his resignation, he would have been ninety-six—but it is more likely that in 328 he was approaching sixty, which would make him younger than many who were actively campaigning. His mother was the Achaemenid princess Apame, whom Artaxerxes II had given in marriage to Pharnabazus in 387, and Artabazus himself had had a checkered career under the successive Persian kings, though he was essentially loyal to the crown.[75] But his political friendships and his past actions probably set him at odds with many of the Persian leaders—notably Bessus and thus also Spitamenes and his supporters.[76] Bringing in an outsider from the western edge of the empire to serve as satrap in Central Asia proved counterproductive. Alexander may have made the administrative change for political rather than personal reasons, but his choice of a replacement, the cavalry commander Cleitus, was equally ill advised.[77] At a drinking party in Maracanda,

---

73. Arr. 4.16.4-7. This attack is not mentioned by Curtius. Peithon son of Sosicles was taken alive by the Scythians: Heckel 195, s.v. "Peithon [2]"; Berve II 311-12 no. 622. Aristonicus the harpist was honored with a statue at Delphi, showing him with a spear in one hand and a lyre in the other (Plut. *Mor.* 334e-f). It was his *aristeia* that probably formed the basis for the poem recited by Pierion (or Pranichus), which Black Cleitus considered a mockery of Macedonian valor (thus Holt 1988, 78 n. 118; Plut. *Alex.* 50.8: the reference to defeated *strategoi* does not vitiate this theory).

74. Bosworth II 115.

75. Son of the Achaemenid Apame and Pharnabazus, and thus a grandson of Artaxerxes II: Plut. *Artox.* 27.4; Xen. *HG* 5.1.28, Plut. *Ages.* 3.3; cf. Plut. *Alex.* 21.9; *IG* II² 356 = Tod II 199. Curtius' claim (6.5.3) that he was in his ninety-fifth year in 330 is therefore impossible. He was probably born in 387. See Judeich, *RE* s.v. "Artabazos (3)"; Berve II 82-84 no. 152; Heckel 55; also Briant 2008, 151-58.

76. Artabazus was clearly an opponent of Bessus: Curt. 5.9-10; 5.12.18.

77. Curt. 8.1.19, 35.

Cleitus' displeasure spilled over into brutally frank criticism of Alexander's policies in general, especially those that involved his new role as King of Asia. The argument ended in tragedy, when the king murdered Cleitus as the banquet was breaking up. The effect was devastating—for the army and its leadership and for the king, in terms of both his policies and his psyche.[78] After a brief period of "mourning," the best remedy was to complete the subjugation of Sogdiana.

The army of occupation prepared to settle in for the winter of 328/7. Hephaestion was sent with a portion of the army to gather provisions in Bactria and winter there. Alexander remained in the region of Nautaca[79] in central western Sogdiana, a place that gave easy access to the main centers and potential trouble spots. But before winter came on, he directed his forces to Xenippa, an area dotted with villages, which bordered on the Scythian lands and was a haven for Bactrian exiles.[80] These fled the territory on news of Alexander's approach and withdrew to the south. Here they made a surprise attack on a contingent of Alexander's army led by Amyntas, the newly appointed Macedonian satrap.[81] The exiles, some 2,500 horsemen, fought with the fury of desperate men, who had no expectation of leniency on the Conqueror's part. In the end, having lost 700 men (of whom 300 were taken prisoner), they fled from the battlefield, leaving 80 Macedonians dead and 350 wounded. Nevertheless, Curtius claims, Alexander was willing to grant them a pardon.[82]

One is tempted, however, to wonder if the battle described by Curtius is the same one Arrian says was fought between Spitamenes and his Scythian allies against Coenus and Amyntas son of Nicolaus.[83] These insurgents had been driven out of Bactria by Craterus and crossed back into Sogdiana, where they picked up

---

78. The Cleitus affair is discussed at length in chapter 12.

79. Curt. 8.2.19: *in regionem, quam Nataca appellant.* Perhaps there was a region that took its name from the town.

80. Curt. 8.2.14: *ipse Xenippa pervenit. Scythiae confinis est regio habitaturque pluribus ac frequentibus vicis, quia ubertas terrae non indigenas modo detinet, sed etiam advenas invitat.* Seibert 1985, 140, puts Xenippa north of Maracanda; Treidler, *RE* IX A2 (1967) 1380–84 between Maracanda and Nautaca.

81. It is unclear exactly where this battle occurred and who Amyntas was. Curtius (8.2.14) had just recorded that Alexander had made a man named Amyntas satrap of Bactria-Sogdiana, and the term *praetor* is used by Curtius to mean either a military commander or a satrap (see, for example, Curt. 3.11.10: *Sabaces, praetor Aegypti*; and 6.9.28: *Amyntas, regius praetor*, one of Alexander's commanders).

82. Curt. 8.2.15-18.

83. Amyntas had apparently been left in Maracanda with Coenus and Meleager (both in command of their battalions of *pezhetairoi*), 400 of the Companion cavalry, all the *hippakontistai* (mounted javelin men), and the loyal Bactrians and Sogdianians (Arr. 4.17.3).

3,000 additional Scythian horsemen at Gabae.[84] From there, they moved to attack Amyntas, Coenus, and their forces, who emerged from Maracanda to engage them. But the details are different in virtually every respect:

> When Coenus and his troops learned of the approach of Spitamenes and his cavalry, they went forth themselves to meet them. A hard-fought battle ensued, and the Macedonians were victorious, with more than 800 of the barbarian horsemen falling in the clash, but of Coenus' men only twenty-five cavalry and twelve infantry. In the flight the Sogdianian forces still with Spitamenes, and most of the Bactrians, deserted their leader and came to Coenus to surrender. The Massagetan Scythians had been badly beaten in the fighting, and they now pillaged the baggage of the Bactrians and Sogdianians who had fought alongside them, after which they proceeded to flee into the desert. But when the news reached them that Alexander was on his way and heading toward the desert, they decapitated Spitamenes and sent the head to Alexander, hoping this act would keep the king from pursuing them. (Arr. 4.17.5-7)

Those who participated in the battle described by Arrian were Bactrians, Sogdianians, and Massagetae, all under the leadership of Spitamenes. They came from the south into Sogdiana, whereas the insurgents described by Curtius were Bactrians alone, coming from the north or northwest, and without a named leader. Their losses were 700 horsemen (of whom only 400 were killed). But they inflicted heavier casualties on the Macedonian force. In Arrian's account, 800 barbarians were killed, compared with only a handful of Macedonians. Hence, despite the superficial resemblance, the two passages appear to describe different engagements.

What opposition remained was restricted to the southeastern portion of Sogdiana, a mountainous area north of the Oxus and along the Wakhsh River. In this region were the lands of Oxyartes and Sisimithres. The latter was the lord of the fortress known as the Rock of Chorienes, where he lived with his wife and

---

84. Craterus' attack on Spitamenes and the Massagetae: Arr. 4.17.1-2. Curt. 8.1.6 only adds to the confusion: "News of the disaster [i.e. of Attinas and his men] was swiftly brought to Craterus, who arrived on the scene with his entire cavalry force only to find that the Massagetae had already fled. A thousand Dahae were cut down, and their defeat terminated the insurrection throughout the area." Again the accounts of Arrian and Curtius cannot be reconciled. Furthermore, Curtius regularly speaks of the Dahae, although these appear only three times in Arrian: at Gaugamela (3.11.3), with Bessus in flight (3.28.8, 10), and as *hippotoxotai* in the Indian campaign (5.12.2).

their five children.[85] He took his official name from the region he ruled, and thus he appears in the sources as both Sisimithres and Chorienes. When Alexander moved into Choriene, the local barons deposited their families and their belongings on the Rock. Since it was well provisioned, it may be that it was the regular practice for the natives to winter there. Oxyartes himself, bowing to necessity and the Conqueror, made his peace with Alexander at that time, if not before.[86] He soon served as an intermediary for the Macedonians and Sisimithres, for it was in the interests of both parties to bring about a negotiated settlement. At the time, there was probably not the slightest inkling of where this would lead:

> Alexander then pushed ahead against the Pareitacae, since large numbers of the barbarians were said to be also occupying a stronghold—another rocky ridge—in their country. This was called the "Rock of Chorienes," and to it had fled Chorienes himself and no small number of his underlings. The height of the ridge was some twenty stades, its circumference about sixty, and it had a sheer drop on every side and only one way up. This ascent, being narrow and not an easy climb—its formation was such as to be out of line with the place's natural features—was thus difficult, even if one faced no opposition and even in single file. A deep ravine all around also protected the ridge, so that anyone who intended bringing an army up to it would first have to see to a lot of filling in of that ravine in order to advance his army for an assault from level ground. (Arr. 4.21.1-2)

Alexander nevertheless attempted to besiege the Rock, the men laboring in relays and conducting the work day and night. Eventually, the rampart that was constructed brought the army into arrow range, where they continued their work behind protective screens:

> Panic-stricken at what had happened, Chorienes sent an envoy to Alexander, imploring him to send Oxyartes to him, and Alexander did send Oxyartes. When Oxyartes arrived, he urged Chorienes to surrender

---

85. She was both his mother and his wife, in accordance with local practice (Curt. 8.2.28); cf. Lane Fox 1973, 315: "Sisimithres, a baron who had married his own mother, perhaps because he was a Zoroastrian." On Zoroastrian next-of-kin marriage, see Boyce 1979, 53. Curt. 8.2.19, 33: Sisimithres had two sons by his own mother. Chorienes had three sons (Curt 8.4.21); Sisimithres had two sons and three daughters (*Metz Epit.* 19). He probably had more children by other wives or concubines.

86. Oxyartes may have surrendered to Alexander around the time that he prepared to winter at Nautaca.

himself as well as the stronghold to Alexander; there was, he told him, no place whatsoever that could not be taken by force by Alexander and his army, but if Chorienes accepted the man's word and his friendship, he had high praise for the king's word and just dealing—and among other things to confirm what he said, he adduced in particular his own treatment.

Accepting this, Chorienes himself came to Alexander with a number of his relatives and close friends, and on his arrival, Alexander gave him a warm response and a guarantee of his friendship. He then kept him there but instructed him to send a number of the men who had accompanied him down to go up to the ridge to order its surrender. . . . So far was Alexander from inflicting any harsh treatment on Chorienes that he handed over to him that very same stronghold and made him viceroy of his former subjects. (Arr. 4.21.6-9)

VI

For Spitamenes, the successful incursion into the heart of Bactria was to be his last. Pursued by Craterus, he and his Scythian horsemen fled in the direction of the desert, where they were joined by an additional 1,000 Massagetae. Nevertheless, they were defeated by the Macedonian force and lost 150 men.[87] Determined to make a counterattack, Spitamenes led his Scythians against Coenus, who was now in Sogdiana with the newly appointed satrap Amyntas son of Nicolaus. At a place called Gabae, located in the southwest of the region (it is said to have bordered on the lands of the Massagetae), he collected an additional force of 3,000 Scythian horsemen. As he approached Maracanda, Coenus and Amyntas brought their forces against him and inflicted another defeat, in which his allies lost more than 800 men.[88] For the Scythians, this was enough. Not much later, they turned on the Bactrians and Sogdianians, most of whom took flight and surrendered to the Macedonians. According to one version, the Massagetae killed Spitamenes and sent his head to Alexander.[89] His partner in the insurrection, Dataphernes, was arrested by the Dahae and brought by his captors

---

87. Arr. 4.17.1-2. Curt. 8.1.6, however, talks about Craterus defeating and killing about 1,000 of the Dahae.

88. Arr. 4.17.6.

89. Arr. 4.17.7 says they sent the head to Alexander in order to keep him away from them (τὴν κεφαλὴν παρὰ Ἀλέξανδρον πέμπουσιν, ὡς ἀποτρέψοντες ἀπὸ σφῶν αὐτῶν τούτῳ τῷ ἔργῳ).

to the Macedonian camp.[90] It was the end of Scythian involvement in the fight against the invader. The campaign of 328 had all but crushed the resistance.

A more sensational account of the death of Spitamenes is given by Curtius (8.3.1-15), and this is similar in many respects to the version of the *Metz Epitome* (20–23). Spitamenes had a burning love for his wife (her name is unknown), and since he could not bear to be parted from her, he took her on endless campaigns with him. She, however, was exhausted by this itinerant life and begged Spitamenes to surrender to Alexander. But this only aroused the jealousy of her husband, who assumed that "her desire to surrender to Alexander . . . arose from her confidence in her beauty."[91] It was only because her brothers intervened that Spitamenes did not kill her. Eventually, the woman invited her husband to a banquet and, having plied him with drink, murdered him as he slept. Later she brought the severed head into Alexander's camp:

> Alexander was now prey to conflicting thoughts as he considered the various aspects of the matter. He believed it a great benefit to himself that a treacherous deserter had been assassinated, a man whose continued existence would have proved an obstacle to his great designs, but he was also repelled by the enormity of the crime—a woman treacherously murdering a man who had treated her well and who was the father of their children. The savagery of the deed carried more weight with him than the gratitude for the favor, however, and he had her ordered from the camp. He did not want her tainting the character and civilized temperament of the Greeks with this example of barbarian lawlessness. (Curt. 8.3.14-15)

Once again, Arrian's version of events differs from those of Curtius and those who followed the same source.[92] Whereas Arrian calls Spitamenes' Scythian allies the Massagetae and attributes his beheading to the tribesmen, Curtius speaks of the Dahae and ascribes the treachery to Spitamenes' wife. Now, it is clear that

---

90. Curt. 8.3.16. *Metz Epit.* 23 says that both Dataphernes and Catanes were arrested by the Scythians. Curt. 8.5.2 and Arr. 4.22.2 say that Craterus hunted down Catanes and his accomplice Haustanes, taking the latter prisoner and killing the former. This represented the end of the resistance in the satrapy. I am reluctant to accept Bosworth's view (II 140) that "there were two Sogdian nobles named Catanes, one Spitamenes' partner in rebellion and the other a local magnate in Pareitacene."

91. Curt. 8.3.4.

92. In this case, we have only *Metz Epit.* 20–23, which gives a similar account but suggests that Alexander dismissed her from the camp lest people think he was motivated to keep her there by lust for her beauty. Burstein 1999 thinks that Cleitarchus' version of the story may have influenced the biblical story of Judith.

Curtius is aware of the difference between these two branches of Scythians: he mentions the Massagetae on several occasions.[93] These tribes were located to the west of Bactria and along the Oxus River, the Dahae occupying the lower Oxus and the Massagetae the lands somewhat to their east.[94] Why he substitutes the Dahae for the Massagetae is unclear, but it is doubtful that if the murder of Spitamenes occurred among the Dahae, they were ignorant of the fact until after the wife had brought her husband's head to Alexander. Curtius continues the account quoted above: "On learning of Spitamenes' murder, the Dahae imprisoned Dataphernes, his partner in the rebellion, and surrendered him along with themselves to Alexander."[95] Can the two versions be reconciled? To begin with, Curtius' statement that Alexander moved against the Dahae because he learned that "Spitamenes was among them" does not rule out the likelihood of his previous campaigning with the Massagetae. These are named by Curtius as participating in the attack on Attinas.[96] It appears that both tribes were involved in the resistance and that Spitamenes worked in conjunction with the Massagetae, while Dataphernes and Catanes were with the Dahae. Now, since we are told that after the debacle against Coenus' forces, the Massagetae turned on their allies, causing the Bactrians and Sogdianians to flee from their camp and surrender to Alexander, it may be that Spitamenes also distanced himself and moved into the territory of the Dahae. Here he was killed. We do not know by whom,[97] but Curtius attributes the act to his wife. Whether at the instigation of the Scythians or on her own initiative, the woman took her husband's head to Alexander's camp in an attempt to win a pardon. The mission proved successful, and it inspired the Dahae to follow suit by arresting Dataphernes. Catanes, in all likelihood, fled to join what remained of the resistance. Some role for Spitamenes' wife is made all the more plausible by the fact that her daughter—if we may assume that she was the mother of Apame—remained in Alexander's entourage (perhaps even in the company of Roxane) and later married Seleucus, for it is otherwise unusual that

93. 4.12.7, 15.2; 6.3.9; 8.1.3 (attacking Attinas). The Massagetae and Dahae are mentioned together at 6.3.9 and 8.1.6, 8.

94. Curt. 8.1.8 says the Chorasmians bordered on the lands of the Dahae and the Massagetae.

95. Curt. 8.3.15; cf. *Metz Epit.* 23: "When the Dahae heard what had happened, they arrested Catanes and Dataphernes and brought them to Alexander."

96. Curt. 8.1.3, naming the Massagetae, the Bactrian "exiles" (*exsules*), and Attinas but omitting Spitamenes; Arr. 4.16.4-5, naming Spitamenes, the Massagetae, and "Sogdianian fugitives" (τῶν Σογδιανῶν τινες φυγάδων) but omitting the name Attinas. Both writers refer to the same event.

97. Strabo 11.11.6 C518 says that Spitamenes was killed by the barbarians (Σπιταμένους ὑπὸ τῶν βαρβάρων διαφθαρέντος).

the daughter of a dangerous enemy, who had been faithless to the king, should be given a prestigious marriage and subsequently be held in honor.[98]

Of the prominent leaders of Bactria and Sogdiana, there remained only Haustanes (hitherto unmentioned by the sources) and Catanes. These, as we have noted, were soon brought to heel by Craterus. One other notable, Oxyartes, is somewhat of an enigma. He owes his importance to the fact that his daughter Roxane became Alexander's wife, but he is attested only once before the events of 328/7. Nothing indicates that he was ever in the entourage of Darius III, and there is no good reason to assume that he had been previously acquainted with the family of Artabazus. Hence, the assumption that he and his family were captured at the Rock of Ariamazes but spared because of their associations with Artabazus can be no more than speculation, even if this helps to explain why Arrian associates Roxane with the Rock of Sogdiana.[99]

VII

The end of the struggle for Bactria and Sogdiana came as an anticlimax. The capture of Ariamazes' rock, the sweep campaign in Sogdiana, and the surrender of the Scythian allies left the Macedonian army in control of most of the satrapy. This control was tightened by garrisons imposed in existing towns and a network of new military colonies. Arrian adds that Chorienes gave supplies to Alexander's army and thus concludes the story. But it appears that he collapses two episodes in the career of Chorienes (and Alexander's campaign) into one.[100] It is clear from Curtius that Alexander conducted a second campaign in the region at the end of winter 328/7 in an attempt to put an end to resistance in Sogdiana. Western Sogdiana had been subdued in 329, but a second rebellion arose in 328, which was put down mainly through the efforts of Coenus and the satrap Amyntas son of Nicolaus. Before that second rebellion, most of the Pamir region had been secured, leaving only those who held out on the Rock of Chorienes. When its

---

98. Whether there is an element of Seleucid propaganda in all this is unclear.

99. He appears once in the company of Bessus at the beginning of 329 (Arr. 3.28.10). Bosworth's view that his family was captured at the Rock of Sogdiana but the marriage was delayed (II 131: "She may have been in Alexander's entourage for several months before the king noticed and married her") strikes me as unnecessary and implausible. Given the chronological disagreements between Arrian and the vulgate, it is more likely that Arrian misunderstood the place of Roxane's capture. Arr. 4.18–19.5, dated to the spring of 327. The date is probably correct, but the location is not (pace Bosworth 1981).

100. Arr. 4.21.10.

commander Sisimithres surrendered over the winter of 328/7, all that remained of the resistance north of Pareitacene and the borderlands of the Sacae.

Weather hampered the Macedonian effort in that region. Curtius refers to the area in question as Gazaba, but the location is uncertain, though clearly it must have been around the headwaters of the Polytimetus and perhaps even between that river and the Iaxartes. The winter conditions cost Alexander "the lives of 2,000 soldiers, camp followers and servants."[101] But the crisis was averted when Sisimithres appeared with much-needed aid: pack animals and 2,000 camels, no doubt carrying dry goods, as well as sheep and cattle which represented "food on the hoof." The Conqueror in gratitude reciprocated by looting the lands of the Sacae and presenting 30,000 head of cattle as a gift to his recent benefactor.[102]

At this point, the Alexander historians descend into chaos, for the simple reason that it was unclear to them—at least to the extant historians—that Sisimithres and Chorienes were one and the same person.[103] Arrian knows only the latter, Strabo only the former, and Curtius and the *Metz Epitome* assume that they are different individuals. Hence, in the last case, when Alexander comes to Chorienes, where he is lavishly entertained, it is assumed that he has come to a new region and to a new "satrap." In fact, the aid given to Alexander by Sisimithres and the recompense paid by the king to his benefactor were followed by a lavish banquet on the Rock of Chorienes. It celebrated the all-but-complete subjugation of Sogdiana. On that occasion, Alexander met and married Oxyartes' daughter Roxane. Because the text of Curtius is corrupt at this point, we may turn to the account given by the *Metz Epitome*, which made use of the same primary source:

> Chorienes entertained Alexander at his house and introduced as dancers at the banquet his own unmarried daughters along with the unmarried daughters of his friends. Among them was the daughter of Oxyartes, Roxane, who was the most beautiful of all. Enchanted by the sight of her and fired with lust, Alexander asked who she was and who her father was, to discover that she was the daughter of Oxyartes, also a guest at the dinner. He took his cup, made a prayer to the gods, and then proceeded to declare that many people often found that many things happen contrary to their expectations, that many kings had had sons by captives or sent

---

101. Curt. 8.4.13.

102. Curt. 8.4.19-20.

103. I am no longer certain that Sisimithres' (Chorienes') stronghold was located as far south as Koh-i-nor. The sources suggest two things: it was not far from Nautaca, and it was near the lands of the Sacae.

daughters to foreign nations to get married, using such a bond to ratify alliances. "So," he continued, "I do not consider the Macedonians your betters in terms of race, and no more would I consider you unworthy of intermarriage with us, even if you had sought alliance with us after a defeat. I am going to make such a match, and I shall ensure that the rest of the Macedonians follow my example." After these words of exhortation from Alexander, each of his friends took away a girl as his bride, to the great delight of Oxyartes and the other barbarians. (*Metz Epit.* 28–31)[104]

Smitten by the beauty of Roxane—at least, so the story goes—Alexander decided to marry her, conducting the ceremony (at least in part) according to local tradition.[105] His local commanders (probably those who acted as *phrourarchoi* of the military colonies) also took natives wives.[106] And thus, peace and stability

---

104. See Heckel 1986. The text of Curtius should thus read: *Inde pervenit in regionem, cui* Chorienes, *satrapes nobilis, praeerat, qui se regis potestati fideique permisit. Ille imperio ei reddito haud amplius, quam ut duo ex tribus filiis secum militarent, exegit. Satrapes etiam eo, qui penes ipsum reliquebatur, tradito barbara opulentia convivium, quo regem accipiebat, instruxerat. Id cum multa comitate celebraret, introduci XXX nobiles virgines iussit. Inter* quas erant <filiae suae virgines et> filia Oxyartis, *Roxane nomine, eximia corporis specie et decore habitus in barbaris raro.* Chorienes is the correct emendation of *cohortandus* (recognized by Geiger, *Feldzüge* 37), but Bardon, in the Budé, changed it to *Oxyartes*, which makes little sense. See also Strabo 11.11.4 C517: ἐλεῖν δὲ καὶ πέτρας ἐρυμνὰς σφόδρα ἐκ προδοσίας, τήν τε ἐν τῇ Βακτριανῇ, τὴν Σισιμίθρου, ἐν ᾗ εἶχεν Ὀξυάρτης τὴν θυγατέρα Ῥωξάνην, καὶ τὴν ἐν τῇ Σογδιανῇ τὴν τοῦ Ὤξου, οἱ δ' Ἀριαμάζου φασί. τὴν μὲν οὖν Σισιμίθρου πεντεκαίδεκα σταδίων ἱστοροῦσι τὸ ὕψος, ὀγδοήκοντα δὲ τὸν κύκλον· ἄνω δ' ἐπίπεδον καὶ εὔγεων, ὅσον πεντακοσίους ἄνδρας τρέφειν δυναμένην, ἐν ᾗ καὶ ξενίας τυχεῖν πολυτελοῦς, καὶ γάμους ἀγαγεῖν Ῥωξάνης τῆς Ὀξυάρτου θυγατρὸς τὸν Ἀλέξανδρον· τὴν δὲ τῆς Σογδιανῆς διπλασίαν τὸ ὕψος φασί. ("They say that Alexander captured, through treachery, two rocky outcrops that were extremely well defended, that of Sisimithres in Bactriana, where Oxyartes kept his daughter Roxane, and that of the Oxus in Sogdiana (though some call this one the Rock of Ariamazes). According to the accounts of it, the Rock of Sisimithres is fifteen stades in height, with a circumference of eighty stades, and its top is level and fertile enough to support 500 men. Here Alexander met with a warm welcome and married Oxyartes' daughter Roxane. The outcrop in Sogdiana is said to be twice the height of the other.") The ancients were either confused by the geography or careless in their use of the terms *Bactria* and *Sogdiana. Metz Epit.* 19, for example, says that Nautaca is "in Bactria."

105. Thus Schwarz *Feldzüge* 82; Lane Fox 1973, 317.

106. Diod. 17 contents: ὡς Ἀλέξανδρος ἐρασθεὶς Ῥωξάνης τῆς Ὀξυάρτου ἔγημεν αὐτὴν καὶ τῶν φίλων πολλοὺς ἔπεισε γῆμαι τὰς τῶν ἐπισήμων βαρβάρων θυγατέρας. Cf. Baynham 1995, 70: "it is quite likely that the garrison forces would regularly have taken local wives." But the reference to *philoi* (= *hetairoi*) suggests that these husbands may have been of a higher rank than even the *phrourarchoi.*

returned to the region, something that two years of campaigning had failed to bring about.[107]

It was left to Craterus and a group of phalanx commanders to tie up the loose ends. Craterus defeated and killed Catanes and took Haustanes prisoner. Attalus and Polyperchon also contributed to the final subjugation of the insurgents. At the end of this last campaign, they joined Alexander in Bactra. When the dust settled, military outposts dotted the satrapy, and not fewer than 10,000 Greek mercenaries were deposited in Central Asia. Ultimately, it proved to be an unshakeable outpost of Hellenism, despite attempts in 325/4 and 323 to uproot the population. But in the same spring as he put an end to the resistance in Sogdiana, Alexander was forced to confront the Macedonian reaction to his orientalizing policies.

107. Müller 2012, 299, notes an interesting sidelight to the effectiveness of the political marriage to Roxane: "After the wedding, Roxane vanished from the scene to reappear only in the last days of Alexander's life. . . . As a guarantee of Oxyartes' loyalty, she lost her symbolic aura as soon as the revolt in Bactria and Sogdiana came to an end. In the light of the Macedonian resentment, Alexander will have had even less interest in giving her a public profile."

12

Persianizing and the Internal Enemy

BEFORE HIS EXECUTION, Hermolaus, one of the royal Pages (*paides basilikoi*), defended his actions—he and several of his cohorts had plotted to murder Alexander while he slept—by saying that he and every Macedonian who valued freedom could no longer tolerate the king's behavior: "the unconscionable killing of Philotas and the even more monstrous killings of Parmenion and the others who died at the time; the murder of Cleitus in his cups; the Median clothing; the obeisance that Alexander wanted and still had not abandoned as an idea; and the king's excesses in drinking and sleeping."[1] This conspiracy in 327 was—for the time being—the last in a line of confrontations between Alexander and his men that had their origins in the changing attitudes and practices of the Macedonian king. The effective propaganda of Panhellenism and vengeance was a double-edged sword. What had served the needs of the expedition and the member states of the League of Corinth in the years leading up to Persepolis and the death of Darius, which followed soon afterward, had now become a liability. Hence Alexander demobilized the allied troops, retaining only those who wished to remain with the army as mercenaries and the Macedonian troops, who served at the king's pleasure. Defeat of the Achaemenid king and the pretender Bessus meant that Alexander needed to make the conquest his own, that he must now work on reconciliation and present a new image to the people of *his* empire. Among the barbarians, there were those who made their peace with the Conqueror, though some played him false or engaged in futile resistance. For the victors, any attempt to accommodate their former enemies was regarded as betrayal, an elevation of the conquered, which tarnished their victories and personal accomplishments.

---

1. Arr. 4.14.2.

In the Path of Conquest. Waldemar Heckel, Oxford University Press (2020). © Oxford University Press.
DOI: 10.1093/oso/9780190076689.001.0001

I

The death of Darius and the flight of his assassins to the Upper Satrapies left Alexander with one final windfall. Not only had the "loyalists" submitted to him, but the securing of Ecbatana and the capture of Darius' wagons, laden with booty, left him with all the trappings of the Persian royalty. Now the virtually undisputed ruler of Asia—he had not yet learned that Bessus had assumed the upright tiara and was demanding to be recognized as King Artaxerxes—he succumbed to the temptations of the tangible symbols of victory. Persepolis would have been a hollow victory had he not been able to run down the fleeing Achaemenid ruler. But now, with Darius' corpse in his possession, the entire mandate of the expedition needed to be revisited. No longer the avenger of Greece (*ultor Graeciae*), he was suddenly faced with a dilemma: should he turn back—an unlikely scenario— or move forward, placing the remnants of the Persian Empire firmly in the hands of the new "King of Asia"? The first visible changes in style and attitude occurred in Zadracarta. At that time, the transformation of the Conqueror was visible in his imitation of the Persian kings, who the Macedonians wrongly thought had "quasi-divine status."[2] He adopted Persian dress and the diadem[3]—although he did not wear trousers or assume the upright tiara—and this was mirrored by his arrogant demeanor;[4] it was even alleged that he used Darius' seal for letters written to his subjects in Asia.[5] Furthermore, he now consorted with his predecessor's 365 concubines—surprising, and perhaps fictitious, behavior on the part of one thought to have had little physical intimacy with women—and eunuchs.[6]

---

2. Curt. 6.6.2: *Persicae regiae par deorum potentiae fastigium aemulabatur*.

3. Curt. 6.6.4. Cf. 3.3.19. On the diadem, see Ritter 1965 and 1987.

4. Curt. 6.6.5: "with the clothes he had also adopted Persian habits, and a contemptuous demeanor accompanied by ostentatious dress."

5. Full discussion in Baldus 1987; Hammond 1995 attempts a refutation of the idea that Alexander used two seals, based on nine passages from the ancient sources. The question of whether Alexander actually used "Darius' seal" on documents intended for Persians cannot be answered with certainty on the basis of this evidence. Hammond points out that Alexander's "policy was one of assimilation and partnership" (1995, 202) and that the use of separate seals ran counter to this. But we are dealing with an ongoing transformation, not unlike Alexander's approach to court ceremonial. Atkinson II 203 allows for the use of a second ring, at least initially.

6. For similar accounts of the king's transformation, see Diod. 17.77.4-6; Justin 12.3.8-12; *Metz Epit.* 1–2; Plut. *Alex.* 45.1-3. I do not subscribe to the view that the king had no interest in women, but he was clearly no Caesar or Demetrius Poliorcetes when it came to affairs with women.

It was not only the manner of his dress and the adoption of Persian practices that gave offense; even more contentious was the introduction of barbarians into the court life and the army. According to Diodorus, "he installed ushers of the Asiatic race in his court, and then he ordered the most distinguished persons to act as his guards; among these was Darius' brother Oxyathres."[7] How he spent his nights with concubines and even eunuchs was at least a matter for the imagination. But Persian ushers controlled access to a king who had traditionally been primus inter pares.[8]

At Hecatompylus, Alexander dismissed the allied troops who had remained with him after the first demobilization at Ecbatana. Those who stayed on no longer fought for slogans but for pay. It was a new venture on which the troops embarked, and they followed—as they realized, quickly and to their own disgust— a new leader, whose self-styling as an Eastern potentate troubled the common soldier and the officer alike. If the vulgate sources can be trusted, the troops saw the transformation as a sign of personal degeneration instead of a shift in policy. For them, all their previous victories were for naught, as the king's actions appeared to elevate the vanquished over the victors—and indeed, the king, too, had, in their opinion, seemed to demote himself "from king of Macedon to satrap of Darius."[9] The orientalizing policy of the king, which was reaping political rewards, was treated by the army and its leaders as an affront. Not surprisingly, opposition to the new Alexander was not slow in manifesting itself.

II

When the army reached Phrada (Farah) in what is today Afghanistan, news of a conspiracy was brought to Alexander. It was reported that a certain *hetairos* of the king, Dimnus of Chalaestra, had joined a group of conspirators which included one of the seven Bodyguards (*Somatophylakes*), a man named Demetrius.[10] The conspirators are often dismissed by modern scholars as nonentities, a complete misrepresentation of the facts. Dimnus himself was a man of higher rank—the *hetairoi* (Companions) comprised a group of nobles who formed the king's

---

7. Diod. 17.77.4 for the ushers: ῥαβδούχους Ἀσιαγενεῖς. Oxyathres: *Metz Epit.* 2.

8. On these, see Olbrycht 2007, 312.

9. Curt. 6.6.10.

10. Several of the conspirators had relatively common names, but this should not lead us to doubt either their historicity or their importance: Peucolaus, Nicanor, Iolaus, Amyntas, Demetrius, Aphobetus, Dioxenus (or Theoxenus), and Archepolis. Not named by Dimnus was another who was convicted of treason: Calis (Calas?).

comitatus;[11] in battle and at court, they held positions of responsibility and priv-
ilege. The *Somatophylakes* were among the highest officials in the kingdom—the
historian and later king of Egypt Ptolemy was inordinately proud of his rank as
Somatophylax[12]—and Dimnus allegedly commented that the conspirators included "brave and illustrious men."[13] The grievances of these conspirators were
clear enough: they resented the king's policy of orientalism. A cavalryman could
be expected to object to the change in dress imposed upon the members of the
Companions, and any one of the king's personal Bodyguards would have found
the creation of a second group of guardsmen,[14] comprising noble Persians, and
the institution of a squad of ushers equally offensive.[15] Philotas, too, may have
understood these concerns. As the commander of the Companions, he would
have been sensitive to the men's objections to Persian attire. This does not mean
that he was an actual participant in the conspiracy, but it, among other things,
explains why he may not have wished it to fail.

It is unfortunate, however, that discussion of this conspiracy has been
sidetracked by the fact that it led to the downfall of Philotas and his father,
Parmenion. Elaborate theories about Alexander's role in the elimination of
Philotas—according to one scholar, it amounted to "framing"[16]—have dominated
modern scholarship, and the underlying causes, as well as the grievances and aims
of the real conspirators, have become of secondary importance. Those theories

11. See Tarn II 137–39 (especially II 138: "The original Companions were nobles, and also landowners, for in a land of somewhat primitive economy like Macedonia a noble could be nothing
else; one might, by analogy, call them the king's 'peers'"). Beckwith 2009, 20, clearly unaware
of Macedonian practices, says that "the Chinese—like the Classical and later Greeks—did not
themselves have the comitatus tradition."

12. See especially Seibert 1969, 8. *Somatophylakia* as a practice (which began with the training
of *paides basilikoi* in θεραπεία τοῦ βασιλέως) and the membership of the unit: Heckel 1986
and *Marshals²* 245–59. Cf. Hammond 1991b, which, although it is often cited with approval,
contains numerous unconvincing conclusions.

13. Curt. 6.7.6: *Tum Dymnus aperit in tertium diem regi insidias conparatas seque eius consilii
fortibus viris et inlustribus esse participem.* Cf. Curt. 6.10.17: Philotas said that if Dimnus' report had proved to be false he would have endangered the lives of many of the king's friends,
that is, of the named "conspirators" (*et ego viderer multis amicorum regis fuisse periculi causa*).

14. These were clearly not members of the Seven, but they may have been a parallel Persian
guard or a "shadow" guard unit (an *antitagma*).

15. One might exclude from this group Hephaestion, who shared Alexander's enthusiasm for
virtually everything, including his Persianizing policy. On the ushers (ῥαβδοῦχοι), see Collins
2017, 75.

16. Badian 1960, reiterated in Badian 2000a.

need not detain us,[17] since they have little bearing on the problem of resistance to Alexander, unless we believe that Philotas and Parmenion were actively hostile to the king, hardly a stance to be taken by "innocent victims."

As it turned out, the conspiracy came to Alexander's attention. Philotas was implicated. Indeed, he incriminated himself by failing to pass the news of the plot on to Alexander. He did not take it seriously, he was later to say in his defense. Historian Guy MacLean Rogers rightly observes:

> If a minor officer in the U.S. Army reported the existence of a conspiracy to assassinate the president, a conspiracy that allegedly included a member of the presidential security detail, to one of the Joint Chiefs of Staff and the chief did not disclose the contents of the report immediately and in full, and this fact was subsequently discovered, the chief would be removed from command and court-martialed without delay.[18]

Hence, it is time to stop feeling sorry for Philotas, who, if he was the victim of this story, was the victim of his own malice or stupidity. We have no reason to discount Demetrius' plot.[19] Philotas admitted that he had heard of it, and he confessed again under torture (hardly a surprise) and finally resorted to weak arguments about how and why he did not take it seriously. The speeches attributed to both Alexander and Philotas by Curtius must be treated with caution because they are rhetorical devices and heavily influenced by episodes in Roman imperial history (even more so in the case of the subsequent trial of Amyntas son of Andromenes). Nevertheless, these speeches and the cloak-and-dagger scenes that precede them have been mined by Alexander's detractors—who have been happy to see him as the precursor of the bad emperor—with little regard for the historical context of the event and the historiographical mindset of the author.

---

17. The most important studies are Adams 2003; Badian 1960 and 2000a; Cauer 1894, 8–38; Heckel 1977b and *Marshals*[2] 55–59; cf. also Heckel 1982; Reames 2008; Rubinsohn 1977.

18. Rogers 2004, 147.

19. Hamilton 1973, 95, expresses some doubt about Demetrius' involvement (as is clear from the scare quotes around the word *plot*) but engages in a little fantasy in his account of events. This reflects his faith in Arrian as the superior source: "The case of Demetrius the Bodyguard well illustrates Alexander's feeling of insecurity and his skill in dealing with those who had incurred his suspicion. Demetrius, when accused of complicity in the 'plot' of Philotas, stoutly denied the charge and Alexander accepted his denial. Evidence of his guilt is clearly lacking. Nevertheless, soon after, Demetrius was removed from his position as Bodyguard and vanishes from our records." This, of course, reverses the positions of Philotas and Demetrius. What Hamilton ought to have said is that Philotas was accused of complicity in the plot of Demetrius.

Why, then, did Demetrius and his accomplices plot to kill Alexander, and what did they hope to achieve? As we have noted, the Panhellenic propaganda, which had served the Macedonian king so well in the first half of the campaign, now proved to be a hindrance to his plans of further conquest. After Persepolis, the Thessalians and the Greek allies were sent home from Ecbatana, with full pay and bonuses, except for those who chose to reenlist and serve as mercenaries.[20] Darius' flight in the direction of the Upper Satrapies required the remaining troops—primarily Macedonians, Thracians, and mercenaries—to pursue him at speeds three and four times greater than the average daily rate.[21] His death at least gave the troops an opportunity to rest. Still Alexander demanded more from them; the continued resistance of Bessus and his followers drew the Conqueror to the fringes of the empire. The Macedonians, although they constituted a standing national army and stood loyally by the king who had brought them so much success (not to mention plunder), could hardly have imagined a campaign that would take them far beyond the Iranian heartland. The obligations to the allies in the west had been met, but the boots on the ground continued to point eastward. With the introduction of Persian style, at the court and in the army, the road of conquest became even longer.

Conspiracies based on emotion are seldom clearly formulated, nor do they give much thought to what will follow the accomplishment of the main objective. Elizabeth Carney, in her discussion of Macedonian conspiracies, notes that in plots of this sort, the conspirators do "not appear to wish to seize the throne for themselves and often seem to desire only the removal of the present king and nothing further, their motivation is unclear, as is the political significance of their act."[22] In this case, that objective was the elimination of a leader whose personality and policies had become objectionable to many of the troops. These men were angry with Alexander and determined to put an end to his actions, even if this

---

20. Darius' death: Arr. 3.21.10; Plut. *Alex.* 42.5; Curt. 5.13.16-25; Justin 11.15.5-15; Diod. 17.73. Demobilization: Plut. *Alex.* 42.5; Arr. 3.19.5-6 (Ecbatana). Arrian does not mention Hecatompylus at all, but it is clear that the final discharge of allied troops took place before Alexander left Zadracarta (north of Hecatompylus) in pursuit of Bessus in August or September 330 (before reaching Phrada, Alexander had spent thirty days subduing Aria; he had left Zadracarta at least twenty-two days earlier).

21. After mopping up the resistance in Hyrcania and in the land of the Mardians, Alexander set out once again from Hecatompylus (where some of the sources say the allied troops were dismissed) on a path that led to Bactria via the Merv Oasis. The march rates were once again brisk, to say the least. Dodge 1890, 439 estimates that the troops moved from Zadracarta to Aria, a distance of more than 500 miles (800+ kilometers) in twenty days, at least two and a half times the normal rate.

22. Carney 1983, 261.

meant jeopardizing the entire campaign. Foremost in the minds of the soldiers who could be expected to support the conspirators—or, rather, condone their actions—was the reversal of the king's Persianizing program and the prospect of marching home, to bask in the glory of their achievement and enjoy the spoils of victory. Of the latter they had already been deprived by Alexander's actions; resuming the march from Zadracarta in pursuit of further conquest, he stripped the army of the burdens of material wealth. The fact that Alexander torched his own baggage before destroying that of the others was small consolation.[23]

Hence, the Persianizing of the king, the favorable treatment of the barbarian nobility, the changes in court practice, the continuation of an unpopular campaign, and the loss of the accumulated booty induced Demetrius and his group to conspire against Alexander. Philotas may have been sympathetic to their cause, but he would not have gained much personal power from the success of the plot. It is absurd to think that Parmenion could have assumed the kingship.[24] If anyone might have replaced Alexander on the throne, it was his namesake from Lyncestis, a man who was already being carried around in chains for a previous act of treason. His execution is depicted as a matter of "housekeeping" after the elimination of the conspirators and Philotas. In fact, the Conqueror must have feared him as a potential candidate for the kingship, a man whose bloodline gave him a legitimate claim to the throne, a rallying point for disaffected Macedonians.[25] Hamilton observes that "Alexander evidently now felt that his namesake, being of royal blood, might become a focus for plots against his own life,"[26] as if his concerns pertained to the future. If ever there was an opportunity to put the Lyncestian on the throne, this had been it. That the present group of would-be

---

23. Curt. 6.6.14-15. Alexander's own sacrifice was, in some ways, a hollow gesture. One is reminded of Xenophon's comment on the younger Cyrus' willingness to part with material things, which was hardly surprising in light of the fact that he had more to give (Xen. *Anab.* 1.9.24: καὶ τὸ μὲν τὰ μεγάλα νικᾶν τοὺς φίλους εὖ ποιοῦντα οὐδὲν θαυμαστόν, ἐπειδή γε καὶ δυνατ ώτερος ἦν).

24. Curtius, who was familiar with the Roman army's ability to create an emperor, makes Alexander say to Dimnus: "what is the vicious crime I have plotted against you to justify your decision that Philotas deserves the rule of the Macedonians more than I myself?" (6.7.30: *quod in te, Dymne, tantum cogitavi nefas, ut tibi Macedonum regno dignior Philotas me quoque ipso videretur?*). Rubinsohn 1977, 418, believes that there were other forces at work: "Parmenio's apparently innocuous—and superfluous—letter [see Curt. 6.9.13-15] may have been a signal to Philotas that agreement with Antipatros had been reached. . . . [T]he execution of Antipatros's son-in-law, Alexander of Lyncestis, who was at hand, and Antipatros's fright at the news, fit into the picture."

25. For Alexander the Lyncestian, see Berve II 17–19 no. 37; Carney 1980; Abramenko 1992a; Heckel 19 s.v. "Alexander [4]" and *Marshals²* 23–31.

26. Hamilton 1973, 95.

assassins had not considered the Lyncestian as the Conqueror's replacement is inconceivable. In short, we may conclude that there was a dangerous conspiracy afoot, one that Philotas deliberately refused to divulge to his king; that the conspirators were not, as is usually stated, nonentities; that they were motivated by Alexander's orientalizing policies; that they probably expected the army to accept the king's death as a welcome fait accompli; that Demetrius the Bodyguard was well placed to assassinate Alexander; and finally, that an acceptable candidate for the kingship was at hand. The whole affair ended badly for the conspirators, for Philotas, Parmenion, and Alexander Lyncestes. But the grievances that gave rise to the conspiracy of Demetrius had not been eradicated.

III

Matters came to a head a second time, almost two years later at a drinking party in Maracanda. The campaigning in Sogdiana had been hard, but there was little in the king's own behavior, besides the continuation of his orientalizing policies, that aggravated the ill will. More disturbing was the memory of Alexander's execution of Philotas and his father, and perhaps also the personnel changes that followed.[27] At any rate, the argument that arose between Alexander and Black Cleitus over their cups escalated to verbal abuse and eventually murder.

Alcohol consumption was the common denominator of the Macedonian banquet, where unmixed wine was imbibed as quickly as it flowed. These parties were generally raucous affairs, too frequently punctuated by gestures, and even overt acts, of aggression which saw the inebriated guests (and even their hosts) reaching for their swords or a nearby spear. Only rarely did they end in tragedy. The banquet in Maracanda was one such exception. Cleitus came to the event brooding over the king's decision to leave him behind as satrap of Bactria and Sogdiana, a position vacated by Artabazus. The reasons for the latter's resignation was not entirely clear, and the official reason (old age) appears to disguise a more serious problem. For a fighting man like Cleitus, satrapal rule was a thankless responsibility. Administrative tasks—even if they included the policing of the province and the suppression of insurgents—had little appeal, and the remoteness of the satrapy, combined with its rude inhabitants, made the "honor"

---

27. Arr. 3.27.4-5 notes that Hephaestion, the king's favorite, was promoted to the command of half the Companion cavalry (the other half was assigned to Cleitus) and that Ptolemy replaced Demetrius as Bodyguard. But the deployment of troops during the campaigns in Central Asia shows that there were more substantial changes in the command structure of the army, particularly a further reorganization of the Companion cavalry. The promotion of Cleitus—and Hephaestion, for that matter—turned out to be only a temporary reward.

unpalatable.[28] In truth, the assignment was a thinly disguised demotion. Heated by wine, Cleitus listened to the king's own comments and those of his sycophants, praising his military prowess, remarking that he was not only superior to his father but a rival of the heroes of old and the immortal gods. But the first of the tensions to be exposed was that between the older traditionalists, who had served under Philip. The younger men cheered the king when he eulogized his own accomplishments and disparaged those of his father. In fact, Alexander went so far as to usurp credit for the victory at Chaeronea, saying that Philip had been wounded during the battle and "lay on the ground, finding that to play dead was the safest course of action," while he himself protected his father with his shield. And he added that Philip "could never bring himself to admit this."[29]

The story about Philip's actions at Chaeronea is almost certainly an invention, either by Curtius or by his source. Alexander and his father were positioned at opposite ends of the battle line in that engagement, and it is said that the praise the Macedonians heaped upon his son for his exemplary actions was a source of pride to the father. Plutarch remarks: "Philip was excessively fond of his son, so that he even rejoiced to hear the Macedonians call Alexander their king, but Philip their general."[30] But what Curtius depicts is a characteristic of Alexander that is hard to refute. He was far less magnanimous than his father, jealous of his own reputation, and sensitive to any slight. And of course, he could never forget that Cleitus had saved *his* life at the Granicus—something that he acknowledged infrequently and with reluctance. The older Macedonians recognized the difference between father and son, and on occasion their faces mirrored the unwelcome demons of his troubled conscience. But the flattery of the younger men and the court parasites gave substance to his illusions. Men like Cleitus—and before him Parmenion—were unpleasant reminders of his roots, of his debts to his father and the previous generation.

According to Curtius, Cleitus began to praise Philip and ranked his exploits in Europe above those of Alexander's Asian campaign, and this was followed

---

28. *Honor exilii.* Schachermeyr 1973, 364: "in Wahrheit aber bedeutete es Entfernung aus dem königlichen Kreis, aus der kämpfenden Truppe, bedeutete es Isolierung und Kaltstellung." Cleitus himself is said to have remarked: "You assign me the province of Sogdiana, which has often rebelled and, so far from being pacified, cannot even be reduced to subjection. I am being sent against wild animals with bloodthirsty natures" (*Sogdianam regionem mihi attribuis, totiens rebellem et non modo indomitam, sed quae ne subigi quidem possit. Mittor ad feras bestias praecipitia ingenia sortitas.* Curt. 8.1.35).

29. Curt. 8.1.22-25, uncorroborated by other sources.

30. Plut. *Alex.* 9.4: Φίλιππος ὑπερηγάπα τὸν υἱόν, ὥστε καὶ χαίρειν τῶν Μακεδόνων Ἀλέξανδρον μὲν βασιλέα, Φίλιππον δὲ στρατηγὸν καλούντων. That this was a consequence of Chaeronea is proved by the preceding paragraph.

by a bitter quarrel between the younger and the older men.[31] Curtius' account takes as its primary focus the clash of generations, pitting the traditionalists (the former soldiers of Philip) against the younger men who admired Alexander and had no need to turn a blind eye to faults they could not see. Arrian's version gives greater attention to the flattery, to which the king listened with pleasure: the deeds of the Dioscuri, Castor and Polydeuces, were no match for his own, they said, while even Heracles paled in comparison. And it was the way in which the message was delivered, more than its meaning, that annoyed Cleitus, who found both the irreverence of the flattery and the king's susceptibility to it offensive. He commented that "Alexander's accomplishments were not, in fact, as great and wonderful as the exaggerated talk made out, and he was not single-handedly responsible for . . . the achievements of the Macedonian people."[32] Finally, he reminded the king of how he had saved his life at the Granicus, when he was being attacked by Spithridates and his brother Rhoesaces. And this, more than anything else, wounded his pride and roused him to anger.

Plutarch, in his *Life of Alexander*, adds one more element, which blends the generational issues with the opposition to orientalism. Cleitus was allegedly offended by the recitation of a poem that he felt mocked a Macedonian defeat at the hands of the barbarians.[33] But the poem by Pranichus or Pierion—the author's identity is uncertain—appears to be a mock epic in praise of the harpist Aristonicus, who distinguished himself in the battle fought near Bactra between Spitamenes' forces and the Macedonians under Peithon son of Sosicles.[34] In spite of its intended purpose, it touched a nerve with men who could by modern clinical standards be diagnosed as suffering from PTSD. The hypervigilance and quickness to anger that one sees in Cleitus was characteristic also of the king himself.[35] Self-deprecation was hardly in Alexander's vocabulary, and overt criticism in public—even though the Macedonians had long been in the habit of speaking frankly to their kings—was voiced by his officers at their own peril. Cleitus, who was quick to quote a line from Euripides, would have done well to recall Homer's remark: "When a king is angry at a lesser man, his is the greater power: even if he

---

31. Curt. 8.1.27-31.

32. Arr. 4.8.2-4.

33. Plut. *Alex.* 50.8-9.

34. First noted, as far as I can tell, by Holt 1988, 78–79 n. 118.

35. See Tritle 2003. On PTSD in general in the ancient world, see Shay 1994. For the symptoms of PTSD, see Shay 1994, xx; Tritle 2000, 58.

holds down his anger for the day, he still keeps resentment in his breast, until he can give effect to it at some other time."[36]

Attempts were made by the Bodyguard to restrain both the king and Cleitus, but the argument had reached its boiling point. It was either in the very banquet hall that Alexander snatched a spear from one of his hypaspists and ran Cleitus through or, as the apologists depicted it, it was when Cleitus, who had been ushered out of the room, returned to continue the quarrel.[37]

III

It is worth noting that Cleitus' grievances, which included a measure of dissatisfaction with Alexander's Persianizing policies, had more to do with court politics, questions of military promotion, and especially the elimination of Philotas and Parmenion.[38] Alexander had not yet married Roxane or attempted to introduce the Persian practice of *proskynesis*. These would be matters that weighed heavily on the minds of his followers shortly before his departure for India.

The union with the barbarian maiden Roxane was the latest step in the transformation of the Conqueror into an Oriental king. He had changed his dress and insinuated various foreign practices and barbarians themselves into his court; Persians served as ushers and guards, while their sons were enrolled in the army; and satrapies had for some time remained in the hands of their former rulers. Now Alexander attempted to introduce a Persian practice that Greeks and Macedonians had long found repugnant. The Achaemenid rulers had adopted

---

36. Homer, *Iliad* 1.80-83, translated by Martin Hammond. The passage refers to Agamemnon, and it is interesting that Cleitus elsewhere makes a remark about Alexander that casts him in the role of Agamemnon—a curious twist for someone who was said to have been an admirer of Achilles (but for Alexander as Agamemnon, see Instinsky 1949, 27). See Curt. 8.1.34: "If someone has to die for you, then Cleitus comes first. But when you come to judge the spoils of victory, the major share goes to those who pour the most insolent insults on your father's memory." Compare *Iliad* 1.165-67: "My hands bear the brunt of the battle's fury, but when the division comes, your prize is by far the greater."

37. For the different versions, see Curt. 8.1.22-52 (excluding the section on Alexander's reaction and remorse); Plut. *Alex.* 50.1–51.10; Arr. 4.8; Justin 12.6.1-4. Modern literature: Schubert 1898; Cauer 1894, 38 ff.; Carney 1981; Clark 1923; Tritle 2003; Müller 2003, 113–22. The view that Alexander was acting against his better nature is debunked by Müller 2003, 121: "Allgemein agieren Menschen unter Alkoholeinfluss enthemmter als in nüchterem Zustand und ihre Handlungsweise unterliegt zwei Grundsätzen: Im Rausch tun sie nichts, was sie grundsätzlich nicht tun wollen, und es fällt ihnen leichter, zu tun, was sie schon immer tun wollten."

38. There is also a hint of dissatisfaction with Alexander's disavowal of Philip as his father and his pretensions to divinity (Plut. 50.11). Curt. 8.1.52 concludes his account with Alexander taunting the mortally wounded Cleitus with the words: "Go now to Philip, Parmenion, and Attalus" (*I nunc ad Philippum et Parmenionem et Attalum*).

the gesture of *proskynesis* from their predecessors, the Medes and the Assyrians. In its crudest form, *proskynesis* involved kowtowing to the king. In the modern age of exploration, Europeans bristled at the thought of debasing themselves in this manner before the Chinese emperor;[39] in the ancient world, the Greeks regarded the act as similarly demeaning. Herodotus described the practice, which recognized the relative status of the individuals involved:

> When they [the Persians] meet in the streets, the following is how one could tell if those meeting each other are equals. Instead of greeting each other, they kiss on the mouth; if one is of a slightly lower class than the other, they kiss on the cheeks; and if one is of much lower birth than the other, he throws himself down and does *proskynesis* before him. (Hdt. 1.134)

The act of prostration was required of nonaristocratic Persians, as well as foreigners, who came into the presence of the Great King, but it is clear that his most powerful nobles made gestures of respect that did not require actual groveling before their monarch.[40] Tithraustes, the Persian chiliarch, is alleged to have told the Athenian admiral Conon, who wanted an audience with Artaxerxes II:

> "For if you come into his sight you must do obeisance to the king (the Greek term is *proskynesis*) but if this is offensive to you, you will still be able to do what you want just by giving me the word." Then Conon said: "It is not offensive for me personally to pay the king any honor whatsoever, but I fear it may be shameful in the eyes of my city-state if I, coming from a society used to commanding other nations, follow the practice of barbarians rather than its own." (Nepos, *Conon* 3.3)

A second example will suffice to demonstrate the Greek attitude toward the practice. In this case, we are told about a Theban named Ismenias, visiting the court of the same king and dealing with the same chiliarch:

---

39. See, for example, the comments of Cohen 2000, 243, 276. Kowtowing was probably a little more extreme than the usual Persian form of prostration. Wright 2001, 93, calls it "a ritual of extreme obeisance that involved prostration and audibly knocking the forehead on the floor. This was symbolic recognition that their countries were humble vassal states of the mighty . . . empire." On the practice, its purpose, and its forms, see Bowden 2013, 56–62.

40. Briant, *HPE* 222–23. See also Richards 1934; Bickerman 1963.

This man was an envoy for his country sent to the Persian king. On arrival he wished personally to meet the Persian to discuss the business for which he had come. The official who took messages into the king and presented petitioners said to him, "But there is, Theban visitor (he spoke in Persian, using an interpreter, and the official's name was Tithraustes), a national custom in Persia that a person who has audience with the king should not converse with him before kneeling in homage. So, if you wish to meet him personally, this is the moment for you to do what custom prescribes. Otherwise, if you do not kneel, the same result will be achieved by us on your behalf." Ismenias said, "Take me in." Entering and coming into full view of the king, he surreptitiously took off the ring he happened to be wearing and let it fall at his feet. Looking down quickly he knelt to pick it up, as if he were performing the act of homage. This gave the Persian king the impression of obeisance, but he had not done anything that causes Greeks a feeling of shame. (Aelian, *VH* 1.21)[41]

Those noble Persians (including the queen mother) who abased themselves before Alexander did so in recognition of their status as subjects through conquest.[42] With the normalization of the relationship between the Conqueror and the nobles whom he had pardoned and raised to higher office, the gesture of respect must have approximated that which had been shown to Darius III. Still, for the Greeks and Macedonians, obeisance was an act appropriate only to a god.[43] Although they knew that this was not the case with the Persian king, the truth was conveniently forgotten. In fact, some ancient writers believed that the most abject form of debasement was what Alexander demanded of his subjects, Greco-Macedonians as well as Persians.

Arrian says that one of Alexander's closest *hetairoi*, Leonnatus, made fun of the Persians as they performed *proskynesis*, believing that the abasement was demeaning and, indeed, humorous to behold. Leonnatus thus earned the king's

---

41. Translation by Nigel Wilson, Loeb Classical Library.

42. The captive Persian queens do obeisance to Hephaestion, mistaking him for Alexander: Curt. 3.12.16-17; Arr. 2.12.6-7; Diod. 17.37.5-6.

43. For this reason, they misunderstood the relationship between the Great King and his subjects. Bickerman 1963, 252–53: "En voyant les Perses le répéter à l'intention de leur souverain, les Grecs conclurent que pour ses sujets le roi était un être surnaturel." Curtius and Justin (that is, Pompeius Trogus) had no doubt that the practice was intended by Alexander as recognition of his divinity. The lack of a notion of "divine kingship" (outside of Egypt) has been generally recognized. For the subordination of the king to a national god, see Kaerst, *Hellenismus* I³ 295: "Es ist ja überhaupt eine im alten Orient weitverbreitete und tiefgewurzelte Vorstellung, daß der Landesgott der eigentliche Herr des Landes ist."

disfavor, since he had scuttled the attempt at integrating Macedonian and Persian practices. Curtius (8.5.22-24) attributes the mockery of *proskynesis* to Polyperchon, who on the author's own evidence was not at the court at the time.[44]

When he did attempt to introduce *proskynesis*, Alexander's intention was to blend Greek and Persian practices, and there were in his inner circle many who understood this and were prepared to do as the king asked.[45] The experiment itself was conducted on a small scale, with only a limited number of the king's *hetairoi* present. It is probably significant that Craterus, who was one of the most reluctant of Alexander's generals to condone his orientalism, was absent from the camp at the time. The event was carefully orchestrated; some have suggested that Hephaestion, the king's alter ego, was the evil genius behind it all. Chares of Mitylene, who himself witnessed these events, claims that Alexander's *hetairoi* took a cup and faced the household altar[46] and that after they took a drink, they did *proskynesis* to Alexander, who then gave them a kiss. But a courtier by the name of Demetrius (known by the surname Pheidon) pointed out to the king that Callisthenes had not performed obeisance and therefore did not deserve a kiss, which the king denied him. Callisthenes merely shrugged and said: "So

---

44. Polyperchon: Heckel 1978. Arr. 4.12.2 says the man who ridiculed the Persians performing *proskynesis* was Leonnatus, but the story of Polyperchon is much closer to the one told by Plut. *Alex.* 74.2-5 about Cassander. It appears to have its origins in the propaganda wars of the Successors: see Heckel, *Marshals*² 203-4.

45. Although the sources say that the Macedonians were expected to perform *proskynesis*, they do not, in fact, specify what this entailed, and from Chares' version (*FGrH* 125 F14), it appears that this was in no way demeaning. I do not understand why Hamilton, *PA* 150, insists that "Alexander proposed to introduce 'prostration.'" The evidence of Curt. 8.5.12 is worthless. The flatterer, Cleon, says that "he would prostrate himself on the ground when the king entered the banquet, and the rest should do the same, especially those who possessed good sense, for it was they who should set the example of worshipping the king." Curtius is clearly equating *proskynesis* with worship of a divinity, and he contrasts the obsequious behavior of Cleon with the sensible response of Callisthenes. As Briant, *HPE* 223, notes, the story of Ismenias and the ring indicates that some form of kneeling or bowing was sufficient to satisfy the Great King. See the useful discussion in Spawforth 2007b, 103-6.

46. The reference to the household altar (ἑστίαν) is a curious feature. It appears that this was a face-saving measure, not unlike Ismenias' ploy with the ring. Since the Greeks and Macedonians regarded *proskynesis* as due only to a god, the act that was seemingly directed toward Alexander could be explained away as reverence to the household deity. But Spawforth 2007b, 105, questions whether "Macedonians would have seen obeisance in religious (as opposed to more broadly cultural) terms." Arr. 4.12.3-4, also from Chares, omits the altar but does agree that the individual who received the cup from Alexander "rose, did obeisance, and received a kiss from Alexander." There is nothing to suggest that the act involved much more than a slight bow or the blowing of a kiss. The mockery of the Persians who performed *proskynesis* occurred on a different occasion.

I shall leave short of a kiss."[47] Callisthenes' overt act of defiance, for which he earned the praise of the Greeks and subsequent writers, scuttled the entire project. But in truth, the experiment was, on a limited scale, much more successful than might have been expected.[48] On the other hand, the audience appears to have been carefully selected, and thus the outcome did not represent the views of the majority of the Macedonian leadership. The common soldier, who played no part in the business, would doubtless have been offended by it.

For Callisthenes, his rejection of *proskynesis* and responsibility for the failure of the king's experiment with cultural blending played no small part in his undoing:

> Next came a piece of vanity characteristic of Persian royalty, the adoption of which Alexander had postponed for fear of provoking undue animosity by changing everything at once:[49] he ordered people to do obeisance before him instead of saluting him. The most outspoken of the objectors was Callisthenes, and this spelled death for him and many prominent Macedonians, *who were all executed, ostensibly for treason.* (Justin 12.7.1-2 emphasis added)

In truth, Callisthenes' failings and his offenses went beyond his objections to *proskynesis*. As the campaign progressed, Callisthenes made the transformation from flatterer—as the official historian, he acted at times as the king's minister of propaganda—to outspoken critic.[50] In part, this was due to the changing nature

---

47. Plut. *Alex.* 54.4-6.

48. Rightly noted by Lane Fox 1973, 323: "The plan could hardly have been tried more reasonably and despite the indignation of Romans, philosophers and others since who have missed its Persian background, Alexander came out of it all remarkably well." Bowden 2013, 68–72, doubts the historicity of the story and believes that Callisthenes' offense at the symposium had nothing to do with an attempt to introduce *proskynesis*. I cannot, however, accept Bowden's conclusion: "The idea of an 'experiment with προσκύνησις'—an experiment that failed and was not repeated—is an invention of the later tradition" (77).

49. Justin 12.3.8-12 discusses Alexander's orientalizing but postpones the *proskynesis* episode to its proper historical context; by contrast, Curt. 6.6.3 looks ahead to the introduction of "prostration" (*iacere humi venerabundos ipsum*). Justin 12.7.1: *Dein, quod primo ex Persico superbiae regiae more distulerat ne omnia pariter invidiosiora essent, no salutari, sed adorari se iubet. Acerrimus inter recusantes Callisthenes fuit. Quae res et illi et multis principibus Macedonum exitio fuit,* siquidem sub specie insidiarum omnes interfecti. The words *multis principibus Macedonum* must refer to the Pages, but they, unlike Callisthenes (about whom the truth cannot be known), were clearly guilty of treason.

50. Brown 1973, 126: "It does seem ironical that the man who wrote about Alexander in such glowing terms should have incurred his hatred over what was chiefly a matter of court etiquette, yet so it was. Willing that Alexander should be accepted as a hero, and later presumably as a god, Callisthenes could not reconcile himself to the servility, as he regarded it, of the

of the expedition. With the end of the Panhellenic phase of the war, Callisthenes' reports, which were probably sent to the west on a yearly basis, were no longer required.[51] And Alexander now had more than his share of flatterers in the form of poets, athletes, philosophers, and courtiers—all were judged sycophants in comparison with the reformed Callisthenes.[52] When he joined the expedition, he regarded himself as Alexander's friend and confidant. He soon discovered that in the king's eyes, he was one of the "hired help." One of his chores, it seems, was to oversee the education of the *paides basilikoi*. His uncle, Aristotle, had performed a similar function at the Macedonian court in Pella (or, more specifically, at Mieza), where the aristocrats who were coeval with Alexander (his *syntrophoi*) were educated with the prince.[53] The views that the sons of noble Macedonians who accompanied Alexander in Asia expressed about politics, loyalty, and freedom were regarded as shaped by their tutor Callisthenes.[54] And although they later failed to implicate him in their conspiracy against Alexander, there was little doubt among those in the camp concerning the role of the Greek who had demonstrated on more than one occasion that he did not know his place.

Persian custom of prostrating oneself before the king on state occasions, and he paid for his unwelcome frankness with his life." Cf. Guthrie 1981, 38. For a sober appraisal of Callisthenes' role, see Zahrnt 2013.

51. Zahrnt 2013, 496, rightly notes that Alexander found no replacement for Callisthenes in his "propaganda department," since this role, at least in relation to the Greeks, was no longer needed: "Dass sich Alexander daraufhin von ihm getrennt und keinen Nachfolger ernannt hat, zeigt, dass er jetzt auf die Haltung der Griechen keine Rücksicht mehr nehmen zu müssen glaubte."

52. For the so-called Peripatetic tradition, see Tarn II 96–99. Hammond 1981, 198–99: "Whatever his contemporaries thought of Callisthenes—and Aristotle regarded him as a man of no sense—his end outraged the Peripatetic School of philosophers, and it was they who were to represent Alexander as the worst of tyrants."

53. Carney 2003, 57–59.

54. Arr. 4.12.7 says that some suspected Callisthenes of inciting the Pages to plot against Alexander, and at 4.13.1, he notes that Hermolaus "was reputed to be a zealous student of philosophy and to be a follower of Callisthenes for this purpose." In fact, Callisthenes was not a philosopher but a historian, but he was probably, like the Athenian statesman Critias, "an amateur among philosophers and a philosopher among amateurs" (Schol. Plat. *Timaeus* 20a = DK 88 A3). Pownall 2018 expresses doubts about Callisthenes' role as tutor. She believes that the only explicit references to Callisthenes as *magister* and Hermolaus as *discipulus* come from Curtius, who "transformed Kallisthenes into a proto-Seneca in order to offer a more pointed commentary on the tyranny of Nero."

IV

It was an institution of the Macedonian state, at least from the time of Philip II, that the sons of the most prominent nobles were educated at the court and brought up with his sons and other relatives. These young men, known as the *paides basilikoi* but often referred to by modern historians as Pages, performed a variety of functions—some of which were reserved in other societies for slaves[55]—for the king. It was their responsibility to guard the king's bedchamber (in shifts) when he slept, and they brought him women by separate entrance. They also accompanied him in the hunt, having received the horses from the grooms and helped the king mount; some appear to have had a limited role in battle. The institution was a training ground for the future generals of the army and governors of the provinces. But the boys were also subjected to corporal punishment at the hands of the king (or, one must suppose, his henchmen) for any dereliction of their duties.[56]

In the spring of 327, Hermolaus son of Sopolis, one of these Pages, struck a boar that was charging at Alexander, possibly saving him from injury but certainly depriving him of the opportunity of spearing the animal. The king, in a fit of anger, ordered Hermolaus to be flogged in front of his cohorts and deprived him of his horse. Whether the Page had been guilty of lèse-majesté by usurping the prerogatives of his master is debatable. There is certainly no explicit evidence of such a rule—although tradition is another matter—but Elizabeth Carney points out that for a young man to make the passage to adulthood, he was required to have killed a boar in the hunt.[57] Without such an achievement, he was not permitted to recline at banquets. The humiliation of Hermolaus went beyond the indignity of flogging and the loss of his horse,[58] and his mind soon shifted from shame and anger to thoughts of vengeance. That, at least, is the incident that gave rise to the conspiracy of Hermolaus (or, as it is often called, the Conspiracy of the Pages). The matter is, however, far more complex.

---

55. Welwei 1977, 62 n. 7, notes that there is a distinction between the "grooms," who were actual slaves, and the *paides basilikoi*, who were not. Diod. 17.76.2 (τῶν τοὺς βασιλικοὺς ἵππους ἀγόντων παίδων) refers to actual slaves. This is clear also from Arr. 4.13.1, where the Pages receive the horses from the grooms (παρὰ τῶν ἱπποκόμων); cf. Curt. 8.6.4: *agenones*.

56. Curt. 8.6.2-6. Cf. Arr. 4.13.1. See Heckel 1986 and *Marshals*² 246–51; Hammond 1990; Carney 1981 and 2008.

57. Carney 2008, 155. Athen. 1.18a, noting that Cassander at the age of thirty-five had not yet earned the right to recline at the symposium. On Persian "rules" for the royal hunt, see Brosius 2007, 44-5; of related interest, Spawforth 2012.

58. Carney 2008, 154–56; Roisman 2003b, 302–3.

Hermolaus enlisted a number of his fellow Pages, including his lover Sostratus son of Amyntas, as members of a conspiracy against the king.[59] Their plan was to murder Alexander as he slept on a night when they were all on duty outside the royal tent. Just how they expected to carry out their plot is unclear, however, since every night there were members of the *Somatophylakes*, men of greater maturity and tested in battle, who slept inside the king's bedchamber.[60] Perhaps they hoped that one of them could reach the sleeping king while the others held the *Somatophylakes* off long enough to allow the assassin to strike. There was little risk that the tumult would awaken Alexander, who would in all likelihood be heavily under the spell of alcohol. Whatever the odds of failure, the conspirators were willing to take their chances.[61] But, like the conspiracy of Demetrius and Dimnus, this conspiracy was revealed by the brother of one of the participants. Epimenes told his lover Charicles, who in turn reported what he had learned to Epimenes' brother Eurylochus. The latter brought the news to Ptolemy and Leonnatus,[62] who informed the king. The conspirators were easily rounded up and put on trial.

That there was more in play than simple vengeance for a personal insult—though we cannot rule out an irrational response to wounded adolescent pride—is almost certain. Two of the Pages were the sons of prominent fathers: Asclepiodorus, father of Antipater, ruled Syria; Hermolaus' father, Sopolis, had been an ilarch in the Companion cavalry. He may have been embittered by what he had seen of Alexander's changes in character and policy; perhaps he resented the fact that he was not promoted within the cavalry, as Demetrius son of Althaemenes was.[63] It is probable that the Pages were influenced by the views

---

59. The other conspirators were Antipater son of Asclepiodorus, Epimenes son of Arsaeus, Anticles son of Theocritus and Philotas son of Carsis (Arr. 4.13.4). Curt. 8.6.9 names Nicostratus (an error for Sostratus: Heckel 1981c, 63–64) and adds Asclepiodorus as a conspirator (*Antipatrum Asclepiodorumque*; cf. *Itinerarium Alexandri* 97: *cum Sostrato et Amynta*). One other individual, Elaptonios, is otherwise unknown. See also Heckel 1992, 289–95; 2003b, 223–24.

60. By comparison, the conspirators could not have been older than eighteen; but Carney 1981, 228, is right in assuming that they were not "young boys."

61. Curtius gives a drawn-out account of the affair. The conspirators had to wait thirty-two days before they were all on guard duty together (8.6.11)—time, of course, being the enemy of all conspiracies (cf. the comment of Darius I in Hdt. 3.76)—and even then, their plans were disrupted by a clairvoyant Syrian woman who had taken to watching over the king (8.6.13-17; cf. Aristobulus *ap.* Arr. 4.13.5-6). Plut. *Alex.* 55.3-5 treats the Hermolaus affair in a few sentences.

62. Arr. 4.13.7 names only Ptolemy, whose *History* was one of his sources. Curt. 8.6.22 adds Leonnatus. On Ptolemy's bias, see Errington 1969; Roisman 1984.

63. Demetrius son of Althaemenes is the only ilarch promoted to the rank of hipparch after the cavalry reforms. This may be due to his family connections (Heckel 1992, 345–46). Curt. 8.7.2

of their fathers or other relatives. Furthermore, whatever Callisthenes taught them, he certainly urged them to fear and be wary of tyrants, to act like free men. When the matter came to trial, Hermolaus defended his actions in the most unapologetic way: "We plotted to kill you because you have begun to act not as a king with his free-born subjects but as a master with his slaves" (Curt. 8.7.1). Yet neither he nor any of the other conspirators implicated Callisthenes in the affair.[64] Hermolaus, in fact, stressed the innocence of his teacher and accused Alexander of harboring a desire to execute him. Then he launched into a speech that summed up all the resentments that went back to the days after Darius' death:

> But you revel in Persian clothes and Persian etiquette; you abhor the customs of your own country. Thus, it was a king of the Persians, not of the Macedonians, we wanted to kill, and, in accordance with the conventions of war, we pursue you as a deserter. You wanted Macedonians to kneel before you and worship you as a God. You repudiate your father Philip. (Curt. 8.7.12-13)

It was the now-familiar refrain: Alexander's Persianizing, lack of sufficient remuneration for the men, the unjust execution of political enemies, the attempt to introduce a court practice that implied (to the Macedonians, at least) the king's divinity, and the disowning of Philip and by extension the traditions of Macedon.[65] Curtius, of course, writes as a man of his own time, and his passages are tainted with *color romanus*. Nevertheless, the sentiments expressed are found in the other sources as well, and they doubtless reflect the feelings of many of the Macedonians in the camp.

---

says that Sopolis was present when Hermolaus was put on trial and "rose to his feet shouting that Hermolaus was also the murderer of his own father and, putting his hand over this son's mouth, stated he should not be heard further because he was crazed by his guilt and misfortune." This is, of course, strongly reminiscent of Coenus' attack on Philotas (6.9.30-31) and points to Curtius' claim that it was a law in Macedonia for family members to be executed along with relatives guilty of treason (6.11.20: *legem Macedonum veriti, qua cautum erat ut propinqui eorum qui regi insidiati essent cum ipsis necarentur*); see Tarn II 270. But Sopolis had been sent from Nautaca (winter 328/7) back to the west on a recruiting mission with Menidas and Epocillus. That he suffered any harm as a result of Hermolaus' plot is unlikely. Asclepiodorus was in the camp when the trial took place, and he reappears as a trierarch of the Hydaspes fleet (Arr. *Ind.* 18.3, as emended by Jacoby).

64. Arr. 4.13.7; Plut. *Alex.* 55.5-6, adding that Alexander himself, in a letter written at the time to Craterus, Attalus, and Alcetas, says that the Pages confessed but implicated no one else.

65. See Müller 2010, 31, who rightly notes that "the shadow of his dead father turned into a political obstacle for [Alexander]." The idealized picture of Philip served only to emphasize Alexander's political and personal metamorphosis and his (perceived) shortcomings.

The conspirators were all executed by stoning.[66] Callisthenes—whether innocent or guilty, it no longer mattered—was arrested and incarcerated. How he died is uncertain, and this in itself indicates that an attempt was made to justify his punishment.[67] The trial of the Pages and the end of Callisthenes sent an unequivocal message through the ranks of the Macedonians. They set out for India relieved of the burden of seditious thoughts.

The Roman historian Livy, writing before Q. Curtius Rufus, tackled the question of whether Alexander could have conquered Rome, a common rhetorical theme in his time. He notes the deleterious effect of the king's Persianizing policies on both himself and his army: "He would then have come to Italy more of a Darius than an Alexander [*Dareo magis similis quam Alexandro*] and brought an army that had forgotten Macedon and was already lapsing into Persian ways."[68]

---

66. Arr. 4.14.3; Curt. 8.8.20 says they were tortured to death by members of their own unit; Plut. *Alex.* 55.7; Justin 12.7.2.

67. For the different versions of Callisthenes' death, see Arr. 4.14.3 and Plut. *Alex.* 55.9 (Chares, *FGrH* 125 F15; Ptolemy, 138 F17, and Aristobulus 139 F33); also Justin 15.3.3-10. Ptolemy said that he was tortured and crucified. The use of torture must have been intended to extort an admission of complicity in the Pages' conspiracy. Bosworth II 100 notes that crucifixion was used primarily for traitors and rebels, and he accepts Ptolemy's version as the correct one, adding: "The drastic and ignominious punishment . . . is a measure of the magnitude of Callisthenes' offence in Alexander's eyes." But the apologists Aristobulus and Chares both mention that he was imprisoned (caged) and died of a disease of lice before his case could be presented to the Greeks. Justin says that Callisthenes was mutilated and placed in a cage and that Lysimachus gave him poison to relieve his misery. For this act, Lysimachus himself was punished. Discussion in Yardley, Wheatley, and Heckel 257–62. Despite its sensational elements, Justin's account supports the view that Callisthenes was imprisoned and that although he was charged with complicity in the conspiracy, his true crime was the rejection of *proskynesis*. See also Brown 1949a.

68. Livy 9.18.3. Cf. Curt. 6.6.10: *ex Macedoniae imperatore Darei satrapen factus*.

13

From the Hindu Kush to the Indus

WHAT THE ALEXANDER historians called India began beyond the satrapy of Parapamisus (or Parapamisadae). The first Indian satrapy, Gandhāra, the Peshawar region, stretched along the Kabul River from the Kunar up to the Indus and may have included (perhaps only nominally) the realm of Taxiles. Hence, it straddled, in the west, what is now the border—formed by the Durand Line—between eastern Afghanistan and western Pakistan and, in the east, the lands along the Indus.[1] The world beyond that was known to the Greeks, for the most part, only by hearsay, as is reflected in their confused descriptions of the geography.[2]

I

The country between the Hindu Kush and the Indus was ruled by local dynasts who must have regarded the end of Achaemenid power as an opportunity to win further independence. Whether they expected Alexander to invade their territory or believed that he would be content to overcome Bessus and pacify

---

1. The dynasts of the Bajaur, Swat, and Buner regions must have been subject to the satrap in Peshawar. Herzfeld 1968, 336, defines Gandhāra (satrapy no. 18) as follows: "in its proper application . . . the plains of the lower Cophen and Swat rivers, as far as and beyond their confluence with the Indus, including Taxila. In a wider application it includes in the north the upper Swat-Σοάστος and Udyāna-Ὀζηνή, and likewise the upper Kabul valley and Ghazni in the west, hence the entire triangle between the Hindukush and the Indus, which touches the Panjāb with its SE point." See also Foucher 1902. Jacobs 1994, maps VI–VI, regards Gandhāra as ending at the Indus and includes Taxiles' realm in Θataguš (also Sattagydia, satrapy no. 19; cf. Herzfeld 1968, 342).

2. Curt. 8.9.2-8 believed that both the Indus and the Ganges flowed into the Red Sea (which in ancient thought was the Persian Gulf, although Curtius or his source may have been thinking of the Arabian Sea; see McCrindle 1896, 183–84 n. 4). Furthermore, he reports that the Ganges meets with the Acesines "before it reaches the sea, the two rivers colliding with great violence." See also Arr. 5.4-5, with Bosworth II 230–41.

In the Path of Conquest. Waldemar Heckel, Oxford University Press (2020). © Oxford University Press.
DOI: 10.1093/oso/9780190076689.001.0001

Bactria and Sogdiana is unclear, but Taxiles (or, rather, his son, who was soon to inherit the kingdom), whose territory was on the eastern bank of the Indus, was taking no chances and had already made submission to Alexander while he was in Sogdiana.[3] Even the hyparch whom the Conqueror had left behind among the Parapamisadae was little concerned with Alexander's return. When he appeared at the beginning of summer 327, after a ten-day crossing of the Hindu Kush, Alexander dismissed the underperforming pair of Niloxenus (*episkopos*) and Proexes (*satrapes*) and replacing the latter with another barbarian, Tyriespis, and entrusting Nicanor with administrative and military oversight of Alexandria-in-the-Caucasus.[4] Heralds had been sent as far as the kingdom of Taxiles (on the eastern bank of the Indus) demanding that the local hyparchs recognize Macedonian authority. Many were prompt in complying and bringing gifts,[5] the people of the hill country less so.

Emerging from the land of the Parapamisadae, Alexander moved into the satrapy of Gandhāra. This had long been subject to Persia—certainly from the

---

3. Diod. 17.86.4. Submission was made by his son Omphis (the form Mophis is found in Diodorus and *Metz Epit.* 49; it is the equivalent of the Sanskrit Ambhi), probably in place of his father and very likely in the hope of gaining Alexander's support against his enemies. Cf. Curt. 8.12.5, who says he was responsible for his father's submission. Omphis, who took his father's official name, Taxiles, upon his accession, remained one of Alexander's most faithful allies.

4. Arr. 4.22.4-5 and 3.28.4 for the first settlement. Despite the difference in terminology, it appears that Nicanor replaced Niloxenus and that Tyriespis was appointed in place of Proexes. Arrian's comment that the *hyparchos* had not performed satisfactorily (ὅτι οὐ καλῶς ἐξηγεῖσθαι ἐδόξε) refers to the administration of the city (τὸν μὲν ὕπαρχον, ὅστις αὐτῷ ἐπὶ τῆς πόλεως ἐτάχθη) and is thus clearly Niloxenus (pace Bosworth II 145; Julien 1914, 42). Both Niloxenus and Proexes were cashiered for their poor performance. What other punishment was meted out we do not know. For the date, see Arr. 4.22.3: ἐξήκοντος ἤδη τοῦ ἤρος (with the comments of Bosworth II 142). Badian 1985, 461, with n. 3, prefers "late summer," noting but not necessarily accepting Fränkel's emendation of ἤρος to θέρους. On the location of Alexandria-in-the-Caucasus and its relationship to Alexandria of Opiane, see the lengthy discussion in Fraser 1996, 140–51, and the conclusion that the city "lay within the wide basin between the southern foot of the Hindu Kush, in the Kūhistān, somewhere between the modern Charikar and the junction of the Ghorband and the Panjshir." Identification with Begram: Seibert 1985, 125, with earlier literature; Bosworth I 370. The old Achaemenid capital was nearby, at Kāpiśī (Eggermont 1975, 175).

5. Arr. 4.22.6 says that Taxiles himself came, along with other hyparchs, bringing twenty-five elephants. Briant, *HPE* 193: "Open refusal to bring gifts was taken as proof of insubordination." They met him at Nicaea. This was either near Jalalabad, probably close to the confluence of the Choes and Cophen (Kabul) rivers (cf. Bosworth II 146) or at Jalalabad itself (Seibert 1985, 146 n. 15).

time of Darius I[6]—although the vicissitudes of Achaemenid fortunes must have strongly affected their commitment to the empire. It seems doubtful that the central government could exercise much direct control over the Indian regions of Gandhāra, Sattagydia (Ɵataguš), and Hinduš, but the presence of Indians in the contingents of Bessus (Bactria) and Barsaentes (Arachosia) suggests that these satraps probably exerted some influence over the satrapies on their eastern borders.[7]

Hephaestion and Perdiccas were sent ahead to Peucelaotis (Pushkalavati, modern Charsada) and ordered to build a boat bridge across the Indus.[8] Taxiles and the hyparchs who had made their submission accompanied the Macedonian force. But at Peucelaotis itself, Astis rebelled and was besieged in his city for thirty days. He was killed in fighting, and the city was entrusted to Sangaeus, who had taken refuge with Taxiles.[9] Alexander turned his attention to the hill tribes— the Aspasians, Guraeans, and Assacenians. In this area, the inhabitants and the local dynasts relied on their strongholds in the hills and hoped to avoid submission to the Conqueror. Their adherence to the Achaemenid kings, at least in the fourth century, had not been strong or sincere. But, as Aurel Stein noted, "the obvious need of securing the flank of his main line of communication explains why Alexander, on arriving in the upper valley of the Kabul River, led one corps of his army into the hill country to the north."[10] Like others before them, these Indian tribes underestimated the tenacity of Alexander and the skill of his army in mountain warfare.

The prominence of local dynasts in the area east of Parapamisus and the absence of any overarching authority suggest that, at least when Alexander entered the area, there was no Achaemenid satrap of Gandhāra.[11] This would support the view that the Persians had effectively lost control over the area. The sources

---

6. See the Persian satrapy lists collected in Briant, *HPE* 173. Gandhāra had already submitted to Persia in the time of Cyrus (Arr. *Ind.* 1.3, but the claim that it had been ruled by the Assyrians and Medes is clearly false).

7. Arr. 3.8.3-4.

8. Peucelaotis: Arr. *Ind.* 1.8 calls it a city of the Assacenians. Hephaestion and Perdiccas' mission and the boat bridge: Arr. 4.22.7, 23.1, 30.9; 5.3.5; Curt. 8.10.2-3, 12.4; *Metz Epit.* 48.

9. Arr. 3.22.8 says that the advance force sent to the Indus had already reached the river and completed its work when Astis rebelled. Bosworth II 153 believes that Astis was one of the hyparchs who met Alexander at Nicaea. If so, he must have formed a very low opinion of the Macedonian military strength. For the chronology of the Peucelaotis campaign, see Badian 1987.

10. Stein 1929, 41.

11. Astis, ruler of Peucelaotis, appears to have been a relatively minor official. But it is possible that he resisted Alexander in his capacity as satrap and that Taxiles, who submitted to

do not name a satrap—Iranian or Indian—who was either defeated or deposed by Alexander or had fled at the news of his coming. There is certainly nothing to support the view that the territory west of the Indus was ruled by Taxiles.[12] Hence, it was imperative that the Conqueror deal with the dynasts one by one. Their lack of coordination in dealing with the invader can be put down to tribal distrust and rivalry. Indeed, it would have been far easier for the Macedonian king to pacify the area if it had been under the authority of an existing satrap.

The dynasts to the north of the Kabul River sent no envoys to the king— although Alexander's agents may have concentrated their efforts on the lowland region of Peshawar and beyond. Hence, the Macedonian king directed his forces against those tribes who inhabited the mountains of the Bajaur, Swat, and Buner regions. O. Caroe writes as follows about Alexander's route:

> Strabo makes it clear for us that Alexander took the northern route on hearing that it was more fertile, while that to the south was either water-less or liable to flood, and thinking that the rivers would be easier to cross towards their sources.
>
> Given this certainty, and given also the whole trend of the account, which shows that he did not descend into the Peshawar plain until after reducing the hill fortresses of Arigaion, Massaga, Bazira, and Ora, a knowl-edge of topography makes his general route clear enough. The rivers he crossed were the Choes, Euaspla and Guraeus, in that order. Between the Euaspla and the Guraeus was a mountain divide. This can only have been the Kunar–Panjkora watershed where the Durand Line now runs, and the Choes would then be the Alishang and the Euaspla the Kunar. The Guraeus is the Panjkora, which appears as the Gauri in the Sanskrit of the sixth book of the Mahabharata. Arigaion would then be Nawagai in Bajaur, which is in fact situated in "a very advantageous site," commanding the Bajaur valleys. After crossing the Panjkora Alexander would neces-sarily take the route through Talash in order to avoid the lower Panjkora and Swat gorges, and so cross the Katgala pass into Adinzai and arrive on

---

the Macedonians, supported an anti-Persian leader in Sangaeus (Arr. 4.22.8). None of the Alexander historians mentions an individual with overarching authority.

12. Noted by Badian 1987, 118. Contra Eggermont 1970, 118–19: "Though Taxila was situated outside the bounds of proper Gandhāra, there is no denying that it held the political prepon-derance in the region. At the time of Alexander's campaign the son of Taxila's king acted as his viceroy at Udabhāṇḍa. The Greeks called him Omphis after the name of his residence. Udabhāṇḍa commanded the ford of the Indus so that the vice-roy was in a position to control the entire traffic along the famous trade-route from Bactria to Taxila. Likewise from there he held sway over the kings of Ariṣṭapura and Puṣkalāvati, the principal towns of Gandhāra."

the banks of the Swat River at Chakdarra. There is nothing to show by which route he left Swat to reach the Peshawar plain.[13]

Certainty is, of course, impossible, but Caroe's synopsis—with the possible exception of the identification of the Choes—appears correct, at least in its general outline.[14] And the route to Nawagai brings the Macedonian force close to the Koh-i-mor, where a major battle occurred and in the shadow of which Nysa—whatever the truth of the story about its Dionysiac connections—may have been located.[15] What we do know is that the Aspasians were the first to feel the Conqueror's wrath. The Macedonian army advanced up the valley of the Choes and attacked the first settlement, whither the Aspasians had fled. The city was protected by a double wall, and although the defenders managed to wound the Macedonian king,[16] their defenses soon collapsed, and some Indians were cut down in flight, though most escaped:

---

13. Caroe 1962, 50–51.

14. The identification of the Guraeus with the Panjkora is virtually certain: the river joins the Swat and thus reaches the Kabul River (Seibert 1985, 150 n. 33; cf. McCrindle 1896, 62 n. 1; Bosworth II 156–57, with additional literature). Curtius (8.10.22) seems to identify the Choaspes with Arrian's Gouraios. But if the Gouraios is the Panjkora, which joins the Swat, the Choaspes cannot be said to debouch into the Kabul, as Strabo 15.1.26 C697 maintains—although this perhaps expects too much precision on the part of the ancients; Arrian knows nothing of the Choaspes (the Choes itself, as far as I can determine, is unique to Arrian), and one must leave open the possibility that the Choes is the Kunar (Choaspes) and that Alexander did not cross this river until he reached the Kunar–Panjkora watershed. Arrian's "Euaspla" (4.23.2), if this is indeed the correct form of the name (cf. *Itiner. Al.* 105, where Mai's emendation of *Euiaique* into *Choeque* may be faulty), may be another name for the same river. One must also consider Alexander's starting point, and this would depend on whether Nicaea was located near Mandrawar (Bosworth II 146) or closer to modern Jalalabad. In the latter case, it is unlikely that Alexander would have backtracked to the Alingar River. Furthermore, it is unclear whether the Aspasians, who lived along the modern Durand Line, extended as far west as the Alingar valley. The Coa of Ptolemy (*Geog.* 7.1.27), on the other hand, is clearly the Cophen (= Kabul). See also the discussion in Seibert 1985, 150, with n. 33.

15. Somewhere between the lands of the Aspasians and the Assacenians, the Macedonian forces were said to have encountered a town called Nysa (the name of the nurse of the god Dionysus), where the countryside was thick with ivy and the natives conducted rituals that recalled Dionysiac worship. In this area, a dynast named Acuphis ruled and came to an amicable arrangement with Alexander. Although Acuphis was, in all likelihood, a historical individual, the entire account of Alexander finding traces of the Greek god in the East is highly suspect. Since it does nothing to illuminate the position of the Indians with respect to the invaders, I have omitted the story from my narrative. For the details, see Curt. 8.10.718; *Metz Epit.* 36–38; Plut. *Alex.* 58.6-9; the story is told in a digression by Arr. 5.1.1–3.4, who concludes ἐμοὶ δ᾽ ἐν μέσῳ κείσθων οἱ ὑπὲρ τούτων λόγοι.

16. Ptolemy and Leonnatus were also wounded (Arr. 4.23.3). These two generals, along with Alexander, were said to have been foremost in the direction of the attack. The source is, however, Ptolemy himself, and we may assume that he did not downplay his own achievements.

Alexander then encamped near the city at a point where the walls seemed easiest to assault. There was a double wall around the city, and as the first of them had not been skillfully constructed, the Macedonians had no difficulty breaking through it, at dawn the following day. At the second, the barbarians briefly mounted resistance, but when the ladders were set up and their front-line fighters were receiving wounds from spears being hurled from all sides, they did not stand their ground but came running out through the gates toward the hills. A number were killed in flight, and the Macedonians dispatched all they caught alive from anger at Alexander having been wounded by them. Most, however, got away to the hills, as these were not far distant from the city. (Arr. 4.23.4-5)[17]

The defenders of Andaca, learning of the defeat, submitted to the Conqueror,[18] and Alexander left Craterus to mop up pockets of resistance while he himself advanced into the heartland of the Aspasians, whose leader appeared with his forces but was killed in combat by Ptolemy son of Lagus. Again, the Egyptian king-turned-historian enhanced his own reputation. Who was there who still lived and even dared to contradict his account?[19] The invading army now crossed the mountains via the Nawa Pass, beyond which the natives of the city of Arigaeum (Nawagai, in Bajaur) set fire to the city and fled. But Alexander, considering its ideal location, had the city rebuilt and repopulated. It was not, however, the end of native resistance in the Bajaur region. A large force of Indians had occupied the mountain near Nawagai (probably Koh-i-mor) and prepared to descend upon the Macedonian forces:

Despite Ptolemy's hostility toward other Macedonian commanders, he appears to have been more generous in his treatment of Leonnatus.

17. Cf. Curt. 8.10.4-6, which places the blame for the slaughter squarely on Alexander's shoulders, and his determination was increased by the arrow wound he had received during the attack. For this wound, see Plut. Mor. 327b (in the land of the Aspasians, although the manuscript reading is corrupt).

18. Metz Epit. 35 appears to refer to the city that was sacked by Alexander as "Silex" and says the next fortified town was garrisoned. This is probably Andaca (Arr. 4.23.5). Unfortunately, the identification of the Silex with the town described in Arr. 4.23.4-5 and Curt. 8.10.4-6 is confounded by the erroneous statement in the Metz Epitome (34) that Alexander "reached the Indus" before his campaign against Silex.

19. Arr. 4.24.3-5. Seibert 1969, 29: "Mit Recht nimmt man an, daß die Schilderung seiner Aristie bei Arrian aus seiner Feder stammt." See also Strasburger 1934, 41; Pearson 1960, 201–2. See Howe 2008, 224–24 for Egyptian elements in Ptolemy's account.

Sent foraging by Alexander, Ptolemy son of Lagus at this point went ahead himself with a few men to reconnoiter, and he reported back to Alexander that he had spotted more fires on the barbarian side than there were in Alexander's camp. Alexander was skeptical about the number of fires, but, aware that there was a body of barbarians in the area, he left part of his force there and encamped as before at the foot of the mountain. He himself took as many men as seemed sufficient in the light of the report. . . .

When they saw the Macedonians approaching—for they were holding higher ground—the barbarians went down to the plain, confident in their numbers and contemptuous of what seemed to be a mere handful of Macedonians; and there was a fierce battle. However, Alexander defeated them with no great difficulty. Those with Ptolemy could not form up on level terrain—the barbarians were holding a hill—so, after marshaling them as companies, Ptolemy led them to the part of the hill most open to attack. He did not completely encircle the hill but left the barbarians room to flee if they so chose. And there was a fierce battle with these as well, because of the difficulty of the terrain and also because the Indians are unlike the other barbarians in the area and are by far the most courageous in those parts. Even they, however, were driven off the hill by the Macedonians, and Leonnatus' men in the third part of the army were equally successful. (Arr. 4.24.8-9, 25.1-3)

Arrian says this battle occurred before Alexander entered the lands of the Assacenians—indeed, before he crossed the Kunar–Panjkora watershed—and notes that those who opposed him on this occasion were the best fighters of those in the region. It is thus unclear whether they were a particularly proficient group of Aspasians or another unnamed tribe who lived between the Aspasians and the Assacenians.[20] Despite their military prowess, more than 40,000 of them were captured, a figure that defies credulity.[21] Since the battle was preceded by a foraging mission by Ptolemy, the capture of 230,000 oxen (an equally amazing number) was a welcome acquisition for the Macedonian army.

---

20. Bosworth II 166 takes ἀλκιμώτατοι τῶν προσχώρων (Arr. 4.25.3) to mean "by far the most warlike of the local population" and assumes that they are also Aspasians. They may, in fact, have been Guraeans, through whose country Alexander marched en route to the Assacenians (Arr. 4.25.6-7). The overwhelming victory may explain their lack of further resistance.

21. Once again, Ptolemy is the source of this episode, in which he participated. The fighting qualities of the Indians, seemingly contradicted by the number of captives, was intended to add luster to his achievements. See Bosworth II 166; cf. Worthington 2016, 55: "Ptolemy, not unexpectedly, makes his particular battle the hardest fought against the toughest opponent." See also Howe 2008, esp. 226.

The resistance of the Aspasians had thus proved ineffective. The failure of the historians to mention administrative details—the names of garrison commanders or newly appointed hyparchs suggests that the campaign, which was both pre-emptive and punitive (for their failure to make submission), was primarily intended to neutralize the hill tribes and dissuade them from engaging in hostile acts against the main trade route, which ran through the lowlands of Peshawar. If that was the desired result, it succeeded: the Aspasians exchanged their menacing defiance for grudging neutrality.

II

Like the Aspasians, the Assacenians took their name from the word for horses (*asvah*), and although we hear little of cavalry warfare, theirs was a land noted for its horse breeding and horsemanship. In numbers and military skill, the Assacenians were a formidable enemy, but their leader, known by the official name Assacenus, had recently died.[22] The Assacenians lived between the Panjkora and the Swat, above the confluence of the rivers, and they had made preparations to defend at least their major settlements.[23] When Alexander marched through the Katgala Pass, he found them firmly entrenched in their capital city of Massaga, now in the hands of the deceased ruler's mother, Cleophis, who acted as regent for her grandson and entrusted the defense of the city to another of her sons, Amminais.[24]

The city was said to have been garrisoned by 38,000 infantrymen and protected by both its walls—made of stone and brick, it had a circumference of thirty-five stades—and a river with steep banks.[25] The mercenaries employed by the ruler of Massaga made a sortie from the town, believing that a feigned retreat

---

22. There is no justification for identifying (as Berve II 89 does) Assacenus with the ruler of the Aspasians (see the discussion in Heckel 58–59). For the Aspasians and Assacenians, see McCrindle 1896, 333–34.

23. The lesser towns: "When the barbarians became aware of his approach, they dared not take their stand in mass for a battle but dispersed to their own cities with the intention of securing the defense and safety of each" (Arr. 4.25.7).

24. Massaga: *Metz Epit.* 39 says that "the king's brother, Amminais, had stirred up against Alexander and armed 9,000 mercenaries, whom he had brought into the state." Arr. 4.26.1 says the mercenaries numbered "about seven thousand." Diod. 17.84 mentions the mercenaries without giving their number (but his account is preceded by a lacuna). Ancient sources for the campaign: Curt. 8.10.22-36; Arr. 4.26.1–27.4 (cf. *Itiner. Al.* 106, where Saccas must be a corruption of the name Mazaga or Massacas or Assacenas); *Metz Epit.* 39–45; Justin 12.7.9-11 (cf. Oros. 3.19.1); Plut. *Alex.* 59.6-7. Modern discussions: Fuller 1958, 245–46; Dodge 1890, 522–25.

25. Curt. 8.10.23.

of the Macedonian forces indicated a loss of nerve. But their disordered charge against what they thought was an enemy in retreat was met by a devastating counterattack, and 200 mercenaries were killed as they fled back to the city walls. They gained a measure of revenge by wounding Alexander in the ankle with an arrow as he came too close to the walls. The defenders held off a Macedonian assault, even though the enemy had made a breach in the wall. It was as well that they did; Alexander was most ruthless with the defeated after suffering a wound—though admittedly this one was not serious.[26] An attack on the second day, when the Macedonians brought up towers and siege engines, was repulsed by the Assacenians. But on the third day, the defenders narrowly escaped an attempt by the Macedonian forces to exploit the breach once more:

> On the third day, Alexander once more brought up the phalanx, and with a device he threw a bridge onto the wall where the breach was located. Over it he led the hypaspists, who had also taken Tyre for him by the same means. But as large numbers pushed forward in eagerness, the bridge became overweighted and collapsed, and the Macedonians fell along with it. When the barbarians saw what had happened, they, with a shout, showered the Macedonians from the walls with stones, arrows, and whatever else a man chanced to have in his hands or could grab right then. Others, running out through the small gates lying between the towers, struck them at close quarters while they were still in disarray. (Arr. 4.26.6-7)

On the fourth day, the resistance of the Assacenians—or at least that of their mercenary garrison—was broken when their leader (hegemon) was killed in the fighting. They asked Alexander for terms, which were granted, allegedly because "Alexander was glad to be able to save the lives of brave men," not a sentiment he was wont to express, despite the views of his idolaters.[27] Indeed, if Arrian's

---

26. Defeat of the mercenary sortie: Arr. 4.26.1-4. Wounding of Alexander: Arr. 4.26.4; Curt. 8.10.28-29; *Metz Epit.* 40. It was apparently on this occasion that a flatterer in Alexander's entourage, the wrestler Dioxippos, remarked that from the king's wound flowed "not blood but ichor" (Aristobulus, *FGrH* 139 F47 = Athen. 6.251a); the story is also told by Plut. *Mor.* 180e, 341b; and *Alex.* 28.3-4, attributing the remark to Anaxarchus. For Alexander's increasingly brutal nature, see Lonsdale 2007, 64.

27. Arr. 4.27.2-3 (cf. the comments of Bosworth II, 174-75). The identity of the hegemon is uncertain. It is doubtful that he was Amminais, the former ruler's brother. Berve II 26 identifies him with the "brother of Assacenus" who opposed the Macedonians in the Buner region (Arr. 4.30.5). It is perhaps best to see him as the mercenary captain, although the fact that Alexander dealt with Cleophis, the queen or dowager queen, when the city surrendered may suggest otherwise.

account is accurate, Alexander was quick to slaughter the mercenaries after their surrender, whereafter he took the city by storm. That he made a pact with the mercenaries and subsequently massacred them is supported by other sources,[28] but these relate that the city itself surrendered voluntarily. The attack on the mercenaries, who left the city under truce, was another miscalculation on the part of the Conqueror, who did little more than stiffen the resistance of the native population who learned of his atrocities. Whether he was blind to the fact that such actions were counterproductive or his actions simply showed that the years of hard campaign had turned him into a bloodthirsty killer is hard to say. Rightly, the mercenaries objected that he was breaking his promise to them and his oath to the gods, but their pleas had no effect. The intensity of the confrontation between the Macedonians and the Indian mercenaries is captured by Diodorus and, although heavily dramatized, is worth quoting:

> The mercenaries were not terrified by the enormity of the danger they were facing. They closed ranks, formed their entire squadron into a circle, and set the children and women in the center so they could safely face the enemy, who was attacking them from all sides. They were desperate themselves and had put up a fierce fight by their daring and bravery in previous encounters, while the Macedonians were anxious not to be bested by the barbarians' fortitude. The battle thus provided an absolutely amazing scene. With the fighting all hand-to-hand and the combatants locked together in the struggle, death and wounds were many and of every kind. For the Macedonians, breaking through the small shields of the barbarians with their *sarissai*, would drive the iron spearheads into their lungs, while the mercenaries hurled their javelins into the massed ranks of their enemy and did not miss, their target being closely packed.
>
> Since many were wounded and not a few killed, the women seized the weapons of those who had fallen and joined their men in the fight. For the perilous situation and critical stage of the action obliged them to show strength contrary to their nature. Thus, some even armed themselves and stood in line with their own husbands, while others rushed to the attack without weapons, seized the shields of the enemy, and thereby greatly hindered their fighting ability. (Diod. 17.84.3-6)[29]

---

28. Arrian's version: 4.27.3-4. Other accounts: Diod. 17.84; *Metz Epit.* 43–45; Polyaenus 4.3.20; omitted by Curtius. Abramenko 1994 believes that the story of the Indian mercenaries is misplaced and belongs to the Aornus campaign.

29. Hammond 1983, 53 sees his Alexander as a victim of character assassination—easily dismissed as Cleitarchan fiction—and observes: "the narrative consists of imagined pictures rather than

Arrian alleges that the city of Massaga was taken by force, after the episode with the mercenaries, and that Alexander accepted the surrender of Assacenus' mother and daughter.[30] About her and the child, he says nothing more. But Justin, Curtius, and the *Metz Epitome* tell a different story. The queen's name is given as Cleophis—it is attested only in the Latin sources—and she was remarkable for her beauty. Rumor held that Alexander had an affair with the queen, whose name and actions recall the famous seductive queen of Egypt, and that she later bore the Conqueror a son, also named Alexander.[31]

The news of Alexander's treatment of the Indian mercenaries must have reached the other Assacenians, and it is little wonder that they continued to resist. Bazira, almost certainly Bir-kot,[32] was the next target of the invader. Again, Alexander's hopes that news of the fall of Massaga would induce the city to surrender were disappointed. Although Coenus pressed the attack on Bazira, the natives were tenacious in their defense, as were the inhabitants of Ora (Udegram), who were besieged by Polyperchon. Here the locals were expecting help from Abisares, ruler of the Kashmir and an enemy of Alexander's new ally Taxiles. As a result, Alexander told Coenus to leave a force to guard Bazira and then follow him to Ora, which Alexander took on the first assault.[33] In the absence of both

---

of participants' memories of actual events, as at Thebes . . . and after Issus. . . . The purpose is to show the brutality of the Macedonians and the treachery of A[lexander] 'shouting in a great voice' (84.2)—for all the world to know!" Tarn II 53 could scarcely do better: "Cleitarchus had a taste either for inventing massacres or for retailing massacres invented by others."

30. Arr. 4.27.8: τὴν μητέρα τὴν Ἀσσακάνου καὶ τὴν παῖδα ἔλαβεν.

31. She is named by Curtius and Justin (cf. Oros. 3.19.1: Cleophylis). Gutschmid 1882, 553–54, believes that she, or at least her name, was invented by a later source to recall Cleopatra VII. Seel 1972, 181–82, believes Curtius took the story from Pompeius Trogus, whose history Justin abbreviated. Compare Pliny, *HN* 9.119, calling Cleopatra *regina meretrix*; cf. Propertius 3.11.39. Justin 12.7.11 says: *Cleophis regina propter prostratam pudicitiam scortum regium ab Indis exinde appellata est.* Curt. 8.10.35 says that Cleophis surrendered to Alexander and put her own son on Alexander's knee. Nevertheless, she is consistently identified as the mother of Assacenus. The story forms part of a pattern of Alexander's relationships with older women: his mother, Ada of Halicarnassus, Sisygambis, and now Cleophis.

32. For the location: Stein 1929, 46–48; Eggermont 1975, 184; Seibert 1985, 152; Bosworth II 176–77.

33. Curt. 8.11.1 says that Polyperchon defeated the natives who made a sortie from Ora and then captured the city. Arr. 4.27.9 writes that Alexander himself attacked the city at once and captured it on the first attempt, capturing also the elephants that were left there. One suspects that Arrian was basing his account on Ptolemy, who in the years after Alexander's death (and perhaps earlier) was not well disposed toward Polyperchon. In fact, in an early passage (4.27.5), he omits Polyperchon from the list of commanders sent against Ora, although the others (Attalus and Alcetas) were on occasion associated with Polyperchon (Heckel, *Marshals*[2] 204; on Ptolemy's bias, see Errington 1969; Roisman 1984).

the king and Coenus, the Bazirans made a sortie from their city, believing themselves more than equal to the besieging force. In the ensuing battle, some 500 of
them were killed and 70 taken alive. When they learned of the fall of Ora, they
abandoned all hope of holding out against the invaders and fled during the night
to the nearby rock, known as Aornus, where they were joined by the inhabitants
of the neighboring towns.[34] Unable to defeat the invader in the field or withstand
his siege engines, the Assacenians placed their faith in the natural defenses of the
mountains, and even these failed them.

As the Assacenians prepared to make their last stand on Aornus, the invader
strengthened and garrisoned their captured cities—Massaga, Bazira, and Ora—
as well as another, Orobatis, which was fortified by Hephaestion and Perdiccas on
their way to the Indus. Nicanor was appointed satrap of Gandhāra.[35] Peucelaotis
was also received in surrender, and a certain Philip was appointed as the commander of its citadel. Now that the satrapy was all but subdued, the king made his
way to Embolima and Aornus.

Aornus (Pir-Sar) was an imposing mountain spur bounded on one side by the
Indus River:[36]

> They say the rock's circumference is roughly 200 stades, and its height
> from bottom to top 11 stades, with the only means of ascent handmade
> and difficult. On the rock's summit (it is said), there is also water, plentiful
> and pure—a spring that is constantly flowing, with water even streaming
> forth from it. There is also wood and enough good, workable land for even
> a thousand men to cultivate. (Arr. 4.28.3)

---

34. Arr. 4.27.8, 28.1.

35. Arr. 4.28.4-6. Nicanor: Heckel 177 s.v. "Nicanor [6]"; Berve II 275–276 no. 556. He is probably the same man whom Alexander had left in charge of Alexandria in the Caucasus (Arr.
4.22.5). The appointment of Nicanor suggests that at that time, Gandhāra did not include
Taxiles' realm, where Alexander subsequently installed Philip son of Machatas as satrap (Arr.
5.8.3).

36. Aornus as Pir-Sar: The identification was made by Sir Aurel Stein (Stein 1927 and 1929,
113–54) and is now generally accepted (Seibert 1985, 153; earlier literature in Seibert 1972a,
152–53; Lane Fox 1973, 3443–46). The alternative, Mount Ilam (Tucci 1977, 52–55; Eggermont
1984, 191–200; Badian 1987, 117 n. 1), does not match the geographical descriptions, the most
important of which is that the Indus flowed at the foot of Aornus. See Bosworth II 178–80.
Military action: Fuller 1958, 248–54; English 2009, 122–29. Ancient sources: Curt. 8.11.2-25;
Diod. 17.85.1–86.1; Plut. *Alex.* 58.5; *Metz Epit.* 46–47; Justin 12.7.12-13 (cf. Oros. 3.19.2); Arr.
4.28.1–30.4.

According to rumor, Heracles had made an unsuccessful attempt to take the rock, something that was said to have heightened the king's desire to outdo his mythical ancestor.[37] Using Embolima as the base of his operations, the Conqueror turned his attention to a stronghold that rivaled anything he had encountered in Sogdiana. Once again, he made use of local informants to gain the high ground,[38] and he filled the chasm that separated him from the defenders, building over the space of three days a mound upon which he could mount his catapults. Having overcome the natural obstacles, his army fell upon the defenders, many of whom fell to their deaths in their scramble to escape. Those who did survive death and avoided capture fled to the kingdom of Abisares on the other side of the Indus. Alexander and his army rejoined Hephaestion at the boat bridge on the river, having dealt with the last holdouts in a little more than two weeks.[39]

Unrest continued after the Macedonians moved into the Punjab. Sisicottus, who had been established as commandant of the garrison at Aornus and ordered to govern the surrounding territory, sent word to Alexander that the Assacenians had risen in revolt and killed the satrap of Gandhāra. Philip, the *phrourarchos* of Peucelaotis, who was now elevated to the position of satrap of Gandhāra, combined forces with Tyriespis of Parapamisus and reestablished order. Pressure was exerted from the western fringe, and by the time of Alexander's death, Gandhāra appears to have come under the rule of the satrap of the Parapamisadae.[40]

---

37. Arr. 4.28.2, voicing doubts that the Theban or Tyrian Heracles ever went to India (cf. Bosworth II 180–81). Diod. 17.85.2-3; *Metz Epit.* 46–47; Curt. 8.11.2; Justin 12.7.12-13; Strabo 15.1.8 C688. Heracles had been driven off by an earthquake.

38. Arr. 4.29.4: a deserter from the Indians. The episode again highlights the role of Ptolemy son of Lagus. Diod. 17.85.4-6: an old man and his sons who lived in poverty in a cave; cf. Curt. 8.11.3-4: Alexander gave the old man a reward of eighty talents. As Bosworth II 186 notes, this is strongly reminiscent of the episode at the Persian Gates.

39. *Metz Epit.* 48: he returned on the sixteenth day. In the confused accounts of these final days, we hear of some final opposition by the Assacenians under a brother of Assacenus in the vicinity of Dyrta (Arr. 4.30.5); he is probably identical with Aphrices (or Erices), who had a force of 20,000 and fifteen elephants but was murdered by his own troops, who were taken into Alexander's service (Diod. 17.86.2-3; Curt. 8.12.1-3; see Heckel 40; Berve II 97–98 no. 191; also Eggermont 1975, 183–84).

40. See especially Jacobs 1994, 76–79, who argues convincingly that the Philip who replaced Nicanor (the satrap who was killed by the Assacenians) was not the son of Machatas and that Alexander did not temporarily join Gandhāra to the lands east of the Indus, since such an arrangement would have been politically and military unviable. Bosworth II 322 does not believe that the ruler (Arr. 5.20.7 calls him *hyparchos*, but he clearly refers to the satrap) killed by the Assacenians was Nicanor; rather, he identifies him as a native ruler. But this view only creates further problems, and we cannot place much faith in Arrian's careless use of terminology.

14

From the Punjab to Pattala

THE DYNAST OF the lands immediately to the east of Gandhāra set out, with a splendid force, from his capital of Taxila[1] to meet Alexander, who had just subdued the valleys of the Kabul River and its tributaries and crossed the Indus on a boat bridge prepared by his generals Hephaestion and Perdiccas. He had first sent an envoy to the Conqueror in Sogdiana, at a time when he was still the heir to the kingdom and known by his personal name Omphis (Ambhi).[2] When he met Alexander in person, near Nicaea on the eastern fringe of Parapamisadae, he was apparently still a king in waiting—though some sources call him Taxiles, probably in anticipation of events to come.[3] Now he met the Macedonian king on his own soil, reporting his father's death and seeking the Conqueror's approval for his accession to the throne. It was, of course, a diplomatic formality but politically expedient. The new Taxiles—he took the official name of rulers in his region—had dangerous enemies on all sides: Abisares to the north, Porus to the east, and the Oxydracae to the south.[4] Only the west was relatively secure, and that was due in part to the appointment of Sangaeus as Astis' successor in Peucelaotis.[5]

---

1. Modern Shakidheri (Seibert 1985, 156), about thirty kilometers northeast of Rawalpindi. See Marshall 1951; Karttunen 1990.

2. Curt. 8.12.5 says that Omphis was responsible for his father's surrender to Alexander; cf. Diod. 17.86.4.

3. Arr. 4.22.6. Although Arrian calls him Taxiles, there is no indication that he asked for recognition as his father's successor on that occasion. Hence, we may assume that his father was still alive.

4. Abisares and Porus: Heckel 1–2 s.v. "Abisares [1]" and 231–32 s.v. "Porus [1]"; Berve II 3–4 no. 2 and 340–45 no. 683. The kingdom of Taxila: Karttunen 1990.

5. Sangaeus, before his appointment as hyparch of Peucelaotis, had fled from his enemy, Astis, and taken refuge with Taxiles (Arr. 4.22.8). Brunt I 415 n. 7 believes that Astis was motivated by fear of Taxiles.

In the Path of Conquest. Waldemar Heckel, Oxford University Press (2020). © Oxford University Press.

DOI: 10.1093/oso/9780190076689.001.0001

The presence of the invading army frightened the Kashmir ruler, who had unwisely sent aid to the Assacenians,[6] and Abisares hoped to avoid making submission in person by pleading ill health. Porus, on the other hand, was preparing to meet the invader in force on the banks of the Hydaspes (Jhelum) River. As for the Oxydracae, at that time they regarded Alexander more with curiosity than concern. Within a year, the Punjab would learn the power of the Macedonian war machine, and a fleet would be poised to make its descent of the Indus river system.

I

The campaign along the Kabul River, the Peshawar lowlands, brought the Macedonian invader to the Indus River, which formed the western boundary of the Punjab, the land of the five rivers. This inverted delta was demarcated by mountains in the north, the Satlej River in the east, and the Indus in the west. Between the two were the rivers called by the Greeks the Hydaspes, the Acesines, and the Hydraotes, known today as the Jhelum, the Chenab, and the Ravi. The Hydaspes is the first to join the Acesines, to which the Hydraotes joins its water from the east and farther south. After combining with the Satlej—of which the Hyphasis (Beas) is a northern tributary—their stream has its confluence with the Indus to the southwest of Bahāwalpur. Between each set of rivers were the kingdoms of Taxiles, Porus, the Mallians, and the Oxydracae, respectively. It was here in the Punjab that the invading army had its first experience with monsoon rains, battle with elephants, and snakes of prodigious size and deadly venom.[7] India was indeed wondrous in the telling but terrifying to the European soldiers

---

6. Arr. 4.27.7. He ruled the hill country north of Taxiles' kingdom; Curt. 8.12.13 and *Metz Epit.* 53 both place him beyond the Hydaspes, but his kingdom must have extended to the Indus (cf. Strabo 15.1.28 C698 = Onesicritus, *FGrH* 134 F18a, ὑπὲρ ταύτης is vague; see also Bosworth II 260–61). Bosworth II 177–78 believes the mercenaries who served at Massaga may have come from his territory (Abhisāra, which McCrindle 1896, 375, identifies with Hazara; cf. Stein 1929, 123).

7. Snakes: Onesicritus (*FGrH* 134 F16b = Ael. *NA* 16.39) claimed that Abisares kept two snakes that measured 140 and 80 cubits, respectively. The former, if there is any reason to trust the mendacious Onesicritus, would have been double the length of any snake known today. By contrast, Diodorus' mention (17.90.1; cf. Arr. *Ind.* 15.10) of snakes (probably pythons) measuring 16 cubits or 24 feet is well within reason. The Macedonians also took to sleeping in hammocks to avoid venomous snakes (Diod. 17.90.5-7; cf. Curt. 9.1.12). Elephants were present at Gaugamela (Arr. 3.8.6, 11.6; see also Charles 2008) but played no significant role in the battle. Monsoons: Strabo 15.1.17 C691 = Aristobulus, *FGrH* 139 F35); Diod. 17.94.2-3 for their demoralizing effect. The rain was a factor in the Hydaspes battle, and the swollen rivers were difficult to cross.

who had now marched to the edges of the known world. Farther to the east were the Ganges lands, the numbers of its inhabitants, although inflated by rumor, sufficient to crush the spirits of the army and even the most adventurous of leaders.

With the crossing of the Indus, the Macedonian conquest reached the eastern edge of the Achaemenid Empire. Those who resisted Alexander were now fighting for their families, their homes, and the autonomy of their regions. The Indian philosopher Kautilya aptly summed up international relations when he said that "your neighbor is your enemy and your neighbor's neighbor is your friend." It was just such a checkerboard of enemies and friends that the invader could use to his advantage. Indeed, it was fortunate that the ruler of the eastern bank of the Indus—at least, the part that bordered on Gandhāra—was anxious to use the foreign army for his own ends. Opposition was hopeless, but collaboration would almost certainly prove advantageous. Hence, he welcomed the Conqueror and placed the resources of his kingdom at his disposal:

Beyond the river lived a certain Mophis,[8] son of Taxiles, who even during his father's lifetime had been eager to conclude an alliance with Alexander because of the latter's achievements. After the death of his father, Mophis sent a deputation to treat with Alexander and to report back whether Alexander wished Mophis himself to assume control of his father's kingdom or preferred to send someone in his stead. When Alexander heard this, he was full of admiration for Mophis' intelligence and his remarkable judgment on this occasion. Mophis, however, would neither change his name nor assume royal robes and so awaited Alexander's arrival.

Alexander then distributed provisions to the men, embarked the army on the ships, and took them across the river.[9] Hearing that Alexander had arrived, Mophis gladly set out toward him with his army and some elephants. When Alexander saw him coming to meet him in battle formation, he was afraid that it was an enemy approaching, and he had instructions issued immediately for his men to take up their arms and go to their positions in the battle line. Agitated by the disturbing turn of events, the Macedonians nevertheless halted on the spot in silence, and when Mophis realized this, he ordered his men to stop and put up their lances. He then rode forward alone, far ahead of his troops. Seeing this,

8. The form "Mophis" is found also in Diod. 17.86.4. Curt. 8.12.5 calls him Omphis (Sanskrit: Ambhi).

9. This is a mistake; the Indus was crossed on foot over a boat bridge, the construction of which was discussed in a digression by Arrian (5.7.1–8.1).

Alexander likewise went ahead of his men, for he believed himself a match for Mophis in single combat. Then the two men met, shook hands, and formed an alliance, following which Mophis turned over to Alexander all his infantry and cavalry, fifty-eight elephants, 600 talents of silver, ... bulls decorated with sacrificial fillets,[10] many vessels of gold and silver, clothing of all kinds, and several uncommon animals of the wild. Alexander accepted these and asked Mophis why he had mobilized an army. Mophis replied that it was because he had intended doing whatever Alexander would have wished, at which Alexander further inquired of him whether any neighbor of his was causing him trouble. Mophis answered that two kings beyond the river were preparing to make war on him: Abisares, who lived in the mountains, and Porus, whose kingdom was in the plain adjacent to the river.

Alexander thanked him for his generosity, declaring that he should succeed to his father's throne and ordering that his name be changed to Taxiles. (*Metz Epit.* 49–54)

Arrian says that Taxiles' realm was enlarged but refers to him as the hyparch of Taxila.[11] He placed a garrison in the city and appointed Philip son of Machatas satrap of the region. In the short term, it appears that Taxiles' powers were restricted by the Conqueror, but this may have been a precautionary measure that allowed Alexander to secure his lines of communication. Abisares made at least

---

10. Curt. 8.12.11: fifty-six elephants, 3,000 bulls, and a large number of sheep. Arr. 5.3.5: 200 talents of silver, 3,000 cattle, more than 10,000 sheep, thirty elephants. He also sent 700 cavalrymen to form an auxiliary force (Arr. 5.3.6). Plut. *Alex.* 59.1-5 refers to the earlier surrender of Taxiles, when the king was at Nicaea (cf. Curt. 8.12.5); it precedes an account of the slaughter of the Indian mercenaries.

11. Arr. 5.8.2; cf. Plut. *Alex.* 60.15, who calls Porus a satrap. The extension of his territory does not mean that Taxiles' territory had been restricted to the area around Taxila, although the reference to "the Indians of this region" (καὶ ἐδέχετο αὐτὸν Ταξίλης ὁ ὕπαρχος τῆς πόλεως καὶ αὐτοὶ οἱ τῇδε Ἰνδοὶ φιλίως) suggests that there were other hyparchs as well. Plut. *Alex.* 59.1 says Taxiles ruled a portion of India "as large as Egypt" (οὐκ ἀποδέουσαν Αἰγύπτου τὸ μέγεθος). Bosworth II 260 thinks Taxiles' territory was now extended west of the Indus. The exact status of the Indian rulers is unclear. Curt. 8.12.4 says that *regnabat in ea regione Omphis*. That is, Omphis/Taxiles was a *rex* (king). Diod. 17.86.4 calls Omphis' father *basileus; Metz Epit.* 49 talks about his reluctance to assume *vestem regiam* (royal attire). But Arr. 5.8.2 calls him ὕπαρχος and makes him subject to Philip, who is called σατράπης (5.8.3). By contrast, Abisares is called τοῦ τῶν ὀρείων Ἰνδῶν βασιλέως (cf. Curt. 8.12.12-13). Arr. 5.19.1 says that Porus fought for his "kingdom" against another king (ὑπὲρ βασιλείας τῆς αὐτοῦ πρὸς βασιλέα ἄλλον). The distinction may be that Taxiles' father had been a subject of the Persian king; hence the title *hyparchos*. Although Taxiles was subordinate to a Macedonian satrap, it is clear that in most other respects, his status was roughly the same as that of Porus and Abisares.

token submission,[12] but the most dangerous enemy occupied the lands east of the Hydaspes.

Abisares and Porus responded to Alexander's demands in different ways: Abisares prevaricated, and Porus had the Macedonian envoy, Cleochares, whipped when he demanded that he pay tribute (and give hostages).[13] The story of Porus' treatment of Cleochares is intended to depict the Indian king as arrogant and to justify Alexander's campaign against him. And this arrogance is displayed in an invented letter to Alexander:

> Porus, King of India, has this to say to Alexander: No matter who you are— and I am told that you are a Macedonian—it is better for you to remain at a distance and to reflect upon your own misfortunes rather than envy another. Porus is declared undefeated up to this time, and Darius causes me no alarm. So, imbecile, don't give me orders! Just set one foot in my territory with hostile intent, and you shall learn that I am King of India, that none but Jupiter is my master. And Porus swears this oath by the great fire that rules the heavens: if I catch any of your men in my territory, I shall have his blood on my lance, and I shall distribute your goods among my slaves—for I have an abundance of riches myself. I shall do only one thing that you demand—to be ready and waiting for you, in arms, at my borders." (*Metz Epit.* 56–57)

Indeed, Porus prepared to receive the invader at the borders of his kingdom with a force of eighty-five elephants of exceptional size, 300 chariots, and about 30,000 infantry.[14] This army was poised to contest Alexander's crossing of the Hydaspes (Jhelum), probably near modern Haranpur.[15] Porus' army occupied the eastern banks of the river, which was, at any rate, not easy to cross. He would defeat the

---

12. *Mez Epit.* 55–56, 65; Curt. 8.13.1

13. *Metz Epit.* 55–56; Curt. 8.13.1-2, who says nothing about the whipping. The agent sent to Abisares was Nicocles, perhaps a Cypriote in Alexander's entourage (Heckel 179 s.v. "Nicocles [3]"; Berve II 278–79 no. 566).

14. Porus will meet Alexander on the borders of his kingdom: Curt. 8.13.2. The size of his army: Curt. 8.13.6 (identical numbers in *Metz Epit.* 54); Diod. 17.86.2, mentions 50,000 infantry, 3,000 cavalry, more than 1,000 chariots, and 150 elephants; Arr. 5.15.4: 30,000 infantry, 4,000 cavalry, 300 chariots, 200 elephants. Plut. *Alex.* 62.2 shows that Porus' army was vastly inferior to Alexander's army (20,000 infantry, 2,000 horse) but that the battle was nevertheless discouraging to the Macedonians: μόλις γὰρ ἐκεῖνον ὠσάμενοι δισμυρίοις πεζοῖς καὶ δισχιλίοις ἱππεῦσι.

15. Alexander's route to Haranpur is supported by Strabo 15.1.32 C700 and Pliny, *HN* 6.17; cf. Seibert 1985, 156. There are two main routes: "the northern road through the Bakāla Pass, past Rohātas, to Jihlam; or . . . the road 20 miles farther south through the Bunhār Pass to Jalālpur" (Smith 1914, 63 n. 1). Sir Aurel Stein surveyed the terrain in 1931 and suggested that Alexander

attacking units in detail as they emerged from the river. The physical obstacles were daunting: the river was four stades in width, the riverbed was deep, with no sign of shallows, and despite its width, the current "rushed ahead as a torrential cataract, just as if it had been narrowly constricted by its banks, and the waves rebounding at several points indicated the presence of unseen rocks." On the opposite shore, Porus had stationed his elephants, which inspired fear in both the horses and their Macedonian riders, who had thus far had little exposure to the beasts.[16]

Porus also kept a watchful eye on the movements of the enemy army; as Alexander marched north along the banks, looking for an alternative crossing point, a detachment of Porus' forces followed him on the other side of the river. The enemy plan was to leave a holding force opposite Porus' main army—this, as so often in the past, was to be commanded by Craterus—while another contingent hoped to cross farther north and catch Porus in a pincer movement. If Porus moved to deal with Alexander, Craterus was instructed to make the river crossing at the point the Indians had evacuated or, at least, weakened their defenses. Another Macedonian force encamped upstream (but south of the planned crossing point) served as a further distraction and could quickly move to support either Alexander or Craterus.[17]

The defensive measures were sound, taking advantage of the terrain and the onslaught of the monsoon rains. Porus also kept a careful eye on the enemy, who on a nightly basis pretended to be launching a flanking maneuver. But when these turned out to be nothing more than feints, he let up his guard, an action that contributed to his defeat.[18] For the invader, too, used the weather to his advantage, as the heavy rains obscured both the defender's view and the noise of the

---

took the road to Haranpur and later marched the seventeen and a half miles north to Jalalpur, where he made the crossing of the river and Admana Island (see Stein 1932, summarized by Fuller 1958, 184; cf. Brunt II 458; Bosworth II 265–69). See the discussion of earlier views in Seibert 1972a, 158–60. The course of the Indus river system has changed dramatically over the centuries, and it is impossible to determine with certainty the true location of the Battle of the Hydaspes (Bosworth 1996, 13 n. 34).

16. Curt. 8.13.8-11.

17. Ancient accounts of the battle: Curt. 8.13.5–14, 33; Diod. 17.87-88; Arr. 5.8.4–18.5; Plut. *Alex.* 60; Justin 12.8.1-8 (cf. Oros. 3.19.3); *Metz Epit.* 53–60; Polyaenus 4.3.9, 22; Frontinus, *Strat.* 1.4.9. Modern discussions: Dodge 1890, 541–65; Veith 1908; Delbrück I, 220–29; Breloer 1933; Hamilton 1956; Fuller 1958, 180–99; Lonsdale 2007, 86–90; Devine 1987; Bosworth 1996, 5–21; Ashley 1998, 318–29; English 2011, 180–215; Worthington 2014, 243–50. Further bibliography in Seibert 1972a, 156–60.

18. Arr. 5.10.3-4. Curt. 8.13.18-27 describes diversionary actions by Ptolemy, whose force was separate from that of Alexander. In all likelihood, this account, which gives prominence to the future king, did not feature in his own *History*, despite the fact that Ptolemy was not shy about exaggerating or even inventing his achievements (cf. Bosworth II 273). Seibert 1969 omits the incident entirely ("Porus" is not to be found in his index; similarly silent is Worthington 2016,

Macedonian troop movements. Alexander marched north to a bend in the river, where a wooded island—apparently Admana—helped to conceal his crossing. He achieved a measure of surprise, and Porus' outpost was overrun, despite a brief but futile attempt to repel the invader:[19]

> Ptolemy says that the son[20] was indeed sent by Porus, but not at the head of a mere sixty chariots. (And, in fact, that Porus would have sent out his son with only sixty chariots, after being told by his scouts that Alexander had crossed the Hydaspes, or that some part of his army had crossed, is somewhat implausible. If these chariots were on an intelligence-gathering mission, their number was large and lacking the flexibility needed for the withdrawal. If, on the other hand, their goal was to prevent the crossing of those of the enemy who had not yet made it over, and to attack those who had already landed, they were insufficient for the operation.) Ptolemy actually says that Porus' son came on the scene with 2,000 cavalry and 120 chariots, but that Alexander stymied them, having already made his final crossing from the island. (Arr. 5.14.5-6 = Ptolemy, *FGrH* 138 F20)

The pickets now turned back to warn Porus, who began his march north to engage Alexander. What ensued was primarily a cavalry engagement on treacherous ground.

Porus' army, when it arrived, was quickly drawn up with 3,000 cavalry on each wing and the infantry in the center. In front of the infantry, elephants were stationed at intervals of about fifteen meters. The Macedonians, on the other

---

58, although the remark that "Ptolemy must have been with Alexander, as he writes of the conflict when they finally crossed the river," suggests that he rejects the role attributed to him by Curtius.

19. Diodorus and Justin say nothing about the turning maneuver, even though it was the essential tactic employed by the invaders. Curtius does not mention Indian pickets—although the Latin is somewhat ambiguous: *vacua erat ab hostibus ripa quae petebatur* (8.13.27)—and makes it clear that Porus' focus was on the force with Ptolemy. This, of course, did not exist as a separate entity. Ptolemy crossed the river on a triacontor with Alexander (Arr. 5.13.1).

20. Arrian does not name him, but he is apparently the same person whom Curtius calls Porus' brother. "These forces [100 chariots and 4,000 cavalry] which he sent ahead were led by his brother Spitaces, and their main strength lay in the chariots, each of which carried six men, two equipped with shields, two archers stationed on each side of the vehicle, and finally the two charioteers who were, in fact, well armed themselves; for when it came to fighting at close quarters, they would drop the reins and fire spears upon the enemy" (8.14.2-3). Arr. 5.18.2 calls Spitaces an Indian nomarch and says nothing of any relationship with Porus; the son, however, died in the engagement (5.15.2; cf. 5.18.2: two sons of Porus, and Spitaces, died). Polyaenus 4.3.21 says a certain "Pittacus" (clearly a corruption of Spitaces) was a nephew of the Indian king. See Heckel 253–54; Berve II 358 no. 716; cf. Bosworth II 303–4.

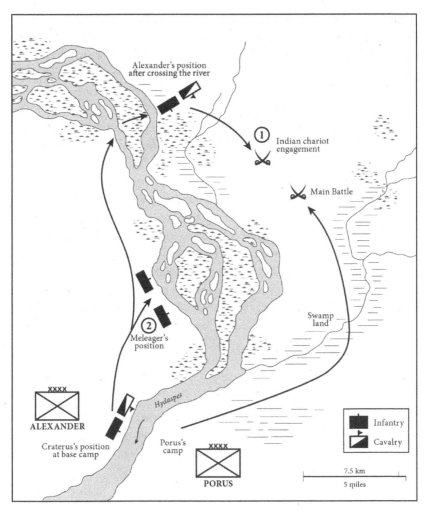

MAP 14.1 Map of the Battle of the Hydaspes River.

hand, had crossed with cavalry and lightly armed forces and were waiting for the phalanx that had been stationed halfway upstream with Meleager, Gorgias, and Attalus to come up. Coenus, with his cavalry, was kept in reserve and concealed from view on the Macedonian left, while Alexander, with the Companion cavalry and the *hippotoxotai* (the mounted archers) and supported by the hypaspists, began to put pressure on the Indian left. This induced the Indian cavalry from the other side of the line to ride behind their own infantry to counter Alexander's attack. But the Indian horsemen who vacated their position on the left were now pursued by Coenus' cavalry, which appeared from its concealed position. In the cavalry engagement, the Macedonians prevailed, while the infantry and the elephants found themselves under pressure in the center from the *pezhetairoi*, the Agrianes, and the Thracians. Whatever advantages the elephants gave the defender, these were soon negated, as the wounding of the beasts turned them back into the ranks of the Indians in their torment and frenzy, until they succumbed to their wounds.[21]

Porus himself was attacked relentlessly by the mounted archers[22] and suffered many wounds before he was finally induced to surrender.[23] His troops had fought valiantly, and the Conqueror spared both the survivors and their leader. But Alexander's generous treatment of the defeated enemy was motivated less by respect for their fighting qualities and the courage of Porus than by the fact that he needed a strong ally in the Punjab to continue his conquests and secure his borders. In an earlier time, under different circumstances, Porus might have suffered the fate of a Batis or Bessus.[24] His treatment of Porus was simple pragmatism in the guise of magnanimity. The Conqueror allowed him to continue to rule his kingdom, which he enlarged, but the title of satrap, used by the Alexander historians though perhaps not proclaimed, indicates his subordination; he was, in short, a vassal king.[25] There is no mention, however, of a Macedonian garrison or military overseer.

II

The story that Porus killed with his javelin the brother of Taxiles, calling him a traitor to his people, may be nothing more than invention for dramatic effect.[26] But it underscores the enmity and rivalry between the neighboring rulers. Hence,

21. Curt. 8.14.24-30. Cf. Diod. 17.88.1-3; Arr. 5.17.5-7. Kistler 2007, 31–37. The elephants feature prominently on the so-called Porus decadrachm and tetradrachm (Bosworth 1996, 6–8; see Goukowsky 1972; Price 1982 and 1991, 51, 452, 456–57; Mørkholm 1991, 52–54; Miller 1994; Lane Fox 1996; Holt 2003.

22. *Metz Epit.* 60; cf. Diod. 17.88.5.

23. *Metz Epit.* 60 says he raised his hands in surrender when he saw that the battle was lost. Curt. 8.14.35-40 gives a lengthy account in which Porus first kills the brother of Taxiles, who urges him to surrender, and then is finally overcome by his wounds and believed to be dead.

24. When asked how he wished to be treated, Porus responded, somewhat audaciously: "Like a king" (Plut. *Alex.* 60.14).

25. Arr. 5.19.3; Plut. *Alex.* 60.15.

26. Curt. 8.14.35-36. Arr. 5.18.7 says that it was Taxiles himself who rode up and urged Porus to surrender and that he narrowly evaded the javelin hurled in his direction. Thereafter, other Indians appealed to him in turn, until Meroes, an old friend, finally induced him to surrender.

before he continued his journey to the south, Alexander induced them to secure their friendship through a marriage alliance. No further details are known, but it appears to have had the desired effect, at least in Alexander's lifetime.[27] Porus now became a faithful ally of the Conqueror, who built two cities on the banks of the Hydaspes, naming one Nicaea in commemoration of the victory and the other Bucephala as a tribute to his beloved horse, who had only recently died.[28] In Porus' kingdom, a massive fleet was constructed for the purpose of carrying the supplies and at least a portion of the army downstream to the ocean.[29] It was a clear indication that the Conqueror had decided to move south once his position in the Punjab was consolidated.[30]

Porus, by his own admission, had failed to submit to Alexander because he trusted in the superiority of his own military forces. Probably, he believed that his ally Abisares would still arrive in time to secure victory. But that was not to be. The Kashmir ruler sent envoys to announce his submission, but he feared to meet the Conqueror in person.[31] Alexander proceeded against the neighboring Indian tribes, and it was clear that he planned a military demonstration in the remainder

---

27. Curt. 9.3.22; *Metz Epit.* 70.

28. Arr. 5.18.4; Plut. *Alex.* 61.1-2: the horse died after the battle and not as a result of it. Curt. 9.1.6, 3.23; Justin 12.8.8; *Metz Epit.* 62; Strabo 15.1.29 C698.

29. The area was forested and ideal for shipbuilding: Strabo 11.7.4 C510; Curt. 9.1.3-4; Diod. 17.89.4.

30. Curt. 9.1.4 (*ut, cum totam Asiam percucurrisset, finem terrarum, mare, inviseret*) is a gross exaggeration. Cf. 9.1.1 (*sibi Orientis finis apertos esse*) suggesting further conquest beyond the Hydaspes, but Diod. 17.89.3 implies that this was a thank-offering for conquests already made. When Diodorus 17.89.5 says that Alexander intended to reach the limits of India and, having subdued its people, to sail down the river to the ocean (τέρμα τῆς Ἰνδικῆς), he means an advance to the eastern boundary of the Punjab followed by a return to the Hydaspes in order to sail south (διενοεῖτο γὰρ ἐπὶ τὸ τέρμα τῆς Ἰνδικῆς παραγενόμενος καὶ πάντας τοὺς ἐγχωρίους καταστρεψάμενος διὰ τοῦ ποταμοῦ καταπλεῖν εἰς τὸν Ὠκεανόν). Had he believed that the ocean was to the east, both the shipbuilding program at the Hydaspes and his political settlement of the eastern Punjab—where he did nothing to secure his lines of communication—are inexplicable (Heckel 2003a, 162–64). We must judge Alexander's intentions at this point in the light of his understanding of Indian geography. What he subsequently learned about India at the Hyphasis did not form part of his calculations. On the falsification of geography to enhance Alexander's achievements, see Strabo 11.7.4 C509.

31. Curt. 9.1.7-8: "Abisares, who had sent a deputation to Alexander before the battle with Porus, now sent a second promising to follow all the king's commands on the one condition that he should not be forced to surrender himself, for he was prepared neither to live without royal power nor to rule as a prisoner. Alexander had word sent to him that if he were reluctant to come to him, then Alexander would come to Abisares." Cf. Arr. 5.20.5-6, who adds that Abisares sent his own brother with money and a gift of forty elephants to Alexander. *Metz Epit.* 65 translates this threat into action: "Alexander led the army against him and brought him to heel."

of the Punjab.[32] Other peoples and minor dynasts, including another Porus, who was to play him false, offered their submission.[33] The invader now advanced eastward to the Acesines River:

> For where Alexander crossed with his army on boats and animal skins, the current of the Acesines is swift, running over large, sharp rocks from which the water is violently carried down seething and roaring, and the width here may be as much as fifteen stades. The crossing was easy for those who were making it on animal skins, says Ptolemy, but not for those going over in the boats: more than a few lost their lives there in the water when these ran onto the rocks and were smashed to bits.
>
> Thus, anyone basing his estimate on this account would judge that those writers are not far from the truth who think that the width of the River Indus is some forty stades on average, but contracts to about fifteen stades where it is at its narrowest and, because of its narrowness, is also at its deepest, and also think that this is the Indus' breadth in many places. In fact, I hypothesize that Alexander chose the widest part of the Acesines for his crossing so as to benefit from a slower current. (Arr. 5.20.8-10)

Porus was instructed to bring elephants and the most warlike of his people to help subdue the adjacent areas. The first objective was to deal with the other Porus, against whom he sent a force under Hephaestion, who, despite his shortcomings as a military leader, enjoyed Alexander's favor.[34] In the event, he did not disappoint, though Diodorus' remark that he returned "having conquered a large part

---

32. While the new foundations of Bucephala and Nicaea and the Indus fleet were being constructed, Alexander left Craterus behind with a military force, lest Porus give any thought to tergiversation (Arr. 5.20.2).

33. Among these were the Glausae (Glauganicae, according to Aristobulus; cf. McCrindle 1896, 111 n. 2), who surrendered only when Alexander's forces invaded their territory. Their thirty-seven towns, ranging in population from 5,000 to more than 10,000, were turned over to Porus (Arr. 5.20.2-4). Defection of the other Porus: Diod. 17.91.1. He had surrendered, but upon learning of the honors heaped upon his enemy and namesake, he rebelled (Arr. 5.20.6, 21.3).

34. Arr. 5.21.5; Diod. 17.91.1. For Hephaestion's career and relative lack of military accomplishment, see Heckel, *Marshals*[2] 75–100; cf. Reames 2010; Müller 2018b. Brunt II 461–62, following Aspach, believes that Alexander first marched north, on the western bank of the Acesines, to deal with the Glausae (Arr. 5.20.2), threatening Abisares in the process. When he did cross the Acesines, the territory of the so-called bad Porus was located to his right (i.e., the south), whither he sent Hephaestion. For the location of the bad Porus' kingdom, see Strabo 15.1.30 C699.

of India" does him more than justice.[35] The so-called bad Porus had fled with his leading supporters to the Gandaridae, in effect abandoning his kingdom to the invader. It was handed over to his namesake, who now became the most dominant power in the northern Punjab. Whether, as it has been suggested, the bad Porus remained in the Gangetic kingdom as an agitator at the court of Sandrocottus (Chandragupta) is nothing more than speculation.[36]

Beyond the Hydraotes, the Adrestae and the Cathaeans proved equally reluctant to surrender.[37] They realized that submission to Alexander was, in effect, recognition of Porus' authority. Whether the Adrestae were won over by negotiation or force is unclear. The Cathaeans, as their name suggests, were warlike people, and they not only prepared to defend themselves but also called upon the other autonomous cities to do likewise:[38]

> Meanwhile, a report came to Alexander that a number of the independent Indians, and especially the ones called Cathaeans, were preparing for battle in case he marched on their country, and were also urging other independent tribes bordering them to take the same precautions; there was a powerful city named Sangala at which they intended to put up a fight. The Cathaeans themselves were also renowned for outstanding courage and strength in battle, as, along with them, were the Oxydracae, another Indian tribe, and yet another Indian tribe, the Malli. For it turned out that Porus and Abisares had also marched on them slightly earlier with their own forces, after stirring up against them many other independent Indians, but had withdrawn after achieving no result worth the effort put into it. (Arr. 5.22.1-2)

---

35. Diod. 17.93.1: πολλὴν τῆς Ἰνδικῆς καταπεπολεμηκώς. Perhaps he had the support of another commander, as he did when he secured the crossing of the Indus.

36. Flight of bad Porus: Arr. 5.21.3; Diod. 17.91.1 says he fled to the Gandaridae, but Strabo 15.1.30 C699 says that this Porus' realm was called Gandaris (καλοῦσι δὲ Γανδαρίδα τὴν ὑπὸ τούτῳ χώραν). Associations with Chandragupta: Bosworth II 325. Chandragupta: Heckel 244–45 s.v. "Sandrocottus"; Berve II 349 no. 695; and Wheatley's excellent discussion in Yardley, Wheatley, and Heckel 275–91, with additional literature.

37. Adrestae: Arr. 5.22.3-4; Diod. 17.91.2; Justin 12.8.9. The Adrestae (Adraïstrai in Arrian) may be the Aratta of the *Mahabharata*. The Cathaeans are wrongly located by Strabo 15.1.30 C699 between the Hydaspes and the Acesines.

38. The name Cathaeans (Greek: Καθαῖοι) is thought to be identical with Kshatriya, the name of the military caste (McCrindle 1896, 347). Their people practiced suttee (or sati), in which a man's widow was cremated with her husband—in the case of multiple wives, they vied for the "honor": Diod. 17.91.3; Strabo 15.1.30 = Onesicritus, *FGrH* 134 F21; cf. Heckel and Yardley 1981.

The Cathaeans, who offered fierce resistance, are dealt with in cursory fashion by the popular tradition. Curtius gives some detail but does not even name them, and Diodorus says only that "Alexander captured their greatest and strongest city after much fighting."[39] In fact, they were more interested in the appearance and the customs of the people of the kingdom of Sopeithes (Sophytes). But Arrian shows that some of the hardest fighting in the Indian campaign involved the Cathaeans and their defense of the city of Sangala.

Sangala lay three days' march from Hydraotes, one day beyond Pimprama, the capital of the Adrestae.[40] Situated on a hill, the city was surrounded by the Cathaeans and their allies, who placed a barricade of wagons in three concentric rings around it, so that the wagons "formed a triple palisade."[41] Behind this, they took up their positions. In a scene evocative of the old American West, the defenders were assailed by the mounted archers, who fired arrows at them in order to prevent them from moving to the attack and in the hope of picking off many of those within the defensive barrier. Alexander's army was coming up in its marching column, and the attack of the *hippotoxotai* gave him time to deploy his forces. Cavalry and light-armed troops were sent to the wings, and the phalanx was placed solidly in the center. Alexander led the cavalry on the right to a position where he saw gaps in the barricade, but he was driven back by heavy fire. The Cathaeans resisted the Macedonians' attempt to draw them out, and this forced the invader to revise his battle plan. The king dismounted and prepared to fight in hoplite fashion. For once, the brunt of the fighting was borne by the infantry, with the cavalry reduced to a protective role on the flanks:

> The Macedonians forced the Indians back from the first line of wagons without difficulty. The Indians, however, formed themselves up before the second line and found it easier to defend themselves, standing as they were in closer order in a smaller circle; and the Macedonians, meanwhile, instead of attacking them over open ground as before, were now dragging off the first wagons and also making a disordered charge through such gaps as each man could find between them. However, the Indians were dislodged from the second line, too, forced back by the phalanx, and they

39. Diod. 17.91.4.

40. Arr. 5.22.3-4. Pimprama is mentioned only by Arrian; it may have been located in the general vicinity of Lahore. See McCrindle 1896, 116 n. 1; Bosworth II 328–29. Sangala has been tentatively identified with Lahore or Amritsar, but Bosworth II 327 objects that the courses of the rivers of the Punjab have changed dramatically over the last two millennia.

41. Arr. 5.22.4. The Sangala campaign: Arr. 5.22.4–24.5; Diod. 17.91.3-4; Curt. 9.1.13-23; Justin 12.8.9; *Metz Epit.* 66 (general); Polyaenus 4.3.20; Fuller 1958, 255–58; English 2009, 129–35.

no longer attempted to remain at the third line but beat a hasty retreat and barricaded themselves within the city. (Arr. 5.23.2-3)

Curtius misunderstands the defensive measures taken by the Cathaeans and recounts a bizarre tale of the preliminaries to the siege of Sangala. Curtius says that "the barbarians came forth to fight with chariots lashed together; some of them were equipped with spears and others with lances, and they would jump nimbly from chariot to chariot."[42] The underlying truth may be that the Cathaeans lashed together the stationary wagons, in order to strengthen the barricade, and that defensive measures involved moving from one wagon to another as the need arose. But in the end, they suffered 8,000 killed and withdrew into the city.

The city, now under siege, was too large to be surrounded entirely by the Macedonian infantry, and a marsh or shallow lake to one side was guarded by cavalry outposts. The Cathaeans, as the enemy expected, attempted to escape from the city around the time of the second watch. But they were overwhelmed by the cavalry, and those who were not killed were driven back inside. After being surrounded by a stockade in all areas but the lake, the defenders planned a second breakout at the point where the stockade ended and left a gap between it and the lake. They were, however, betrayed by collaborators within the city. Ptolemy the historian once again points the spotlight on Ptolemy the general,[43] who took measures to contain the second attempt of the Cathaeans to escape. This time, some 500 Indians were cut down. Finally, with the arrival of Porus' forces and the construction of siege engines, the Macedonians made a final assault on the city. In fact, the siege engines were unnecessary, since the brick walls were undermined by sappers and thus breached; in other places, the walls were scaled on ladders. A desperate defense ensued, and 17,000 Indians were killed, while more than 70,000 were captured. But they had not sold their lives cheaply: in one of the bloodiest engagements in the Punjab, 100 Macedonians were killed, but 1,200 were wounded, including the *Somatophylax* and future king of Thrace (and, briefly, Macedon), Lysimachus.[44]

---

42. Curt. 9.1.15.

43. Arr. 5.23.7–24.3. Although Arrian does not refer to Ptolemy's *History*, the ultimate source is not in doubt. *FGrH* 138 F35; Strasburger 1934, 35; cf. Pearson 1960, 202–4; Bosworth II 327. Seibert 1969, 25, rightly concludes that "daß auch hier Ptolemaios seine Leistungen ausführlich darstellte."

44. Casualties: Arr. 5.24.3: 500 killed trying to break out of the city; 5.24.5: 17,000 killed when the city fell; Diod. 17.91.4 says only that Alexander captured the city at great risk and burned it (τὴν μεγίστην καὶ ὀχυρωτάτην πόλιν μετὰ πολλῶν κινδύνων ἐκπολιορκήσας ἐνέπρησεν). Diodorus adds that a second city was besieged but surrendered. Curt. 9.1.17 says that 8,000 Indians (he does not name them as Cathaeans) were killed before the siege began. Curtius also speaks

It appears that the Conqueror resorted once again to terror, making an example of Sangala in order to intimidate the remaining cities. Polyaenus, not always the most reliable of sources, records the following:

> Alexander put all the adult Cathaeans to death since, through desperation, they resisted him, and he completely destroyed their most powerful city, Sangala. A nasty rumor then pervaded the Indian population to the effect that Alexander's way of war was savage and barbarous. Alexander, however, wanted to alter this reputation of his, and when he captured a second Indian city, he took hostages and struck a treaty; then, on reaching a third city, which was large and well populated, he lined the hostages up in front of the phalanx—old men, children, and women. The people recognized that they were members of their own race and, seeing the humanity in Alexander's actions, they threw open their gates and welcomed him with the olive branches of suppliants. Word of this immediately spread, convincing the Indians to give Alexander a warm welcome. (Polyaenus 4.3.30)

It is hard to believe that the parading of captives in front of the army was a sign of philanthropy.[45] Alexander appears to have used them to threaten the enemy with captivity—significantly, the "hostages" were noncombatants—or as human shields, as the Mongols were later to do.[46] Even Arrian's account, which is so often sanitized for the sake of Alexander's image, shows that the treatment of the remaining Cathaeans was hardly "philanthropic." The king sent Eumenes to demand their surrender,

> but, since the report had already reached them that Alexander had taken Sangala by assault, they became fearful and fled, abandoning their cities. When their flight was reported to Alexander, he set off in hot pursuit; but most got away in good time because the pursuit was long delayed. Even so, after their departure, those left behind through disability were put to death by the army, some five hundred in all. Abandoning the idea of pursuit of the fugitives, Alexander went back to Sangala, completely

---

of more merciful treatment of the enemy, which induced other towns to surrender (9.1.20-23). Lysimachus: Heckel 153–55 s.v. "Lysimachus [2]"; Berve II 239–42 no. 480; Lund 1992; Landucci Gattinoni 1992; Heckel 1992, 267–75.

45. οἱ δὲ τοὺς ὁμοφύλους γνωρίσαντες καὶ τὰ ἔργα τῆς Ἀλεξάνδρου φιλανθρωπίας ὁρῶντες ἀνοίγουσί τε τὰς πύλας καὶ μετὰ ἱκετηριῶν αὐτὸν ἐδέξαντο.

46. Saunders 1971, 56; Chambers 2003, 13–14.

destroyed the city, and handed over its lands to those Indians who, though long autonomous, had willingly gone over to him. (Arr. 5.24.7-8)

The campaign between the Hydraotes and the Hyphasis resembles in many respects that in Gandhāra, and the slaughter no doubt reflected the heavy losses sustained by the invader.[47] The Indians may have feared Porus, who now joined the Macedonians, as much as they feared the Conqueror himself.[48]

III

Alexander's arrival at the Hyphasis River once again brought to a head the dissatisfaction of his own troops, though in this case it was the common soldiers more than the officers who opposed him. Modern scholars have for the most part accepted the accounts of the extant Alexander historians, which depict the Conqueror as eager to press on into the unknown in his quest for the eastern ocean. Learning of the peoples who lived along the Ganges, he was determined to cross the Hyphasis and wage war against them, giving little thought to the numbers of the enemy or the condition, both physical and mental, of his own troops. The Macedonians, who had followed their leader faithfully and given him countless hard-fought victories, refused to go on. It was, in fact, a strike (*secessio*) rather than a mutiny. The king took it badly, sulked in his tent, but was eventually persuaded by the spokesman of the troops to turn back:[49]

It was, some said, his only defeat, and it came at hands of his own army.

---

47. Macedonian losses were always downplayed by the Alexander historians, but even if one uses their figures, the losses at Sangala, as Bosworth II 334 notes, rivaled those at Gaugamela and the Hydaspes.

48. Despite Arrian's comment that the cities were turned over to those autonomous towns that had surrendered voluntarily, it appears that they were all placed under Porus' authority in the end (see Arr. 6.2.1). After the campaign against the Cathaeans, Alexander came to the kingdom of Sophytes (Sopeithes; Saubhuti), who submitted to the Macedonians voluntarily. The episode contributes little to our understanding of Indian resistance, except perhaps to show that intimidation was effective in some instances. See Curt. 9.1.24-35; *Metz Epit.* 66–67; Diod. 17.91.4–92.3; Justin 12.8.10 (cf. Oros. 3.19.5); Arr. 6.2.2 (in a different context); see Heckel 252–53 s.v. "Sophytes"; Berve II 367–68 nos. 734–35, who regards Arrian's Sopeithes as a separate individual.

49. The views of the troops were presented by Coenus son of Polemocrates, one of the most distinguished officers in the army (Curt. 9.3.3-15; Arr. 5.27). For his career, see Heckel, *Marshals²* 67–74; Berve II 169–75. I do not share Spann's view (1999, 68–69) that Coenus was part of the deception. He was, furthermore, not the only officer who supported the troops (Curt. 9.3.17; Arr. 5.28.1 also mentions the hesitation of the other officers: τῷ ὄκνῳ τῶν ἄλλων ἡγεμόνων).

> After the Kophes it was the Indus, then the Hydaspes, then the Acesines and the Hyarotis, and finally the Hypanis. For he was prevented from going further, partly because he was attending to certain oracles and partly through pressure from the army, which was already suffering hardship. Mostly, though, its troubles stemmed from the waters, as they were always being rained on. (Strabo 15.1.27 C697)[50]

The story is far more complex than Strabo's brief summary lets on, but the geographer brings out two interesting points: the role of "oracles" and the effect of the weather on the troops. One points to the official justification of the decision to turn back, the other to the plight of the troops, which Alexander had (apparently) chosen to disregard. And, although this study is concerned with resistance in its different forms, it is impossible to understand the actions of the Macedonian troops without touching on the question of leadership.[51]

Everything that Alexander had done up to this point since the battle at the Hydaspes, suggests that he was consolidating his victories and the borders of his empire. The Indus river system was a natural boundary, and the subjugation of the Punjab left its eastern portion in the hands of Porus, now a powerful vassal and ally. The true aims of the Conqueror are revealed by the fact that he was already building a fleet on the Hydaspes for the journey south and by the addition of the conquered territories beyond the Acesines to the realm of Porus. He seems to have placed very few restrictions on his powers: there were no satraps, hyparchs, or *phrourarchoi*; there were no Macedonian garrisons. The conquest of the Punjab served an additional purpose in that it kept the troops occupied during the monsoon season. In truth, those who campaigned formed only a portion of the force. Others were engaged in foraging or in the construction of the fleet.

But the strongest indicator that Alexander had no intention of continuing eastward can be found in the manner in which he treated the information about the land and the people he was (allegedly) planning to conquer. His informant, a local dynast named Phegeus or Phegelis (Sanskrit: Bhagala), reported that the

---

50. The Greek names for the rivers of the Punjab take various forms: the Hyarotis (cf. Hiarotis: Curt. 9.1.13) is the Hydraotes. The Hypanis (Hypasis: Curt. 9.1.35) is, of course, the Hyphasis (Beas). See Karttunen 1997, 113–18.

51. For the question of Alexander's true intentions at the Hyphasis, see Heckel 2003a; cf. Spann 1999; Howe and Müller 2012; Müller 2018a, 187–89. The issue was raised earlier by Niese I 138–39; Endres 1924, 12–15; and Hampl 1954, 102–6; but the majority of scholars take the sources on face value (Carney 1996b, 33–37, with *King and Court* 57–59; Anson 2013171–74 and 2015a). See Seibert 1972a, 160–62; cf. Badian 1985, 467, discussed below, and Holt 1982. For the Macedonians' opposition to kings, and Alexander in particular, see Roisman 2015, who does not accept my views on the Hyphasis "mutiny"; cf. Roisman 2012, 31–60.

Gangetic kingdom beyond the Hyphasis was in disarray and that the current king, Xandrames (Chandramas), was the son of a former barber and usurper. Nevertheless, he had considerable forces at his disposal: 20,000 cavalry, 200,000 infantry, 2,000 chariots, and 4,000 war elephants.[52]

These extravagant numbers allegedly inflamed Alexander's desire to march to the Ganges—an implausible reaction, even for a megalomaniac. What is more incredible, however, is that the Conqueror revealed this news to his troops, exhausted and ill equipped as they were, as if to inspire them. As he must have expected, it had the opposite effect. The information was made public, not to motivate but to dissuade. The king wanted the troops to make a decision that suited his own purpose but one that, if he had made it himself, might have him appear timid[53] and thus tarnish the well-crafted image of an adventurous and invincible commander.

Alexander stressed the magnitude of a campaign against the Gandaridae to troops who were in no condition take on such a project. Nor did he reveal to them the imminent arrival of 25,000 new suits of armor. When he looked out at the soldiers, he could not fail to notice their condition and their despair:

> Alexander could see that his men were exhausted from their perpetual campaigns and that after they had now endured almost eight years of hardship and peril, he needed to boost the morale of the troops with appropriate language to urge them on to the campaign against the Gandaridae. For casualties among the men had been considerable, and there was no prospect of any letup in the fighting. Moreover, the horses' hooves had been ground down by the interminable marching, most of the weapons were worn out, and all their Greek clothing gone (they had to resort to barbarian dress, recutting garments of the Indians). It also so happened that the fierce winter storms had been raging for seventy days, with incessant thunder and lightning breaking out over them.[54] (Diod. 17.94.1-3)

---

52. The numbers of cavalry, infantry, and chariots are the same in Diodorus, Curtius, and the *Metz Epitome*; cf. Justin 12.8.10: 200,000 infantry. Diod. 17.93.2 says there were 4,000 elephants; Curt. 9.2.4 has 3,000; the corrupt passage in the *Metz Epit.* 68 seems to refer to 180 elephants. Plut. *Alex.* 62.3: 200,000 infantry, 80,000 cavalry, 8,000 chariots, and 6,000 elephants.

53. Thus Endres 1924, 13: "Er wußte zu gut, daß logische Erörterungen bei der Masse ohne Wirkung sind und die Umkehr ihm in jedem Falle als Schwäche ausgelegt wird."

54. Not only were the "bad omens" clear to all, but, as Arr. 5.24.2 reports, Alexander knew that the men were meeting in groups throughout the camp and expressing their unwillingness to follow him any longer (ξύλλογοί τε ἐγίγνοντο κατὰ τὸ στρατόπεδον τῶν μὲν τὰ σφέτερα ὀδυρομένων, ὅσοι ἐπιεικέστατοι, τῶν δὲ οὐκ ἀκολουθήσειν, οὐδ᾽ ἢν ἄγῃ Ἀλέξανδρος, ἀπισχυριζομένων).

Diodorus goes on to say that the king attempted to bribe the troops by allowing them to ravage the countryside and with promises of support for their wives and children. This may have been an invention ex post facto, a further attempt to improve Alexander's image, and it has little support in the other sources.[55] And what good would these measures do if they followed him on a suicidal mission? Why the Conqueror chose this form of enticement and yet withheld the fact that much-needed new equipment was on its way is puzzling. One cannot help but think that he was doing everything in his power to scuttle the campaign. Equally baffling is his failure to garrison the newly conquered territory and thus secure his lines of communication.

Instead, Alexander made his insincere appeal to the troops who were predisposed to reject it. He begins his "exhortation" by referring to rumors it was in his power to suppress (Curt. 9.2.12-14, 16-17). It was the very fact that rumor had such an impact on the common soldier that he did not do so. His words did nothing to allay the troops' concerns. He said that even if the reports were accurate, the soldiers should not be frightened by them. Elephants, he reminded them, had proved a greater danger to their own forces than to the men they were supposed to attack. Whether the number of such animals at the Ganges was "equal to those that Porus had or whether there are 3,000 of them" made no difference, "since we see that they all turn to flight after one or two have been wounded." Even the large numbers of enemy infantry and cavalry were dismissed as "a disorderly horde." The speech continued in a similar vein, adding that the soldiers should think more about accomplishments and glory—both theirs and the king's—and not let the opportunity slip from their grasp, for the "rewards are greater than the dangers." To argue that Alexander believed what he said, or even that he misled his troops to gain his desired purpose, is to demean his true military genius. In truth, he had set himself up for "failure," and the conclusion of his oration made it clear to his men that the blame would fall on their shoulders.[56]

The troops reacted as the Conqueror knew they would. His response was feigned anger and disappointment. But in the end, he was persuaded to do what he had intended all along. The failure was blamed on the men, and the historians invented further excuses for the decision to turn back. The king himself was a master of deception, rivaled only by his propagandists.[57] Ptolemy gives one final

---

55. Only Justin 12.4.2-11 mentions such provisions for the soldiers' family in a completely different context (after the death of Darius and the fictitious Amazon episode); Plut. *Alex.* 71 and Arr. 7.12.1-2 report similar measures at Opis in 324.

56. Alexander's "motivational" speech: Curt. 9.2.12-30; Arr. 6.25.3-26.8.

57. Smith 1914, 76: "The soothsayers judiciously discovered that the omens were unfavourable for the passage of the river, and Alexander, with a heavy heart, gave orders for retreat."

justification for Alexander's withdrawal, saying that he "nevertheless made sacrificial offerings for the crossing, but in the sacrifice the victims proved unfavorable."[58] The *Metz Epitome* sums the matter up, omitting the confrontation with the troops altogether:

> The king refused to believe [what he had been told by Phegeus] until he questioned Porus and got exactly the same details from him. After establishing the facts, Alexander set up a number of altars along the river and ordered the construction of towers to serve as monuments of his campaign. Then, after sacrificing, he ordered the digging of ditches greater than their camp warranted and the making of sedan-chair frames larger than a human's stature required, of oversized shields of all kinds and horse bridles of dimensions greater than what was practical, and he commanded that these be left at various points in the camp. He himself then returned to the River Acesines. (*Mez Epit.* 69)

There could be no better monument to the sham of the Hyphasis episode than the fraudulent, supernatural camp and altars by the river.[59] When the troops returned to the Hydaspes, having reunited with their colleagues in other contingents, they found that the fleet had been built—in order to be used in a Gangetic campaign, they would have needed to be dismantled for transport.[60] The cities that

---

58. Arr. 5.28.4 = Ptolemy, *FGrH* 138 F23. Bosworth II 356: "For Arrian the king had already capitulated, and the sacrifices could only be a contrived sham."

59. Cf. Curt. 9.3.19: *posteritati fallax miraculum praeparans.* Pliny, *HN* 6.21.62: *arisque in adversa ripa dicatis*; cf. Philostratus, *Life of Apollonius* 2.43 (cf. Oikonomides 1988, 31–32). For the location of these altars, Smith 1903, 686 puts them in the Gaurdāspur District. See also Wood 1997, 197.

60. For the practice, see Arr. 5.8.4. But if Alexander had planned to use these ships for the Hyphasis crossing and the Ganges campaign, they ought to have been ready for transport by the time of the *secessio*. Furthermore, the construction of the fleet began before Alexander ever learned of the Gangetic kingdom. The importance of the fleet is noted by Niese I 139: "es geht aus den Thatsachen hervor, daß Alexander nicht daran dachte, bis an den Ganges und weiter zu gehen; denn da er schon im Gebiete des Taxiles und Poros die Anstalten zum Bau einer Flotte hatte treffen lassen, so muß er damals schon das beabsichtigt haben, was er später ausführte, die Fahrt den Hydaspes und Indus hinab." The ships in question were not those of the Indus boat bridge, as Anson 2015a, 71, implies, nor was it simply enlarged "after the retreat from the Beas." Badian 1985, 467 n. 2, is similarly discomfited by the evidence of the completed (or nearly completed) fleet: "C. ix.1.3f and D. 89.4f relate the building of the fleet straight after the victory over Porus. Curtius, characteristically, shows that he could make no sense of this. He adds: '. . . ut, cum totam Asiam percucurrisset, finem terrarum mare inviseret.' In view of his attested plans for advancing eastwards, Alexander can hardly have ordered a fleet to take him south to be built at this point. . . . If ships were built earlier, they were meant for different purposes: for supplies, of course, and perhaps for exploration, in connection with the

would be landmarks of Alexander's victory were also completed and populated.[61] Reinforcements arrived, as did 25,000 new suits of armor:

> Alexander then returned with his entire force to the River Acesines, marching along the same roads by which he had come. Finding there the ships that he had ordered to be built, he equipped them and had further ships constructed. At just this juncture there arrived from Greece, under their own commanders, allied troops and mercenaries—more than 30,000 infantry and slightly fewer than 6,000 cavalry—and with them were brought fine suits of armor for 25,000 infantry and 100 talents of medicines. These he, naturally, distributed among his soldiers. His naval force now assembled and 200 vessels without hatches made ready for action, he gave names to the two cities that he had established on each side of the river: Nicaea to one because of his victory in the war and Bucephala to the other to commemorate the horse that died in the battle with Porus. (Diod. 17.95.3-5)

Diodorus had made a few factual errors: like the other authors who used the same (now lost) source, he confuses the Acesines with the Hydaspes;[62] the numbers of the reinforcements from Europe are grossly exaggerated;[63] and the observation that Bucephalus died in the battle against Porus is probably incorrect.[64] But it is hard to ignore the fact that the king failed to tell his disheartened troops about the very things that would have raised their spirits: the expectation of reinforcements, medical supplies, and new suits of armor. All these had, in fact, been intended for the campaign to the Indus Delta. In preparation for

---

momentary idea that he had found the sources of the Nile." But Badian fails to consider that rivers that flow south cannot supply an army marching east, nor does he take into account the sheer size of the fleet—far too large for either supply or exploration.

61. They were, in fact, damaged by the heavy rains and restored (Arr. 5.29.5).

62. *Metz Epit.* 69; Curt. 9.3.20. It is clear from Strabo 15.1.29 C698 and Arr. 5.29.5 that the river is the Hydaspes (cf. Arr. *Ind.* 18).

63. This would constitute a new army in itself. Curt. 9.3.21 says there were 7,000 infantry and 5,000 horse, the latter brought from Thrace by Memnon.

64. The story that he died in the battle is common: Arr. 5.14.4; Plut. *Alex.* 61.1; Justin 12.8.4; *Metz Epit.* 62. Onesicritus, *FGrH* 134 F20 = Plut. *Alex.* 61.1 says the horse died of old age after the battle. Diodorus' statement that Alexander returned by the same route probably explains the sudden appearance of envoys from Abisares and Arsaces with gifts and confirmation of Abisares' illness. Alexander added Arsaces' territory to that of Abisares (Arr. 5.29.4-5).

this journey, the realm of Porus had been enlarged to form a buffer state on the eastern edge of the empire.[65]

IV

If the Macedonian troops thought the retreat at the Hyphasis signaled the end of their labors, they were soon to find more dangerous foes awaiting them to the south. The Sibi, who lived near the junction of the Hydaspes and the Acesines and were—in the imagination of the Alexander historians—descendants of Heracles, were forced to surrender.[66] Their crime, it appears, was to have been situated astride the Macedonian lines of communication, and the attack on their city was a rearguard action.[67] By contrast, the Agalasseis mustered 40,000 infantry and 3,000 cavalry, only to be defeated on the field of battle and blockaded within their city walls. When the city was taken, all men of military age were executed and the rest sold into slavery.[68] Once again, the tactics of terror served only to make the defenders more determined. When another of their cities was about to fall to the Macedonians, the natives set fire to it, intent on burning themselves along with their women and children. Curtius remarks upon a bizarre spectacle in which the inhabitants were torching their city while the attackers sought to extinguish the flames. This act clearly was motivated not by kindness but by concern for the loss of booty. Given its location and the stubborn resistance of the natives, Alexander garrisoned the citadel, which had been rescued from the conflagration.[69]

---

65. Arr. 6.2.1 says that Alexander convened a meeting of the Indian dynasts and proclaimed Porus king (*basileus*) of the newly conquered territory, placing more than 2,000 cities under his authority.

66. Sibi (also Sibae): Diod. 17.96.1-3; Curt. 9.4.1-4; Justin 12.9.2; Strabo 15.1.8 C688, 15.1.33 C701. For their location, see also Eggermont 1993, 21–24. Whether they did so voluntarily, as Diod. 17.96.2 suggests, or only after Alexander besieged their capital (Curt. 9.4.4) is unclear. They were descended from those who had attacked Aornus with Heracles (Strabo. 15.1.8 C688; Diod. 17.96.2).

67. Cf. Smith 1903, 689; 1914, 93. Since they had not moved against the invader in an aggressive fashion, they were treated leniently and allowed to remain autonomous. Arr. 6.4.2 may refer to the Sibi.

68. The Agalasseis (Diod. 17.96.3) are the Agensones of Justin 12.9.2 and the "other tribe" mentioned by Curt. 9.4.5. Arr. 6.4.2 may refer to the campaigns against the Sibi and the Agalasseis. The latter are difficult to locate (although they are associated with the Acesines River; Eggermont 1993, 24–25), but they clearly lived above the confluence of the Acesines and the Indus and thus north of the Mallians.

69. Thus Curt. 9.4.6-8. Diod. 17.96.4-5 tells a different story. The defenders were said to have numbered 20,000. Alexander himself burned the city, because he had lost many (οὐκ ὀλίγους)

The Oxydracae and the Mallians lived to the south of Porus' kingdom, the former between the Hyphasis-Satlej and the Hydraotes, the latter near the confluence of the Acesines and the Indus.[70] According to reports, they could muster as many as 100,000 infantry and at least 10,000 cavalry.[71] An earlier campaign against them by Porus and Abisares had failed, and they were not inclined to submit to the latest invader.[72] Rumor was, of course, more potent than reality, and it was not long before resentment resurfaced in the Macedonian camp. The perils they had avoided by not advancing to the Ganges were now matched by those encountered during the descent of the Indus.[73]

Alexander divided his army in order to sweep up the remnants of resistance in the lands between the various rivers that were to converge as they moved south, with Craterus in the west, Hephaestion in the middle, and Philip son of Machatas in the east.[74] Despite their reputation as a numerous and warlike people, the Mallians did not have their forces in the field and ready to oppose the Macedonians. They were certainly concerned about a possible incursion into

---

men in the house-to-house fighting. The inhabitants who fled to the citadel finally surrendered and were spared.

70. Smith 1903, 692, puts the Mallians on both sides of the Hydraotes (Ravi) River. Curt. 9.7.14 suggests that the two peoples had under Achaemenid rule paid tribute to the satrap of Arachosia.

71. Numbers: 100,000 infantry, 20,000 cavalry (*Metz Epit.* 75); 90,000 infantry, 10,000 cavalry, 900 chariots (Curt. 9.4.16); 80,000 foot, 10,000 horse, 700 chariots (Diod. 17.98.1); 80,000 infantry, 60,000 cavalry (Justin 12.9.3).

72. For their war with Porus and Abisares, see Arr. 5.22.2. The two tribes (Kshudraka and Malava) are often named together. In Sanskrit, they appear jointly as the Kshudraka-mālava. Curt. 9.4.15 calls the former the Sudracae and notes that the two peoples were often at war with each other (as we should expect from warlike neighbors) but were united in the face of a common enemy. Diod. 17.98.1-2 says that they had formerly been at war but that their reconciliation was sealed by 10,000 marriages between the two tribes, though even this did not prevent further dissension. They appear in the manuscripts of a very corrupt passage of Justin 12.9.3 as *ambros et sugambros*, which in Seel's text is rendered *Mandros et Sudracas*. Eggermont 1975, 188 n. 736, however, asserts that "Sudracae is no tribal name, they are called after the Sutlej river, Sanskrit: Śutudru" (cf. Eggermont 1993, 34).

73. Curt. 9.4.17: *Gangem amnen et quae ultra essent coactos transmittere non tamen finesse, sed mutasse bellum.* Rolfe in the Loeb edition translates the passage: "after being compelled to cross the Ganges and the regions beyond it, they had nevertheless not ended but only shifted the war." This would be blatantly false, since the army had not, in fact, crossed the Ganges or even the Hyphasis. Reading *coactum* instead of *coactos* makes Alexander the subject. Hence, "Alexander had been made to forgo the Ganges and what lay beyond it . . . but he still had not terminated the war, only changed its location."

74. The Mallian campaign: Diod. 17.98-99; Plut. *Alex.* 63 and *Mor.* 327b, 341c, 343d-e and 344c-d; Justin 12.9.1-10.1; Curt. 9.4.15-5.20; Arr. 6.4.3-11.2. See also Breloer 1941, 29-56, which is still worth reading, despite the unfair remarks of Brunt II 443. See also Fuller 1958, 259-63.

their territory, for they sent their women and children to the safety of fortified cities. Clearly, they were frightened by the news of the fate of the Agalasseis. The Mallians were nevertheless caught off guard, either because of the speed of the Macedonian advance or by the unexpected route taken by the invader. They assumed that Alexander would advance into their territory by marching up the Hydraotes River from its confluence with the Acesines.[75] But the king led his troops through the waterless region of the Sandar-Bar and attacked them from the west. The invader caught the first of the Mallians outside their town and un-armed. Many were killed, as they were unable to offer any meaningful resistance. What followed was a relentless campaign by the Macedonians that spread terror among the Mallians; they overwhelmed their cities and drove them on in head-long flight, killing many who had neither the power to resist nor the ability to elude the Conqueror's mobile forces.[76]

The Mallians made one last attempt at resistance in their capital,[77] where they were quickly blockaded. Here they were given a glorious opportunity to bring the Macedonian invasion to an abrupt and disastrous conclusion, as the Conqueror pressed the attack with characteristic abandon:

> To Alexander . . . it appeared that the Macedonians bringing the ladders were slacking, and so he snatched a ladder from one of the carriers, set it against the wall himself, and clambered up under the cover of his shield. Peucestas followed him, bearing the sacred shield that Alexander had taken from the temple of Athena at Troy and which he always kept with him and had carried before him in battle. He was followed up the same ladder by Leonnatus the Bodyguard and, on a different ladder, by Abreas, one of the *dimoiritai*.[78]
>
> By now, the king was close to the battlement on the summit of the wall. He propped his shield on it and pushed off a number of Indians

75. The direction of Alexander's march: Arr. 6.6.2-3.

76. First stages of the Mallian campaign: Arr. 6.4.3–6.6. Very different is Curt. 9.4.23-26, who says the enemy was the Sudracae and describes topographical features that do not suit the re-gion. Eggermont 1993, 37, says that "the phenomenon of mountains in the midst of the Rechna Doab is highly suspect" and explains the error as resulting in the belief that the Sudracae were descended from Dionysus, who was in turn associated with Mount Meros. For the confusion of the Mallians and the Sudracae, see Arr. 6.11.3; cf. Plut. *Alex.* 63.2.

77. Identification of the city with Multan (thus Lane Fox 1980, 340; Wood 1997, 199–200), which Smith 1914, 96 n. 1, regards as "absolutely baseless"; cf. Engels 1978a, 110 n. 53, following Mughal 1967. Multan is too far south. Bosworth 1988a, 135 n. 348 puts the city "in the general area north-east of modern Multan."

78. A *dimoirites* was a man who received double pay.

inside the wall, and others he also killed with his sword, clearing the wall in that area, The hypaspists, who then became very fearful for their king, swiftly pushed their way up the same ladder and broke it, and as a result, those already climbing it fell down, and they made an ascent impossible for the others.

As Alexander stood on the wall, he was the target of weapons coming from all directions from the towers close by—for none of the Indians dared close in on him—and also from those inside the citadel who, since there happened to be earth piled up against the wall at that point, were not launching them at long range, either. Just who Alexander was both the brilliance of his armor and his outstanding courage made clear. He therefore decided that he would be in danger remaining there and bringing off no noteworthy action but that he could, by jumping down inside the wall, possibly create panic among the Indians or, failing that—if he had to face danger anyway—bring off mighty feats that future generations would consider worth knowing about, and he would not die an ignoble death. Having decided on this, he jumped down from the wall into the citadel.

There, propped against the wall, he struck and dispatched with his sword a number of Indians who advanced on him too incautiously, together with their leader. Others who were approaching he kept off one at a time by throwing stones at each of them, and anyone getting too near by again using his sword. The barbarians were then no longer willing to come close and, instead, surrounded him on all sides and hurled at him whatever projectile came to hand.

Meanwhile, Peucestas and Abreas, the *dimoirites*, and behind him Leonnatus, the only men who had succeeded in climbing to the top of the wall before the ladders collapsed, had also jumped down and were now defending the king. Abreas (the *dimoirites*) fell there, struck in the face by an arrow; and Alexander was himself also hit by an arrow that went through his corselet and into his chest above the breast, which resulted, in Ptolemy's account, in a discharge of air as well as blood. However, while his blood was still warm, he kept on defending himself despite his poor condition, but when a great deal of blood came flooding out as he exhaled, he succumbed to dizziness and a blackout, slumping over his shield.

Peucestas stood over him as he lay prostrate and held over him the sacred shield from Troy, while Leonnatus stood on his other side, both of them facing the oncoming projectiles while Alexander was at death's door from loss of blood. (Arr. 6.9.3–10.2)

The pattern of Macedonian behavior had by now become well established. As the wounded king was carried from the battlefield, the army vented its fury with unrestrained bloodletting. Whether their king died or survived the incident, the Macedonians would make sure that the defenders paid the ultimate price, soldiers and civilians.[79] The Alexander historians share the indignation of the troops[80] and their crazed response to the actions of peoples who sought merely to defend themselves against the aggressions of an enemy who had no legitimate reason for attacking them.[81]

One is tempted to assume that the reputation of the Mallians was deliberately exaggerated to explain the king's near-fatal wounding and to justify the terrible retribution. There are, in fact, various indicators that the Indians were not as prepared for the struggle as the sources let on, for the same writers who comment on their warlike nature describe them as helpless in many cases and more prone to flee than to stand their ground.[82] Arrian depicts them as anything but heroic or intimidating. Caught off guard and outside their town unarmed (6.6.3), most offered no resistance. The ones in the city deserted to the citadel out of despair (6.6.5). Those of another city, attacked by Perdiccas, abandoned the place, and many were killed in flight or in the marshlands (6.6.6); others who fled across the river were killed in the crossing or hunted down and slaughtered (6.7.1-3). Yet others deserted the walls of a major city, drawing back once again into the citadel (6.7.4), although they did kill some twenty-five Macedonians who pressed them too hard. They were driven to set fire to their own homes, and many perished therein, but in their last stand, Arrian credits them with some courage, in that they chose to die fighting rather than endure captivity (6.7.6).[83] Of the remaining Mallians, most abandoned their cities and were hunted down in the desert or in

---

79. Curt. 9.5.19-20: "[The Macedonians] smashed through the wall with pickaxes, and, bursting into the city where they had made the breach, they cut down the Indians, more of whom took flight than dared engage the enemy. Old men, women, children—none was spared. Anyone the Macedonians encountered they believed responsible for their king's wounds. Mass slaughter of the enemy finally appeased their just rage." Arr. 6.11.1 confirms the slaughter but describes it in only a few words: οἱ μὲν ἔκτεινον τοὺς Ἰνδούς, καὶ ἀπέκτεινάν γε πάντας οὐδὲ γυναῖκα ἢ παῖδα ὑπ᾽ ελείποντο.

80. Curt. 9.5.20 (quoted above) speaks of their *iusta ira*.

81. Badian 1985, 468, calls it a "fierce and (on strict military grounds) avoidable campaign" but ventures into the realm of fantasy when he alleges that Alexander's intention was "to punish the army for their mutiny [at the Beas]."

82. Numerous and warlike people: Arr. 6.4.3 (πλείστους τε καὶ μαχιμωτάτους); cf. Diod. 17.98.1 (μετὰ δὲ ταῦτα στρατεύσας ἐπὶ Συδράκας καὶ τοὺς ὀνομαζομένους Μαλλούς, ἔθνη πολυάνθρωπα καὶ μάχιμα); Curt. 9.4.24 (*validissimae Indorum gentes erant et bellum impigre parabant*).

83. ζῶντες δὲ δι᾽ ἀνδρ<ε>ίαν ὀλίγοι ἐλήφθησαν.

the woods, where they were rounded up or killed (6.8.1-3); this was followed by further desertions, and one attempt at resistance by a force of 50,000[84] ended with the Mallians turning in flight from terror of the Macedonians (6.8.4-8). Finally, they were driven into the city in which Alexander was seriously wounded. Was the king's peril the result of a determined and deadly enemy or caused by his own recklessness?

There were those in the chain of command who had already questioned—if not openly, then in private discussions with their fellow commanders—the purpose of the military actions along the Indus river system. Craterus, one of the most accomplished and loyal of Alexander's commanders, spoke to his king in a way that must have caused him to consider the wisdom of Coenus' speech at the Hyphasis. The fates of the king and the army were inseparable, and it was reasonable for the troops to advise their commander to show restraint and prudence when the contest had, in fact, already been won. The struggle with Darius had come to an end, and with it the need to take risks. And Alexander should not endanger his life for places that were of no consequence: "a reputation swiftly fades when one's foes are undistinguished, and nothing is more unworthy than squandering it on operations where it cannot be displayed to advantage."[85]

The Alexander historians, it seems, invented for the Mallians a reputation for martial prowess that was proved false by their actual performance. This chapter in the history of the conquest of India reveals the plight of the victims of a brutal campaign. The Mallians, as we have seen, were wrongly confused with the Sudracae (or Oxydracae), but the latter never engaged the invader militarily. They lived farther to the north and the east, between the Ravi and the Beas-Satlej, and the Macedonians would have gained little by attacking them.[86] In the event, they had no need to do so; the lesson of the Mallians was sufficient to induce their formal submission.[87] Perhaps the last of the Punjab tribes—who appear in the

---

84. The poor performance of the Mallians may perhaps be explained by Diodorus' story that although they had settled their differences with the neighboring Sudracae, they failed to agree on questions of leadership (17.98.1-2). The withdrawal of the Sudracae left the Mallians vulnerable. It also explains why Arr. 6.8.6 attributes to them only 50,000 men. The account by Smith 1914, 94–96, sums up the inadequacy of the Mallian resistance, as it is presented by the ancient historians.

85. Curt. 9.6.14. For Craterus' entire speech, doubtless Curtius' own creation: 9.6.6-14. Ptolemy and others expressed similar opinions (9.6.15).

86. I do not understand what group Lane Fox 1980, 480, has in mind when he speaks of Alexander attacking the "Mallians allies." Given the starting point and the direction of his march, these cannot have been the Oxydracae.

87. Arr. 6.14.1-3 (for their alleged connections with Dionysus, see also Strabo 15.1.8 C687); Curt. 9.7.12-14. The Oxydracae and the Mallians agreed to pay the tribute and contribute

sources as the Abastanes, Sabarcae, or Sambastae—submitted en masse, apparently overawed by the size and appearance of the Macedonian flotilla.[88]

Some scholars have attributed Alexander's bloody campaign in India to his resentment at having been forced to turn back at the Hyphasis:[89]

> From this point on it seems Alexander's fury at his enforced return from the Hyphasis was taken out on the Indians, for, savage as were his actions in Bactria and Sogdia, his ruthless murderousness along the rivers of India was greater. He had absolutely no regard for human life or suffering, but it must also be admitted that he had as little for his own. Unfortunately, however, those he ruthlessly destroyed had not his own paranoiac obsession of kinship with the gods and the intense conviction that he would at last sit with them on high. He is described, now, as a man of dark and gloomy thoughts, having no regard for human life, and facing death with a complete unconcern.[90]

But in fact, the Conqueror needed no justification, and it is doubtful that his motives were different from those that led to his slaughter of those who resisted him in Central Asia. Those who did not submit voluntarily were brutally punished. Such measures did indeed influence the actions of other groups but not in the way that Alexander imagined. Acts of terror merely strengthened opposition. In areas that he could not expect to hold once he moved on, the king's policy (if indeed it was policy and not simply bloodlust) amounted to little more than gratuitous violence.[91]

2,500 horsemen to Alexander's campaign (Curt. 9.7.14). Arr. 6.14.3 says they gave 1,000 men as hostages, as well as 500 chariots with drivers, and agreed to accept the Macedonian satrap, Philip.

88. Arr. 6.15.1 says that Alexander was joined at the junction of the Acesines and the Indus by Perdiccas, who had subdued the Abastanes. Hence, they are to be located above the confluence. It is reasonable to assume that the Sabarkai and Sambastae are the same people as the Abastanes (cf. Eggermont 1993, 67, though I do not accept his equation of the Abastanes with the Oxydracae). Curt. 9.8.3-7 and Diod. 17.102.1-3 say they could muster 60,000 infantry, 6,000 cavalry, and 500 chariots, but they chose to surrender when they saw the Macedonian forces.

89. Some (e.g., Badian 1985, 468) have gone so far as to suggest that Alexander took his resentment out on his own men.

90. Cummings 2004, 365.

91. Lane Fox 1973, 384, estimates the number killed in this region at a "quarter of a million." By the highest reckoning, on the basis of figures in the sources, the Indus campaign, from the confluence of the Hydaspes and the Acesines, accounted for about 150,000 lost lives. See Heckel and McLeod 2015, 247. Whether the ancient authors exaggerated or understated (through omission of details) the extent of the slaughter is unclear.

V

From the southern point of the Punjab to the Indus Delta, the various Indian tribes resorted to resistance, submission, or ill-advised perfidy according to their perceptions of the enemy and their own strength. Unfortunately, the identities and locations of the tribes who lived between the Punjab and the bifurcation of the Indus in the south are at best uncertain, and the information provided by the extant Alexander historians is as varied and shifting as the ancient courses of the Indus and its tributaries.[92] In succession, the kingdoms of Musicanus (ruler of the Mushikas), Oxicanus, Porticanus, and Sambus fell to the invader. Musicanus surrendered and was allowed to retain his kingdom, although the citadel of his capital was fortified and garrisoned.[93] Porticanus, ruler of the Praesti, died in an attempt to resist. His defenses were destroyed, his people enslaved.[94] The Macedonians captured another rajah, Oxicanus, the ruler of Azeika who is (wrongly?) identified with Porticanus. His fate is unrecorded, but in this heartless campaign it can easily be surmised.[95]

---

92. Diod. 17.102.4 mentions the Sodrae and the Massani as living between the Sambastae and the kingdom of Musicanus; Arr. 6.15.1 speaks of a people called the Ossadii (who may be identical with Diodorus' Massani); Curt. 9.8.8 mentions only "other tribes" (*alias gentes*). Arr. 6.15.4 mentions the royal city of the Sogdians, who may be identical with Diodorus' Sodrae (thus Seibert 1985, 167 n.40). The Xathri sent ships, built on Alexander's orders, which joined him at the junction of the Indus and the Acesines (Arr. 6.15.1), Smith 1914, 99 n.1 thought the name "looks like a transcription of the Sanskrit Kshatriya; they may be identical with the Cathaeans (cf. Eggermont 1993, 101–103); the ships must have come from upstream, from territories already conquered. Justin mentions no other tribes between the Mallians and the land of King Sambus (12.10.2; cf. Oros. 13.19.11). The difficulty of making sense of all this is perhaps reflected in the brevity of the treatment which Badian 1985, 469–70 accords this portion of Alexander's campaign: "The journey down the Indus was combined with the ruthless subjugation of the inhabitants on both banks, in the east probably as far as the edge of the great desert. The Brahmins, who had already been the centre of resistance among the Malli, inspired constant major revolts in Alexander's rear, and only the planting of numerous garrisons and, at times, a policy of extermination secured the frontier."

93. Arr. 6.15.5-7; Curt. 9.8.10 (very brief). Diod. 17.102.5 says that Musicanus was killed.

94. Porticanus: Curt. 9.8.11-12; Diod. 17.102.4-5. Ruler of Pardabathra: Ptol. *Geog.* 7.1.58. Oxicanus: Arr. 6.16.1-2.

95. Identification with Porticanus: Berve II 293 no. 587 s.v. Ὀξυκανός. Cf. Seibert 1985, 167: "ins Reich des Oxykanos oder Porikanos [*sic*]." But see Eggermont 1975, 9–15. Against the identification, see Heckel 187, 231; cf. Heckel 1997, 214. Oxicanus: Arr. 6.16.1-2. Ruler of Azeika: Ptol. *Geog.* 7.1.57; Eggermont 1975, 12. Curt. 9.8.11 calls Porticanus *rex*, whereas Arr. 6.16.1 designates Oxicanus as *nomarches*. But although it is tempting to see Oxicanus as a subordinate of Porticanus, Arrian's comment (6.16.2) that the rest of the cities of the region surrendered without a fight rules this out.

Sambus did not await the arrival of the invaders but fled. His cities were taken with little resistance, including Sindimana, which was surrendered by the ruler's relatives. These explained that Sambus had fled out of fear of his rival Musicanus, whose power had not been diminished by the Macedonian conquest. Alexander indicated his willingness to pardon Sambus,[96] but another of his cities, under the influence of the Brahmans, held out against the Conqueror; its citizens and the fomenters of revolt were subjected to unrestrained slaughter. Curtius claims that Cleitarchus reported the deaths of 80,000 Indians and selling of many captives into slavery.[97]

What it was that precipitated a rebellion by the Musicani is unclear, though it appears that the native rulers feared their neighbors and longtime rivals more than they feared the foreign invader. The rising was easily suppressed, its leaders arrested by Alexander's general Peithon, and all, along with their ruler, were crucified.[98] Another factor, which cannot be discounted, is the influence of Brahmans, intellectuals who served as counselors of the king.[99] We are told of another city of the Brahmans, sometimes referred to as Harmatelia (or Harmata), where resistance by some 3,000 Indians was easily overcome, at the loss of 600 Indian dead, although the poisoned arrows of the defenders inflicted an excruciating death on the Macedonians.[100]

---

96. Arr. 6.16.3 says that Alexander had appointed Sambus satrap of the Indian hillmen (τῶν ὀρείων Ἰνδῶν σατράπην) who lived in the region west of Alor (Eggermont 1975, 22; identification of Sindimana with Sehwan seems unlikely). He may be identical with Curtius' Samaxus, who had earlier come to Alexander at Taxila in the company of Barsaentes (Curt. 8.13.3-4). Barsaentes had indeed fled to the hill tribes of India who bordered on Drangiana, and it appears that he was given refuge by Sambus (Curt. 6.6.36). Curt. 8.13.4 says Sambus (Samaxus) was brought as a prisoner, but this may be a mistake. It appears that Sambus saw an opportunity, betrayed Barsaentes, and gained reinstatement in his satrapy.

97. Curt. 9.8.13-15; Cleitarchus, *FGrH* 137 F25. The 80,000 were not restricted to this city alone, as the words *in ea regione* indicate. Cf. Diod. 17.102.6.

98. Curt. 9.8.16; Arr. 6.17.1-2. Alexander was equally brutal in suppressing the revolt of the Musicani, razing their cities, planting garrisons, and selling the inhabitants into slavery.

99. Strabo 15.1.66 C716: Νέαρχος δὲ περὶ τῶν σοφιστῶν οὕτω λέγει. τοὺς μὲν Βραχμᾶνας πολιτεύεσθαι καὶ παρακολουθεῖν τοῖς βασιλεῦσι συμβούλους. In this capacity, they induced their kings to make militarily unsound decisions.

100. Cummings 2004, 386 n. 1, identifies this city with Brahmanabad (properly called Bahmanābād; see Smith 1914, 103 n. 1), which was destroyed by an earthquake in the late tenth or early eleventh century A.D., and locates it on the Indus (337, map), very close to Pattala. Eggermont 1975, 148-62, places it in the land of the Oreitai and identifies it with Rhambacia. His arguments are primarily linguistic: "As I have shown that according to Indian sources Roruka *alias* Ora *alias* Rambacia *alias* Harmatelia was the capital of the Sauvīras, and as, moreover, I have made it probable that the Sauviras occupied the territory of the ancient Oritan district, it is *not too far-fetched* to conclude that the Sauri *alias* Surae *alias* Sires mentioned by the Roman sources are identical with the Indian Sauviras. The only reason why

Farther south, the *hyparchos* of Pattala fled with most of his tribesmen and left the region virtually uninhabited. Alexander sent his most mobile troops to track them down and persuade them to return.[101] With the exception of isolated attacks by Indians who then escaped to the desert, it was the end of organized resistance on the Indus. Alexander nevertheless had his land forces march alongside the fleet as he explored the delta. The army had secured the eastern boundary of the empire and, at last, reached the ocean.[102]

the Alexander historians called the inhabitants of the district Oritans is that Roruka *alias* Ora was the largest village in the region, and that, therefore, Alexander founded his Alexandria of the Oritans there" (emphasis added). Seibert 1985 omits the place entirely. For their resistance, see Diod. 17.103.1-3; Curt. 9.8.17-19 (in addition to 600 killed, 1,000 were captured). Poisoned weapons: Curt. 9.8.20-27; Diod. 17.103.4-8. Ptolemy was among the wounded, and Strabo 15.2.7 C723 gives some support to Eggermont's view that this occurred among the Oreitae (ἐν τοῖς Ὠρείταις).

101. Arr. 6.17.5-6; but Curt. 9.8.28-29 speaks of the flight of King Moeris or Soeris (*rex erat Moeris, qui, urbe deserta, in montes profugerat*) and of Alexander's occupation of Pattala and plundering of the countryside. Diod. 17.104.2 says that Pattala, like Sparta, had two kings and a council of elders but mentions neither flight nor resistance.

102. Not all the Macedonians who completed the expedition with Alexander looked out toward the "end of the world" (*terminos mundi*: Curt. 9.9.1). Craterus had been sent to the west earlier; he rejoined Alexander in Carmania. The final organization of India saw the Sind region assigned to Peithon son of Agenor, while Philip son of Machatas governed the western Punjab, supporting the dynast Taxiles. Gandhāra's satrap was killed, and Philip assumed control of the area. Oxyartes replaced Tyriespis as satrap of the Parapamisadae (Arr. 6.15.2-4). Discussion in Bosworth 1983; Julien 1914, 44-52.

15

Return to the West

PROBLEMS OF CONSOLIDATION AND THE REVIVAL OF OLD GRIEVANCES

> *However, the difficulty he had been facing with the return journey, the wound he had received among the Mallians, and his reportedly heavy troop losses raised doubts about his safety. This prompted subject states to rebel and gave rise to widespread injustice, greed, and wonton violence among his generals and satraps. Turmoil and revolution permeated everywhere. (Plut. Alex. 68.3)*

WITH THE REDUCTION of Sind, Alexander could now explore the Indus delta and prepare for Nearchus' voyage along the Indian Ocean (Arabian Sea) to the Strait of Hormuz and beyond.[1] The supply problems of the army were mitigated to some extent by the division of forces. Before reaching Pattala, Craterus had been sent through the Mullah (or Bolan) Pass and the satrapies of Arachosia and Drangiana, leading some of the heavy infantry, the elephants, and troops who were either unfit (*apomachoi*) or thought to deserve a break from the rigors of campaigning.[2] His task was to patrol the area and mop up remnants of resistance there before reuniting with the king in Carmania. The fleet, which skirted the coast of the Makran desert, could solve logistical problems but created new ones of its own. For the main force, the joy of returning to the West was diminished

---

1. Nearchus' voyage is described in Arrian's *Indica*, based on the *History* of Nearchus himself (Jacoby, *FGrH* 133, and Pearson 1960, 112–49), and not treated in detail here. See also Heckel 1992, 228–34; Berve II 269–72 no. 544; Badian 1975; Tomaschek 1890; Capelle, *RE* s.v. "Nearchos"; Seibert 1985, 182–83; Sofman and Tsibukidis 1987; see also Engels 1978a, 115–16 n. 83.

2. Arr. 6.17.3, erroneously reported also at 6.15.5; cf. Bosworth 1976, 127–32. Justin 12.10.1 names Polyperchon, who may have accompanied Craterus; see also Strabo 15.2.5 C721. Reunion in Carmania: Arr. 6.27.3; cf. Strabo 15.2.11 C725. For his mission, Heckel, *Marshals*[2] 140. The Bolan Pass appears to have formed the eastern boundary of Arachosia (Herzfeld 1968, 336).

In the Path of Conquest. Waldemar Heckel, Oxford University Press (2020). © Oxford University Press.

DOI: 10.1093/oso/9780190076689.001.0001

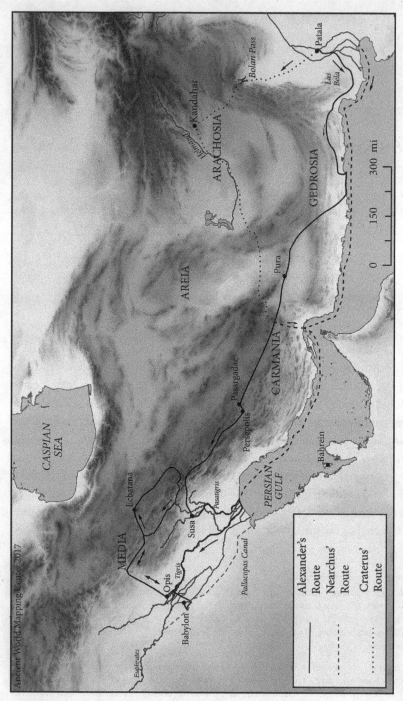

MAP 15.1 Map of Alexander's march from India to Babylon, 325–323.

by the perils of the trackless Gedrosian wasteland, where it faced the final serious challenges—both natural and human—of the campaign. For the natives of the region, Alexander's march proved an unexpected and unwanted hardship.[3]

I

The departure date for the journey home—and at this point, home meant Babylon—was determined by the weather, more precisely the monsoon season (July to September), which made sailing in the ships of the day virtually impossible. Since a coordination of land and naval forces was essential, the army marched ahead, probably at the end of August,[4] with the intention of digging wells and creating supply dumps. It was necessary for Nearchus to postpone the sailing until the setting of the Pleiades.[5] In all, from the time of the king's historic venture into the ocean, this entailed a delay of three months. For the army, which marched ahead, the conditions were less than ideal, as Alexander advanced to the Arabis River (Hab), the western limit of India in those parts. Beyond this point lived the independent tribes of the Oreitae and the Arabitae. The latter lacked the means to resist the invader and fled into the desert.[6] The Oreitai, however, were a danger to both the land army and the fleet, which needed to put in for supplies and water, but they, too, were ultimately no more successful.[7] Alexander split his army into three groups and subdued the Oreitae, killing many of them and

---

3. Eloquently noted by Bosworth 1988a, 146: "Alexander's army was not the worst afflicted. One should spare a thought for the wretched inhabitants of the Makran, whose harvest was stripped bare by Alexander's passage inland and Nearchus' along the coast. . . . Their prospect of starvation was more certain and the ordeal would be longer than sixty days."

4. Thus Seibert 1985, 170. The chronology is problematic. Engels 1978a, 135, dates Alexander's departure from Pattala to mid-July and the beginning of Nearchus' voyage to late October. Nearchus, however, left earlier (Arr. *Ind.* 21.1: on the twentieth day of Boëdromion and thus almost a month earlier than Engels proposes), only to be forced to wait out the winds early in the voyage, a delay of twenty-four days at Sangada (Arr. *Ind.* 21.11-13). But Strabo 15.2.5 C721 says that the king was already completing his journey (ἤδη τοῦ βασιλέως τελοῦντος τὴν ὁδόν) when Nearchus set out (presumably referring to his second departure). Since the journey from the Oreitan lands to Pura lasted sixty days (Plut. *Alex.* 66.7; Strabo 15.2.7 C723), that portion of the journey must have begun in late September. Pliny, *HN* 6.26.100, claims that Alexander reached Susa in the seventh month after leaving Pattala (Engels 1978a, 136, says six months from Pattala to Tepe Yahya in Carmania) and that Nearchus reached Alexander there after a three-month voyage. This would put Alexander in Susa in March 324. See also Beloch III² 2.320-21.

5. Arr. 6.21.1-2.

6. Arr. 6.21.4; Curt. 9.10.5; Diod. 17.104.4 (Abritai).

7. Arr. 6.21.3 says Alexander attacked the Oreitai for their lack of friendly support (ὅτι μηδὲν φίλιον αὐτοῖς ἐς αὐτόν τε καὶ τὴν στρατιὰν ἐπέπρακτο). They offered organized resistance near the borders of Gedrosia (Arr. 6.22.1-2).

carrying off booty. Curtius says that the three contingents "were simultaneously looting the Indians, and rich spoils were carried off." Nevertheless, it is difficult to imagine what precious items the conquerors might have carried off from this economically depressed region.[8] Attempts were made to put the area firmly under Macedonian control, with city foundations and the concomitant planting of garrison forces.[9] As Alexander continued his march in the direction of Gedrosia, he left Leonnatus with Apollophanes, whom he had appointed as satrap of the region, to complete the subjugation of the Oreitae, who, despite their limited resources, proved to be tenacious opponents.[10]

The physical difficulties of the coastal region and the Gedrosian desert took their toll on the Macedonian army, but the Oreitae were the last of the former subjects of Persia to stand up to the Conqueror. After a difficult march of sixty days,[11] Alexander reached Pura, the capital of Gedrosia, where he was able to distribute provisions to the troops. Many had died on the journey, the greatest hardships falling on the supernumeraries and the camp followers.[12] It is difficult to estimate the actual human losses, since we do not know how many accompanied Alexander on the march, but Plutarch's claim that less than a quarter of his fighting force survived out of a number of 120,000 infantry and 15,000 cavalry is grossly exaggerated.[13] Whatever the true number of losses, it was a calamity and

---

8. Curt. 9.10.7: *tria simul agmina populabantur Indos, magnaeque praedae actae sunt.* The Oreitae were not Indians (thus Arr. *Ind.* 22.10: μέχρι μὲν τοῦδε Ἀράβιες, ἔσχατοι Ἰνδῶν ταύτῃ ᾠκισμένοι, τὰ δὲ ἀπὸ τοῦδε Ὠρεῖται ἐπεῖχον). But the manuscripts of Arr. 6.21.3 have τοῖς Ὠρείταις τοῖς ταύτῃ Ἰνδοῖς αὐτονόμοις. Organized resistance at the borders of Gedrosia: Arr. 6.22.2.

9. The city of Rhambacia was resettled by Hephaestion, with the customary *synoikismos* (drawing the neighboring peoples into the city). Arr. 6.21.5; Curt. 9.10.5 says the settlers were Arachosians. The imposition of a garrison is a reasonable assumption.

10. In a major battle, 6,000 of the Oreitae were killed; the Macedonians lost 15 cavalrymen but also the Gedrosian satrap (Arr. *Ind.* 23.5; cf. Arr. 6.22.2-3; Curt. 9.10.19).

11. Alexander's Gedrosian march: Arr. 6.22-23; Curt. 9.10.5-18; Diod. 17.104.4–106.1; Plut. *Alex.* 66.4-7; Justin 12.10.7; Strabo 15.2.3-8 C721-724. Also Stein 1943; Strasburger 1952 and 1954; Seibert 1985, 171–80; Engels 1978a, 137–43; Lane Fox 1980, 348–55, and Wood 1997, 210–17 (both with stunning photographs); Bosworth 1988a, 142–46.

12. Cf. Atkinson and Hammond 2013, 315.

13. Plut. *Alex.* 66.4-5. The number 120,000 is given by Curt. 8.5.4 for the army at the beginning of the Indian campaign and must have included allies, mercenaries, camp followers and sailors of various nationalities. Arr. *Ind.* 19.5 gives the same number for the beginning of the voyage down the Indus, many of whom would have manned the 800 (Arr. *Ind.* 19.7) to 2,000 (Arr. 6.2.4) ships and boats of the river fleet. The Indian allies would have returned home when the army marched west, and many of the mercenaries were deposited in the conquered cities as garrison troops. Furthermore, the army was divided (Strabo 15.2.5 C721-722). Craterus' force must have numbered at least 10,000. Those who manned the fleet could have been as numerous, but we have no figures for either ships or men. Clearly, the bulk of the vessels in the Indus fleet

a black mark on the king's reputation if it is true—and most likely it is not—that his motive was to surpass the achievements of Cyrus the Great and Semiramis.[14] Alexander may have reflected on the nature of his achievement when the army was convalescing in Carmania, but such fantasies should be left to those who created his image in the years after his death.

II

Pura, the capital of Gedrosia, was a welcome sight for the bedraggled army of the Conqueror. The satrapal center had ample resources, augmented by supplies summoned by the king on the march. But with the supplies came news of defection or malfeasance on the part of satraps and generals who, after Alexander's crossing of the Hindu Kush in 327, gave little thought to his return or the consequences of their own actions. There came to light cases of insubordination on the part of his Macedonian and Greek officials or of Persians who had sworn allegiance to the Conqueror.[15] Power unbridled by oversight was intoxicating for some, whereas others familiar with the Achaemenid system believed that punishment could be averted by a combination of appeasement and feigned contrition. The social/familial networks that had protected delinquent satraps under Achaemenid rulers had been disrupted, if not eradicated, and for the Greco-Macedonian officials, they were nonexistent or ineffectual.[16] For once, it is difficult to see those who opposed the king as justified in their actions or as innocent victims of an imagined "reign of terror." They were, in fact, guilty of the charges brought against them,

were unsuitable for the coastal voyage. Tarn's estimate (I, 107) of 8,000 to 10,000 fighting men is probably too low (although we must deduct the troops with Leonnatus, who must have been properly supplied on their return). Bosworth 1988a, 142: "the absolute minimum cannot have been less than 30,000" (but this would include the noncombatants). See also the discussion in Brunt II 481–83; also I, 530–31.

14. Arr. 6.24.2-3; Strabo 15.1.5 C686 and 15.2.5 C722, based on Nearchus.

15. Some Persian satraps had been instrumental in arresting pretenders to the throne: Atropates arrested Baryaxes, who had assumed the upright tiara (Arr. 6.29.3). Phrataphernes, who proved to be particularly loyal to Alexander, had earlier dealt with fellow Persians who were found to be treasonous. Müller 2003, 196–98, sees three categories of malefactors: those who had openly rebelled (e.g., Autophradates and Astaspes), those who had committed crimes against their subjects (e.g., the Macedonian generals), and those who had failed to supply the army during the Gedrosian march.

16. It should be noted, however, that up to this point, there were no recorded cases of malfeasance on the part of Macedonian governors, and, with the exception of Cleomenes of Naucratis, Greeks were not appointed as satraps until the latter part of the campaign.

and perhaps even greater crimes, often directed as much against their native subjects as against their absent overlord.

Among the Macedonians, the worst offenders were men who had been part of Alexander's army or entourage, one of them a close personal friend. The facts that they had all been present in Ecbatana in 330 and that most had participated in the execution of Parmenion have led to the mistaken assumption that their actions (or those of Alexander) could be interpreted as residual effects, and indeed a continuation, of a purge of the army by the king. The conduct of the treasurer Harpalus and the generals Cleander, Heracon, Sitalces, and Agathon should not be viewed as resistance or rebellion but rather as a combination of insubordination and neglect. Their activities were not coordinated with the misdeeds of their Persian counterparts, nor was Alexander engaged in a purge based on trumped-up charges. The case against the Macedonians was clear and indefensible:

> When Alexander had already reached Carmania, Craterus arrived with the rest of the army and the elephants, and also with Ordanes, whom he had captured after the man rebelled and instigated an insurgency. To this region also came Stasanor, satrap of the Arians and Zarangians, and with him Pharismanes son of Phrataphernes, satrap of the Parthians and Hyrcanians, as well as Cleander, Sitalces and Heracon, the generals left behind with Parmenion in command of the army in Media, and these also brought with them most of their army. Both the region's inhabitants and the army itself brought numerous accusations against Cleander and Sitalces and their followers, charging them with looting temples, tampering with ancient tombs, and other wrongful acts that were outrageous and wicked against their subjects. When this was reported to him, Alexander had both men executed in order to strike fear in the others—all the remaining satraps, hyparchs, and nomarchs—of also suffering a fate like theirs should they commit similar offenses. And it was this more than anything that kept in order the nations that had been taken in war by Alexander or had voluntarily come over to him, so numerous though they were and so widely separated—that in Alexander's realm the mistreatment of the ruled by the rulers was not permitted. (Arr. 6.27.3-5)

The story is elaborated by Curtius, who says the crimes of these men included sexual assault and that Cleander himself "had raped a virgin of noble birth and then given her to his slave as a concubine."[17]

---

17. Alexander objected to the rape of native women (of good families) by his subordinates in Media in a time of peace. Curt. 10.1.3-5: "After plundering everything in the secular sphere, they

By far the worst offender was the king's personal friend Harpalus son of Machatas. A relative of one of Philip II's wives, he and other members of the Elimeiot royal house had served with Alexander since the beginning of the campaign. Harpalus was physically unfit for the rigors of military life and was relegated to less glamorous (though not unimportant) forms of service. He was one of the *hetairoi* of the young prince who, in 337/6, had encouraged him to enter into negotiations with Pixodarus, for which he (along with his colleagues Ptolemy, Nearchus, Erigyius, and Laomedon) were exiled by Philip. In 333, before the Battle of Issus, he fled from Alexander's camp, probably having embezzled money in his role as treasurer. Inexplicably, he was encouraged to return and forgiven by the king. But corruption and hedonism were woven into the fabric of his character, and he proved to be a faithless friend.[18] In Alexander's absence, he used the treasury to fund his personal life of debauchery, including "the violation of women and illicit affairs with native girls."[19] But he went beyond this by bringing to Babylon the Athenian courtesan Pythionice—she bore him a daughter who was later raised by Charicles son of Phocion—and, after her death, another hetaira named Glycera, whom he treated like a queen. By comparison, his taste for delicacies from the Red Sea and his attempts to cultivate ivy can be dismissed as frivolous eccentricities.[20]

The barbarian malefactors were punished for a variety of "crimes." There were those who had actively rebelled in the king's absence, some of them even assuming the upright tiara and thus challenging his right to rule. Others had either ignored or been slow to respond to Alexander's call for supplies during his

had not even refrained from what was sacred: virgins and *women of the highest breeding* had been sexually assaulted and were bemoaning the physical abuse they had suffered. The greed and lust of these men had made the barbarians abhor the Macedonian name. Worst of all was the lust-crazed Cleander, who had raped *a virgin of noble birth* and then given her to his slave as a concubine." Cf. the crimes of Harpalus, which included ὕβρεις γυναικῶν καὶ παρανόμους ἔρωτας βαρβάρων (Diod. 17.108.4). The rape of nonnoble women in the course of war was apparently regarded as normal and acceptable. Timoclea of Thebes, who murdered the Thracian commander who had raped her, was acquitted by Alexander not because the man's crime justified Timoclea's actions but because she was a woman of rank and dignified bearing (Plut. *Alex.* 22.4, 41.9-10; *Mor.* 181a, 339c-d).

18. Life and career: Stähelin, *RE* VII.2 (1912) 2397–401 no. 2; Heckel 129–31 and *Marshals*² 218–27; Berve II 75–80 no. 143. For his famous (second) flight and its context and consequences, see Badian 1961; Jaschinski 1981, 23 ff.; Blackwell 1999; also Worthington 1986.

19. His amours with native women: Diod. 17.108.4. Athenian courtesans: Paus. 12.37.4; Plut. *Phoc.* 22.1-2; Theopompus, *FGrH* 115 F253 = Athen. 13.595a-c, and F254. Cf. Müller 2006, 81–92; Heckel 126, 240.

20. Daughter of Pythionice: Plut. *Phoc.* 22.3. Delicacies from the Red Sea: Diod. 17.108.4. Gardening: Plut. *Mor.* 648c-d; *Alex.* 35.15; Theophrastus, *HP* 4.4.1; Pliny, *HN* 16.144.

Gedrosian march. And at least one was in open rebellion when the Macedonian force entered Carmania. The housecleaning—it was neither a "purge" nor a "reign of terror"[21]—took place over an extended period, perhaps beginning in Pura and concluding in Susa.[22]

Craterus met Alexander in Carmania, bringing two hitherto unknown rebels by the names of Ordanes and Zariaspes.[23] These were probably the leaders of the residual opposition that had its origins in the uprisings of 328/7, with Drangiana as the base of their operations. Their actions were in all likelihood directed against the satrap Stasanor, whom Alexander had placed in charge of Aria and Drangiana after his experiment with barbarian rule there failed. Stasanor may have captured them and handed them over to Craterus, but it is possible that they remained a thorn in the satrap's side until the larger Macedonian force appeared. At any rate, Stasanor was summoned to Carmania, presumably to apprise the king of events that occurred in his absence. The rebels were executed by Alexander, as was Astaspes, who had been left as satrap of Carmania in 330 and was now believed to be plotting rebellion.[24]

When the Macedonian army reached Persis, other rebels were brought to him, most notably Baryaxes, who, after the deposing of Oxydates in Media, was arrested by Atropates because "he had assumed the upright tiara and called himself king of the Persians and the Medes."[25] This appears to have been an attempt to revive Median nationalism or perhaps an indication of factional strife between the former supporters and enemies of Darius III.[26] Atropates brought Baryaxes

---

21. See the sensible discussion by Higgins 1980.

22. Atkinson in Atkinson and Yardley 2009, 109.

23. Arr. 6.27.3: Ordanes; Curt. 9.10.19: Orzines and Zariaspes. The latter name suggests connections with Bactra (also known as Zariaspa); see Heckel 273; Berve II 162–63 no. 335. Despite the superficial resemblance of the names Zariaspes and Baryaxes, the historical circumstances rule out an identification of the two. Ordanes and Ozines are almost certainly the same person (cf. Justi 351); Heckel 185. Berve II 282 no. 579 and 293–94 no. 590 distinguish the two; cf. Badian 1961, 19, who lists them separately in his catalog of Persian rebels in Badian 2000a, 93 (nos. 5–6).

24. Curt. 9.10.21, 29. For Astaspes' career: Heckel 59; Berve II, 89 no. 173; Badian 2000a, 90–91. For the satrapal changes in this area, see Heckel 2017c.

25. Arr. 6.29.3: ὅτι ὀρθὴν τὴν κίδαριν περιθέμενος βασιλέα προσεῖπεν αὐτὸν Περσῶν καὶ Μήδων. See Heckel 70.

26. Median nationalism: Badian 2000a, 92. Oxydates is identified as Persian by both Arr. 3.20.3 and Curt. 6.2.11, as well as a personal enemy of Darius, who had imprisoned him and threatened him with execution. Atropates remained with Darius until his death. Oxydates' failure to obey Alexander's orders (Arr. 4.18.3: ἐθελοκακεῖν) may be an indicator of more widespread opposition in Media. Of course, we must keep in mind that the ambitions of leaders do not necessarily reflect the attitudes of their subjects.

to Parsagadae, where the rebel was executed along with his associates. One last malefactor, Orxines, who had taken over the satrapy of Persis upon the death of Phrasaortes and without the king's permission, made what he considered to be a credible defense: he had taken control of the satrapy, believing himself to be the most worthy candidate, in order to protect Persia for Alexander. Curtius claims that he was descended both from the Seven and from Cyrus the Great,[27] which would explain his presumption. On the other hand, it casts doubt on the official charge that he had desecrated the tomb of his ancestor. Curtius' account of his fate was clearly designed to discredit the eunuch Bagoas and, by extension, the king himself.[28]

This charge, we are told, resulted in Orxines' execution. Curtius was fond of such cloak-and-dagger scenes—most likely, they were the product of his own experiences with political life in imperial Rome—and his accounts have resonated with scholars who are otherwise more critical in their use of sources. That Orxines was guilty of plundering the tomb of his distinguished ancestor defies credulity, especially when one considers that he made political capital from his pedigree. Others were, indeed, punished for the sacrilege, but no other source mentions Orxines in this connection. But the veracity of this particular charge matters little; his crime was the usurpation of the satrapy and his subsequent attempt to retain it through bribery. If Bagoas played a role in his demise—and, despite the topos of the malicious eunuch, it would not be an unprecedented act—it may have to do with the fate of Nabarzanes, who had close relations with Bagoas. He may have lost Darius' trust after the Battle of Issus and been replaced, at least in a military capacity, by Orxines. Like many other disputes that came to be regarded as rebellions, the roots of conflict may be found in Persian factional strife.[29]

The punishment of recalcitrant satraps did not end in Persis. When he reached Susa, Alexander summoned Abulites and charged him with failure to

---

27. Curt. 4.12.8; 10.1.23.

28. Curt. 10.1.24-35. Compare the case of Dioxippos, who was also "framed" for theft (Diod. 17.100-1; Curt. 9.7.16-26).

29. Nabarzanes at Issus: Curt. 3.9.1. Orxines at Gaugamela: Arr. 3.8.5; Curt. 4.12.7-8, giving Orxines supreme command. For suspicions about Nabarzanes' disfavor, see Badian 2000a, 84, who asks the question ("Did the King no longer trust him?") but assumes instead that Nabarzanes was left in charge of Susa, where Artabazus could not be trusted, and replaced by Mazaeus. Badian draws attention to a problem, but his solution is not satisfactory. Furthermore, Nabarzanes, who was with Darius in flight, appears to have been with him all along. An interesting picture emerges of "rebels" who were not only hostile to Alexander but had previously opposed Darius as well.

send provisions to the army in (or emerging from) Gedrosia. The confrontation is summed up by Plutarch:

> Of Abulites' sons, Alexander ran one through with a spear and killed him; and after Abulites failed to procure any of their vital supplies but instead brought him 3,000 talents, he threw the money to his horses and when the horses refused to eat it declared: "Of what benefit to us, then, is your provisioning?" and he had Abulites imprisoned. (Plut. *Alex.* 68.7)

III

Few in the Macedonian army or in Alexander's entourage would have had much sympathy for Cleander and his fellow generals, much less for Harpalus, who probably had few friends outside the king's narrow circle. There were many who felt that Cleander and the others who had fallen from grace had finally paid for their treachery toward Parmenion, despite the fact that they had acted on Alexander's orders. For, in fact, it was easier to blame the agents than the perpetrator of the action. The old general's complicity in the conspiracy of Demetrius the Bodyguard had never been proven—indeed, he had been convicted and executed without the benefit of a trial and, certainly, without forewarning. The fact of their criminality in other matters, to which several of the troops who accompanied them to Carmania testified, created the illusion that the real culprits had been brought to justice and freed them from conflicting thoughts about their king, whose transformation since Parmenion's death was even more troubling. About the celebration of marriages of more than ninety of the king's *hetairoi* to aristocratic Persian women they were equally ambivalent. There were clearly financial and/or political advantages, but there were some who found the practice objectionable.[30]

---

30. For the supposed economic benefits of the interracial marriages, see Heckel 2008, 137–39. There is among Alexander scholars a persistent fiction that the Macedonians were opposed to the marriages and that they were all—except for that of Seleucus and Apame—repudiated after Alexander's death. This recorded exception is matched by Craterus' repudiation of Amastris, possibly a reflection of his personal views but certainly dictated by his political arrangements (including his agreement to marry Phila, the daughter of Antipater). But the evidence of Arr. 7.6.2 makes it clear that most of those who objected to the marriages were not those who took Persian brides and that only some of the grooms were displeased by the arrangement (τοὺς γάμους ἐν τῷ νόμῳ τῷ Περσικῷ ποιηθέντας οὐ πρὸς θυμοῦ γενέσθαι τοῖς πολλοῖς αὐτῶν, οὐδὲ τῶν γημάντων ἔστιν οἷς, καίτοι τῇ ἰσότητι τῇ ἐς τὸν βασιλέα μεγάλως τετιμημένοις). Furthermore, it is not altogether clear whether it was the marriage or the Persian manner of the wedding ceremony that was objectionable to some of the bridegrooms. In the case of repudiations, there were usually political reasons. See Müller 2013.

Even the common soldiers who took barbarian wives—there were said to have been 10,000 of these—resented the changes to the power structure and believed themselves to be subjects of an elite that now included their former enemies.

The arrival of 30,000 newly minted troops from the provinces, the so-called *epigonoi*, or descendants, only helped to put their grievances into context.[31] The result was a full-scale mutiny at Opis on the Tigris River.[32] The men, who now (rightly) believed that the king was planning to establish Babylon or some other Eastern capital as the seat of his power, demanded release from military service. It was not for this result that he had endured so much hardship, shed their own blood, and watched their comrades die. They objected to the integration of barbarian troops into existing units in Alexander's army.[33] For the king selected a force of 13,000 infantry and 2,000 cavalry, which he planned to retain in Asia, and demobilized the remainder, in accordance with their demands. But this, too, was viewed as rejection.

Alexander, of course, upbraided them for their unruliness and their ingratitude,[34] swaying the troops with an emotional appeal that left them questioning their decision, despite its underlying soundness. With rhetorical skill, he turned the tables on the mutineers.[35] And, like prodigal children who had been justly chastised by a parent, they begged forgiveness from the very man they were determined to resist. The king, without fear, jumped into the crowd of soldiers and laid his hands on some thirteen of the ringleaders, whom no one was now prepared to defend. These were handed over to the hypaspists—a portion of which unit formed the king's military police—to be thrown in chains into the Tigris.[36] At the Hyphasis, it had been his intention from the start to cave in to the soldiers' demands. But there was no element of sham in this matter; it was terminated to no one's satisfaction with the acquiescence of all. Alexander understood crowd psychology.

---

31. The Macedonian grievances are spelled out by Arr. 7.6, and it is clear that they were, for the most part, a revival of complaints that went back to 331.

32. Arr. 7.8.1-12.3; Curt. 10.2.8–4.3; Diod. 17.108-110; Plut. *Alex.* 70-72; Justin 12.11.–12.6; Polyaenus 4.3.7. Wüst 1953/4a-b; Carney 1996b, 37–42.

33. On the mixed phalanx, see Arr. 7.23.3-4; Bosworth 2010, 96–97.

34. On this point and Curtius' Roman models for Alexander's speech, see Atkinson in Atkinson and Yardley 2009, 132.

35. On the speech, see Wüst 1953/4a and Nagle 1996.

36. Curt. 10.2.30; Arr. 7.8.3; Justin 12.11.8; cf. Diod. 17.109.2. Execution by drowning (Curt. 10.4.2) appears to have Near Eastern precedents.

Tension within the army was lessened by the departure of 10,000 veterans under the leadership of Craterus, whom Alexander had appointed to replace Antipater as regent of Macedon and overseer of Greek affairs. It was a move, combined with the Exiles' Decree, to limit the power of the old regent, who, according to (admittedly biased) reports from Alexander's mother, was insubordinate. The demobilized troops included the most conservative element, men who were least likely to look with favor on the king's orientalizing policies. A similar precaution—though one that ultimately backfired—was the disbanding of virtually all mercenary armies in the satrapies. Whether this was intended to prevent mercenary uprisings of the sort that had taken place in Bactria or to limit the military powers of the satraps, it was clearly aimed at strengthening the central authority, now headquartered in Babylon. What resistance remained was motivated primarily by Alexander's new role as king of an empire based in Asia and adapting to Persian practices. Not only in matters of policy and presentation had the king invited opposition; psychologically, he was no longer the man who set out from Europe in 334. Megalomania had always been in his nature, but the trials of leadership—the stress of battle, the dangers of conspiracy, and the burden of ruling a diverse population—coupled with wounds, illness, and immoderate drinking, had exacerbated existing mental instability. The adulation he received from his troops on account of his military prowess had changed to resentment of his growing aloofness and his pretensions to divinity. He became a deeply disturbed and embittered man, insensitive to the suffering of his troops. He had abandoned his Macedonian roots—one could not say he ever had a strong sense of Macedonian nationalism—and his circle of true friends grew ever smaller. The sudden death of his dearest friend Hephaestion in Ecbatana was devastating and marked by extravagant tributes to the dead man and a maniacal search for scapegoats. That he was the victim of a plot to poison him in Babylon is almost certainly false, but one can understand why the rumor, which spread after his death, was easily believed.[37]

---

37. The full story is told in the *Liber de Morte Testamentumque Alexandri Magni*, Ps.-Call. A 3.30.1–33.25 and other versions of the *Alexander Romance* (texts collected in Heckel 1988, 86–107). Curt. 10.10.5, 14–19 (with Atkinson 2009, 229–30, 234–42); Diod. 17.117.5–118.2; 19.11.8; Plut. *Alex.* 77.2–5. Discounted as literary fiction by Seibert 1984; cf. the idiosyncratic work of Grant 2017, 552–612.

IV

On the evening of June 10/11, 323,[38] Alexander died in Babylon after a lengthy illness contracted after, and perhaps even caused by, a night of heavy drinking at the house of Medius of Larissa, a Thessalian in the king's entourage.[39] A description of the events of that evening and the subsequent illness was found in what purported to be an excerpt from the *Ephemerides* or *Royal Diary* of the king.[40] The authenticity of this work, attributed in antiquity to either Eumenes of Cardia or Diodotus of Erythrae (possibly even both), has been much debated. Was it a genuine account taken from official records, or was it a later fabrication intended to suppress the rumor that a powerful cabal of officers had murdered the king?

Alexander's death was attributed to poison, administered by one of Antipater's sons, Iolaus, who was the king's chief cupbearer (*archioinochoos*). The story goes that Antipater feared that Craterus had been sent back to Macedonia with a group of veterans in order to kill him[41] and that he sent another son, Cassander, with the poison—so strong that it "had the power to consume even iron and that only an ass's hoof was resistant to the fluid"[42]—which Iolaus mixed into the king's drink. It is virtually certain that a pamphlet claiming to preserve an accurate account of the events that led to the king's death and also the text of the testament he dictated in his final days was a propaganda work of the years after 323 written for the benefit of one of Alexander's Successors in order to discredit his political opponents. The exact date of the work and the camp in which it was

---

38. Date of Alexander's death: Daisios 28 on the Macedonian calendar (but see Aristobulus, *FGrH* 139 F3b = Plut. *Alex.* 75.6, with Hamilton, *PA* 209–10). Ps.-Call. 3.35 says Pharmouthi 4, according to the Egyptian calendar (June 13), but a Babylonian tablet dates it to the twenty-ninth day of the second month of the Babylonian calendar, which Depuydt 1997 equates with June 10/11. See also Koch 2000. For a summary of earlier literature, see Seibert 1972a, 173–75.

39. The cause of Alexander's death has been the subject of considerable speculation: Engels 1978b (malaria); Borza and Reames-Zimmerman 2000 (perforated ulcer and compromised immune system); Marr and Calisher 2003 (West Nile Virus); O'Brien 1980 and 1992, 217–30 (alcoholism); Milns 1968, 255–58 (strychnine poisoning); Schep 2009 (hellebore poisoning); Hall 2018 (Guillain-Barré syndrome). See also Yardley, Wheatley, and Heckel 43–46, with additional literature.

40. Arr. 7.25.1–26.1; Plut. *Alex.* 76.1–77.1; Aelian, *VH* 3.23; Jacoby, *FGrH* 117 F2a and 3a-b.

41. On Craterus and Antipater, see now Pitt and Richardson 2017, with earlier literature.

42. Curt. 10.10.16: *ungulam iumenti*. Justin 12.13.7: *nec aliter ferri nisi in ungula equi potuerit*. Plut. *Alex.* 77.4: ὄνου χηλήν. When Plut. *Alex.* 73.6 notes that "a lion, which was the largest and finest of his [Alexander's] animals reared in captivity, was attacked by a domesticated ass, which killed it with a kick" (καὶ γὰρ λέοντα τῶν τρεφομένων μέγιστον καὶ κάλλιστον ἥμερος ὄνος ἐπελθὼν καὶ λακτίσας ἀνεῖλεν), the kick of the ass's hoof is almost certainly meant to symbolize the poison, and the lion is Alexander himself.

produced remain a matter of debate.[43] The pamphlet gives insight into the political turmoil following Alexander's death, and it confirms—if such confirmation is
needed—that the aspirations of the Successors reflected support for or rejection
of his policies and leadership.[44]

---

43. Ausfeld 1895 and 1901, followed by Merkelbach 1977, argued that the pamphlet was written
in the interests of Perdiccas and thus very soon after the king's death. My own view (Heckel
1988 and 2007, the latter now placed in question by new evidence for the date of Cleitarchus;
see Prandi 2012), that the work was published c. 318/17 for the benefit of Polyperchon and his
supporters, has been challenged by Bosworth 2000, whose argument has won the approval of
many scholars (see Meeus 2014, 293, with n. 113). Bosworth believes that the pamphlet served
the political aspirations of Ptolemy in 308; the testament indicates that it was Alexander's wish
that he should marry Cleopatra. The issue, in my opinion, is whether the aim of the publica-
tion was simply to lend (false) legitimacy to Ptolemy's actions or, in the case of Polyperchon, to
persuade others to form an alliance against Antigonus and Cassander.

44. See Errington 1976 and, for a different view, Meeus 2009a.

16

Epilogue

RESISTANCE TO ALEXANDER'S conquests has been viewed in the preceding pages for the most part from the vantage point of individual peoples and areas. The conquered were in many cases subject to other overlords or engaged in long-term struggles with traditional enemies. In some areas, there was resistance at the grass-roots level, a direct reflection of the rights (and obligations) of citizens. In others, where populations lived by brigandage or pillage, subjugation threatened economic prosperity, or at least sustainability, and the traditional way of life. But the satrapies of the Achaemenid Empire were administered by, and to the benefit of, the Persian ruling class, who in addition to employing mercenary forces drew upon native troops with little training, inadequate equipment, and inept leadership. For these conscripts, exchanging political masters was preferable to prolonged military service or even death, especially when such sacrifices contributed only to the preservation of a system that offered minimal benefit—and that benefit was continuity.

In the Eastern and Western bookends of the new empire, the conquered, if they cared to seek the cause of their subjugation, could find it in their political fragmentation and long-standing enmities. The Greeks in the West remained stubbornly hostile to the Conqueror despite the reality of defeat, as if past greatness could once more be harnessed to the cause of liberation. But such thinking was the conceit of orators, who inspired mobilization without guaranteeing success. Three great powers—Athens, Sparta, and Thebes—were hampered by suspicion and envy and would not cooperate if they thought one would gain more than the rest. The bitter struggle for supremacy after the Peloponnesian War had driven a wedge between Sparta and Thebes, and Athens' attempt to revive its power through the Second Athenian League alienated many of its erstwhile

In the Path of Conquest. Waldemar Heckel, Oxford University Press (2020). © Oxford University Press.
DOI: 10.1093/oso/9780190076689.001.0001

allies.[1] Defeat at Chaeronea demanded sober reflection, but the lesson was learned only when Alexander destroyed Thebes utterly and frightened the Athenians into submission. The hegemon of the Corinthian League did not impose obedience on Sparta, which remained proud, isolated, and impotent. In the early fifth century, Darius I and Xerxes had found the fringe areas troublesome, even when portions of it were incorporated into the empire; in the West, the Greeks had at least set aside their differences—and even then there were dissenters—in the face of a foreign enemy. But it was less productive to characterize the Macedonians as barbarians, even though the extent of their Hellenism was a moot point,[2] and impossible to resist the military juggernaut. Xerxes' hordes had indeed been numerically superior, but the Macedonian army was a force unparalleled in Greek history up to this point.

In the East, the Indus lands had been added to the Persian Empire in the time of Darius I. Gandhāra, because of its proximity to Bactria, was the most secure.[3] Those who lived beyond the Indus paid tribute to the Achaemenids but formed a checkerboard of dynasts whose rivalries negated any threat to Persian control. But Achaemenid authority in this area had weakened by the time of Alexander's expedition. The basic political structures remained intact, and although Alexander made administrative changes, these proved to be cosmetic and ephemeral.[4] The imposed friendship of Porus and Taxiles, sealed by a marriage alliance, was of short duration, and Porus himself was murdered by Eudamus and his troops.[5] The rise of Sandrocottus (Chandragupta) rendered the question of loyalty to the Macedonians meaningless.

In the middle were the lands that had been subjected to Persian authority since the reigns of Cyrus and Cambyses, and these retained over two centuries a degree of cohesion, despite the Great Satraps' Revolt, which had, at any rate,

---

1. Since Athens supplied the majority of the ships in Alexander's allied fleet, one wonders whether this might not have induced Cos and other former members of the Second Athenian League to resist Alexander in 334.

2. Despite the recognition of Alexander I Philhellene as Greek (which allowed him to participate in the Olympic festival: Hdt. 5.22.1-2), Demosthenes persisted in calling Philip II and the Macedonian royal house "barbarians" (Dem. 3.16-17, 24). For problems of ethnicity, see Hall 2002, 154–56. The question of the identity of the ancient Macedonians has long ceased to be a purely academic pursuit and has instead been used to serve modern political interests and fuel ethnic hatreds.

3. For the importance of Bactria, see Holt 1988, 42: "it is clear that Bactria occupied a prominent place in the empire of the Achaemenid Kings, and was perhaps the key satrapy of the eastern frontier."

4. See Julien 1914, 44–50; Bosworth 1983.

5. Marriage alliance: Curt. 9.3.22. Murder of Porus: Diod. 19.14.8.

been confined to the West. Although theories of Persian decadence and decay have been debunked by scholars, the empire had, paradoxically, contributed to its own demise by means of its meddling in Greek affairs and its reliance on mercenary armies. The intervention of the Great King as arbiter of the Common Peace promoted Greek disunity, furthered by the generous distribution of bribes and subsidies.[6] In the end, it only paved the way for Macedonian domination. Persian power ended abruptly with the death of the Achaemenid ruler and the usurper Bessus. Still, the empire did not collapse. Such was the strength of its institutions and administrative organization that it was merely subjected to what in business terminology would be called a hostile takeover, with Alexander as the new CEO overseeing the middle managers (the satraps and *hyparchoi*), some newly appointed, others retained from the previous administration. Where Achaemenid rule had been viewed as oppressive, Alexander replaced Persian satraps with Greeks or Macedonians. Local dynasts (e.g., the Hecatomnids of Caria) were retained, and some places were exempted from taxation. In the Iranian heartland, the Persian satraps were allowed to remain in office, but garrisons under a *phrourarchos* or *strategos* were imposed. The claim that Alexander showed no interest in administrative matters is patently false.[7] Rebels continued to test the resolve of the King of Asia, but such uprisings were probably no more frequent than they had been in the Achaemenid era.[8] The same is true of malfeasance, which Alexander punished with (some would say excessive) severity. Given the large

---

6. The Peace of Antalcidas, aptly called the King's Peace, in 387/6 was reincarnated in subsequent decades, favoring first the Spartans and then the Thebans. See Ryder 1965. The power of Persian money, bribes, and subsidies: Hdt. 9.2.2-3; 9.5; 9.41; Diod. 11.28.3; Thuc. 1.109.2-3; 8.46.1-2; Plut. *Ages.* 15.1; Dem. 9.36-40; Xen. *HG* 3.5.1-2; Paus. 3.9.7-8; Plut. *Ages.* 15.6, *Artox.* 20.3, *Lys.* 27; Hellenica Oxyrhynchia 6.3–7.2; Polyaenus 1.48.3; Nepos, *Epam.* 4.1-2; Plut. *Pelop.* 30; Diod. 17.4.8; Justin 11.2.7; Paus. 3.9.2; Diod. 14.81.6; 14.84.5, 85.2; Xen. *HG* 4.8.12; Nepos, *Conon* 4.1, 5; Justin 6.1.4-9, 2.16; Diod. 16.40.1-2, 44.1-2; Justin 11.3.9.

7. See, for example, Grainger 2007, 82, who turns virtue into vice: "in the empire he was moving from challenge to challenge without providing a real government for it other than a temporary continuation of the old system." But did Alexander regard these arrangements as temporary? Almost certainly not. The Indian campaign Grainger describes as "escapism," adding that "Alexander's motives for this invasion were pathetic" (83); "[Alexander] had steadily avoided the more unexciting decisions such as organizing a government" (85). These views are shared by Billows 2018, 181: Alexander's conquests "went well beyond [his father's] plans in ways that, while immediately successful, made little strategic sense"; "he showed no interest in organizing his conquests into a coherent, functioning empire, merely continuing the Persian system for the sake of convenience"; and he "seems to have lived for the thrill of the fight and of conquest for its own sake."

8. The most serious challenges came from Persians (often claiming to belong to the families of the Seven) who sought the kingship for themselves or were suspected of doing so. This is perhaps the true reason for the execution of Orxines (see Heckel 186; Berve II 294 no. 592).

number of officials who qualified as "Achaemenids" and "Relatives" (*syngeneis*), there was doubtless a culture of corruption. Persian kings had been more lenient in their treatment of such offenders—though not always. But Alexander's punitive measures were directed against Greek and Macedonian malefactors as well. In the period of transition, there were seismic shifts—many of them not entirely unpredictable—but the structure held firm.[9] Blame for the disintegration of Alexander's empire falls squarely on the shoulders of the Diadochi and their epigones, even if the king gave too little thought to producing and naming an heir. He was, after all, far too young and narcissistic to contemplate his own mortality. It took the ambitions of his former generals to rend the fabric of the Achaemenid tent.

The very fact of the empire's structural stability made the conquest easier and, in the heartland, less bloody. For, with the exception of the slaughter in major battles at Issus and Gaugamela, the bloodiest years of the campaign were those of 329–325, when Alexander was in the less stable fringe areas—Bactria and Sogdiana and the lands east of the Hindu Kush.[10] Here the inhabitants would not abandon what they could either carry with them or store in secure fortresses. But even then, for the barbarian horsemen and their families, personal property counted for little and could be as easily recouped as it was lost. Yet, paradoxically, the efficiency of the Persian Empire proved to be its undoing. The system of roads and communication instituted by the Achaemenids[11] aided the conquest, as the

---

9. I am not persuaded by the view of Brosius 2003, 169: "it is doubtful that the Macedonians and Greeks had any in-depth knowledge of the geographical extent and geophysical extremes of the empire, of the careful balance between exercising royal power and accepting the ethnic, cultural and religious diversity of the empire's population, or of the power structures between the king, his relatives, the satraps, and the Persian nobility—issues which were of vital importance for the stability of the empire, and which determined how successfully the empire could be held after a military conquest." The Greco-Macedonian knowledge of Eastern geography was certainly inadequate, at least *before* the invasion. Some questions concerning the nature of the Caucasus and the Tanais, which was regarded as the dividing line between Europe and Asia, persisted (to say nothing of theories concerning the Indus and the Nile; cf. Högemann 1985, 65–67), but the Macedonian soldier and his leaders probably covered more kilometers of terrain in the empire than most Persian monarchs ever did. And it is simply not true that Alexander was ignorant of "ethnic, cultural and religious diversity." I would go so far as to suggest that it was the Conqueror's appreciation of these factors (along with an understanding of the administrative structures) that explains his so-called orientalizing policies, the ones that were greeted by the Macedonian soldiery (and some of the generals) with disapproval. Alexander's administrative and political measures have been unjustly underrated, perhaps even misunderstood. The disintegration of the empire after his death had, in my opinion, little to do with the Conqueror's measures—even if we allow for the fact that in some places, the conquest was superficial or incomplete.

10. Casualty figures provided in chapter 15.

11. Kuhrt, *Corpus* 730–62; Graf 1994; and especially Seibert 1985, 15–27.

Macedonian army moved quickly into lands where mobilization was comparatively slow and satraps distrusted their neighbors and their mercenaries almost as much as they distrusted the enemy. Those satraps who had continued eastward in flight with Darius lost their territories to the underlings who surrendered them or other prominent defectors—sometimes only temporarily but often for good. With the fall of the core region, the accumulated gold and silver of Achaemenid treasure houses was used to fund invasion and occupation, as well as the suppression of insurgency.[12] The ability to harness the empire's own resources against itself allowed the conquering army to be less of a burden on the nations in its path, thus lessening the impact on the defeated, who were, consequently, less hostile to their new masters.

Such was the situation on land. Those peoples who depended upon the sea for their defense, communications, and livelihood were the ones who had been annexed by force. It was an inconvenient truth for the Achaemenid rulers that theirs was a landlocked state that relied for its maritime defense on the ships and sailors of subjects whose loyalty to the empire was uncertain: Ionian Greeks, Phoenicians, Cypriotes, and Egyptians.

---

12. Thus Briant, *HPE* 867: "now he [i.e., the invader] was the one who was able to take advantage of the organization of the Achaemenid strategic space around strongholds, treasuries, and storehouses—places where the Great King's enemy could find ample supplies of money and materiel that had originally been created for the defense of the imperial territories." On Alexander's accumulated wealth, see Holt 2016.

Sources for the History of Alexander the Great

Virtually everything we know about the history of the Conqueror comes from Greek and Roman sources.[1] And this makes it extremely difficult for us to view the conquest from the vantage point of the defeated. That is not to say that such an endeavor is impossible, for this would render any such attempt futile. It is important to bear in mind that what the extant sources say about the motives and objectives of Alexander's enemies is little more than conjecture, though some of the views expressed go back to the lost primary histories, which may have made use of eyewitness sources (e.g., mercenaries who fought against Alexander).[2] The thoughts attributed to Darius and his subordinates are even more conjectural, as are those of Alexander and his Macedonians. For the Greeks who resisted the conquest, there is at least the evidence of the Athenian orators and, in places, "official" documents on stone—though even these (the former especially) must be vetted for bias. The barbarians, on the other hand, have left us very little to work with: some official documents, such as the requisitioning of supplies for Bessus in the Upper Satrapies or astronomical diaries and prophesies revealed ex post facto. The best one can do is tease inferences from the Greco-Roman sources, and even here it is difficult to separate truth from fiction. These are the limitations of the evidence that offers

---

1. I exclude from this discussion the various versions of the *Alexander Romance* (often referred to as Ps.-Callisthenes), on which see the excellent work of Richard Stoneman, especially Stoneman 2008, 230–45. Many works on Alexander provide discussions for sources. That of Müller 2019, 11–33, is particularly useful.

2. I do not mean to revive the debunked theory of the "mercenaries source," at least in the way imagined by Tarn II 71–74 (rejected by Brunt 1962; further literature in Seibert 1972a, 10–11, 233; but see Rzepka 2009). See also the comments in the introduction.

explicit testimony, but inferences can nevertheless be drawn, and these amount to far more than speculation. Hence, it is necessary to say a few words about the nature of the sources, both lost and extant.

I

For the reign of Alexander the Great, there are four full-scale extant accounts, written anywhere from about three hundred to five hundred years after the death of the Conqueror. These are, in order of appearance, the seventeenth book of the *Bibliotheca* of Diodorus of Sicily (Loeb edition by C. Bradford Welles; OWC, Robin Waterfield tr.; Budé edition by P. Goukowsky); the *Historiae Alexandri Magni* by Q. Curtius Rufus (Loeb edition by J. C. Rolfe; Penguin Classics, J. C. Yardley trans.; Budé edition by H. Bardon; see also Baynham 1998; Atkinson I–II and *Curtius 10*); Plutarch's *Life of Alexander* (Loeb translation by B. Perrin; commentary by Hamilton, *PA*); and Arrian's *History of Alexander* (possibly called the *Anabasis Alexandrou*, Brunt I–II (Loeb); Penguin Classics, A. de Sélincourt trans.; Oxford World's Classics, Martin Hammond trans., with an excellent introduction by J. E. Atkinson; commentary by Bosworth I–II; also Stadter 1980; Bosworth 1988b). For the title of Arrian's work, see Bosworth I 7–8. It may simply have been called τὰ περὶ Ἀλεξάνδρου. *Anabasis Alexandrou* is the title commonly used by scholars.

Diodorus' seventeenth book (Commentary by Prandi 2013) is marred by a lacuna that obliterates the events after the death of Bessus up to Alexander's siege of Massaga (Diod. 17.83-84). To these we may add the work of a certain M. Junianus (or Junianius) Justinus, better known as Justin, who abbreviated the *Historiae Philippicae* of Pompeius Trogus, which covered the years 336–323 in its eleventh and twelfth books (translation and commentary in Yardley and Heckel; see also Seel 1972; Alonso-Núñez 1992; Yardley 2003; Bartlett 2014). Trogus himself belonged to the Augustan age, and Justin is now dated to the late second or early third century A.D. (Yardley and Heckel 13; Yardley 2003, 5, "about 200 A.D."; also Yardley 2010). A late-fourth-century date, proposed by Syme 1988 and endorsed by Barnes 1991, 343 (cf. Mineo and Zecchini 2016, 51–59), is untenable. Justin's epitome (or, perhaps more rightly, florilegium) provides uneven coverage of the period and is marred by errors in fact that are almost certainly due to sloppy abbreviation. It also exhibits Roman elements (*color romanus*), though this undoubtedly reflects the work of Trogus himself. One other work, which survived only in a single manuscript from Metz—and that, too, was lost in a bombing raid during the Second World War—dealt with the history of Alexander from the events after Darius' death to the Indian campaign of 326/5. Known simply as the *Metz Epitome*, it clearly belongs to the same tradition as the works of Diodorus and Curtius, with which it has a great deal in common (Geissendörfer 1967; Baynham 1995). A few other extant sources add useful information: the *Geography* of Strabo, Plutarch's *De Alexandri Magni fortuna et virtute* I–II, and Pliny's *Historia Naturalis*, as well as Polyaenus' *Stratagemata*, Aelian's *Varia Historia*, and the *Deipnosophistae* of Athenaeus. This list is not exhaustive (see, for example, Polybius' long digression on Callisthenes and Issus; cf. also Billows 2000), but these works make up the bulk of what we know about Alexander and his campaigns beyond what is found in the Alexander historians proper. By contrast, very little contemporary evidence survives. The inscriptional evidence is scant by comparison with other periods (Heisserer 1980), and the numismatic evidence is subject to a variety of interpretations (Bellinger 1963; Price 1982 and 1991; Dahmen 2007) though often valuable for the establishment of dating criteria or as instruments of propaganda.

The literary sources are based on contemporary accounts, all lost, written by men who either accompanied the expedition (though not always in a military capacity) or, as in the case of Cleitarchus of Alexandria, drew upon the recollections, written or oral, of those who did. The fragments of the lost historians have been collected by F. Jacoby, *FGrH* IIB and *BNJ* (a work in progress), supplemented by English and French translations in Robinson 1953 and Auberger 2001, respectively (cf. Fraenkel 1883; Pearson 1960; Pédech 1984; Hammond 1983 and 1993). Auberger's omission of Callisthenes makes little sense: "Nous n'avons pas pris en compte son récit dans notre ouvrage car le lecteur dispose de plusieurs traductions de son *Roman d'Alexandre*" (2001, 13). This confuses the *Praxeis Alexandrou* with the work of Pseudo-Callisthenes (on which, see Merkelbach 1954 and 1977; Stoneman 2008). For our purposes, a brief sketch of the historiographic tradition for Alexander will serve as an underpinning of the preceding discussion.

A record of day-to-day activities was preserved in the *Royal Journal* or *Diary* known also as the *Ephemerides* (Jacoby, *FGrH* 117; Robinson 1932; Pearson 1955 and 1960, 185–86, 260–61; Samuel 1965; Hammond 1988; Anson 1996. See esp. Bosworth 1971a and 1988b, 157–84). This was compiled by the king's secretary Eumenes of Cardia (and/or Diodotos of Erythrai). Diodotos of Erythrai may have been a pseudonym for Eumenes of Cardia. One is reminded of Xenophon's reference (*Hell.* 3.1.2) to the story of the Ten Thousand written by Themistogenes of Syracuse, almost certainly a reference to at least an earlier version of his *Anabasis*. The exact form of the *Ephemerides* is unclear; some scholars believe the work contained records of military activity, but two of the three passages that purport to come from this source deal with the circumstances leading up to Alexander's death (*FGrH* 117 F2a-b and 3a-b). It has even been proposed that the *Ephemerides* were fabricated to cover up the truth behind the king's death (Bosworth 1971a, 120–23). It is, however, unlikely that the Macedonian kings did not keep such official records, and in addition to the *Ephemerides* (whatever their actual value), there is the history composed by Callisthenes of Olynthus, a nephew of Aristotle. This work, entitled *Praxeis Alexandrou* ("Deeds of Alexander"), appears to have been published in installments that covered each campaigning season (Jacoby, *FGrH* 124; Corssen 1917; Prentice 1923; Brown 1949a; Pearson 1960, 22–49; Plezia 1972; Golan 1988; Devine 1994; also Bosworth 1970). Intended as a work of propaganda (Pearson 1960, 22; Devine 1994), it was probably used to justify the Panhellenic crusade to the Greeks west of the Aegean and perhaps even to serve as a recruiting tool. As the title implies, the king himself was very much at the center of events. Callisthenes was later executed for his defiance of the king—he opposed the attempt to introduce *proskynesis* at the Macedonian court and was thought (rightly or wrongly) to have incited Hermolaus and his fellow Pages to plot regicide (both events in 327)—but in his early years, as the author of an "official" history, he presented a flattering picture of the young Conqueror, one in which the sea at Mount Climax did obeisance to Alexander (*FGrH* 124 F31). The contents of the last book of the *Praxeis Alexandrou* are unknown, though it appears that it did not go beyond the events of 329/8. Robinson 1929 believes that the disappearance of Aristander of Telmissus, who last appears in the extant Alexander historians at the time of the Cleitus episode (Plut. *Alex.* 50.3-5), indicates that Callisthenes' *Praxeis Alexandrou* came to an end soon thereafter. Two passages naming Aristander in connection with prophecies relating to the Successors (Ael. *VH* 12.64; App. *Syr.* 64.338) are almost certainly invented or due to confusion with Peithagoras of Amphipolis.

All other accounts appeared after Alexander's death, though it seems that some were being composed during his lifetime. Chares of Mitylene (*FGrH* 125), a court official (Plut. *Alex.* 46.2 calls him εἰσαγγελεύς, "usher"), must have been keeping notes during the course of the campaign. Marsyas of Pella (*FGrH* 135/6) may have written his *Makedonika* (of which the τὰ περὶ Ἀλεξάνδρου appears to have been a part) during the king's lifetime, while he was with his brother Antigonus the One-Eyed in Phrygia. For his history, see Heckel 1980b and Howe, *BNJ* "Marsyas (135–136)." The story in Lucian's *How to Write History* 12 (= *FGrH* 139 T4) that Aristobulus read his version of Alexander's single combat with Porus to the king as they were sailing down the Hydaspes and that the king snatched the script from him and threw it overboard is almost certainly an invention and chronologically unlikely. Cf. Plut. *Alex.* 46 (= *FGrH* 134 T8) for a similar story concerning Lysimachus and Onesicritus. This was clearly a topos, like Alexander's disapproval of the epic poem of Choirilos of Iasos. Ephippus of Olynthus (*FGrH* 126; cf. Spawforth 2012) wrote a work critical of Hephaestion and Alexander (almost certainly based on personal observations; hence, it is unlikely that he was identical with the Ephippus of Arr. 3.5.3; see Heckel 118) after the latter's death.

We know, for example, that in the last days of the king's life, Nearchus read out loud to Alexander an account of the progress of the fleet from India to Mesopotamia (Plut. *Alex.* 76.3; but Hamilton, *PA* 211, expresses doubts; for Nearchus' history, see Jacoby, *FGrH* 133; Pearson 1960, 112–49). We are also told that he wrote with the intention of correcting the mendacities of his rival Onesicritus (Jacoby, *FGrH* 134; Brown 1949b; Pearson 1960, 83–111; Winiarczyk 2007), but this appears to refer to the final version of Nearchus' history. Onesicritus may have modeled his work on Xenophon's *Cyropaedia* (Diog. Laert. 6.84; for Onesicritus and Xenophon, see also Brown 1949b, 13–23); Nearchus' account was the primary source for Arrian's *Indica* and appears to have concentrated on the descent of the Indus River and the voyage to the Persian Gulf. Both histories were published relatively soon after 323 and, along with the *Praxeis Alexandrou*, were used by Cleitarchus of Alexandria, a writer noted for his bombastic style (Jacoby, *FGrH* 137; Brown 1950; Pearson 1960, 212–42; Prandi 1996). It was, until relatively recently, thought that he wrote at some point between 310 and 305, but this has been challenged by a recently discovered papyrus fragment that suggests that he belonged to the middle of the third century. On the other hand, he was allegedly the son of Deinon, a fourth-century writer of *Persika* ("Persian Affairs"), and made use of such material in his *History of Alexander* (Pliny, *HN* 10.136: *Dinon Clitarchi celebrati auctoris pater*; see Parker 2009; but also the salutary remarks of Prandi 2012). It is Cleitarchus' history that most scholars regard as the common source of what has been called the Alexander Vulgate (Rüegg 1906, 5, traces the idea back to Raun 1868), the popular tradition that comprises the works of Diodorus of Sicily, Curtius Rufus, Justin, and the *Metz Epitome*. A good deal of the historical narrative of Plutarch's *Life of Alexander* is also based on Cleitarchus, although the biographer used (or, at least, was familiar with) a wide range of authors. Plut. *Alex.* 46 (cf. Hamilton, *PA* 126–27), for example, cites fourteen authors who discussed the Amazon story: Cleitarchus, Polycleitus, Onesicritus, Antigenes, Ister, Aristobulus, Chares, Ptolemy, Anticleides, Philon, Philip of Theangela, Hecataeus of Eretria, Philip the Chalcidian, and Duris of Samos. These sources contain numerous sensational episodes and are often critical of Alexander's actions. Consequently, it has been the practice of some historians to reject their information as fictitious or embellished, coming from late and unreliable sources. The truth is not so simple.

In contrast to the Vulgate, there is the apologetic tradition that omits or whitewashes those incidents that do not redound to Alexander's credit. The chief representative of this tradition is Arrian and the derivative *Itinerarium Alexandri* (see the edition and commentary by Tabacco 2000; English translation by Davies 1998; also Lane Fox 1997), based on the works of Ptolemy son of Lagus and Aristobulus of Cassandrea. Arrian's methodology and his somewhat simplistic approach to his sources are spelled out in the preface of the work:

> Wherever the accounts of Ptolemy son of Lagus and Aristobulus son of Aristobulus are in agreement in what they have written about Alexander son of Philip, I myself record them as being factually correct; where this is not so, I have chosen what seems to me to be the more reliable version and *at the same time a better read*. Now, other writers have given varying accounts of Alexander, and there is no one about whom more writers are in disaccord with one another. In my view, however, Ptolemy and Aristobulus are the ones to have provided the more authoritative accounts, the latter, Aristobulus, because he campaigned with Alexander, and Ptolemy because, apart from campaigning with him, *he was a king himself and more than anyone would have found untruthfulness particularly dishonorable*. Moreover, since they were both writing when Alexander was already dead, there was no pressure or profit involved in their writing anything other than what occurred. Some accounts also given by others I have, however, included because they struck me as noteworthy and *not totally unreliable*—but included them only as apocryphal material on Alexander. (Arr. *proem.* 1–3)

Aristobulus had accompanied Alexander as an engineer of some sort and was entrusted in 325/4 with the restoration of the tomb of Cyrus the Great in Pasargadae (*FGrH* 139 F51a-b). His date and place of birth are unknown, but he must have become a resident of Cassander's new city, Cassandrea (founded in 316). He was perhaps a Phocian in origin (see Pearson 1952 and 1960, 151; Pédech 1984, 332 postulates: "Il est même probable qu'il participa à la fondation de Cassandreia en tant qu'ingénieur et architecte"). Ps.-Lucian says that he began writing at the age of eighty-four and lived beyond the age of ninety (*Macrob.* 22 = *FGrH* 139 T3; see Pearson 1960, 150–87; Tarn II 29–43; Pédech 1984, 331–405). That he published his work before the death of Cassander (297), who was reputedly hostile to Alexander, seems unlikely. His account of Alexander was flattering and apologetic.

The fragments of his work—these number sixty-two and one doubtful passage—suggest he was interested in practical matters of engineering and distances, as well as geography, local history, and customs, even the variants of names. As such, he was a good choice for Arrian, since he provided material that balanced Ptolemy's military narrative. But it is impossible to say whether he wrote before or after Ptolemy—who was equally concerned about Alexander's reputation—since the date of that man's *History* is also debated. It is, however, reasonably certain that Aristobulus wrote in the third century. Ptolemy, on the other hand, appears to have written late in life, perhaps after elevating his son, who would come to be known as Ptolemy II Philadelphos, to a share of the throne in 285. The view of Errington that Ptolemy wrote much earlier, with the intention of either denigrating his political rivals or, at least, passing over their achievements in silence, has had a relatively short "shelf life" (Errington 1969; Roisman 1984; Heckel 2018a; cases of Ptolemy's bias have been noted at various points in the preceding narrative). The bias of the work is clear, as are the individuals targeted by his pen, but the disservice he does to his former enemies is not stinging and extensive enough to justify labeling the *History* as polemic (Heckel and Yardley 1984, 5). Far more, it serves as a means to glorify Ptolemy's own role in the campaigns and to emphasize his relationship with the king, who is the unblemished hero of the piece (Ptolemy's *History*: Jacoby, *FGrH* 138; Strasburger 1934; Kornemann 1935; Pearson 1960, 188–211; Pédech 1984, 215–329). But the result is that we do not learn as much about the activities and motives of the opposing side as we should like.

II

It remains to note those passages in the extant historians that give us some insight into the affairs of the enemy, evidence for which appears to have come from a Greek (mercenary?) or Persian source. See also the detailed discussion in Brunt 1962. There were also countless oral sources: various mercenaries who served the Great King; Greek ambassadors captured in Persia; spies, scouts, and prisoners of war (many interrogated by Laomedon son of Larichos); and numerous notable men (and women) known by name, among them Abulites, Ada, *Amminapes*, Antibelus (or Artiboles), Ariobarzanes,

Arsaces, Arsames, *Artabazus, Atropates*, Autophradates, Bagisthanes, *Bagoas, Barsine, Calanus, Cleophis* (if historical), *Cophen, Glaucus, Hystaspes, Itanes, Mazaeus, Melon, Mithrenes*, Nabarzanes, Orxines (Orsines), Oxathres, *Oxyartes, Oxyathres*, Oxydates, *Patron*, Pharnabazus, Phegeus, Phrasaortes, Phratapbernes, *Porus, Roxane*, Sabictas, *Taxiles*, Tiridates, the wife of Spitamenes, and others captured at Issus and Damascus. The names in italics indicate those who would have had extended exposure to Alexander and/or his historians. The passages in the following list (which is not exhaustive) must, however, be used with caution, since some ascribe motives that may or may not be correct but are nevertheless inferred by the author who reported them (or by his source). Furthermore, some passages are clearly historical fiction and do not stand up to scrutiny. But the references given below indicate just how much information could possibly have been collected from the losing side, even if this was often suppressed or distorted.

Diodorus. 17.2.3-6 (Attalus in Asia Minor); 17.3.3–4.9 (Greek reaction to Philip's death); 17.2.4, 5.3–7.2 (events leading up to and including Darius' accession; cf. 16.89, 91.2); 17.7.1-10 (activities of Memnon before Alexander's invasion); 17.8.1–9.1 (uprisings in the north and at Thebes); 17.10 (Theban decision to resist Alexander); 17.11. (Thebans reflect upon their past glory); 17.14.2 (Medism of the Thebans; cf. 17.9.5); 17.18.2-4 (Persian strategy decisions); 17.20.3 (names of Persian dead at the Granicus); 17.23.4-6 (Memnon's supreme command); 17.24.5–26.7, 27.5 (defense of Halicarnassus, mainly from the Persian vantage point); 17.28 (actions of the Marmares); 17.29 (Memnon's countermeasures in the Aegean); 17.30.1–31.3 (Darius' deliberations; news of Memnon's death); 17.34.5 (names of Persian dead at Issus); 17.40.3 (Tyrians decide to resist; most of the Tyrian measures taken in defense of the city [17.42–46] were easily observable from the Macedonian side; I have not included descriptions of actions taken by the resisters when they were clearly reported from the invader's point of view); 17.41.1-2 (Tyre and Carthage); 17.48.2-5 (Amyntas in Egypt); 17.48.5-6 (Persian countermeasures in Anatolia); 17.55 (Persian defensive measures at the Tigris); 17.59.5-8 (action on the Persian right at Gaugamela); 17.62-63 (Agis' war and rebellion in Thrace); 17.61.1-2 (Darius at Ecbatana); 17.73.1-4 (flight and death of Darius); 17.74.1-2 (Bessus assumes power); 17.78 (rebellion of Satibarzanes); 17.83.7-8 (Bessus and Bagodaras = Gobares); 17.93 (Alexander learns of the Ganges and the Nanda dynasty from Phegeus); 17.108.4-8 (crimes and flight of Harpalus; affairs in Athens); 17.111.1-4 (prelude to Lamian War).

Justin. 10.1-3 (Persian Empire from Ochus to Darius); 11.2.7-10 (unrest in Greece); 11.4.1-6 (speech of Cleadas); 11.10.10-14 (affairs in Tyre); 11.14.3-4 (Darius' flight from Gaugamela); 11.15.1-5 (arrest and death of Darius); 12.1.4-11 (Agis' war and Thrace); 12.10.8 (crimes of Alexander's governors).

Curtius. 3.2.1–3.25 (Darius' army; deliberations in his camp; death of Charidemus; appointment of Pharnabazus; details of the Persian procession); 3.8.1-15 (the Persian camp; discussion with Greek mercenaries; Darius moves against Alexander); 3.8.24-27 (Persian reaction to Alexander's approach); 3.9.1-6 (Persian battle order); 3.11.10-12 (names of Persian dead; flight of Darius); 4.1.27–33 (Amyntas and the mercenaries, from Tripolis to Egypt); 4.1.34-37 (Persian countermeasures in Anatolia and the Aegean); 4.1.38-40 (Spartan unrest in Greece); 4.3.19-23 (situation in Tyre; Carthaginian delegation); 4.5.13-22 (affairs in Asia Minor in Alexander's absence); 4.6.1-4 (renewal of Darius' war effort; summoning of Bessus); 4.9.1-10 (Darius' camp; Mazaeus at the Tigris); 4.10.25-34 (Darius receives news of his wife's death); 4.12.6-12, 18 (Persian deployment at Gaugamela); 4.13.11-14 (Darius keeps his troops under arms during the night); 4.16.1-7 (actions of Mazaeus; his escape to Babylon); 5.1.2-9 (Darius at Arbela; deliberations; Persians move into Media); 5.8–13 (Darius at Ecbatana; Persian strategy; dissension at Darius' court and in the camp; the Greek mercenaries; Artabazus supports Darius against Bessus and Nabarzanes; arrest and death of Darius); 6.1 (Agis' war); 6.4.8-14, 6.5.22-23 (negotiations for Nabarzanes' surrender); 6.4.23–5 (surrender of Phrataphernes, Artabazus; Greek ambassadors); 7.4.1-21 (Bessus and Gobares; Bessus flees across the Oxus); 7.5.19-26 (betrayal and extradition of Bessus); 7.6.14-16 (Spitamenes and Catanes reject Alexander's peace offer); 7.11 (siege and capture of the Rock of Arimazes; negotiations conducted by Cophen son of Artabazus); 8.2.25-32 (Sisimithres' surrender negotiated by Oxartes/Oxyartes); 8.3.1-16 (Spitamenes' wife; if the story is true, the episode tells us something about the motives of the rebels in Sogdiana, and we may assume that the woman was a source of further information about the situation.); 9.2.1-7 (Phegeus informs Alexander about the Ganges and the Nanda dynasty); 9.4.15 (preparations of Sudracae); 9.7.1-11 (uprising in Bactria; Biton and Boxus); 10.1.1-5 (crimes of Alexander's governors); 10.2.1-7 (Harpalus; affairs in Athens).

   Metz Epitome. 3–6 (Bessus assumes the kingship; his arrest and extradition); 17–18 (Ariomazes; negotiations by Dares); 20–23 (wife of Spitamenes).

   Arrian. 1.12.8-10 (Persian commanders and strategy at the Granicus); 1.16.3 (names of Persian dead at the Granicus); 1.17.9-12 (affairs in Ephesus before Alexander's arrival); 1.19.1-2 (embassy of Glaucippus of Miletus); 1.20.3, 23.1-3 (Memnon at Halicarnassus); 2.1-2 (Persian counterattack in the Aegean); 2.6.1–7.2 (Darius' camp at Sochi; his advance into Cilicia); 2.11.8 (names of Persian dead at Issus); 2.13.1-6 (Darius' flight; Amyntas in Egypt; Persian countermeasures in the Aegean); 3.2.3-7 (report of activities in the Aegean); 3.7.1-4 (Persian action at the Euphrates and Tigris; 3.7.4: information from captured scouts); 3.8.3-6 (Persian forces at Gaugamela); 3.11.3-7 (Persian deployment, from document captured after the battle); 3.16.1-2 (Darius' flight to Media and his motives; probably from Patron or Glaucus, the mercenary captains); 3.19.1-5 (Darius at Ecbatana and his subsequent flight; deserters come to Alexander); 3.20.3 (arrest and imprisonment of Oxydates); 3.21.1 (events in the Persian camp reported by Bastanes and the son of Mazaeus); 3.23.4 (Nabarzanes and Phrataphernes surrender to Alexander; potential sources of information; cf. 3.23.7, surrender of Artabazus and his sons; 3.24.4-5, surrender of Greek ambassadors and mercenaries); 3.25.3 (usurpation of Bessus, from Persian sources: Περσῶν τινες, οἳ ἤγγελλον); 3.28.9-10 (Bessus crosses the Oxus); 3.29.6 (arrest of Bessus, reported by agents of Spitamenes and Dataphernes; cf.

3.30.1-2); 4.18.4–19.4 (capture of Rock of Sogdiana through agency of Oxyartes; confused by Arrian; cf. 4.21.6-9: Chorienes and Oxyartes); 5.25-27 (reports of the land beyond the Hyphasis); 6.4.3 (measures taken by the Mallians and Oxydracae); 6.273-5 (malfeasance and crimes of Alexander's governors); 6.29.2–30.1 (Persian misdeeds in Alexander's absence).

Glossary

Achaemenidae (Achaemenids) Descendants of Achaemenes. The Persian royal house.

Aeacidae (Aeacids) Descendants of Aeacus. The Epirote royal house.

agema The elite unit of infantry (hypaspists) or cavalry in the Macedonian army.

akontistes (akontistai) Javelin man.

Alexander Vulgate See **vulgate**.

antitagma A unit (*tagma/taxis*) set up as a counter-balance to another.

apologia A defense. Sometimes a "whitewashing" of events.

apomachoi Those unfit for military service on account of illness, wounds, or age.

archihypaspistes The supreme commander of the hypaspists.

archioinochoos Chief cupbearer. Distinct from the *edeatros*, who was the king's "taster."

archon A military or political leader.

Argeadae (Argeads) The Macedonian royal family.

argyraspides The Silver Shields. A unit of 3,000 former hypaspists.

asthetairoi The name may mean "closest companions"; a subset of the Macedonian phalanx generally known as the *pezhetairoi*.

ataktoi Literally, "those without discipline." A unit of troops made up of men whose loyalty or discipline is suspect.

cataphract A heavily armed cavalryman.

chiliarch The commander of 1,000 men. In Persia, the chiliarch was the commander of the king's cavalry and/or his chief courtier.

color romanus Literally, Roman coloration. Passages (descriptions) that reflect Roman life or practices and thus the origin and attitudes of the author.

Companion cavalry The Macedonian cavalry, numbering 1,500–1,800 and divided into squadrons known as *ilai*.

diphtheria Skins or hides. These were stuffed with straw to make flotation devices for the crossing of rivers. Cf. Bloedow 2002.

epigonoi Successors or descendants. Specifically, the 30,000 barbarian troops recruited in the empire and trained in the Macedonian fashion.

episkopos A political or financial overseer.

epistoleus A letter carrier.

euergetai Benefactors. Specifically, the Ariaspians of the Helmand region.

gazophylax Treasurer. Guardian of the treasury. In Persia, such an official was often a eunuch.

harmamaxai "Covered wagons," used by the Persians to transport women and dignitaries.

harmost A Spartan garrison commander.

hegemon A general or military leader. Also a commander-in-chief.

hetairoi (**sing.** ***hetairos***) The king's "Companions." Members of the Macedonian nobility or distinguished men from other states (e.g., Demaratus of Corinth).

hippakontistai Mounted javelin men.

hipparch Cavalry commander, normally of a unit larger than the *ile*. In Greek, the word appears as either *hipparchos* or *hipparches*.

hippokomoi Grooms. Those responsible for preparing the horses and helping the king and nobles mount them. Some of the tasks of the *hippokomoi* were shared by the *paides basilikoi*.

hippotoxotai Mounted archers.

hippeis Cavalrymen.

hoplite Greek or Macedonian infantryman armed with a large shield (*hoplon*) and a thrusting spear (*dory*).

hyparchos A lieutenant. Also used as a substitute for satrap or regional governor.

hypaspists A 3,000-man Macedonian infantry guard.

ilarch (***ilarches***) Commander of an *ile*.

ile (**plur.** ***ilai***) A cavalry squadron, ranging in size from about 150 to 300. Also *eile/eilai*.

ile basilike The Macedonian "Royal Squadron." Alexander's cavalry guard.

Kardakes Persian troops—there were said to be 60,000 of them at Issus—of uncertain origin and fighting style. Sometimes identified as hoplites, though some have considered them peltasts.

koine eirene Common Peace.

lithobolos (**plur.** ***lithoboloi***) A siege engine. Stone thrower.

misthophoroi Mercenaries.

misthophoroi hippeis Mercenary cavalry.

monomachia A duel. Single combat.

Pages See *paides basilikoi.*

paides basilikoi Young men of the Macedonian aristocracy raised at the court and trained in military arts and leadership.

Panhellenism The idea of Greekness based on common customs, religion, language, and traditions.

pelta A smaller shield carried by some cavalrymen or by lightly armed infantry (i.e., peltasts).

pezhetairoi Macedonian infantrymen, usually armed with the eighteen-foot *sarissa.* Literally, "foot companions."

phalanx The Macedonian heavy infantry.

philoi (sing. *philos*) Friends. In the technical sense, "Companions" of the King (*hetairoi*).

phrourarchos Commandant. Garrison commander.

prodromoi Also called *skopoi*. Mounted scouts.

proskynesis

psiloi Lightly armed infantrymen (such as archers, javelin men, slingers, peltasts).

sarissa (**also** *sarisa*) The Macedonian pike, roughly eighteen feet in length. A cavalryman could carry a shorter *sarissa*.

sarissophoroi Those who carried the *sarissa*, often referring to a cavalry unit.

satrap (*satrapes*) A Persian "provincial" governor.

secessio In Roman military terminology, a "strike," or a failure on the part of the troops to respond to orders. But this falls short of mutiny.

Somatophylakes basilikoi Members of a royal bodyguard; young men of aristocratic background. Also known as *hypaspistai basilikoi* ("royal hypaspists").

Somatophylax A member of the Macedonian seven-man Bodyguard.

strategos A general or a military overseer.

syntrophoi Those who were brought up at the court along with the king's sons.

taxiarches Commander of a *taxis*.

taxis A generic term for a military unit of varying size.

tetrarchy Cavalry unit made up of four squadrons. The term occurs rarely.

topos A common feature or theme in writing (including historical writing), usually appropriate to the situation but seldom historically accurate.

toxotes (*toxotai*) Archers.

vulgate An outdated but not entirely obsolete term for the popular Alexander tradition thought to be based primarily on Cleitarchus of Alexandria. The so-called vulgate authors are Diodorus, Q. Curtius Rufus, Justin (and to a certain extent Plutarch, in his *Life of Alexander*).

xenoi Mercenaries.

xyston (**plur.** *xysta*) A cavalryman's thrusting spear.

Bibliography

Abe, Takuji. 2012. "Dascylium: An Overview of the Achaemenid Satrapal City." *Kyoto Journal of Ancient History* 12: 1–17.

Abramenko, Andrik. 1992a. "Die Verschwörung des Alexander Lynkestes und die 'μήτηρ τοῦ βασιλέως'. Zu Diodor XVII 32, 1." *Tyche* 7: 1–8.

———. 1992b. "Die zwei Seeschlachten vor Tyros. Zu den militärischen Voraussetzungen für die makedonische Eroberung der Inselfestung (332 v. Chr.)." *Klio* 74: 166–78.

———. 1994. "Alexander vor Mazagae und Aornus: Korrekturen zu den Berichten über das Massaker an den indischen Söldnern." *Klio* 76: 192–207.

Adams, W. L. 2003. "The Episode of Philotas: An Insight." In Heckel and Tritle, 113–26.

———. 2007. "The Games of Alexander the Great." In Heckel, Tritle, and Wheatley, 125–38.

Ager, S. 2018. "Building a Dynasty: The Families of Ptolemy Soter." In Howe 2018b, 36–59.

Akamatis, I. M. 2011. "Pella." In Lane Fox, 393–408.

Alonso Troncoso, V., and E. M. Anson, eds. 2013. *After Alexander: The Time of the Diadochi (323–282 B.C.)*. Oxford and Oakville.

Alonso-Núñez, José Miguel. 1992. *La historia universal de Pompeyo Trogo*. Madrid.

Ameling, W. 1988. "Alexander und Achilleus: Ein Bestandsaufnahme." *Zu Alex. d. Gr.*, 595–603.

———. 1990. "KOINON ΤΩΝ ΣΙΔΩΝΙΩΝ." *ZPE* 81: 189–99.

Amitay, O. 2008. "Why Did Alexander the Great Besiege Tyre?" *Athenaeum* 96: 91–102.

Anson, E. 1989. "The Persian Fleet in 334." *CP* 44: 44–49.

———. 1996. "The *Ephemerides* of Alexander the Great." *Historia* 45: 501–4.

———. 2013. *Alexander the Great: Themes and Issues.*

———. 2015a. "Alexander at the Beas." In Wheatley and Baynham, 65–74.

———. 2015b. "Counter-Insurgency: The Lesson of Alexander the Great." In Howe, Garvin, and Wrightson, 94–106.

———. 2015c. "'Shock and Awe' à la Alexander the Great." In Heckel, Müller, and Wrightson, 213–32.

Antela-Bernárdez, B. 2012. "Philip and Pausanias: A Deadly Love in Macedonian Politics." *CQ* 62: 423–39.

Archibald, Z. 2010. "Macedonia and Thrace." In Roisman and Worthington, 326–41.

Asheri, D., A. B. Lloyd, and A. Corcella. 2007. *A Commentary on Herodotus: Books I–IV.* Oxford.

Ashley, James R. 1998. *The Macedonian Empire: The Era of Warfare under Philip II and Alexander the Great, 359–323 B.C.* Jefferson, NC.

Atkinson, J. E., and M. Hammond. 2013. *Arrian. Alexander the Great. The* Anabasis *and the* Indica, translated by Martin Hammond, with notes by J. E. Atkinson. Oxford.

Atkinson, J. E., and J. C. Yardley. 2009. *Curtius Rufus. Histories of Alexander the Great. Book 10*. Introduction and historical commentary by J. E. Atkinson; translation by J. C. Yardley. Oxford.

Auberger, J. 2001. *Historiens d'Alexandre.* Paris.

Ausfeld, A. 1895. "Über das angebliche Testament Alexanders des Großen." *RhM* 50: 357–66.

———. 1901. "Das angebliche Testament Alexanders des Großen." *RhM* 56: 517–42.

Austin, M. M. 1993. "Alexander and the Macedonian Invasion of Asia: Aspects of the Historiography of War and Empire in Antiquity." In Rich and Shipley, 197–223.

Aymard, A. 1950. "Basileus Makedonon." *RIDA* 4: 61–97.

Badian, E. 1958. "The Eunuch Bagoas: A Study in Method." *CQ* 8: 144–57.

———. 1960. "The Death of Parmenio." *TAPA* 91: 324–38.

———. 1961. "Harpalus." *JHS* 81: 16–43.

———. 1963. "The Death of Philip II." *Phoenix* 17: 244–50.

———. 1966. "Alexander the Great and the Greeks of Asia Minor." In *Ancient Society and Institutions: Studies Presented to Victor Ehrenberg.* Oxford: 37–69.

———. 1967. "Agis III." *Hermes* 95: 170–92.

———. 1975. "Nearchus the Cretan." *YCS* 24: 147–70.

———, ed. 1976. *Alexandre le Grand. Image et réalité.* Geneva.

———. 1977a. "The Battle of the Granicus: A New Look." *AM* 2: 271–93.

———. 1977b. "A Document of Artaxerxes IV?" In Kinzl, 40–50.

———. 1981. "The Deification of Alexander the Great." In Dell, 27–71.

———. 1985. "Alexander in Iran." In *Cambridge History of Iran* II, edited by I. L. Gershevitch, 420–501. Cambridge.

———. 1987. "Alexander at Peucelaotis." *CQ* 37: 117–28.

———. 1994. "Agis III: Revisions and Reflections." In Worthington, 258–92.

———. 1996. "Alexander the Great between the Two Thrones and Heaven: Variations on an Old Theme." *Journal of Roman Archaeology* supp. 17: 11–26.

———. 1999. "A Note on the 'Alexander Mosaic.'" In Titchener and Moorton, 75–92.

———. 2000a. "Conspiracies." In Bosworth and Baynham, 50–95.

———. 2000b. "Darius III." *HSCP* 100: 241–68.

———. 2007. "Once More the Death of Philip II." *AM* 7: 389–406.

———. 2012. *The Collected Papers on Alexander the Great.* London and New York.

Bagnall, R. S. 1979. "The Date of the Foundation of Alexandria in Egypt." *AJAH* 4: 46–49.

Bakir, T. 1995. "Archäologische Beobachtungen über die Residenz in Daskyleion." In Briant, 269–85.

———. 2006. "Daskyleion." *Byzas* 3: 61–71.

Balcer, J. M. 1978. "Alexander's Burning of Persepolis." *Iranica Antiqua* 13: 119–33.

Baldus, H. R. 1987. "Die Siegel Alexanders des Großen. Versuch einer Rekonstruktion auf literarischer und numismatischer Grundlage." *Chiron* 17: 395–449.

Barnes, T. D. 1991. "Latin Literature between Diocletian and Ambrose." *Phoenix* 45: 341–55.

Bartlett, B. 2014. "Justin's Epitome: The Unlikely Adaptation of Trogus' World History." *Histos* 8: 246–83.

Bauer, A. 1899. "Die Schlacht bei Issos." *Öst. Jb.* II: 105–28.

Baumbach, A. 1911. *Kleinasien unter Alexander dem Großen.* Weida.

Baynham, Elizabeth. 1995. "An Introduction to the Metz Epitome: Its Traditions and Value." *Antichthon* 29: 60–77.

———. 1998. *Alexander the Great: The Unique History of Quintus Curtius Rufus.* Ann Arbor.

———. 2015. "Cleomenes of Naucratis: Villain or Victim?" In Howe, Garvin, and Wrightson, 127–34.

Bean, George E. 1971. *Turkey beyond the Maeander.* London.

Bearzot, C. 1987. "La tradizione su Parmenione negli storici di Alessandro." *Aevum* 61: 89–104.

Beckwith, C. 2009. *Empires of the Silk Road.* Princeton.

Bellinger, A. 1963. *Essays on the Coinage of Alexander the Great.* ANS Numismatic Studies 11. New York.

Bernhardt, R. 1988. "Zu den Verhandlungen zwischen Dareios und Alexander nach der Schlacht bei Issos." *Chiron* 18: 181–98.

Berthold, Richard M. 1984. *Rhodes in the Hellenistic Age.* Ithaca and London.

Bettenworth, Anja. 2016. "'Jetzt büßten die Nachfahren die Schuld ihrer Ahnen.' Das Problem der Branchidenepisode bei Curtius Rufus." In Wulfram, 189–208.

Bickerman, E 1963. "À propos d'un passage de Chares de Mytilène." *La Parola del Passato* 18: 241–55.

———. 1988. *The Jews in the Greek Age.* Cambridge, MA.

Billows, Richard A. 1990. *Antigonos the One-Eyed and the Creation of the Hellenistic State.* Berkeley and Los Angeles.

———. 2000. "Polybius and the Alexander Historiography." In Bosworth and Baynham, 286–306.

———. 2018. *Before and After Alexander: The Legend and Legacy of Alexander the Great.* New York and London.

Bing, Daniel J. 1998. "Datames and Mazaeus: The Iconography of Revolt and Restoration in Cilicia." *Historia* 47: 41–76.

Blackwell, C. 1999. *In the Absence of Alexander: Harpalus and the Failure of Macedonian Authority.* Bonn.

Blänsdorf, J. 1971. "Herodot bei Curtius Rufus." *Hermes* 99: 11–24.

Blocdow, Edmund F. 1991. "Alexander the Great and Those Sogdianaean Horses: Prelude to Hellenism in Bactria-Sogdiana." In Seibert, 17–32.

———. 1995. "Diplomatic Negotiations between Darius and Alexander: Historical Implications of the First Phase at Marathus in Phoenicia 333/332 BC." *AHB* 9: 93–110.

———. 1996. "On 'Wagons' and 'Shields': Alexander's Crossing of Mount Haemus in 335 B.C." *AHB* 10: 119–30.

———. 1998. "The Siege of Tyre in 332 BC: Alexander at the Crossroads in His Career." *La Parola del Passato* 73: 255–93.

———. 2002. "On the Crossing of Rivers: Alexander's διφθέραι." *Klio* 84: 57–75.

———. 2003. "Why Did Philip and Alexander Launch a War against the Persian Empire?" *L'Antiquité Classique* 72: 261–74.

———. 2004. "Egypt in Alexander's Scheme of Things." *Quaderni Urbinati di Cultura Classica* 77: 75–99.

Bonnet, C. 1988. *Melqart. Cultes et mythes de l'Héracles Tyrien en Méditerranée.* Leuven.

Borza, E. N. 1967. "Alexander and the Return from Siwah." *Historia* 16: 369.

———. 1971. "The End of Agis' Revolt." *CP* 66: 230–35 = Borza 1995, 201–10.

———. 1972. "Fire from Heaven: Alexander at Persepolis." *CP* 67: 233–45 = Borza 1995, 217–38.

———. 1990. *In the Shadow of Olympus: The Emergence of Macedon.* Princeton.

———. 1995. *Makedonika: Essays by Eugene N. Borza*, edited by Carol G. Thomas. Claremont, CA

Borza, E. N., and J. Reames-Zimmerman. 2000. "Some New Thoughts on the Death of Alexander the Great." *AncW* 31: 22–30.

Bosworth, A. B. 1970. "Aristotle and Callisthenes." *Historia* 19: 407–13.

———. 1971a. "The Death of Alexander the Great: Rumour and Propaganda." *CQ* 21: 112–36.

———. 1971b. "Philip II and Upper Macedonia." *CQ* 21: 93–105.

———. 1974. "The Government of Syria under Alexander the Great." *CQ* 24: 46–64.

———. 1975. "The Mission of Amphoterus and the Outbreak of Agis' War." *Phoenix* 29: 27–43.

———. 1976. "Arrian and the Alexander Vulgate." In Badian, 1–33.

———. 1980. "Alexander and the Iranians." *JHS* 100: 1–21.

———. 1981. "A Missing Year in the History of Alexander the Great." *JHS* 101: 17–39.

———. 1982. "The Location of Alexander's Campaign against the Illyrians in 335 B.C." In Barr-Sharrar and Borza, 75–84.

———. 1983. "The Indian Satrapies under Alexander the Great." *Antichthon* 17: 36–46.

———. 1988a. *Conquest and Empire: The Reign of Alexander the Great.* Cambridge.

———. 1988b. *From Arrian to Alexander.* Oxford.

———. 1996. *Alexander and the East: The Tragedy of Triumph.* Oxford.

———. 2000. "Ptolemy and the Will of Alexander." In Bosworth and Baynham, 207–41.

———. 2010. "The Argeads and the Phalanx." In Carney and Ogden, 91–102.

Bosworth, A. B., and E. J. Baynham (eds.). 2000. *Alexander the Great in Fact and Fiction.* Oxford.

Bottéro, Jean. 1992. *Mesopotamia: Writing, Reasoning, and the Gods.* Chicago.

Bowden, H. 2013. "On Kissing and Making Up: Court Protocol and Historiography in Alexander the Great's Experiment with *Proskynesis." BICS* 56: 55–77.

———. 2017a. "The Argeads and Greek Sanctuaries." In Müller et al., 164–82.

———. 2017b. "The Eagle Has Landed: Divination in the Alexander Historians." In Howe, Müller, and Stoneman, 149–68.

———. 2018. "Alexander as Achilles: Arrian's Use of Homer from Troy to the Granikos." In Howe and Pownall, 163–79.

Boyce, Mary. 1979. *Zoroastrians: Their Religious Beliefs and Practices.* London.

Breloer, B. 1933. *Alexanders Kampf gegen Poros.* Stuttgart.

———. 1941. *Alexanders Bund mit Poros. Indien von Dareios zu Sandrokottos.* Leipzig.

Briant, P. 1973. *Antigone le Borgne.* Paris.

———. 1976. " 'Brigandage', dissidence et conquête en Asie achéménide et hellénistique." *DHA* 2: 163–258.

———. 1984. *L'Asie centrale et les royaumes proche-orientaux du premier millenaire (c. VIIIe–IVe siècles avant nôtre ère).* Paris.

———, ed. 1995. *Dans les pays de Dix-Mille: Peuples et pays du proche-Orient vus par un grec: Actes de las Table Ronde Internationale, organisé à l'initiative du GRACO, Toulouse, 3–4 février 1995.* Toulouse.

———. 1999. "The Achaemenid Empire." In Raaflaub and Rosenstein, 105–28.

———. 2008. *Lettre ouverte à Alexandre le Grand.* Arles.

———. 2010. *Alexander the Great and his Empire.* Translated by Amélie Kuhrt. Princeton.

———. 2015. *Darius in the Shadow of Alexander,* translated by Jane Marie Todd. Cambridge, MA, and London.

Brice, Lee L. 2015. "Insurgency and Terrorism in the Ancient World, Grounding the Discussion." In Howe and Brice, 3–27.

Brosius, M. 2003. "Alexander and the Persians." In Roisman, 169–93.

———. 2006. *The Persians.* London.

———. 2007. "New out of Old? Court and Court Ceremonies in Achaemenid Persia." In Spawforth, 17–57.

Brown, B. R. 1978. "Deinokrates and Alexandria." *BASP* 15: 39–42.

Brown, T. S. 1949a. "Callisthenes and Alexander." *AJP* 70: 225–48.

———. 1949b. *Onesicritus: A Study in Hellenistic Historiography.* Berkeley and Los Angeles.

———. 1950. "Clitarchus." *AJP* 71: 134–55.

———. 1973. *The Greek Historians.* Lexington.

Bruce, I. A. F. 1967. *A Historical Commentary on the "Hellenica Oxyrhynchia."* Cambridge.

Brundage, B. C. 1958. "Herakles the Levantine: A Comprehensive View." *JNES* 1: 225 ff.

Brunt, P. A. 1962. "Persian Accounts of Alexander's Campaigns." *CQ* 12: 141–55.

———. 1975. "Alexander, Barsine and Heracles." *RFIC* 103: 27–46.

Buck, R. J. 1994. *Boiotia and the Boiotian League.* Edmonton.

Buckler, J. 1980. *The Theban Hegemony, 371–362 BC.* Cambridge, MA.

———. 1982. "Alliance and Hegemony in Fourth-Century Greece: The Case of the Theban Hegemony." *AncW* 5: 79–89.

———. 1989. *Philip II and the Sacred War.* Supplements to *Mnemosyne* 109. Leiden.

———. 1994. "Philip II, the Greeks, and the King 346–336 B.C." *Illinois Classical Studies* 19: 99–111.

———. 2003. *Aegean Greece in the Fourth Century B.C.* Leiden.

Burn, A. R. 1952. "Notes on Alexander's Campaigns, 332–330." *JHS* 72: 81–91.

———. 1973. *Alexander the Great and the Middle East.* Harmondsworth.

———. 1984. *Persia and the Greeks,* edited by D. M. Lewis. Palo Alto.

Burstein, S. M. 1991. "Pharaoh Alexander: A Scholarly Myth." *Anc. Soc.* 22: 139–45.

———. 1994. "Alexander in Egypt: Continuity or Change." *Achaemenid History* 8: 381–87.

———. 1999. "Cleitarchus in Jerusalem." In Titchener and Moorton, 105–12.

———. 2000. "Prelude to Alexander the Great: The Reign of Khababash." *AHB* 14: 149–54.

Cahill, N. 1985. "The Treasury at Persepolis: Gift-Giving at the City of the Persians." *AJA* 89: 373–89.

Cannadine, D., and S. Price, eds. 1987. *Rituals of Royalty: Power and Ceremonial in Traditional Societies.* Cambridge.

Capomacchia, Anna Maria G. 1986. *Semiramis una femminilità ribaltata.* Rome.

Cargill, J. 1981. *The Second Athenian League: Empire or Free Alliance?* Berkeley and Los Angeles.

———. 1982. "Hegemony Not Empire: The Second Athenian League." *AncW* 5: 91–102.

Carlsen, J. 1993. "Alexander the Great (1970–1990)." In Carlsen et al., 41–52.

Carlsen, J., et al., eds. 1993. *Alexander the Great: Reality and Myth.* Rome.

Carney, E. D. 1980. "Alexander the Lyncestian: The Disloyal Opposition." *GRBS* 20: 23–33 [= Carney, *King and Court* 127–37].

———. 1981. "The Death of Clitus." *GRBS* 22: 149–60 [= Carney, *King and Court* 141–54].

———. 1983. "Regicide in Macedonia." *La Parola del Passato* 211: 60–72 [= Carney, *King and Court* 155–65].

———. 1992. "The Politics of Polygamy: Olympias, Alexander and the Murder of Philip II." *Historia* 41: 169–89 [= Carney, *King and Court* 167–90].

———. 1996a. "Alexander and Persian Women." *AJP* 117: 563–83.

———. 1996b. "Macedonians and Mutiny: Discipline and Indiscipline in the Army of Philip and Alexander." *CP* 91: 19–44.

———. 2000a. "Artifice and Alexander History." In Bosworth and Baynham, 263–85.

———. 2000b. *Women and Monarchy in Macedonia*. Norman, OK.

———. 2003. "Elite Education and High Culture in Macedonia." In Heckel and Tritle, 47–63 [= Carney, *King and Court* 191–204].

———. 2005. "Women and Dunasteia in Caria." *AJP* 126: 65–91.

———. 2006. *Olympias*. London and New York.

———. 2007a. "The Philippeum, Women, and the Formation of Dynastic Image." In Heckel, Tritle, and Wheatley, 27–60 [= Carney, *King and Court* 61–90].

———. 2008. "The Role of the *Basilikoi Paides* at the Argead Court." In Howe and Reames, 145–64 [= Carney, *King and Court* 207–23].

———. 2019. *Eurydice and the Birth of Macedonian Power*. Oxford.

Carney, Elizabeth, and Daniel Ogden, eds. 2010. *Philip II and Alexander the Great: Father and Son, Lives and Afterlives*. Oxford.

Caroe, O. 1962. *The Pathans 550 BC–AD 1957*. London.

Carstens, Anne Marie. 2009. *Karia and the Hekatomnids. The Creation of a Dynasty*. BAR International Series 1943. Oxford.

Cartledge, Paul. 1987. *Agesilaos and the Crisis of Sparta*. Baltimore.

———. 2004. *Alexander the Great: The Hunt for a New Past*. New York.

Cartledge, Paul, and Fiona Greenland, eds. 2010. *Responses to Oliver Stone's Alexander: Film, History, and Cultural Studies*. Madison.

Cartledge, P., and A. Spawforth. 2002. *Hellenistic and Roman Sparta: A Tale of Two Cities*. London and New York.

Cauer, F. 1894. *Philotas, Kleitos, Kallisthenes: Beiträge zur Geschichte Alexanders des Grossen.Jahrbücher für classische Philologie*, Supplbd. 20.

Cawkwell, G. L. 1969. "The Crowning of Demosthenes." *CQ* 19: 161–80.

———. 1976. "Agesilaus and Sparta." *CQ* 26: 62–84.

———. 2005. *The Greek Wars: The Failure of Persia*. Oxford.

Chambers, J. 2003. *The Devil's Horsemen: The Mongol Invasion of Europe*. Edison, NJ.

Charles, Michael B. 2008. "Alexander, Elephants and Gaugamela." *Mouseion* 8: 9–23.

———. 2012. "The Persian ΚΑΡΔΑΚΕΣ." *JHS* 132: 7–21.

———. 2015. "The Chiliarchs of Achaemenid Persia: Towards a Revised Understanding of the Office." *Phoenix* 69: 279–303.

Clark, J. H., and B. Turner, eds. 2017. *Brill's Companion to Military Defeat in Ancient Mediterranean Society*. Leiden.

Clark, L. P. 1923. "Unconscious Motives Underlying the Personalities of Great Statesmen and Their Relation to Epoch-Making Events, III, The Narcism [*sic*] of Alexander the Great." *Psychoanalytic Reveiw* 10: 56–69.

Clauss, Manfred. 1983. *Sparta. Eine Einführung in seine Geschichte und Zivilisation.* Munich.

Clayton, Peter, and Martin Price, eds. 1988. *The Seven Wonders of the Ancient World.* New York.

Collins, A. W. 2001. "The Office of Chiliarch under Alexander and the Successors." *Phoenix* 55: 259–83.

———. 2013. "Alexander the Great and the Kingship of Babylon." *AHB* 27: 130–48.

———. 2017. "The Persian Royal Tent and Ceremonial of Alexander the Great." *CQ* 67: 71–76.

Cohen, S. J. D. 1982–83. "Alexander the Great and Jaddus the High Priest according to Josephus." *Association for Jewish Studies Review* 7–8: 41–68.

Cohen, Warren I. 2000. *East Asia at the Center: Four Thousand Years of Engagement with the World.* New York.

Cook, J. M. 1983. *The Persian Empire.* New York.

Corssen, P. 1917. "Das angebliche Werk des Olynthiers Kallisthenes." *Philologus* 74: 1–57.

Cowley, Robert, ed. 1999. *What If?* New York.

Cross, G. N. 1932. *Epirus: A Study in Greek Constitutional Development.* Cambridge.

Cummings, Lewis V. 2004. *Alexander the Great.* New York.

Cuyler Young, T., Jr. 1980. "480/479 B.C.: A Persian Perspective." *IA* 15: 213–239.

Dahmen, Karsten. 2007. *The Legend of Alexander the Great on Greek and Roman Coins.* London and New York.

Dandamaev, M. A. 1989. *A Political History of the Achaemenid Empire*, translated by W. J. Vogelsang. Leiden.

Daryaee, T., ed. 2012. *The Oxford Handbook of Iranian History.* Oxford.

Davies, Iolo. 1998. "Alexander's Itinerary." *AHB* 12: 29–54.

Davis, Paul K. 2003. *Besieged: 100 Great Sieges from Jericho to Sarajevo.* Oxford.

Delbrück, H. 1990. *History of the Art of War.* 4 vols. Translated by Walter J. Renfroe, Jr. Lincoln.

Dell, H. J. 1970. "The Western Frontier of the Macedonian Monarchy." *AM* 1: 115–26.

———. 1980. "Philip and Macedonia's Northern Neighbors." In Hatzopoulos and Loukopoulos, 90–99.

———, ed. 1981. *Ancient Macedonian Studies in Honor of Charles F. Edson.* Thessaloniki.

Delling, G. 1981. "Alexander der Grosse als Bekenner des Jüdischen Gottesglaubens." *Journal for the Study of Judaism in the Persian, Hellenistic and Roman World* 12: 1–51.

Depuydt, Leo. 1997. "The Time of Death of Alexander the Great: 11 June 323 B.C. (−322), ca. 4:00–5:00 P.M." *WO* 28: 117–35.

De Souza, Philip. 2003. *The Greek and Persian Wars 499–386 BC.* Oxford: Osprey.

Develin, R. 1981. "The Murder of Philip II." *Antichthon* 15: 86–99.

Devine, A. M. 1975. "Grand Tactics at Gaugamela." *Phoenix.* 29: 374–85.

———. 1980. "The Location of the Battle of Issus." *Liverpool Classical Monthly* 4: 3–10.

———. 1984. "The Location of Castabalum and Alexander's Route from Mallus to Myriandrus." *Acta Classica* 27: 127–29.

———. 1985a. "Grand Tactics at the Battle of Issus." *AncW* 12: 39–59.

———. 1985b. "The Strategies of Alexander the Great and Darius III in the Issus Campaign (333 BC)." *AncW* 12: 25–38.

———. 1986a. "The Battle of Gaugamela: A Tactical and Source-Critical Study." *AncW* 13: 87–115.

———. 1986a. "Demythologizing the Battle of the Granicus." *Phoenix* 40: 265–78.

———. 1987. "The Battle of the Hydaspes: A Tactical and Source-Critical Study." *AncW* 16: 91–113.

———. 1988. "A Pawn-Sacrifice at the Battle of the Granicus, the Origins of a Favourite Stratagem of Alexander the Great." *AncW* 18: 3–20.

———. 1989. "The Macedonian Army at Gaugamela: Its Strength and the Length of Its Battle-Line." *AncW* 19: 77–80.

———. 1994. "Alexander's Propaganda Machine: Callisthenes as the Ultimate Source for Arrian, *Anabasis* 1–3." In Worthington, 89–103.

Dietrich, M., and O. Loretz, eds. 1993. *Vom Alten Orient zum Alten Testament.* Neukirchen-Vluyn.

Dittberner, W. 1908. *Issos, ein Beitrag zur Geschichte Alexanders des Grossen.* Berlin.

Dodge, T. A. 1890. *Alexander: A History of the Origin and Growth of the Art of War from the Earliest Times to the Battle of Ipsus, 301 BC, with a Detailed Account of the Campaigns of Alexander the Great Macedonian.* Boston.

Dreyer, Boris. 2009. "Heroes, Cults, and Divinity." In Heckel and Tritle, 218–34.

Dusinberre, Elspeth R. M. 2013. *Empire, Authority and Autonomy in Achaemenid Anatolia.* Cambridge.

Eddy, Samuel K. 1973. "The Cold War between Athens and Persia, ca. 448–412 B.C." *CP* 68: 241–258.

Edmunds, L. 1971. "The Religiosity of Alexander the Great." *GRBS* 12: 363–91.

Eggermont, P. H. L. 1970. "Alexander's Campaign in Gandhara and Ptolemy's List of Indo-Scythian Towns." *OLP* 1: 63–123.

———. 1975. *Alexander's Campaign in Sind and the Siege of the Brahmin Town of Harmatelia.* Leuven.

———. 1984. "Ptolemy the Geographer and the People of the Dards." *OLP* 15: 191–233.

———. 1993. *Alexander's Campaign in Southern Punjab.* Leuven.

Ehrhardt, C. 1967. "Two Notes on Philip of Macedon's First Interventions in Thessaly." *CQ* 17: 296–301.

Elayi, J. 2013. *Histoire de la Phénicie.* Paris.

Ellis, J. R. 1971. "Amyntas Perdikka, Philip II and Alexander the Great: A Study in Conspiracy." *JHS* 91: 15–24.

———. 1976. *Philip II and Macedonian Imperialism.* Princeton.

Endres, H. 1924. *Geographischer Horizont und Politik bei Alexander den Grossen in den Jahren 330–323.* Würzburg.

308 Bibliography

Engels, D. W. 1978a. *Alexander the Great and the Logistics of the Macedonian Army.* Berkeley and Los Angeles.

———. 1978b. "A Note on Alexander's Death." *CP* 73: 224–28.

English. S. 2009. *The Sieges of Alexander the Great.* Barnsley.

———. 2011. *The Field Campaigns of Alexander the Great.* Barnsley.

Errington, R. M. 1969. "Bias in Ptolemy's History of Alexander." *CQ* 19: 233–42.

———. 1974. "Macedonian Royal Style and Its Significance." *JHS* 94: 20–37.

———. 1975. "Arybbas the Molossian." *GRBS* 16: 41–50.

———. 1976. "Alexander in the Hellenistic World." In Badian, 137–79.

Erskine, A., and L. Llewellyn-Jones, eds. 2011. *Creating a Hellenistic World.* Swansea.

Erzen, Afif. 1940. *Kilikien bis zum Ende der Perserherrschaft.* Leipzig.

Fawcett, B. 2006. "The Battle of Arbela." In B. Fawcett, ed. *How to Lose a Battle. Foolish Plans and Great Military Blunders.* New York: 1–10.

Fears, J. Rufus. 1975. "Pausanias, the Assassin of Philip II." *Athenaeum* 53: 111–35.

Fischer, Klaus. 1987. "Bessos im Gelände zwischen Areia und Bactria. Landschaft und Siedlung an Wegestrecken der Zeit Alexanders III. von Makedonien." *Zu Alex. d. Gr.* 1: 457–66.

Flower, M. A. 2000. "Alexander the Great and Panhellenism." In Bosworth and Baynham, 96–135.

Foss, C. 1977. "The Battle of the Granicus: A New Look." *AM* 2: 495–502.

Foucher, A. 1902. *Notes sur la géographie du Gandhāra.* Hanoi.

Fraenkel, A. 1883. *Die Quellen der Alexanderhistoriker.* Breslau.

Franke, P. R. 1992. "Dolmetschen in hellenistischer Zeit." In Müller, Sier and Werner, 85–96.

Franz, D. 2009. "Kriegsfinanzierung Alexanders des Großen." In Müller, 115–50.

Fraser, P. M. 1972. *Ptolemaic Alexandria,* 3 vols. Oxford.

———. 1996. *Cities of Alexander the Great.* Oxford.

French, V., and P. Dixon. 1986. "The Pixodarus Affair: Another View." *AncW* 13: 73–82.

Frye, R. N. 1972. "Gestures of Deference to Royalty in Ancient Iran." *Iranica Antiqua* 9: 102–7.

———. 1984. *The History of Ancient Iran.* Munich.

Fuller, J. F. C. 1958. *The Generalship of Alexander the Great.* London.

Funke, S. 2000. *Aiakidenmythos und epeirotisches Königtum.* Stuttgart.

Gaebel, Robert E. 2002. *Cavalry Operations in the Ancient Greek World.* Norman, OK.

Galewicz, C., J. Pstrusińska, and L. Sudyka, eds. 2007. *Understanding Eurasia from Ancient Times to the Present Day.* Krakow.

Garnand, B. 2002. "From Infant Sacrifice to the ABC's: Ancient Phoenicians and Modern Identities." *Stanford Journal of Archaeology.* Online.

———. 2006. "The Use of Phoenician Human Sacrifice in the Formation of Ethnic Identities." PhD diss., University of Chicago.

Geissendörfer, Dieter. 1967. "Die Quellen der Metzer Epitome." *Philologus* 111: 258–66.

Golan, D. 1988. "The Fate of a Court Historian: Callisthenes." *Athenaeum* 66: 99–120.

Goukowsky, P. 1972. "Le Rôi Poros et son éléphant." *BCH* 96: 473–502.

Graf, D. F. 1994. "The Persian Royal Road System." *Achaemenid History* 8: 167–89.

Grainger, John D. 1991. *Hellenistic Phoenicia*. Oxford.

———. 2007. *Alexander the Great Failure*. London.

Graninger, D. 2010. "Macedonia and Thessaly." In Roisman and Worthington, 306–25.

Grant, David. 2017. *In Search of the Lost Testament of Alexander the Great*. Dexter, MI.

Graßl, H. 1987. "Alexander der Große und die Zerstörung Thebens." *Zu Alex. d. Gr.* 1: 271–78.

Grayson, A. K. 1993. "Eunuchs in Power: Their Role in the Assyrian Bureaucracy." In Dietrich and Loretz, 85–98.

Green, P. 1991. *Alexander of Macedon, 356–323 B.C.: A Historical Biography*. Berkeley and Los Angeles. [Originally published Harmondsworth, 1974.]

———. 2003. "Politics, Philosophy, and Propaganda: Hermias of Atarneus and His Friendship with Aristotle." In Heckel and Tritle, 29–46.

Greenwalt, W. S. 1982. "A Macedonian Mantis." *AncW* 5: 17–25.

———. 1988. "Amyntas III and the Political Stability of Argead Macedonia." *AncW* 18: 35–44.

———. 1999. "Why Pella?" *Historia* 48: 453–62.

———. 2010. "Macedonia, Illyria and Epirus." In Roisman and Worthington, 279–305.

Griffith, G. T 1947. "Alexander's Generalship at Gaugamela." *JHS* 67: 77–89.

Groningen, B. A. van. 1925. "De Cleomene Naucratita." *Mnemosyne* 53: 101–30.

Gruhn, A. 1905. *Das Schlachtfeld von Issos. Eine Widerlegung der Ansicht Jankes*. Jena.

Guthrie, W. K. C. 1981. *A History of Greek Philosophy*, VI: *Aristotle: An Encounter*. Cambridge.

Gutschmid, A. von. 1882. "Trogus und Timagenes." *RhM* 37: 548–55.

Habicht, C. 1970. *Gottmenschentum und griechische Städte*, 2nd ed. Munich.

Hackmann, F. 1902. *Die Schlacht bei Gaugamela*. Halle.

Hall, Edith. 1989. *Inventing the Barbarian: Greek Self-Definition through Tragedy*. Oxford.

Hall, Jonathan. 2002. *Hellenicity: Between Ethnicity and Culture*. Chicago.

Hall, Katherine. 2018. "Did Alexander the Great Die from Guillain-Barré Syndrome?" *AHB* 32: 106–28.

Hamilton, Charles D. 1979. *Sparta's Bitter Victories*. Ithaca and London.

———. 1982. "Agesilaus and the Failure of Spartan Hegemony." *AncW* 5: 67–78.

———. 1991. *Agesilaus and the Failure of Spartan Hegemony*. Ithaca, NY.

Hamilton, Charles D., and Peter Krentz, eds. 1997. *Polis and Polemos: Essays on Politics, War, and History in Ancient Greece in Honor of Donald Kagan*. Claremont, CA.

Hamilton, J. R. 1953. "Alexander and His So-Called Father." *CQ* 3: 151–57.

———. 1956. "The Cavalry Battle at the Hydaspes." *JHS* 76: 26–31.

———. 1965. "Alexander's Early Life." *Greece & Rome* 12: 117–24.

———. 1971. "Alexander and the Aral." *CQ* 21: 106–11.

————. 1973. *Alexander the Great*. London.

————. 1984. "The Origins of Ruler-Cult." *Prudentia* 16: 3–16.

Hammond, N. G. L. 1966. "The Kingdoms of Illyria *circa* 400–167 B.C." *ABSA* 61: 239–53.

————. 1967. *Epirus*. Oxford.

————. 1974. "Alexander's Campaigns in Illyria." *JHS* 94: 66–87.

————. 1978. "'Philip's Tomb' in Historical Context." *GRBS* 19: 331–50.

————. 1980a. "The Battle of the Granicus River." *JHS* 100: 73–88.

————. 1980b. "The March of Alexander the Great on Thebes in 335 B.C." In Μέγας Ἀλέξανδρος 2000 χρόνια ἀπὸ τὸν θάνατόν, 171–81. Thessaloniki.

————. 1981. *Alexander the Great: King, Commander, Statesman*. London.

————. 1983. *Three Historians of Alexander the Great*. Cambridge.

————. 1986. "The Kingdom of Asia and the Persian Throne." *Antichthon* 20: 73–85.

————. 1988. "The royal journal of Alexander." *Historia* 37: 129–50.

————. 1990. "Royal Pages, Personal Pages and Boys Trained in the Macedonian Manner during the Period of the Temenid Monarchy." *Historia* 39: 261–90.

————. 1991a. "The Macedonian Defeat Near Samarcand." *AncW* 22: 41–47.

————. 1991b. "The Various Guards of Philip II and Alexander III." *Historia* 40: 396–418.

————. 1992a. "Alexander's Charge at the Battle of Issus in 333 B.C." *Historia* 41: 395–406.

————. 1992b. "The Archaeological Evidence for the Burning of the Persepolis Palace." *CQ* 42: 358–64.

————. 1993. *Sources for Alexander the Great: An Analysis of Plutarch's* Life *and Arrian's* Anabasis Alexandrou. Cambridge.

————. 1994a. "Illyrians and North-West Greeks." In *CAH²* VI 422–43.

————. 1994b. "One or Two Passes at the Cilicia-Syria Border?" *AncW* 25: 15–26.

————. 1994c. *Philip of Macedon*. Baltimore.

————. 1995. "Did Alexander Use One or Two Seals?" *Chiron* 25: 199–203.

————. 1998. "The Branchidae at Didyma and in Sogdiana." *CQ* 48: 339–44.

Hampl, F. 1954. "Alexander der Große und die Beurteilung geschichtlicher Persönlichkeiten in der modernen Historiographie." *La Nouvelle Clio* 6: 91–136.

Hanson, Victor Davis. 2005. *A War Like No Other: How the Athenians and Spartans Fought the Peloponnesian War*. New York.

Harden, D. 1963. *The Phoenicians*, rev. ed. London.

Harl, Kenneth W. 1997. "Alexander's Cavalry Battle at the Granicus." In Hamilton and Krentz, 303–26.

Hatzopoulos, M. B., and L. D. Loukopoulos, eds. 1980. *Philip of Macedon*. Athens.

Hauben, H. 1970. "The King of the Sidonians and the Persian Imperial Fleet." *Anc. Soc.* 1: 1–8.

————. 1972. "The Command Structure in Alexander's Mediterranean Fleets." *Anc. Soc.* 3: 55–65.

————. 1976. "The Expansion of Macedonian Sea-Power under Alexander the Great." *Anc. Soc.* 7: 79–105.

———. 1977. "Rhodes, Alexander and the Diadochi from 333/332 to 304 B.C." *Historia* 26: 307–39.

Hauben, H., and A. Meeus, eds. 2014. *The Age of the Successors and the Creation of the Hellenistic Kingdoms (323–276 B.C.)*. Leuven.

Heckel, W. 1977a. "Asandros." *AJP* 98: 410–12.

———. 1977b. "The Conspiracy *against* Philotas." *Phoenix* 31: 9–21.

———. 1978. "Leonnatos, Polyperchon and the Introduction of *Proskynesis*." *AJP* 99: 459–61.

———. 1980a. "Alexander at the Persian Gates." *Athenaeum* 58: 168–74.

———. 1980b. "Marsyas of Pella: Historian of Macedon." *Hermes* 108: 444–62.

———. 1981a. "Philip and Olympias (337/6 B.C.)." In Shrimpton and McCargar, 51–57.

———. 1981b. "Polyxena, the Mother of Alexander the Great." *Chiron* 11: 79–86.

———. 1981c. "Some Speculations on the Prosopography of the *Alexanderreich*." *LCM* 6: 63–70.

———. 1982. "Who Was Hegelochos?" *RhM* 125: 78–87.

———. 1986. "Chorienes and Sisimithres." *Athenaeum* 74: 223–26.

———. 1988. *The Last Days and Testament of Alexander the Great: A Prosopographic Study*. Historia Einzelschriften. Heft 56. Stuttgart.

———. 1992. *The Marshals of Alexander's Empire*. London and New York.

———. 1994. "Notes on Q. Curtius Rufus' *History of Alexander*." *Acta Classica* 37 67–78.

———. 1997. "Resistance to Alexander the Great." In Tritle, 189–227.

———. 2002. "The Case of the Missing Phrourarch: Arr. 3.16.6-9." *AHB* 16: 57–60.

———. 2003a. "Alexander the Great and the Limits of the 'Civilised World.'" In Heckel and Tritle, 147–74.

———. 2003b. "King and 'Companions': Observations on the Nature of Power in the Reign of Alexander." In Roisman, 197–225.

———. 2005. "*Synaspismos*, Sarissas and Thracian Wagons." *Acta Classica* 48: 189–94.

———. 2006. "Mazaeus, Callisthenes and the Alexander Sarcophagus." *Historia* 55: 385–96.

———. 2007. "The Earliest Evidence for the Plot to Poison Alexander." In Heckel, Tritle and Wheatley, 265–75.

———. 2008. *The Conquests of Alexander the Great*. Cambridge.

———. 2015. "Alexander, Achilles, and Heracles: Between Myth and History." In Wheatley and Baynham, 21–33.

———. 2017a. "Dareios III's Military Reforms before Gaugamela and the Alexander Mosaic: A Note." *AHB* 31: 65–69.

———. 2017b. "Geography and Politics in Argead Makedonia." In Müller et al., 67–78.

———. 2017c. "Was Sibyrtios Ever Satrap of Karmania?" *Anabasis* 8: 36–41.

———. 2018a. "Ptolemy: A Man of His Own Making." In Howe, 1–19.

Heckel, W. 2018b. "Artabazus in the Lands beyond the Caspian." *Anabasis* 9: 93–109.

Heckel, W., Timothy Howe, and Sabine Müller. 2017. "'The Giver of the Bride, the Bridegroom, and the Bride': A Study of the Murder of Philip II and Its Aftermath." In Howe, Müller, and Stoneman, 92–124.

Heckel, W., and J. L. McLeod. 2015. "Alexander the Great and the Fate of the Enemy: Quantifying, Qualifying and Categorizing Atrocities." In Heckel, Müller and Wrightson, 233–67.

Heckel, W., S. Müller, and G. Wrightson, eds. 2015. *The Many Faces of War in the Ancient World*. Newcastle upon Tyne.

* Heckel, W., and L. Tritle, eds. 2003. *Crossroads of History: The Age of Alexander*. Claremont, CA.

* ———, eds. 2009. *Alexander the Great: A New History*. Oxford and Malden.

* Heckel, W., L. Tritle, and P. Wheatley, eds. 2007. *Alexander's Empire: Formulation to Decay*. Claremont, CA.

Heckel, W., C. Willekes, and G. Wrightson. 2010. "Scythed Chariots at Gaugamela: A Case Study." In Carney and Ogden, 103–9, 272–75.

Heckel, W., and J. C. Yardley. 1981. "Roman Writers and the Indian Practice of Suttee." *Philologus* 125: 305–11.

———. 1984. *Quintus Curtius Rufus: The History of Alexander*, translated by J. C. Yardley, notes and introduction by W. Heckel. Harmondsworth.

Heisserer, A. J. 1980. *Alexander the Great and the Greeks: The Epigraphic Evidence*. Norman, OK.

Herzfeld, Ernst. 1968. *The Persian Empire: Studies in Geography and Ethnography of the Ancient Near East*, edited from the posthumous papers by Gerold Walser. Wiesbaden.

Heskel, J. 1988. "The Political Background to the Arybbas Decree." *GRBS* 29: 185–96.

Higgins, W. E. 1980. "Aspects of Alexander's Imperial Administration: Some Modern Methods and Views Reviewed." *Athenaeum* 48: 129–52.

Höbl, G. 2001. *A History of the Ptolemaic Empire*. London and New York.

Högemann, Peter. 1985. *Alexander der Große und Arabien*. Zetemata, Heft 82. Munich.

Holt, F. L. 1982. "The Hyphasis 'Mutiny': A Source Study." *AncW* 5: 33–59.

———. 1988. *Alexander the Great and Bactria*. Leiden.

———. 1994. "Spitamenes against Alexander." *ΙΣΤΟΡΙΚΟΓΕΩΓΡΑΦΙΚΑ* 4: 51–58.

———. 2003. *Alexander the Great and the Mystery of the Elephant Medallions*. Berkeley and Los Angeles.

———. 2005. *Into the Land of Bones: Alexander the Great in Afghanistan*. Berkeley and Los Angeles.

———. 2016. *The Treasures of Alexander the Great: How One Man's Wealth Shaped the World*. Oxford.

Hornblower, Simon. 1982. *Mausolos*. Oxford.

———. 2002. *The Greek World: 479–323 BC*, 3rd ed. London.

Horster, M., and C. Reitz, eds. 2010. *Condensing Texts—"Condensed Texts."* Palingenesia, Band 98. Stuttgart.

Howe, T. 2008. "Alexander in India: Ptolemy as Near Eastern Historiographer." In Howe and Reames, 215–33.

———. 2015a. "Alexander and the 'Afghan' Insurgency: A Reassessment." In Howe and Brice, 151–82.

———. 2015b. "Cleopatra-Eurydice, Olympias and a 'Weak' Alexander." In Wheatley and Baynham, 133–46.

———. 2015c. "Introducing Ptolemy: Alexander at the Persian Gates." In Heckel, Müller, and Wrightson, 166–95.

———. 2017. "Plain Tales from the Hills: Illyrian Influences on Argead Military Development." In Müller et al., 99–111.

———. 2018a. "A Founding Mother? Eurydike I, Philip II and Macedonian Royal Mythology." In Howe and Pownall, 1–28.

———, ed. 2018b. *Ptolemy I Soter: A Self-Made Man*. Philadelphia.

Howe, T., and Lee L. Brice, eds. 2015. *Brill's Companion to Insurgency and Terrorism in the Ancient Mediterranean*. Leiden.

Howe, T., E. E. Garvin, and G. Wrightson, eds. 2015. *Greece, Macedon and Persia: Studies in Social, Political and Military History in Honour of Waldemar Heckel*. Oxford and Philadelphia.

Howe, T., and S. Müller. 2012. "Mission Accomplished: Alexander at the Hyphasis." *AHB* 26: 21–38.

Howe, Timothy, Sabine Müller, and Richard Stoneman, eds. 2017. *Ancient Historiography on War and Empire*. Oxford and Philadelphia.

Howe, Timothy, and Frances Pownall, eds. 2018. *Ancient Macedonians in the Greek and Roman Sources: From History to Historiography*. Swansea.

Howe, T., and J. Reames, eds. 2008. *Macedonian Legacies: Studies in Ancient Macedonian History and Culture in Honor of Eugene N. Borza*. Claremont, CA.

Huber, Irene. 2005. *Rituale der Seuchen- und Schadensabwehr in Vorderen Orient und Griechenland. Formen kollektiver Krisenbewältigung in der Antike*. Stuttgart.

Hyland, John O. 2013. "Alexander's Satraps of Media." *JAH* 1: 119–44.

———. 2017. "Achaemenid Soldiers, Alexander's Conquest, and the Experience of Defeat." In Clark and Turner, 74–95.

———. 2018. *Persian Interventions: The Achaemenid Empire, Athens and Sparta, 450–386 BCE*. Baltimore.

Instinsky, H. U. 1949. *Alexander am Hellespont*. Würzburg.

Isager, J., ed. 1994. *Hekatomnid Caria and the Ionian Renaissance*. Halicarnassan Studies I. Odense.

Jacobs, B. 1992. "Der Tod des Bessos—Ein Beitrag zur Frage des Verhältnisses der Achämeniden zur Lehre des Zoroastres." *Acta praehistorica et archaeologica* 24: 177–86.

———. 1994. *Die Satrapienverwaltung im Perserreich zur Zeit Dareios' III*. Wiesbaden.

Jaeger, W. 1934. *Aristotle. Fundamentals of the History of his Development*. Translated by R. Robinson. Oxford.

Janke, A. 1904. *Auf Alexanders des Grossen Pfaden*. Berlin.

———. 1910. "Die Schlacht bei Issos." *Klio* 10 137–77.

Jaschinski, S. 1981. *Alexander und Griechenland unter dem Eindruck der Flucht des Harpalos*. Bonn.

Jehne, M. 1994. *Koine Eirene: Untersuchungen zu den Befriedungs und Stabilisierungsbemühungen in der griechischen Poliswelt des 4. Jahrhunderts v. Chr.* Stuttgart.

Jouguet, P. 1940. "La date Alexandrine de la fondation d'Alexandrie." *REA* 42: 192–97.

Julien, P. 1914. *Zur Verwaltung der Satrapien unter Alexander dem Grossen*. Weida.

Kagan, Donald. 2003. *The Peloponnesian War*. New York.

Kahn, D. 2008. "Inaros' Rebellion against Artaxerxes I and the Athenian Disaster in Egypt." *CQ* 58: 424–40.

Karttunen, K. 1990. "Taxila: Indian City and a Stronghold of Hellenism." *Arctos* 24: 85–96.

———. 1997. *India and the Hellenistic World*. Helsinki.

Keegan, J. 1987. *The Mask of Command*. New York.

Keen, Antony G. 1996. "Alexander's Invasion of Lycia: Its Route and Purpose." *AHB* 10: 110–18.

———. 1998. *Dynastic Lycia: A Political History of the Lycians and Their Relations with Foreign Powers, c.545–362 BC*. Leiden.

Kelly, D. 1990. "Charidemos' Citizenship: The Problem of *IG* II2 207." *ZPE* 83 96–109.

Kennell, Nigel. 2010. *Spartans: A New History*. Oxford and Malden.

Kern, Paul Bentley. 1999. *Ancient Siege Warfare*. London.

Kholod, M. 2011. "Persian Political Propaganda in the War against Alexander the Great." *IA* 46: 149–60.

———. 2017. "The Financial Administration of Asia Minor under Alexander the Great." In Howe, Müller, and Stoneman, 136–48.

———. 2018. "The Macedonian Expeditionary Corps in Asia Minor (336–335 BC)." *Klio* 100: 407–46.

King, Carol J. 2018. *Ancient Macedonia*. London and New York.

Kinzl, K. H., ed. 1977. *Greece and the Eastern Mediterranean in Ancient History and Prehistory: Studies Presented to Fritz Schachermeyr*. Berlin.

Kistler, John M. 2007. *War Elephants*. Lincoln and London.

Klęczar, Aleksandra. 2012. "The Kingship of Alexander the Great in the Jewish Versions of the Alexander Narrative." In Stoneman, Erickson, and Netton, 339–48.

Kleinow, H.-G. 1987. "Lysias im panhellenischen Vorfeld Alexanders d. Gr." In Will and Heinrichs, 89–122.

Koch, H. 2000. "Todesmonat oder Lebensdauer Alexanders des Großen? Textkritische Bemerkungen zu Iust. 12.16.1." *RhM* 143: 326–37.

Köhler, U. 1892. "Über das Verhältniss Alexanders des Grossen zu seinem Vater Philipp." *SB Berlin* 497–514.

Kornemann, E. 1935. *Die Alexandergeschichte des Königs Ptolemaios I. von Aegypten. Versuch einer Rekonstruktion.* Leipzig and Berlin.

Kosmetatou, E. 1997. "Pisidia and the Hellenistic Kings from 323 to 133 BC." *Anc. Soc.* 28: 5–37.

Kraft, K. 1971. *Der "rationale" Alexander.* Frankfurter Althistorische Studien. Heft 5. Frankfurt.

Kraus, A. ed. 1984. *Land und Reich, Stamm und Nation: Festgabe für Max Spindler zum 90. Gerburtstag.* Munich.

Kuhrt, A. 1987. "Usurpation, Conquest, and Ceremonial: From Babylonia to Persia." In Cannadine and Price, 48–52.

———. 1995. *The Ancient Near East c.3000–330 BC*, 2 vols. London and New York.

Kuhrt, A., and Susan Sherwin-White, eds. 1987. *Hellenism in the East.* Berkeley and Los Angeles.

LaBuff, Jeremy. 2017. "The Achaemenid Creation of Karia." In Müller et al., 27–40.

Lancel, S. 1995. *Carthage: A History*, translated by Antonia Nevill. Oxford.

Landucci Gattinoni, F. 1992. *Lisimaco di Tracia. Un sovrano nella prospettiva del primo ellenismo.* Milan.

Lane Fox, R. 1973. *Alexander the Great.* London.

———. 1980. *The Search for Alexander.* Boston and Toronto.

———. 1996. "Text and Image: Alexander the Great, Coins and Elephants." *BICS* 41: 87–108.

———. 1997. "The Itinerary of Alexander: Constantius to Julian." *CQ* 47: 239–52.

———. 2007. "Alexander the Great: 'Last of the Achaemenids'?" In Tuplin, 267–311.

———, ed. 2011. *Brill's Companion to Ancient Macedon: Studies in the Archaeology and History of Macedon, 650 BC–300 AD.* Leiden.

Lenfant, D. 2012. "Ctesias and His Eunuchs: A Challenge to Modern Historians." *Histos* 6: 257–97.

Lesky, A. 1966. *A History of Greek Literature*, translated by James Willis and Cornelis de Heer. New York.

Leuze, Oscar. 1935. *Die Satrapieneinteilung in Syrien und im Zweistromlande von 520–320.* Halle.

Lewis, David M. 1977. *Sparta and Persia: Lectures Delivered at the University of Cincinnati, Autumn 1976, in Memory of Donald W. Bradeen.* Leiden.

Licia, Vasile, ed. 2006. *Philia. Festschrift für Gerhard Wirth.* Galați.

Llewellyn-Jones, Lloyd. 2010. "'Help Me, Aphrodite!': Depicting the Royal Women of Persia in *Alexander*." In Cartledge and Greenland, 243–81.

Llewellyn-Jones, L., and James Robson. 2010. *Ctesias' History of Persis: Tales of the Orient.* London.

Lloyd, A. B. 1982. "The Inscription of Udjahorresnet: A Collaborator's Testament." *JEA* 68: 166–80.

———. 2011. "From Satrapy to Hellenistic Kingdom: The Case of Egypt." In Erskine and Llewellyn-Jones, 83–105.

Lock, R. A. 1972. "The Date of Agis III's War in Greece." *Antichthon* 6: 10–27.

Lonsdale, David J. 2007. *Alexander the Great: Lessons in Strategy*. London and New York.

Lott, J. Bert. 1996. "Philip II, Alexander, and the Two Tyrannies at Eresos of *IG* XII.2.526." *Phoenix* 50: 26–40.

Loukopoulou, L. D. 2011. "Macedonia and Thrace." In Lane Fox, 467–76.

Lund, Helen S. 1992. *Lysimachus: A Study in Early Hellenistic Kingship*. London and New York.

Ma, John. 2008. "Chaironeia 338: Topographies of Commemoration." *JHS* 128: 72–91.

MacDermot, B. C., and Klaus Schippmann. 1999. "Alexander's March from Susa to Persepolis." *Iranica Antiqua* 34: 283–308.

Mahaffy, J. P. 1899. *A History of Egypt*. Volume 4: *Under the Ptolemaic Dynasty*. London.

Mairs, Rachel. 2014. *The Hellenistic Far East. Archaeology, Language, and Identity in Greek Central Asia*. Berkeley and Los Angeles.

Marr, J. S., and C. H. Calisher. 2003. "Alexander the Great and West Nile Virus Encephalitis." *Emerging Infectious Diseases* 9.12: 1599–1603.

Marsden, E. W. 1964. *The Campaign of Gaugamela*. Liverpool.

Marshall, F. S. 1905. *The Second Athenian Confederacy*. Cambridge.

Marshall, J. 1951. *Taxila*, 3 vols. Cambridge.

Maurice, F. 1930. "The Size of the Army of Xerxes in the Invasion of Greece 480 B.C." *JHS* 50: 210–235.

McCoy, J. W. 1989. "Memnon of Rhodes at the Granicus." *AJP* 110: 413–33.

McCrindle, J. W. 1896. *The Invasion of India by Alexander the Great*. London.

McGregor, M. F. 1987. *The Athenians and their Empire*. Vancouver.

McQueen, E. I. 1978. "Some Notes on the Anti-Macedonian Movement in the Peloponnese in 331 B.C." *Historia* 27: 40–64.

Meeus, A. 2009a. "Alexander's Image in the Age of the Successors." In Heckel and Tritle, 235–50.

———. 2014. "The Territorial Ambitions of Ptolemy I." In Hauben and Meeus, 263–306.

Meiggs, R. 1972. *The Athenian Empire*. Oxford.

Merkelbach, R. 1954. *Die Quellen des griechischen Alexanderromans*. Munich.

———. 1977. *Die Quellen des griechischen Alexanderromans*, 2nd enlarged ed. Zetemata. Heft 9. Munich.

Merker, I. L. 1965. "The Ancient Kingdom of Paionia." *Balkan Studies* 6: 35–55.

Michels, Christoph. 2017. "The Persian Impact on Bithynia, Commagene, Pontus, and Cappadocia." In Müller et al., 41–55.

Mikrojannakis, E. 1970. "The Diplomatic Contacts between Alexander III and Darius III." *AM* 1: 103–8.

Mildenberg, L. 1993. "Über das Münzwesen im Reich der Achämeniden." *Archaeologische Mitteilungen aus Iran* 26: 55–79.

Miller, M. C. J. 1994. "The 'Porus' Decadrachm of Alexander and the Founding of Bucephala." *AncW* 25: 109–20.

Milns, R. D. 1966. "Alexander's Pursuit of Darius through Iran." *Historia* 15: 256.

———. 1968. *Alexander the Great*. London.

Mineo, B., and G. Zecchini. 2016. *Justin. Abrege des Histoires Philippiques de Trogue Pompee*. Tome 1. *Livres I–X*, text and translation by B. Mineo, historical notes by G. Zecchini. Paris.

Mócsy, A. 1966. "Die Vorgeschichte Obermösiens im hellenistisch-römischen Zeitalter." *Acta Antiqua Academiae Scientiarum Hungaricae* 14: 87–112.

Moloney, E. 2015. "Neither Agamemnon nor Thersites, Achilles nor Margites: The Heraclid Kings of Ancient Macedonia." *Antichthon* 49: 50–72.

Momigliano, A. 1979. "Flavius Josephus and Alexander's Visit to Jerusalem." *Athenaeum* 57: 442–448.

Mørkholm, O. 1991. *Early Hellenistic Coinage from the Accession of Alexander to the Peace of Apamea (336–186 B.C.)*. Cambridge.

Morris, I., and W. Scheidel, eds. 2009. *The Dynamics of Ancient Empires: State Power from Assyria to Byzantium*. Oxford.

Mortensen, K. 1991. "The Career of Bardylis." *AncW* 22: 49–59.

Moysey, Robert A. 1991. "Diodorus, the Satraps and the Decline of the Persian Empire." *AHB* 5: 113–22.

———. 1992. "Plutarch, Nepos and the Satrapal Revolt of 362/1 B.C." *Historia* 41: 158–66.

Mughal, Muhammad R. 1967. "Excavations at Tulamba, West Pakistan." *Pakistan Archaeology* 4: 1–152.

Müller, Carl Werner, Kurt Sier, and Jürgen Werner, eds. 1992. *Zum Umgang mit fremden Sprachen in der Griechisch-Römischen Antike*. Stuttgart.

Müller, H., ed. 2009. *1000 & 1 Talente. Visualisierung antiker Kriegskosten. Begleitband zu einer studentischen Ausstellung*. Gutenberg.

Müller, Sabine. 2003. *Maßnahmen der Herrschaftssicherung gegenüber makedonischen Opposition bei Alexander dem Großen*. Frankfurt am Main.

———. 2006. "Alexander, Harpalos und die Ehren für Pythionike und Glykera: Überlegungen zu den Repräsentationsformen des Schatzmeisters in Babylon und Tarsos." In Licia, 71–106.

———. 2010. "In the Shadow of His Father: Alexander, Hermolaus and the Legend of Philip." In Carney and Ogden, 25–32.

———. 2012. "Stories of the Persian Bride: Alexander and Roxane." In Stoneman, Erickson, and Netton, 295–309.

———. 2013. "The Female Element of the Political Self-Fashioning of the Diadochi: Ptolemy, Seleucus, Lysimachus, and Their Iranian Wives." In Alonso Troncoso and Anson, 199–214.

———. 2014. *Alexander, Makedonien und Persien*. Berlin.

———. 2016. *Die Argeaden. Geschichte Makedoniens bis zum Zeitalter Alexanders des Großen*. Paderborn.

———. 2018. "Hephaistion—A Re-assessment of His Career." In Howe and Pownall, 77–102.

———. 2019. *Alexander der Große. Eroberung—Politik—Rezeption.* Stuttgart.

Müller, Sabine, Tim Howe, Hugh Bowden, and Robert Rollinger, eds. 2017. *The History of the Argeads: New Perspectives.* Wiesbaden.

Murison, C. L. 1972. "Darius III and the Battle of Issus." *Historia* 21: 394–423.

Myśliwiec, Karol. 2000. *The Twilight of Ancient Egypt: First Millennium B.C.E.* Translated by David Lorton. Ithaca, NY.

Nagle, D. Brendan. 1996. "The Cultural Context of Alexander's Speech at Opis." *TAPA* 126: 151–72.

Naiden, Fred. 2019. *Soldier, Priest, and God: A Life of Alexander the Great.* Oxford and New York.

Nawotka, K. 2003. "Freedom of Greek Cities in Asia Minor in the Age of Alexander the Great." *Klio* 85: 15–41.

———. 2010. *Alexander the Great.* Newcastle upon Tyne.

Neuhaus, O. 1902. "Der Vater des Sisygambis und das Verwandtschaftsverhältniss des Dareios III Kodomannos zu Artaxerxes II und III." *RhM* 57: 145–59.

Neumann, C. 1971. "A Note on Alexander's March-Rates." *Historia* 20: 196–98.

Nice, Alex. 2005. "The Reputation of the 'Mantis' Aristander." *Acta Classica* 48: 87–102.

Noethlichs, Karl Leo. 1987. "Sparta und Alexander: Überlegungen zum 'Mäuerkrieg' und zum 'Sparta-Mythos.'" *Zu Alex. d. Gr.* 1: 391–412.

Nudell, Joshua P. 2018. "Oracular Politics: Propaganda and Myth in the Restoration of Didyma." *AHB* 32: 44–60.

Nylander, Carl. 1993. "Darius III—The Coward King: Points and Counterpoints." In Carlsen et al., 145–60.

Oates, J. 1986. *Babylon.* Revised ed. London.

Ober, J. 1999. "Conquest Denied: The Premature Death of Alexander the Great." In Cowley, 37–56.

O'Brien, J. M. 1980. "The Enigma of Alexander the Great: The Alcohol Factor." *Annals of Scholarship* 1: 31–46.

———. 1992. *Alexander the Great. The Invisible Enemy.* London and New York.

Ogden, D. 1999. *Polygamy, Prostitutes and Death: The Hellenistic Dynasties.* London.

———, ed. 2002. *The Hellenistic World.* Swansea and London.

Oikonomides, A. N. 1988. "The Real End of Alexander's Conquest of India." *AncW* 18: 31–34.

Olbrycht, M. J. 2007. "The Military Reforms of Alexander the Great during His Campaigns in Iran, Afghanistan and Central Asia." In Galewicz, Pstrusińska, and Sudyka, 309–21.

———. 2011. "Ethnicity of Settlers in the Colonies of Alexander the Great in Iran and Central Asia." *Bulletin of IICAS* 14: 22–35.

Olmstead, A. T. 1948. *History of the Persian Empire.* Chicago.

Osborne, M. J. 1973. "Orontes." *Historia* 21: 515–51.

Özet, M. Aykut. 1994. "The Tomb of a Noble Woman from the Hekatomnid Period." In Isager, 88–96.

Palagia, O. 2010. "Philip's Eurydice in the Philippeum at Olympia." In Carney and Ogden, 33–41.

———. 2017. "The Argeads: Archaeological Evidence." In Müller et al., 151–61.

———. 2018. "Alexander the Great, the Royal Throne and the funerary Thrones of Macedonia." *Karanos* 1: 23–34.

Papazoglou, F. 1965. "Les origines et la destinée de l'état illyrien: Illyrii proprie dicti." *Historia* 14: 143–79.

Parke, H. W. 1933. *Greek Mercenary Soldiers from the Earliest Times to the Battle of Ipsus.* Oxford.

———. 1985. "The Massacre of the Branchidae." *JHS* 105: 59–68.

Parker, Victor. 2009. "Source-Critical Reflections on Cleitarchus' Work." In Wheatley and Hannah, 29–55.

Pearson, L. 1952. "Aristobulus the Phocian." *AJP* 73: 71–75.

———. 1955. "The Diary and the Correspondence of Alexander the Great." *Historia* 3: 429–55.

———. 1960. *The Lost Histories of Alexander the Great.* Philadelphia.

Pédech, P. 1984. *Historiens compagnons d'Alexandre.* Paris.

Perlman, S. 1957. "Isocrates' 'Philippus'—a Reinterpretation." *Historia* 6: 306–17 = Perlman 1973: 104–15.

Perlman, S., ed. 1973. *Philip and Athens.* Cambridge.

Petsas, P. 1978. *Pella: Alexander the Great's Capital.* Thessaloniki.

Pitt, E. M., and W. P. Richardson. 2017. "Hostile Inaction? Antipater, Craterus and the Macedonian Regency." *CQ* 67: 77–87.

Plezia, M. 1972. "Der Titel und der Zweck von Kallisthenes' Alexandergeschichte." *Eirene* 60: 263–68.

Potts, D. T. 2012. "The Elamites." In Daryaee, 37–56.

Pownall, F. 2007. "The Panhellenism of Isocrates." In Heckel, Tritle and Wheatley, 13–25.

———. 2018. "Was Kallisthenes the Tutor of Alexander's Royal Pages?" In Howe and Pownall, 59–76.

Prag, A. J. N. W., and R. A. H. Neave. 1994. "Who Is the 'Carian Princess'?" In Isager, 97–109.

Prandi, L. 1996. *Fortuna e realtà dell'opera di Clitarco.* Historia Einzelschriften, Heft 104. Stuttgart.

———. 1998. "A Few Remarks on the Amyntas 'Conspiracy.'" In Will, 91–101.

———. 2012. "New Evidence for the Dating of Cleitarchus (*POxy* LXI, 4808)?" *Histos* 6: 15–26.

———. 2013. *Diodoro Siculo. Bibliotheca storica. Libro XVII. Commento storico.* Milan.

Prentice, W. K. 1923. "Callisthenes, the Original Historian of Alexander." *TAPA* 54: 74–85.

Price, M. J. 1982. "The 'Porus' Coinage of Alexander the Great: A Symbol of Concord and Community." In Scheers, 75–85.

———. 1991. *The Coinage in the Name of Alexander the Great and Philip Arrhidaeus.* London.

Raaflaub, K, and N. Rosenstein, eds. 1999. *War and Society in the Ancient and Medieval Worlds: Asia, the Mediterranean, Europe, and Mesoamerica.* Cambridge, MA.

Raun, C. 1868. *De Clitarcho Diodori, Iustini, Curtii auctore.* Bonn.

Rawlinson, G. 2005. *Phoenicia.* London and New York. [Originally published in 1889.]

Reames, J. 2008. "Crisis and Opportunity—The Philotas Affair Again." In Howe and Reames, 165–81.

———. 2010. "The Cult of Hephaestion." In Cartledge and Greenland, 183–216.

Redford, Donald B. 2010. *City of the Ram-Man: The Story of Ancient Mendes.* Princeton.

Rehork, J. 1969. "Homer, Herodot und Alexander." In Stiehl and Stier, 251–60.

Renault, Mary. 1975. *The Nature of Alexander.* New York.

Rich, John, and Graham Shipley, eds. 1993. *War and Society in the Greek World.* London and New York.

Richards, C. G. 1934. "Proskynesis." *CR* 48: 168–70.

Riginos, A. S. 1994. "The Wounding of Philip II of Macedon: Fact and Fabrication." *JHS* 114: 103–19.

Ritter, H.-W. 1965. *Diadem und Königsherrschaft.* Munich.

———. 1987. "Die Bedeutung des Diadems." *Historia* 36: 290–301.

Robinson, C. A., Jr. 1929. "The Seer Aristander." *AJP* 50: 195–97.

———. 1932. *The Ephemerides of Alexander's Expedition.* Providence.

———. 1953. *The History of Alexander the Great,* Vol. 1. Providence.

Rochette, B. 1997. "Les armées d'Alexandre le Grand et les langues étrangères." *L'Antiquité Classique* 66: 311–318.

Roebuck, C. 1948. "The Settlements of Philip II with the Greek States in 338 B.C." *CP* 43: 73–92.

Rogers, Guy MacLean. 2004. *Alexander. The Ambiguity of Greatness.* New York.

Roisman, J. 1984. "Ptolemy and His Rivals in His History of Alexander." *CQ* 34: 373–85.

———, ed. 2003a. *Brill's Companion to Alexander the Great.* Leiden.

———. 2003b. "Honor in Alexander's Camp." In Roisman, 279–321.

———. 2012. *Alexander's Veterans and the Early Wars of the Successors.* Norman, OK.

———. 2015. "Opposition to Macedonian Kings: Riots for Rewards and Verbal Protests." In Howe, Garvin, and Wrightson, 77–86.

Roisman, J., and I. Worthington, eds. 2010. *A Companion to Ancient Macedonia.* Oxford and Malden.

Romane, J. Patrick. 1987. "Alexander's Siege of Tyre." *AncW* 16: 79–90.

———. 1988. "Alexander's Siege of Gaza—332 B.C." *AncW* 18: 21–30.

Rop, J. 2019. *Greek Military Service in the Ancient Near East, 401–330 BCE.* Cambridge.

Roy, J. 1994. "Thebes in the 360s B.C." In *CAH²* VI 187–208.

Rubinsohn, Z. 1977. "The 'Philotas Affair': A Reconsideration," *AM* 2: 409–20.

Rüegg, August. 1906. *Beiträge zur Erforschung der Quellenverhältnisse in der Alexandergeschichte des Curtius.* Basel.

Rutz, W. 1984. "Das Bild des Dareios bei Curtius Rufus." *Würzburger Jahrbücher* 10: 147–59.

Ruzicka, S. 1983. "Curtius 4.1.34–37 and the 'Magnitudo Belli.'" *CJ* 79: 30–34.

———. 1985. "A Note on Philip's Persian War." *AJAH* 10: 84–95.

———. 1988. "War in the Aegean, 333–331 B.C.: A Reconsideration." *Phoenix* 42: 131–51.

———. 1992. *Politics of a Persian Dynasty: The Hecatomnids in the Fourth Century B.C.* Norman, OK.

———. 1997. "The Eastern Greek World." In Tritle, 107–36.

———. 2010. "The 'Pixodarus Affair' Reconsidered Again." In Carney and Ogden, 3–11.

———. 2012. *Trouble in the West: Egypt and the Persian Empire 525–332 BCE.* Oxford.

Ryder, T. T. B. 1965. *Koine Eirene: General Peace and Local Independence in Ancient Greece.* Oxford.

Rzepka, J. 2009. "Conspirators-Companions-Bodyguards: A Note on the So-Called Mercenaries' Source and the Conspiracy of Bessus (Curt. 5,8,1-11)." *AHB* 23: 19–31.

Samuel, A. E. 1965. "Alexander's 'Royal Journals.'" *Historia* 14: 1–12.

Sancisi-Weerdenburg, H. 1993. "Alexander and Persepolis." In Carlsen et al., 177–88.

Saunders, J. J. 1971. *The History of the Mongol Conquests.* Philadelphia.

Schachermeyr, Fritz. 1973. *Alexander der Grosse. Das Problem seiner Persönlichkeit und seines Wirkens.* Vienna.

———. 1976. "Alexander und die unterworfenen Nationen." In Badian, 47–86.

Schaefer, A. 1887. *Demosthenes und seine Zeit,* 3rd ed. Leipzig.

Scheers, S., ed. 1982. *Studia Paolo Naster I: Numismatica Antiqua.* Louvain.

Schep, Leo. 2009. "The Death of Alexander the Great: Reconsidering Poison." In Wheatley and Hannah, 227–36.

Schramm, W. 1972. "War Semiramis assyrische Regentin?" *Historia* 21: 513–21.

Schubert, R. 1898. "Der Tod des Kleitos." *RhM* 53: 98–117.

Schultz, P. 2007. "Leochares' Argead Portraits in the Philippeion." In von der Hoff and Schultz, 205–33.

Seel, O. 1972. *Eine römische Weltgeschichte.* Nuremberg.

Seibert, J. 1969. *Untersuchungen zur Geschichte Ptolemaios' I.* Munich.

———. 1972a. *Alexander der Grosse.* Erträge der Forschung 10. Darmstadt.

———. 1972b. "Nochmals zu Kleomenes von Naukratis." *Chiron* 2: 99–102.

———. 1983. *Das Zeitalter der Diadochen.* Erträge der Forschung 185. Darmstadt.

———. 1984. "Das Testament Alexanders, ein Pamphlet aus der Frühzeit der Diadochen?" In Kraus, 247–60.

———. 1985. *Die Eroberung des Perserreiches durch Alexander den Grossen auf kartographischer Grundlage.* Wiesbaden.

———. 1987. "Dareios III." *Zu Alex. d. Gr.* 1: 437–56.

———, ed. 1991. *Hellenistische Studien. Gedenkschrift für Hermann Bengtson.* Munich.

———. 1998. "'Panhellenischer' Kreuzzug, Nationalkrieg, Rachefeldzug oder makedonischer Eroberungskrieg?—Überlegungen zu den Ursachen des Krieges gegen Persien." In Will, 5–59.

Seibt, Gunter F. 1977. *Griechische Söldner im Achaimenidenreich*. Bonn.

Sekunda, N. 1988. "Some Notes on the Life of Datames." *Iran* 26: 35–53.

———. 1992. *The Persian Amry 560–330 BC*. London.

Shäfer, P. 2003. *The History of the Jews in the Greco-Roman World*. London and New York.

Shahbazi, A. Shapour. 2012 "The Achaemenid Persian Empire (550–330 BCE)." In Daryaee, 120–41.

Shay, J. 1994. *Achilles in Vietnam: Combat Trauma and the Undoing of Character*. New York.

Shayegan, M. R. 2007. "Prosopographical Notes: The Iranian Nobility during and after the Macedonian Conquest." *Bulletin of the Asia Institute* 21: 97–126.

Sherwin-White, Susan. 1987. "Seleucid Babylonia: A Case Study for the Installation and Development of Greek Rule." In Kuhrt and Sherwin-White, 1–31.

Shrimpton, G. S. 1991. *Theopompus the Historian*. Kingston and Montreal.

Shrimpton, G. S., and D. J. McCargar, eds. 1981. *Classical Contributions: Studies in Honour of Malcolm Francis McGregor*. Locust Valley, NY.

Siewert, P. 1972. *Der Eid von Plataiai*. Munich.

Smith, M. 2009–10. "The Failure of Alexander's Conquest and Administration of Bactria-Sogdiana." *Hirundo* 8: 64–72.

Smith, Vincent A. 1903. "The Position of the Autonomous Tribes of the Panjāb Conquered by Alexander the Great." *JRAS*: 685–702.

———. 1914. *The Early History of India from 600 B.C. to the Muhammadan Conquest, Including the Invasion of Alexander the Great*, 3rd ed. Oxford.

Snowden, Frank M., Jr. 1970. *Blacks in Antiquity: Ethiopians in the Greco-Roman Experience*. Cambridge, MA.

———. 1983. *Before Color Prejudice: The Ancient View of Blacks*. Cambridge, MA.

Sofman, A. S., and D. I. Tsibukidis. 1987. "Nearchus and Alexander." *AncW* 16: 71–77.

Sordi, M. 1958. *La lega tessala*. Rome.

Spann, Philip O. 1999. "Alexander at the Beas: A Fox in a Lion's Skin." In Titchener and Moorton, 62–74.

Spawforth, A. J. S., ed. 2007a. *The Court and Court Society in Ancient Monarchies*. Cambridge.

———. 2007b. "The Court of Alexander between Europe and Asia." In Spawforth, 82–120.

———. 2012. "The Pamphleteer Ephippus, King Alexander and the Persian Royal Hunt." *Histos* 6: 169–213.

Speck, Henry. 2002. "Alexander at the Persian Gates: A Study in Historiography and Topography." *AJAH* n.s. 1: 1–234.

Squillace, Giuseppe. 2010. "Consensus Strategies and Philip and Alexander: The Vengeance Theme." In Carney and Ogden, 69–80.

Stadter, Philip A. 1980. *Arrian of Nicomedia.* Chapel Hill.

Stark, Freya. 1956. "Alexander's Minor Campaigns in Turkey." *GJ* 122: 294–304.

———. 1958a. "Alexander's March from Miletus to Phrygia." *JHS* 78: 102–20.

———. 1958b. *Alexander's Path from Caria to Cilicia.* New York.

Stein, A. 1927. "Alexander's Campaign in the Indian North-west Frontier." *GJ* 70: 417–540.

———. 1929. *On Alexander's Track to the Indus.* London.

———. 1932. "The Site of Alexander's Passage of the Hydaspes and the Battle with Porus." *GJ* 80: 31–46.

———. 1938. "An Archaeological Journey in Western Iran." *GJ* 92: 314–18.

———. 1942. "Notes on Alexander's Crossing of the Tigris and the Battle of Arbela." *GJ* 1942: 155–64.

———. 1943. "On Alexander's Route into Gedrosia: An Archaeological Tour in Las Bela." *GJ* 102: 193–227.

Stenton, Frank M. 1971. *Anglo-Saxon England,* 3rd ed. Oxford.

Stewart, A. 1993. *Faces of Power. Alexander's Image and Hellenistic Politics.* Berkeley and Los Angeles.

Stiehl, Ruth, and Hans Erich Stier, eds. 1969. *Beiträge zur Alten Geschichte und deren Nachleben. Festschrift für Franz Altheim zum 6.10.1968.* Berlin.

Stoneman, Richard. 2008. *Alexander the Great: A Life in Legend.* New Haven.

Stoneman, Richard, Kyle Erickson, and Ian Netton, eds. 2012. *The Alexander Romance in Persia and the East.* Groningen.

Strasburger, H. 1934. *Ptolemaios und Alexander.* Leipzig.

———. 1952. "Alexanders Zug durch die Gedrosische Wüste." *Hermes* 80: 456–93.

———. 1954. "Zur Route Alexanders dourch Gedrosien." *Hermes* 82: 251–54.

Strootman, R. 2010/2011. "Alexander's Thessalian Cavalry." *Talanta* 42/43: 51–67.

Stylianou, P. J. 1998. *A Historical Commentary on Diodorus Siculus, Book 15.* Oxford.

Sushko, A. 1936. *Gaugamela: The Modern Qaraqosh.* Chicago.

Syme, R. 1988. "The Date of Justin and the Discovery of Trogus." *Historia* 37: 358–71.

Tabacco, Raffaella. 2000. Itinerarium Alexandri. *Testo, apparato critico, introduzione, traduzione e commento.* Turin.

Tarn, W. W. 1921. "Heracles Son of Barsine." *JHS* 41: 18–28.

Tataki, Argyro. 1998. *Macedonians Abroad: A Contribution to the Prosopography of Ancient Macedonia.* Athens.

Thompson, M. 2007. *Granicus 334 BC: Alexander's First Persian Victory.* Osprey Campaign Series 182. Oxford.

Titchener, Francis B., and Richard Moorton, Jr., eds. 1999. *The Eye Expanded: Life and the Arts in Graeco-Roman Antiquity.* Berkeley and Los Angeles.

Tomaschek, W. 1890. "Topographische Erläuterung der Küstenfahrt Nearchs vom Indus bis zum Euphrat." *SB Wien* 121: 31–88.

Tougher, Shaun. 2008. *The Eunuch in Byzantine History and Society.* London and New York.

Tritle, L. A., ed. 1997. *The Greek World in the Fourth Century: From the Fall of the Athenian Empire to the Successors of Alexander.* London and New York.

———. 2000. *From Melos to My Lai: War and Survival.* London and New York.

———. 2003. "Alexander and the Killing of Cleitus the Black." In Heckel and Tritle, 127–46.

———. 2010. *A New History of the Peloponnesian War.* Oxford and Malden.

Trundle, Matthew. 2004. *Greek Mercenaries from the Late Archaic Period to Alexander.* London and New York.

Tucci, G. 1977. "On Swat: The Dards and Connected Problems." *East and West* 27: 9–85.

Tuplin, C., ed. 2007. *Persian Responses: Political and Cultural Interaction with(in) the Achaemenid Empire.* Swansea.

Urban, R. 1991. *Der Königsfrieden von 387/386 v. Chr. Vorgeschichte, Zustandegekommen Ergebnis und politische Umsetzung.* Stuttgart.

Vacante, S. 2012. "Alexander the Great and the 'Defeat' of the Sogdianian Revolt." *AHB* 26: 87–130.

Veith, G. 1908. "Der Kavalleriekampf in der Schlacht am Hydaspes." *Klio* 8: 131–53.

Velásquez Muñoz, 2013. "Problemas en torno al camino real aqueménida entre Susa y Persépolis: rutas y estaciones." *Gerion* 31: 147–78.

Velkov, Velizar. 1987. "Alexander der Große und Thrakien." In Will and Heinrichs, 257–69.

Venetis, E. 2012. "Iran in the Time of Alexander the Great and the Seleucids." In Daryaee, 142–63.

Vogelsang, W. 1985. "Early Historical Arachosia in South-East Afghanistan: Meeting-Place between East and West." *Iranica Antiqua* 20: 55–99.

———. 2002. *The Afghans.* Oxford and Malden.

Vogt, E. 1971. "Kleomenes von Naukratis—Herr von Ägypten," *Chiron* 1: 153–57.

Von der Hoff, R., and P. Schultz, eds. 2007. *Early Hellenistic Portraiture: Image, Style, Context.* Cambridge.

Vorhis, Justin Grant. 2017. "The Best of the Macedonians: Alexander as Achilles in Arrian, Curtius, and Plutarch." PhD diss., University of California, Los Angeles.

Waters, M. 2014. *Ancient Persia: A Concise History of the Achaemenid Empire, 550–330 BCE.* Cambridge.

Waywell, Geoffrey B. 1988. "The Mausoleum at Halicarnassus." In Clayton and Price, 100–23.

Weiskopf, Michael. 1989. *The So-Called "Great Satraps' Revolt." 366-360 B.C. Concerning Local Instability in the Achaemenid Far West.* Historia Einzelschriften. Heft 63. Stuttgart.

Welles, C. Bradford. 1962. "The Discovery of Sarapis and the Foundation Date of Alexandria." *Historia* 11: 271–98.

Welwei, K.-W. 1977. *Unfreie im antiken Kriegsdienst. Zweiter Teil: Die kleineren und mittleren griechischen Staaten und die hellenistischen Reiche.* Wiesbaden.

Westlake, H.D. 1935. *Thessaly in the Fourth Century B.C.* London.

Wheatley, Pat, and Elizabeth Baynham, eds. 2015. *East and West in the World Empire of Alexander: Essays in Honour of Brian Bosworth.* Oxford.

Wheatley, Pat, and Robert Hannah, eds. 2009. *Alexander and his Successors. Essays from the Antipodes.* Claremont.

Whitehorne, J. 1994. *Cleopatras.* London and New York.

———. 2011. "Early Hellenistic Rhodes: The Struggle for Independence and the Dream of Hegemony." In Erskine and Llewellyn-Jones, 123–46.

Wiesehöfer, J. 1996. *Ancient Persia from 550 BC to 650 AD.* London and New York.

———. 2009. "The Achaemenid Empire." In Morris and Scheidel, 66–98.

———. 2015. "Fourth Century Revolts against Persia: The Test Case of Sidon (348–345 B.C.E.)." In Howe and Brice, 93–112.

Wilkes, John. 1992. *The Illyrians.* Oxford.

Will, E. 1952. "Au sanctuaire d'Héraclès à Tyr." *Berytus* 10: 1–12.

Will, W. 1987. "Ein sogenannter Vatermörder. Nochmals zur Ermordung Philipps." *Zu Alex. d. Gr.* 1.219–32.

———, ed. 1998. *Alexander der Grosse. Eine Welteroberung und ihr Hintergrund. Vorträge des Internationalen Bonner Alexanderkolloquium, 19.–21.12.1996.* Bonn.

Willrich, H. 1899. "Wer ließ König Philipp von Makedonien ermorden?" *Hermes* 34: 174–83.

Winiarczyk, Marek. 2007. "Das Werk *Die Erziehung Alexanders* des Onesikritos von Astypalaea (*FGrHist* 134 F1-39). Forschungsstand (1832–2005) und Interpretationsversuch." *Eos* 94: 197–250.

Wirth, G. 1971a. "Alexander zwischen Gaugamela und Persepolis." *Historia* 20: 617–32 = Wirth 1985, 76–91.

———. 1985. *Studien zur Alexandergeschichte.* Darmstadt.

———. 1989. *Der Kampfverband des Proteas. Spekulationen zu den Begleitumständen der Laufbahn Alexanders.* Amsterdam.

Wiseman, D. J. 1985. *Nebuchadrezzar and Babylon: The Schweich Lectures.* Oxford.

Wood, Michael. 1997. *In the Footsteps of Alexander the Great.* Berkeley and Los Angeles.

Worthington, I. 1986. "The Chronology of the Harpalus Affair." *SO* 61: 63–76.

———, ed. 1994. *Ventures into Greek History.* Oxford.

———. 2003. "Alexander's Destruction of Thebes." In Heckel and Tritle, 65–86.

———. 2008. *Philip II of Macedonia.* New Haven.

———. 2014. *By the Spear: Philip II, Alexander the Great, and the Rise and Fall of the Macedonian Empire.* Oxford.

———. 2016. *Ptolemy I: King and Pharaoh of Egypt.* Oxford.

Wright, David Curtius. 2001. *The History of China.* Westport and London.

Wulfram, Hartmut, ed. 2016. *Der römische Alexanderhistoriker Curtius Rufus. Erzähltechnik, Retorik, Figurenpsychologie und Rezeption.* Wiener Studien Beiheft 38. Vienna.

Wüst, F. 1953/4a. "Die Rede Alexanders des Grossen in Opis." *Historia* 2: 177–88.

———. 1953/4b. "Die Meuterei von Opis." *Historia* 2: 418–31.

Yardley, J. C. 2003. *Justin and Pompeius Trogus: A Study of the Language of Justin's Epitome of Trogus.* Toronto.

———. 2010. "What Is Justin Doing with Trogus?" In Horster and Reitz, 469–90.

Zahrnt, M. 1999. "Alexander der Große und der lykische Hirt. Bemerkungen zur Propaganda während des Rachekrieges (334-330 v. Chr.)." *AM* 6.1: 1381–87.

———. 2013. "Kallisthenes von Olynth—ein verkannter Oppositioneller?" *Hermes* 141: 491–96.

Index